D1414035

DESIGNING AND IMPLEMENTING LOCAL AREA NETWORKS

DESIGNING AND IMPLEMENTING LOCAL AREA NETWORKS

Dimitris N. Chorafas

McGraw-Hill Book Company

*New York St. Louis San Francisco Auckland
Bogotá Hamburg Johannesburg London
Madrid Mexico Montreal New Delhi Panama
Paris São Paulo Singapore Sydney Tokyo Toronto*

Library of Congress Cataloging in Publication Data

Chorafas, Dimitris N.
Designing and implementing local area networks.

Includes index.
1. Computer networks. 2. Electronic data processing
—Distributed processing. I. Title.
TK5105.5.C486 1984 001.64'404 83-11965
ISBN 0-07-010819-6

34567890 DOC/DOC 898765

ISBN 0-07-010819-6

The editors for this book were Stephen G. Guty and Rita Margolies, the designer was Riverside Graphic Studio, Inc., and the production supervisor was Teresa F. Leaden. It was set in Caledonia by Santype-Byrd.

Printed and bound by R. R. Donnelley & Sons, Inc.

CONTENTS

PREFACE

This book was written for the information scientist who wants to know how to put to work to his advantage the best that current technology can offer. Since the concepts which the book conveys have only recently gained widespread acceptance, it starts with fundamentals. What is a local area network (LAN)? Why should we want to interconnect independent microcomputer systems that act as producers and consumers of information? How can we best use personal computers and LAN technology to serve organizational objectives?

A local area network is a communications facility that covers a limited topology and interconnects in an effective manner different types of servers and workstations (WS), more particularly personal and professional computers. In width it varies from 100 m to nearly 10 km depending on the architecture.

The two pillars on which a LAN rests—the physical and logical transport media and the personal computer–based WS—are the reason why today's technical press is filled with announcements of LAN products. In the steady search for productivity at the workbench, new solutions from small firms rival those from billion dollar corporations in a field that is only a few years old but is dynamic and fast-growing.

With computers and a LAN—that is, with a *myriaprocessor*—supported features, prices, and technology are distributed across a broad spectrum. This book describes the environment in which a local area network can best be put to work, its distinguishing characteristics, architectural issues, and the system design associated with them. It also discusses the real-life possibilities of myriaprocessors and the fundamental requirements for a successful application.

When we talk of local area networks, we must always remember that there is nothing about them that is totally new as to software or hardware:

- Personal computers now sell over two million a year.
- The operating system techniques are standard.
- The communications technology is well established.
- There are no applications that specifically arise from local networks per se. Even electronic mail was first implemented with standard mainframe computers.

The innovations lie in the physical-logical connection technology and its engineering to fit the characteristics of the myriaprocessors: speed, ease of use, effective range, and price. The options are many and sometimes confusing, but what particularly handicaps the persons looking toward the selection and implementation of a LAN environment is a clear view of rationality and possible advantages. Chapter 1 aims to supply that view: *The* essence of the PC and LAN revolution is individual access at an affordable price.

How does a local area network fit an office environment? Chapter 2 addresses that question, and by doing so it underscores the range of logical and physical challenges to be faced in an effective solution. Physical connection technology will continue to develop for some time, but the requirements of mass production and the installation perspectives underline the need to face the carrier problem. That is the subject of Chap. 3.

Chapter 4 treats the very important question of broadband versus baseband. First the technical characteristics and then the advantages and disadvantages that each solution will involve are considered. That is followed by Chap. 5 on protocols, synchronous and asynchronous, based on a layered approach and answering different topology requirements through alternative types of LAN architecture.

Three chapters, 6, 7, and 8, are devoted to standardization. In the first we consider the national, regional, and international normalization effort starting with the physical layer. Attention is focused on the standards organizations and their respective authorities and responsibilities. In the second we stress the work accomplished in the United States by the IEEE Project 802. The aim of this committee effort is to establish LAN standards at the two lower layers of the network connection: the physical and the data link. Three media access methods are developed: contention (CSMA/CD), token, and tree structure. They are presented and documented in the book. The third chapter on standardization concerns the Open System Interconnection, the architectural solution advanced by the International Standards Organization, better known as the ISO/OSI model.

Although we may be a long way from the establishment of a firm standard for all manufacturers, any effort in this direction should be welcome. It is senseless to spend time, money, and brainpower on the implementation of translation mechanisms between incompatible "standards." A new era has just dawned. We will do much better in it if we invest our resources in advancing the state of the art.

Chapters 9 through 17 get into the details of alternative LAN architectures available in the marketplace. I have chosen seven LAN architectures as examples:

- Omninet and Cluster One are baseband at or below 1 Mbps (megabits per second) with low-cost interfaces.
- ARC, the evolving IBM Token Ring, and Ethernet also are baseband, but they respectively feature a capacity of 2.5, 4.0, and 10 Mbps, along with more expensive interfaces.
- Wangnet, ALAN, and LocalNet are broadband.

Finally, Chap. 18 has the objective of enlarging the reader's applications horizon. Specific implementation experiences are presented, and the point made is that the larger framework in which we operate involves much more than mechanical action: *the employment of intelligent machines is an act of human intelligence.*

* * *

Let me take this opportunity to thank both the organizations and the executives who participated in my research and made this book possible. Among the users are the St. Paul Insurance Companies, Citibank, Chase Manhattan, the Chemical Bank, and Bank of America. On the manufacturers' side are Wang, 3M/Interactive Systems, Datapoint, Honeywell, Xerox, Olivetti, Sytek, Nestar, Corvus, Fujitsu, and NEC.

The choice of these manufacturers was not accidental. It followed years of analysis of the declining fortunes of the mainframers, particularly those who failed to see the significance of the dropping cost of computer power and the profound transformation which followed. Once again we see the effect of the cutting edge of technology: users and manufacturers must reprogram their design, marketing, and implementation strategies.

Finally, I express my thanks to everybody who contributed to this book: my colleagues, for their advice and the insight which they provided; the people who took part in my seminars, for their puzzling and most interesting questions; and Eva-Maria Binder, for assistance in preparing the drawings and doing the typing.

Dimitris N. Chorafas

PART 1

SOLUTIONS WITH LOCAL NETWORKS

1 MAKING USE OF HIGH TECHNOLOGY

Advanced computer and communications technology has become the key to survival of a great many financial institutions and industrial concerns. No words can better explain its role than General Electric's dictum: "Automate, emigrate, or evaporate."

Having called the able application of high technology "the most important undertaking of this century," GE has engaged in a far-sighted program of retooling its own and other factories into the automated plants of the future. The new, exciting tools and techniques are used in three broad areas of interest:

1. The *technology base*. Here the aim is to accelerate advances in productivity and product quality.
2. The thrust for *generic solutions*: developing standards and recommendations for applications, demonstrating solutions, and providing experimental facilities.
3. *Application support*: developing specialized skills through education by seminars, workshops, and dissemination media.

These are the approaches to the *implementation of the microprocessors that are revolutionizing communications, business systems, manufacturing, technology, and military equipment*. We are becoming a technology-driven society to which the present generation, with its image problems, is adjusting with difficulty. The next generation, however, will take computers, communications, and intelligent workstations for granted. Today, fifth-grade kids learn about computers and sixth-graders start programming and get hands-on experience.

At present the hardware is mindless and acquires an intellectual cast only through software, but by year 2000 the following developments may take us to intelligent machines:

1. Very large scale integration
2. Universal, inexpensive broadband communications
3. Voice recognition and voice answerback
4. Human language man-machine communications
5. Self-sustaining associative databases
6. Cryogenic circuitry approximating biological densities
7. Holographic memories
8. Hardware and software adaptive to environmental stimuli
9. Teachable computers
10. Brain-type metalanguage
11. Automated intuition
12. Brain augmentation through high-level intelligence

While that transition is taking place over 20 or so years, we must remember that, aside from it, the pace of technological development has accelerated and our human capital finds it hard to adjust to the new realities. The two necessities for growth and survival are *to accept change*, which in at least some areas is part of the ongoing evolution, and *to manage information as a vital resource comparable to food and energy.*

Japanese manufacturers are in the forefront in these respects: They believe the time has come to change strategy and not just follow what others are doing in information technology, but do better. They also see clearly the connection between international bargaining power and technology. But where do American and European companies stand?

AN "INDUSTRIAL STRENGTH" MACHINE

Most of the terminals that connect office desks to company mainframes are dumb. In contrast, the personal computer (PC) is developing into an intelligent user-programmable terminal. It is a monotask (*one machine, one man, one terminal*) but multiprocessor; it is a low-cost, high-capacity device. Putting computing power in the hands of end users is therefore the way more companies are going; there is a significant trend toward multifunction workstations as opposed to single-function terminals.

Furthermore, the difference in price between a personal computer and a simple terminal is quite significant—in favor of the PC.

Broadly, the PC line divides into the home and the professional microcomputers. As Fig. 1-1 demonstrates, the latter are more expensive than consumer-oriented machines. The "industrial strength" micros are not always found in walk-in retail stores.

Although off-the-shelf software is widely available, a professional

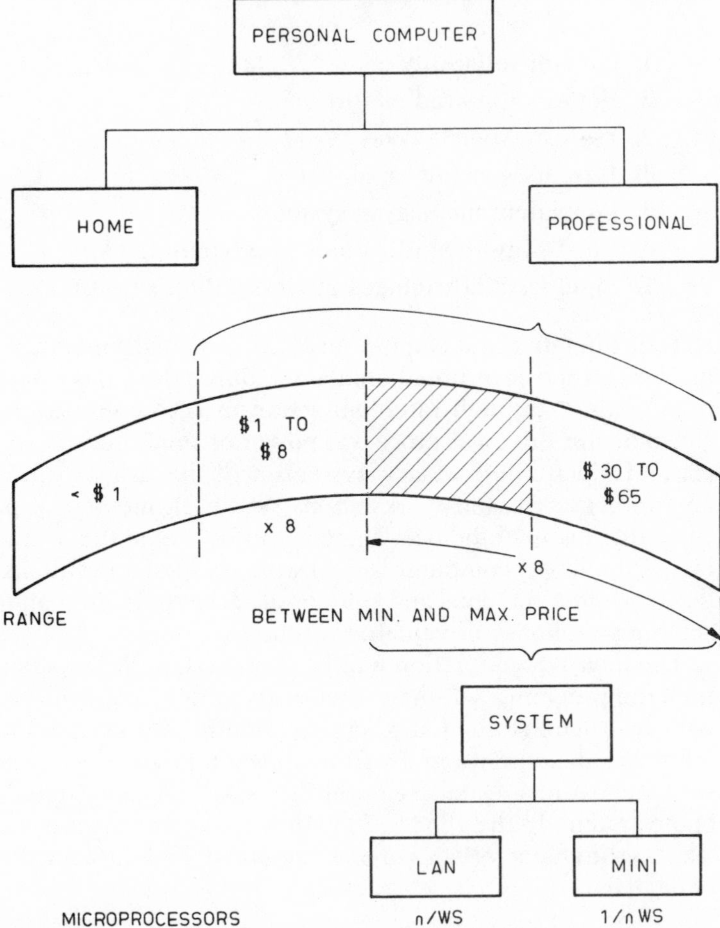

Figure 1-1. Division of the home and professional PC market, price ranges, and comparison of LAN and shared mini solutions in terms of microprocessor power per workstation. The difference in microprocessor power is n^2 per ws.

microcomputer most often runs programs that have been written for or tailored to a particular business. In this respect, an industrial strength micro challenges a dumb terminal because the latter must draw on the power of a bigger, centralized computer. Frequently, the results are delays, downtime, and user unhappiness.

What has been said of centralized mainframes is to a lesser extent true of minicomputers. Whereas microprocessor-based workstations in a local area network (LAN) feature n processors, where $n \geqslant 1$, a number of dumb terminals attached to a mini share a single processor. The difference in computer power is n^2 in favor of the LAN. Furthermore, the LAN provides these user advantages:

1. Greater reliability
2. Better-supported facilities
3. Faster response time
4. Internetworking capabilities
5. Polyvalent messaging systems
6. Flexibility in applications programming (AP)
7. Significant advantages in workstation selection

Today in talk about communications, personal computers are pretty much regarded as terminal emulators. But as the PC takes on networking functions through interconnection in LANs, end users will take advantage of the local processor power of small deskdrawer computers and electronic message systems will flourish and proliferate. A microprocessor-based workstation (WS) with memory capability assures that many of the user's needs can be met at the user's site. This leaves the larger computer free to work on bigger problems, safekeep the user's text and data, and store rarely accessed information and thus act as a warehouse of valuable resources.

The next WS generation will be designed for the separation of data from the programs, will have dictionary addressing, will be equipped with instructions needed to create, modify, destroy, and materialize information elements, and will include a high degree of integrity and security features. Database capabilities will be an outstanding feature of the system. In the 1983 to 1986 time frame, the professional PC will take on the characteristics of one or more of the following three classes of devices:

1. A WS installed under every desk linked to a local text and database and to a long-haul engine (mini, mainframe, text and data warehouse) through a LAN.

2. A small business system of the kind developed since the late 1970s.

3. A communications terminal equipped with a lot of data communication protocols and switchable to different networks.

During the same time period, a significant increase in message exchange will call for other services to be supported through local intelligence. For instance, in electronic message exchange, *smart forms* will become very important. A good deal of mail system capability is not used primarily for messaging; instead it is used for such forms-related tasks as order entry.

This is where the smart forms are valuable. They include user-oriented prompts, flexible (user-defined) programs, and choice of language (QuickComm supports eight languages). A user-defined forms capability in a message system is a way to extend the use of the system and to handle structured information effectively.

Local intelligence will be supported through an impressive range of microprocessor lines. Among the leading current products are Intel's 8086 and 8088. Both are 16-BPW (bits per word) machines, but the 8086 has a 16-bit and the 8088 an 8-bit bus. (The cost difference between the 8- and 16-BPW microprocessors is today quite negligible.) Intel's iAPX 432 has 32 BPW and a 32-bit bus.

Newer developments go well beyond that level. The 80186 is a 16-BPW "board on a chip" compatible with the 8086 but incorporating 55,000 transistors. The 80286 incorporates 130,000 transistors; it is a virtual memory machine and has memory management built into it. In both microprocessors the clock is at the 10-MHz (megahertz) level, but design makes the 80186 twice the 8086 speed and the 80286 four times the 8086 speed. (With the 8086 memory, access takes four cycles; whereas 80186 works at two cycles and 80286 at one cycle. Hence, the 8086 is waiting on memory access).

Furthermore, the 80186 addresses 1 MB (megabyte), and the 80286 addresses 2 MB. These are not in the future; they are currently available machines. The 80186 and 80286 are now being tested on user premises. (The IBM PC employs the 8088, and the persistent rumor is that IBM did the specs for the 80286. IBM is Intel's biggest customer, and since late 1982 a major shareholder.)

To appreciate the generation of microprocessors now in advanced stages of development, note that the IBM 4300 line, the HIS DPS 8, the Univac, and the Burroughs machines work at 8 MHz. In comparison with them the 1 MHz of Apple II and the 2 MHz of Apple III are dwarfish. That is not true of the new machines. The microprocessors currently integrated in PCs compare very favorably with the machines cited above, as Table 1-1 shows. New developments go well beyond the prevailing mainframe level.

The introduction of professional computers to the workplace is challenging in three ways:

1. The first challenge is to plan for one *umbrella technology*, that will furnish a broad array of capabilities directly to users. All of the office and industrial implementation fields we know today will be subsumed in that technology.
2. The second challenge is to *eliminate barriers* even if the traditional separation of technologies is reflected in everything that touches on computer work. Here it is important to understand that the technological basis for separation is crumbling. That should foster a desire to broaden interests and embrace a total view of information technology.
3. The third challenge is to expand *information management* by enriching the information component with color and graphics

TABLE 1-1 A COMPARISON OF MICROPROCESSORS

	Intel 8086	Motorola 68000	Zilog Z8000	National Semi-conductor 16000
Year of introduction	1978	1980	1979	1981
Basic clock	5 (4–8)	5–8	4 (2.5–4)	10
BPW	16	32	16	16
Basic instructions	95	61+	110	100
Use of microcode	No	Yes	No	No
General-purpose registers	14	16	16	8
Floating point	No	No	No	No
Pins	40	64	48/40	48/40
Direct access, in megabytes	1	16/64	48	16
Address size in bits	20	24	16	
Interrupt provisions	Yes	Yes	Yes	Yes
Stacks	Yes	Yes	Yes	Yes
Arrays	No	No	No	Yes
Virtual system structure	No	No	No	16032 only
Debug mode	No	Yes	No	No

and by providing advanced security and protection capabilities. This will lead to a proliferation of nontechnical users and a burgeoning demand for additional functions.

Until now, information management has been the sole interest of computer specialists, but data handling systems are expanding to meet the requirements of management at large. Any approach to the management of information must meet all three challenges. If it does, it will broaden marketing and implementation perspectives.

INCREASING INTELLIGENCE AND EASE OF USE

With ultimately increased intelligence and ease of use, computers and communications will be better able to assist man. Among the prerequisites are the ability to process information by using everyday language, put stored knowledge to practical use, and promote the functions of learning, associating, and inferring. Now, however, the essence of the personal computer revolution is individual access to computing power at an affordable price. Besides cost-effectiveness, a personal computer in the executive and clerical environments has the benefits of:

- Distributed processing
- Local databases
- Gateway to mainframes or minis
- Interconnection through LAN
- Fast response in interaction with a powerful local computer

Good solutions must combine the latest in hardware with innovative software. A major competitive advantage is a variety of compatibles and add-on features developed around the workstation. The current trend is toward a proliferation of workstations with increasingly intelligent features. If a company doesn't supply such supports, it will most likely lose the best of its people and not attract good replacements.

Voice recognition and voice synthesis will be among the most attractive add-on features in coming years. Voice-actuated equipment is bound to get cheaper and have an increased vocabulary. Today the 100-word units are becoming a base offering.

Voice recognition first found a solid application in quality control, where it improves operator accuracy and reduces the chance of errors. Nippon Electric has introduced a voice input processor with a 120-word vocabulary for use with its personal computers. It sells for $500.

By 1985 it is expected that continuous-speech systems with vocabularies of up to 500 words will be available and that the vocabulary will be increased to 1500 words by 1987.

Evaluating voice recognition capabilities is a tricky business because of the signal-to-noise ratio, the random characteristics of the environment, and a change of voice due to emotion or fatigue. Also, the industry is still searching for an accurate continuous-speech recognition algorithm. At present the process requires very large 32- and 64-bit high-speed machines. The issue is that, whereas current commercial systems can recognize a limited number of isolated words, the office environment calls for the recognition of continuous speech and large vocabularies with high accuracy independently of the speaker.

Nevertheless, manufacturers anticipate that speech recognition capability will be the primary feature of the next WS generation. Developers are working to reduce the number of components in a speech recognition preprocessor circuit to one very large scale integrated circuit with both analog and digital components. Until they are successful at an affordable price, however, user-friendly solutions to the man-machine communication problem will be supported by graphic tablets. A graphic tablet, or graphic pad, is a printed circuit board (PCB) whose elements have numeric codes that are defined by PCB records in the database design file. First appearing in computer-aided design (CAD), such pads provided user-friendly capabilities for scaling, rotation, volume accumulation, error message diagnostics, and generally programmable formats. They now find a range of applications in management, including banking, in connection with PCs and LANs.

The tablets are well suited to help in an applications environment which changes very rapidly, because they can be effectively reprogrammed to meet different functional requirements and to help in transition. They are particularly well suited to a structured input, and such solutions can fit the user level if we care to define with precision what we have to do. Understandably, the definition has to be dynamic: environmental changes want it that way.

Alternatively, when PCs and LANs are at a premium, we can use touch-sensing video screens. Rather than pushing buttons, switches, or keyboards, the user points to (touches) a computer-generated display on a terminal screen equipped with a touch-sensing device.

In terms of implementation, voice output is more advanced than voice input. Increasingly, computers vocalize. At a Grand Union supermarket in Stratford, Connecticut, the terminal at the checkout counter records the price of each item and also announces it to the customer, along with the grand total, the money received and the amount of change to be returned.

The point often missed, because of an antiquated image about what the computer can and cannot do, is that when we get a microcomputer on a desk, the whole applications programming perspective changes. Leaving artificial intelligence to some future day, at the present time we find many people with a PC who never heard that "it cannot be done by a computer." New concepts are being developed; there is a leapfrogging over past favorites; and there is a drive toward more workstations properly implemented through user coinvolvement.

It has not escaped the attention of central data processing (DP) operators that the PC explosion is threatening their power base. As a result, new policies are being developed. For instance, the St. Paul Insurance Companies decided that the DP organization will be promoter and vendor to the user departments, but *not* the PC controller. The position taken in this insurance company is that the management information service and data processing organization will promote both PCs and LANs. (St. Paul is one of the largest LAN users; it has 47 operating installations). Although the central DP shop sets the LAN standards, it does not write the applications. A senior St. Paul executive had this comment about the new policy: "We decided that we can't and shouldn't force the user. The user is free to go on. DP will help support, but the user is on his own in terms of AP [applications programming] development. The user buys from DP, but we don't try to control things we can't control anyway."

At the same time, the central computer resources are evolving. The expanding capabilities and the backup they can provide to the distributed environment help coordinate what goes on in the periphery, even under a laissez faire policy like that adopted by St. Paul.

A TIME FOR STANDARDIZATION?

Workstations, local data processing, local area networks, messaging, and file and text retrieval are in full evolution, and the evolution is rapid. The driving force is in the need for a more efficient, reliable, and secure means of communication, timely and accurate access to text and databases, and the impact of information available instantly from different sources.

The PC plays the role of a monitoring system in the network; it provides the user with softcopies and hardcopies without leaving the desk or wasting time on the phone. This is why the communicating capability of the personal computer and the features of the LAN are so valuable. Said the DP director of a leading insurance company, "We are standardizing on the IBM PC. They are more expensive, but can also substitute for the IBM terminals."

IBM has big marketing plans for its PC. For the customer, buying from Sears and Computerworld represents a solution with no heavy overhead and no IBM inflexibility. But still more important is the fact that IBM intends to have the PC as a key part of its office product strategy. It can be a telephone station, an intelligent TV outlet, a data terminal, and a message device, as the 1983 IBM announcements helped document.

The key requirement is software to tie the PC to the telephone system, the minis, and the mainframes. When that can be done, and the PC is integrated with the telephone chores, adoption will be accelerated. The foremost consideration, therefore, is to tie the different functions together. Most important among them is communications; and when we standardize it is in that direction that we should first move. With that in mind, we can talk of six compatibilities with reference to the PC:

1. Communications protocol
2. LAN interface
3. Microprocessor
4. Bus structure
5. Operating system
6. Language

Three data communication protocols come immediately to mind: start/stop, binary synchronous, and packet switching. The latter is increasingly gaining acceptance, particularly since the X.25 standard established by CCITT is becoming the basis of new value-added network designs. But this subject is much broader than short-haul communications. Quite unlike our past ideas, which centered mainly on the carrier lines, the modern way to look at protocols is to cover the whole range from databasing to data communication.

A message is a file in the database, and any message should be structured as a file. That outlook can be implemented if we take care to make databasing, processing, and communications capabilities compatible as to data structures, file structures, bits per word, and instruction sets.

Leading computer users understand this challenge and have established their own standards when there were no generally accepted ones. A company may have hundreds of computers around, but in the absence of standards the data on one machine are not the same as those on another. Communications become twisted, and much power is lost in interminable translations.

The basic assumption behind homogeneity is that a workstation of any kind acts as both local intelligence and an input/output (I/O) device. Through LAN, a PC, a data terminal, a minicomputer or mainframe, a facsimile machine, a word processor, an electronic copier, and a telephone can be linked to one comprehensive system for the transmission and interaction of information. Communications and networks are an inseparable part of the evaluation of an automated office and computer-based message systems at large. Standards are indispensable; our civilization is based on effective communications.

The cutting edge of technology sees to it that local networking is inseparable from the employment of microcomputer systems, and vice versa. A LAN is not an end in itself; it is an essential way for the user to realize the benefits to be derived from semiconductors in his daily work. The same is true of the PC. In a local environment, communicating devices are not far from each other, but there is definite physical separation from a few dozen meters to a few kilometers. Furthermore, communications links may be set up long-haul through a switched or dedicated telephone network among distant LANs.

When it comes to the LAN interface, the best standardization is being done by IEEE Project 802. Three protocols for local networking are favored:

- Carrier-sensing multiple access with collision detection (CSMA/CD)
- Token ring
- Token bus

To these should be added a variation of CSMA/CD with random delays generated after message collision; it is of particular interest in transmission over longer distances such as those in metropolitan areas. That is true of a protocol, originally introduced in about 1960, that has waited until station intelligence has permitted its usage: truth tables, also known as tree structures.

A *bus* is used to interface many different modules. Examples are the S-100/IEEE-696 and the IEEE-488 buses. Both are hardware buses that permit a user to plug in a bus-compatible device, without having to make any other hardware modifications, and have the device operate. The S-100 was first used in one of the early PC kits. In reality, it is a compact 100-pin module. Currently it is the most widely used microcomputer hardware interconnection, and it offers advantages that are not available with any other microcomputer connector. Also, it is processor-independent.

There are already 30 different S-100 central processing unit (CPU) cards that can be plugged into an S-100 bus. Nine 8-bit microprocessors are available: 6502, 6800, 6802, 6809, 2650, F8, 8080, 8085, and Z80. Eight 16-bit and 32-bit microprocessors are compatible: 8086, 8088, 9900, Z8000, 68,000, Pascal Microengine, Alpha Micro (similar to LSI-11), and the AMD 2901 bit slice processor. The S-100 also has great hardware support. There are now over sixty different manufacturers of about 400 different plug-in S-100 boards, and that's greater than any other microcomputer system.

It can be seen why the S-100 bus is most widely used with microcomputers. It has a data transfer rate of up to 10 MHz, and it accommodates the newer 16-bit processors by directly addressing up to 16 MB (megabytes) of memory, 64K I/O ports, 10 vectored interrupts, 16 bus masters, and 23 plug-in slots.

Most new developments in the microcomputer field such as 16-bit microprocessors, dual processors, direct memory access, cache memories, and the CP/M and MS DOS operating systems have an S-100–based solution with two floppy disk drives. Finally, the S-100 bus has been adopted as the IEEE-696 bus standard.

There are also *software buses*; an example is the control program for microcomputers (CP/M) by Digital Research. An operating system is a *logical bus*. In terms of operating systems (OS), the developing de facto "standards" are the CP/M 80 and 86, the USCD Pascal (ISO level O), the MS DOS (disk operating system), which will most likely dominate the 16-BPW market, and Unix, the upcoming OS for a whole range of applications.

Intel realized the CP/M in firmware. Introduced in 1974, this disk operating system is the oldest and most mature DOS for microcomputers. It has been implemented on over 250 different types of equipment. One of its advantages is that it leads to easy emulation; there is no machine-gated problem, and there are no major throughput requirements.

CP/M has been used with hard disk systems as well as with floppy disks. It is supported by two user groups, CP/MUG and SIG/MUG, that have released some 60 volumes containing more than 1600 public domain programs. Those programs can be loaded into and run on systems using the CP/M DOS. To them should be added another 1500 commercially available CP/M software packages. Together the program groups form the largest applications software base in existence. Finally, the CP/M version-to-version compatibility is high and has been maintained as new features have been added.

TABLE 1-2 DE FACTO OS STANDARDS FOR PERSONAL COMPUTERS

	Current and projected utilization, percent	
	1982*	1986†
UNIX	5	14
CP/M 80	70	22
CP/M 86	10	20
MS DOS	15	44

* With about 3 million PC.
† With about 10 to 12 million PC.

Yet the winners with the 16-BPW personal computers will most likely be MS DOS and Unix. The latter will also dominate the 32-BPW market and an impressive range of applications, having become a requirement for procurement (currently, of minicomputers) at the Department of Defense. Table 1-2 outlines the current and projected utilization of the evolved de facto OS standards with PC.

The earliest PC language favorite was Basic, but as the PC usage matures, it leaves much to be desired. Two trends are in evidence:

- Among end users Pascal is taking the lead, as Table 1-3 shows. It is expected that by 1985 Basic and Pascal will be sharing about equally some 85 percent of the market.
- Software developers (particularly of basic and horizontal software) increasingly use the C language designed by Bell Telephone Laboratories. It and the Unix OS, also Bell designed, are becoming an industry standard.

TABLE 1-3 PROGRAMMING LANGUAGE UTILIZATION FOR MICRO-, MINI-, AND PERSONAL COMPUTERS

	Mini to VAX, percent	Pesonal computers, percent	
		1982	1985 (Expected)
Basic	40	70	45
Pascal	15	25	40
C	5	1–2	10
Mod. 2	—	0–0.5	5 (Mod. 2 through Fortran)
Cobol	25	1–2	
Fortran	5	0.5–1	
Other	10	2	

The trend toward computers and communications standardization is now evident. Standardization is promoted by a standards association or just springs up. If the trend persists, there will be two groups:

- *The innovators*, who risk losing their companies in the process of trying to impose de facto standards. The only exception is IBM. Its market share, together with the plug-compatible companies, has made its technical characteristics the de facto industry standard.
- The "*me too'ers*," who, like the Japanese, copy but do it better at lower cost. Purchasers hope to get a better return on their capital.

Because both groups eye the end user and his investment, successful companies will start with the application and move upstream toward design. Determining application priorities is a key element in planning. The first step, of course, is to establish how to plan. The organization must be sure that the right people are involved and that all key points are covered. In developing a strategic standardization and compatibility plan, management should draw up guidelines which the company adopts as a formal policy. This helps ensure the cooperation of all employees from the designers to the production and the marketing people.

A plan must cover a wide range: identification of critical applications, the level of technology to be used, emergency processing, and methods of keeping the end users informed about developments. In all this, the best input is user participation.

IS THERE A ROLE FOR MAINFRAMES?

We have said that the future lies in an intelligent, well-directed workstation implementation with most of the emphasis on PCs and LANs. Does this spell the demise of mainframes and minicomputers? Statistics can help find an answer, but the answer is not a simple yes or no. First, statistics do indicate that in the 1970s the minis reduced the mainframes' market share, but they did not secure all of the market. The mini-micro scenario will no doubt be similar; there is good evidence that PC purchases have led to orders for minicomputers being cancelled.

The defenses of the mainframes, and of the minis on the installed base, have two bastions:

1. The large investments in applications software which companies wisely refuse to throw away every time a new technology

comes around. Such software investments will be mitigated by depreciation and obsolescence, but the change will not be abrupt.

2. Professional mentality, which changes with time and exposure but puts the brakes on fast new developments. Eventually, training, conviction, coercion, or flat orders will peel off the layers of prejudice.

PCs and LANs will dominate the new applications and the revamped projects. They will coexist with the older computer systems solutions until physical, logical, and human pressures overcome the barriers to greater efficiency and modernization. At the same time mainframes will be given a new mission, probably that of central text and database warehouse.

Farther out on the horizon is the fifth generation computer project with the goal of developing, by the 1990s, machines that incorporate and exploit the concepts of artificial intelligence. These computers will have problem-solving functions, sophisticated man-machine interfaces, and inference and knowledge-based expert functions. Innovative computer architectures, substantially different from traditional Von Neumann machines, will be investigated. The goal, however, is solutions in artificial intelligence, not just concepts different than those characterizing the Von Neumann approach to machine design and programming.

Present-day mainframes offer up to 25 million instructions per second (MIPS) and 128 MB of central memory (Fujitsu) and upwards of 40 pins (I/O pins on the chip) packaging. That is up from the 16 and 24 pins of the 1970s. Current developments are toward 160 to 180 pins, and 240 is the next goal.

On the other hand, as we get enough functions inside the chip, the number of I/O pins will start to go down. This development is quite significant for another reason: As the number of gates goes up and the cost of gates sharply decreases, an artificial intelligence machine will become economically feasible. A whole generation of artificial intelligence engines will then show up.

Both mainframes and the PC benefit from the RAM evolution. Between 1972 and 1982 we went from the 1K (1024 bytes) to the 64K chip. The silicon 256K chip was available at the time of publication, and the production yield and associated price drop necessary for wide use was projected for 1984. Quite significantly, the 1-MB silicon chip is in the laboratory. The yield is very low, but chips exist. What's important is that, contrary to earlier predictions, it does not push the laws of physics to the limit. Electronbeam resist in pattern creation eases the masking technology and achieves resolution at the angstrom level.

Another effort concentrates on increasing the number of instructions per second. This calls for:

- Shortening the delay paths to reduce media delay
- Increasing the level of circuit integration
- Building a new central interface unit to allow a larger number of multiprocessors
- Imbedding in the design the ability of the system to reconfigure itself
- Developing powerful logical functions to be created in silicon rather than run in software

New logical development will create a *hypervisor* capability. This sees to it that the machine can run under two different operating systems or two versions of the same OS without interference. Though this facility can also exist in PCs (Apple III allows DOS and USCS to coexist), a dual environment is not advisable with PCs. It may be welcome with mainframes, however.

The most valid projection about the future of mainframes is that they will turn into text and database storage machines. They will continue to run in large numbers because of the amount of text and data that will be generated by PCs and LANs at the workstation level.

LOCAL AREA NETWORKS

Coaxial cable has been successfully used for many years in cable television. In that application it supplied the first cost-effective means of carrying multiple data signals on one medium: up to 30 different channels of the same or different frequency. That was made possible by combining the advantages of coaxial cable with computers and radio frequency communications.

The cable came to be used for local networking when it was appreciated that here was a way to provide business and industry with a simple, economical means of transmitting text, data, voice, and image in digital form and also analog control signals. It met the growing need for generating, processing, transmitting, and storing information of all kinds. To the local area network structures thereby created can be attached personal workstations, microprocessors, microfiles, databases, and interactive graphics. Personal computers are powerful enough for even ambitious user applications when they are integrated into a LAN. By emphasizing a systems rather than a component-by-component approach, LANs can dramatically increase user productivity and also accommodate an organization's changing goals and structure.

Local networks equipped with personal computers can lead to the integration of word processing and data processing and also foster innovative approaches to computer applications. At the core are the microcomputers. Designing PC LANs requires a set of objectives different from those involved in designing long-haul networks for large computer systems.

The fundamental problem is how to create a useful processing, databasing, and communications tool within the cost constraints imposed by the pricing of today's computers and components. We must take advantage of the readily available off-the-shelf desktop units, floppy disks, hard disks, video units, and printers. A similar comment is appropriate to the applications software, which, for a personal computer network, must be designed to cost no more, and preferably much less, than the computers themselves. That is equally applicable to the interfaces to the LAN transport medium. The network interfaces should not be a dominant part of the total system cost; otherwise, they become counterproductive.

The power of the personal computer lies not in the hardware but in the software. That being so, the emphasis of the information system disciplines is changing. For the 1980s, databasing is the most widespread task in computing. The local area network should support an efficient text and database access mechanism. No matter how the user thinks of his data, ultimately it will have to be stored on some medium, retrieved, updated, and made available for *man-information* interactivity and other communications purposes. Together with databases, the 1980s will see a new thrust in the communications disciplines.

Microcomputers, databases, and local networks are the portals to a new era; together they define the *myriaprocessor*. A myriaprocessor's hardware and software should compare very favorably with alternative solutions including all faculties supported: processing, storage, retrieval, transport, and presentation. Design is, of course, at a premium. It must be based on the fact that, in modern business, information is a vital material and the efficiency with which it is handled dramatically affects managerial performance and profits.

LOCAL NETWORKS IN THE OFFICE ENVIRONMENT

Information in an office environment is diverse in form and presentation. It includes:

- Audio components
- Video (softcopy) reports
- Hardcopy confirmations
- Instantaneous query requirements
- Access to text and data warehouses

In classical office applications different protocols are used and the transmission speeds required are nonhomogeneous. Variety in media and procedures necessarily leads to solutions which have characterized office work. To integrate them, we must study the fundamentals, make choices, and experiment to find the most applicable solutions. Three other characteristics are important:

1. Information in the office is nearly simultaneous in use. This leads to online approaches.
2. The new technologies are not text handling but video and graphics. These will be increasingly employed for management reporting, teleconferencing, educational, and security purposes.
3. Office practice cannot be upset through the introduction of new systems. Any such introduction must be carefully planned. Continuity can be preserved by considering the information lines, the corresponding practices, and the prevailing motivations.

In the past, the mechanization of office chores has given us specialized services, but there have been drawbacks. The most notable of the latter have been nonhomogeneous modernization, the proliferation of equipment, and the difficulty of interconnection. The last has led to increasingly high costs and has impeded implementation of the electronic office. The LAN allows us to unify systems and procedures.

Cost-effectiveness is more than a matter of dollars and cents. Many savings can be realized by cabling the office in a unified way and permitting all types of traffic to transit through the cable. But still more important is the continuity to be provided through the implementation of a LAN. It *is* possible to avoid upsetting current practices.

Prerequisite to such an implementation are plug compatibility and agile user interfaces; these have the highest importance. We have had word processors, videos, printers, and telephones for years, but our experience with local area networks is still scanty. Choices and tradeoffs are therefore necessary.

When a function can be implemented with either hardware or software, the PC cost advantage often lies with simple, programmable hardware. Responsibility for most of the function is then assigned to the software. Another decision involving both functionality and cost concerns network speed. The choice should be a network performance level that can be supported at reasonable cost by personal computers.

The text, data, and image terminating equipment, the number of units to be attached to the network, and the volume of traffic help establish the bandwidth requirements. The work to be typically done at the workstations in the network must be established in advance and be both quantified and qualified. It is not enough to say "it's office work." Only when this has been done in an able manner is it possible to study the implementation properly. In the system study due attention must be paid to LAN flexibility. This, too, has its prerequisites. For instance, one kind of flexibility results from the autostart facility of the network.

The system can be so configured that specific workstations, when turned on, automatically download specific programs to themselves or to other stations from a network file server. This makes possible no-operator server stations, easy parametric reconfiguration, turnkey applications, and secure, generally available workstations. Networks able to support these characteristics can be either a local or a long-haul network (LHN). As Table 2-1 shows, the two major classes of networking differ greatly, particularly in cost, capacity, and the attention given to WS design.

Clearly, though, the distinction between a LAN and a LHN is not black or white. Many different network versions are possible: a strictly local application in which baseband solutions, say up to 10 Mbps, are sufficient; an area beyond the local boundaries in which broadband capabilities, say up to 400 Mbps, are necessary; a coast-to-coast long-haul capability; or a global network with internetworking and long-haul networks (Fig. 2-1).

Typically, global networks are satellite-supported and, with current technology, carry about 400 megahertz channels, which is the broadband capacity offered by LANs. Like the coaxial cable and optical fiber installations, a satellite system is characterized by all-digital transmission, which makes possible the integration of voice, data, and image traffic. Both the LAN and the satellite system offer wideband transmission, the former among workstations and the latter to earth stations situated directly on customer premises or linked by high-speed local connections. Both are, furthermore, characterized by switched interconnections among virtually any number of network nodes.

Ten criteria help differentiate the local area architectures:

1. The overall network architecture: supported services and conformity to international standards
2. The number of layers supported by the LAN
3. The gateways to other LANs and LHNs
4. The network structure and topology (ring, ether, star, and so on)

TABLE 2-1 COMPARISON OF LOCAL AND LONG-HAUL NETWORKS

	LAN	LHN
Cost	Low to very low	High
Capacity	High to very high (Mbps)	Low (kbps)
Attention to WS design	Relatively high	Relatively low

5. The bits carried per second (broadband versus baseband)
6. The protocol being used (token, collision detection, slots, etc.)
7. The physical medium (twisted wire, flat wire, coaxial, optical fiber)
8. The way information is transmitted on the carrier
9. The type and cost of the bus interface unit
10. The modems to be used

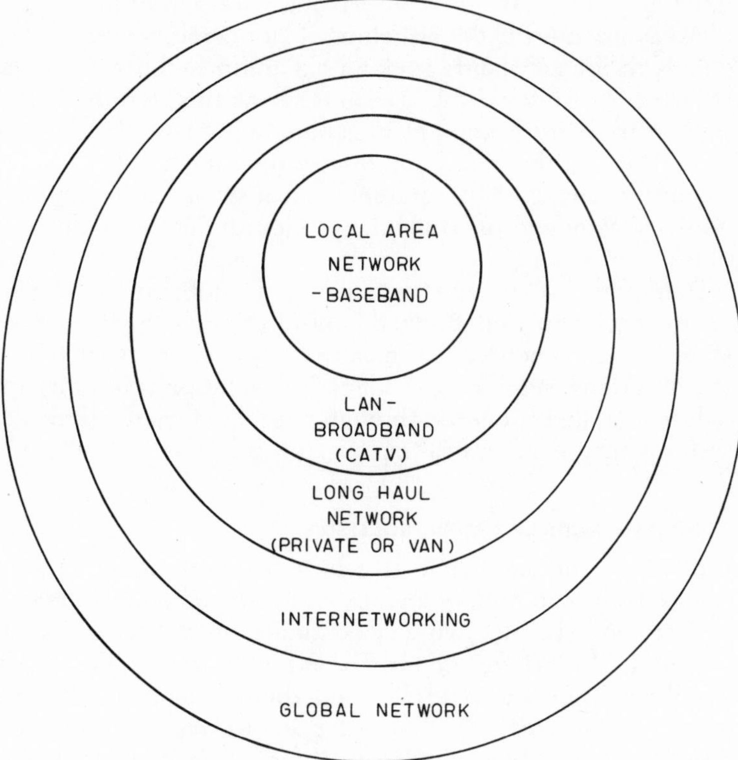

Figure 2-1. Between a baseband LAN and a satellite-based global network there are several intermediate solutions.

There are three basic ways of transmitting information:

1. Audio signals, such as voice transmission on classical telephone lines
2. Video signals, as used in television
3. Binary digits such as the electronic pulses in digital computers

A particular complication in office application is the need for handling all three types of signals. This has led to the countless pairs of telephone wires, one of which is usually dedicated to each function. The variety and multiplicity of office applications—voice signals, closed-circuit television, security alarm, power monitoring, word processing, data processing, copiers, printers, facsimile—led to overlapping networks of wires needed to tie all the elements together. The result has not been a cohesive, integrated communications system. Furthermore, each additional application necessitates adding a minimum of two new wires to an existing wire bundle.

To avoid altering the structure of an operating system, installation engineers are constantly seeking out an unused pair within a bundle, entering existing wiring conduits, installing terminal blocks, and proceeding with a number of other time-consuming and expensive tasks. With all that going on, troubleshooting and fault isolation may require many days to complete because of the complexity of the wiring system and the difficulty of identifying the source of a certain noise.

Aside from time and expense, it is difficult for a company to maintain effective centralized control of a multipath communication system, since each communication application usually has its own specifications and wiring. The modern solution is interdisciplinary in nature, and that is offered through a local area network which aims to assure a total communications capability.

COMPONENT PARTS OF A MYRIAPROCESSOR

With the implementation of a local network architecture, a single coaxial cable can replace an entire network of conventional wires and permit simultaneous two-way communication between workstations in the LAN. When properly monitored, the cable is capable of handling hundreds of high-speed digital channels with text, data, voice, and image signals. For instance, in a coaxial broadband configuration, a single cable provides the information capacity of thousands of twisted pairs of conventional telephone wires.

In an office, the cable is run through an elevated floor or overhead; in factories, the overhead solution is often favored (Fig. 2-2). Office and factory approaches can be similar except that in the factory a baseband system tends to be less advisable because of possible interferences from nearby motors or other equipment. Whether in the office or in the factory, the myriaprocessor requires:

1. An *object-based system.*
2. *Nodes* with memory and processing power that are well defined.
3. *Protocols* for tasks running on one node to access another.
4. *Programs* that are systemwide rather than a program for this or that machine.

Above all, there must be a *strategy*. Where do we wish to go? What do we want to reach? At what cost? Within what time? Having answered these questions, we must look at the mechanics. How can we simulate the complete projected system? What experiment is to be used at each WS? How much memory shall we put at each node?

Many answers are specific to the situation, but basic definitions can be helpful:

- With the *myriaprocessor*, the main contention is *not* in CPU cycles but in access to the disk.

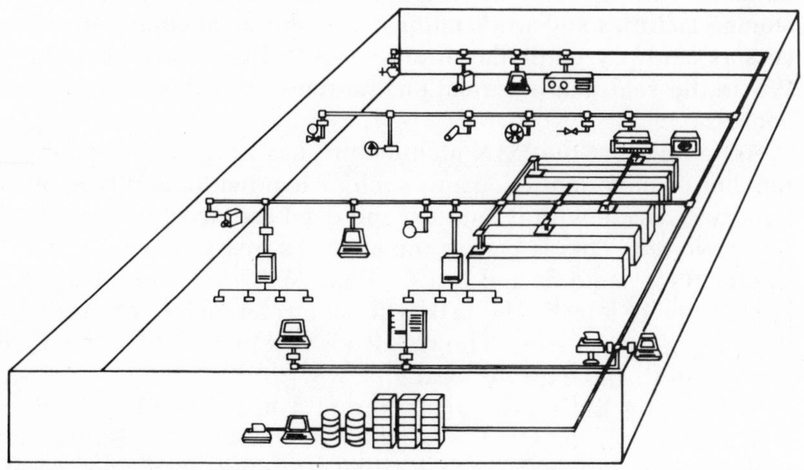

Figure 2-2. Local area network in a factory environment.

- Thus, it may be advantageous that the *database* be distributed to a *number* of nodes which can store information elements (IE).
- The nodes can be workstations or dedicated rear-end machines. What is important to the user is that there be *one logical source* of data.

This is the reason for using *pipes* and associated routing information. Furthermore:

1. The LAN *architecture* must be flexible, easy to implement and to maintain.
2. The chosen *protocols* must provide reasonable assurance of error correction and a guaranteed message delivery.
3. The supported *band* must be wide enough to cover the projected application(s).
4. The *services* being featured must answer the applications requirements in a cost-effective manner.
5. The *strategy* should be to develop a LAN architecture which can promote lots of parallelism—and be open to future developments.

The design must assure that the system is flexible and expandable. Almost certainly, as applications experience accumulates, we will need to increase the number of nodes, accommodate additional storage facilities and workstations, blur the distinction between processors, and pay particular attention to end use considerations. The WS is the real man-information interface, and therefore our major concern.

Assuming that the LAN architecture has been properly drafted, a number of important decisions such as bandwidth and type of cable have been made with it, but text and database structure and distribution have not. This is part of the analyst's mission. A LAN is full of information elements and tasks. At any WS a keystroke leads to the appearance of a task. The task will have reference to objects (stacks, data storage, processes). The task itself will move where the TDB is, fetch from it, and execute locally.

Automating file access, downline and upline loading, and other activities obviously involve network overhead. That is true of the traffic-handling procedures of the network architecture; it is one of the reasons why the choice of an architecture is so fundamental. For instance, for short-term information exchanges, network overhead can be avoided by permitting multiple-packet two-way physical connections on the network. This allows several packets to be sent between a pair of stations without having to free and reallocate the cable between packet transmissions, and it results in a performance increase for an operation that requires the exchange of several small data packets.

While the details of the employed technology should be absolutely transparent to the users, the LAN specialist should clearly understand the software tools available to allow the construction of indivisible operations analogous to a read, modify, write memory cycle necessary for synchronization of multiple independent processes. Among other important technical issues which should be visible to the systems expert is the procedure followed for the acknowledgment of successful transmission to be sent back to the sender with no significant delay.

If the protocols are carefully designed, we can have nodes differing in capacity. Plenty of challenges lie in the logical functions, not in the hardware. An 8086 can easily handle a 50-MB disk; there is cheap computing hardware with powerful features. The applications study should not be too concerned with hardware efficiency in resource utilization. The mission is to assure a consistent TDB image, and much of the complication a system may have is directly related to that problem.

One of the solutions is a mechanism for storing data redundantly. From the system standpoint, our main interest should be not what the packets look like, but what the processors and the processes say to each other. For greater efficiency in this task, each node should have a directory that indicates which other node is interested in an IE and must be informed if this IE is moved or altered.

Regarding the operation of a distributed database, IBM says that 80 percent of our processing is done on 20 percent of our database. When we have properly identified the 20 percent, we can find whether to distribute it personally, locally, or to a text and data warehouse. It is well to remember, however, that with LAN and LHN every distributed database (DDB) level at every post can be accessible to every WS in the system (Fig. 2-3).

The system must provide assurance that microfiles (personal files) will be reserved to their originators (users) and selected, authorized associates. Even a proprietary TDB may be downstream sharing its IE with other users. It is, however, advisable to move sharable IE to a universal TDB, which may be local-area-based, or a text and data warehouse which users typically need a code to access.

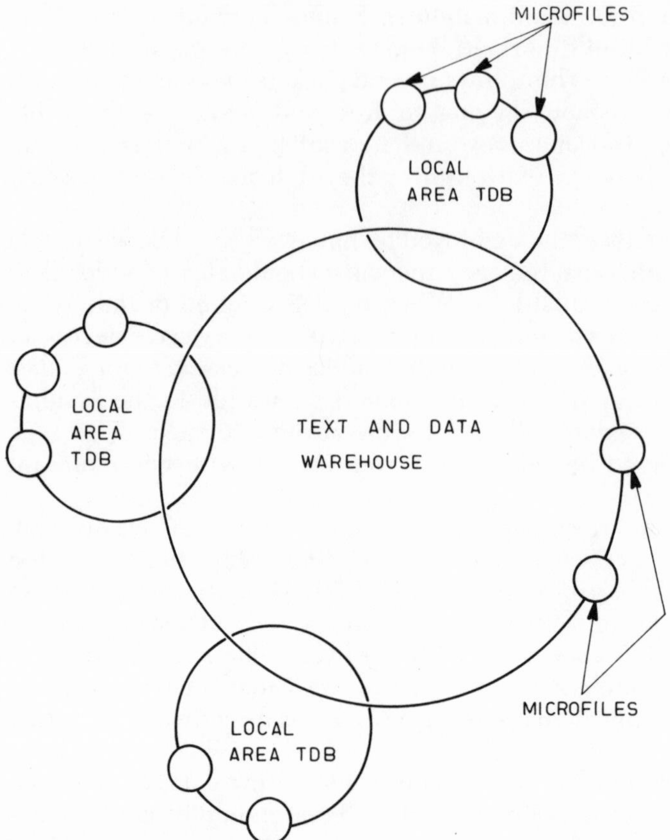

Figure 2-3. Taken together, personal microfiles, local area text and databases, and central text and data warehouses constitute one of the most vital resources of the enterprise.

For its part, the WS should be capable of message transfer to and from the TDB. This implies the existence of software, but just as vital is the training of the communicators. The key is learning to use effectively the kind of interactive faculties a LAN makes feasible. We must learn to access memory—our own and others' microfiles—and get out of paper.

INTERCONNECTION TECHNOLOGY

Interconnection technology is vital for three reasons: local workstations will grow increasingly complex and will themselves constitute tiny networks; the LAN has a horizontal, nonhierarchical structure and a dependability that is increased by interconnecting nodes; and an internetworking capability is needed. Interconnection is one of the key subjects in the 1980s.

Interconnection technology has to do with the ways and means of obtaining a fully connected local area network. Each node may be a LAN on its own, and each may have one or more gateways. During the middle 1980s an impressive amount of interconnection hardware will be offered. The challenge will be in software development.

An important interconnection problem is that of LANs interfacing with minicomputers and mainframes. Since every major company has plenty of minis and mainframes, these are the questions to be answered in a systems study: How can we provide a gateway to our minis? To the mainframes? Can we use existing packages and dedicate one microcomputer to data communication? What's the effect on the LAN disk(s) of mixing languages such as Basic and Pascal?

To a certain degree, it is a matter of seeking out other experiences and obtaining information about them. And since most projects are still in their infancy, the search for efficient solutions will necessarily involve a good degree of experimentation. As Professor Halstead of MIT remarked, "Interacting with the big OS is hopelessly complicated. With micros we can be more specific in doing what we want to do."

The new generation of layered operating systems which is under development may ease current constraints. The principle of such a system affords a novel and efficient approach to the management of computers and communications resources. The imbedded functions in an OS can be separated into layers. Each layer implements a class of real or virtual faculties and manages the following:

- Processes and jobs
- Virtual memory
- Text and data search and retrieval
- Files and messages
- Communications disciplines
- Directories and definitions

Each layer can be implemented with functions toward the levels lower down but not those higher up. The principle is extendable to permit the design of cooperating processes within an integrated methodology. This is roughly the approach taken with the LAN servers. Webster's defines a *server* as "one who serves or assists; a thing used in serving." In LAN technology, a server is a hardware and software package dedicated to the support of common resources. We distinguish the file server, print server, and communications server (gateway, internet). These are basic features in any LAN.

Though the semantic gap from the outermost to the innermost layer may be great, that between any two successive levels is small. Layers are linked through interfaces; each is characterized by a protocol; and many layers may be converted to firmware. The more a given layer takes on a hardware form, the more effective the total system becomes and the more the system resembles an integrated data processing, databasing, data communicating (DP/DB/DC) machine reflected in a local network architecture.

We said above that the main reason why interconnection technology is so important has to do with the workstations to be attached to the LAN. This introduces the subject of the interfaces. An interface has two basic aspects: technology and cost. The interface logic (contained in a bus interface unit, or BIU) is composed of hardware that recognizes its own station address in a data packet on the network. A control line in the cable indicates that there is a station address and triggers a comparator that notifies when the address in the network matches that programmed into the address switch on the interface. (The same control line serves as the carrier signal indicating that a transmission is in progress.)

Typically, the interface of a WS toward the cable of the LAN will be composed of two parts: a tap or attachments on the carrier and a transponder. The latter may be a stand-alone BIU or a card to be inserted in the slot of the personal computer (as in the Apple). More demanding attached resources are the gateway, print server, and disk server (Fig. 2-4).

As stated earlier in this chapter, the cost of the BIU should be a small fraction of that of the personal computer to which it is attached. Choosing a LAN has both technical and financial aspects. Although the cost of the BIU will fall with volume production, as we will see in a later chapter, the interface costs for different LANs today differ by an order of magnitude. In some cases they exceed the cost of the workstation.

Let's consider WS procedures run on a 64K RAM Apple II Plus with a 10-MB Corvus hard disk. The Apple costs $1695; each BIU costs $490; the hard disk costs about $4000; a Pascal language system (with language card, Pascal diskettes, and manuals) is $495. A myriaprocessor of, say, 25 personal computers will then cost $66,275 if there is a 30 percent quantity discount for Pascal, and less if the Apples and the BIUs also are discounted. But if the interface cost were $4500, the cost would be prohibitive and unfavorably comparable to that of a minicomputer.

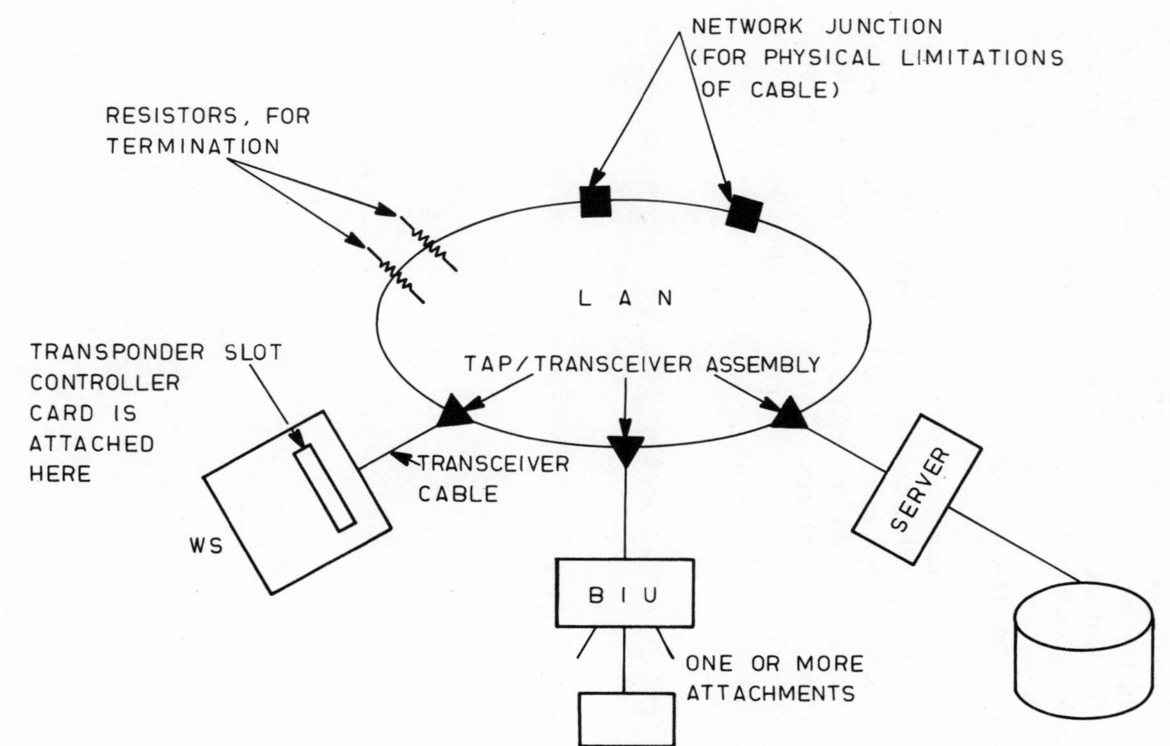

Figure 2-4. A typical LAN structure with taps, workstations, BIU, servers, and shared resources.

The novelty of LAN applications, the importance of effective man-information communications at the WS level, applications requirements, and interconnection characteristics are good reasons why the systems specialist must work with the users to develop a set of solid manuals. The manuals must be well prepared and have many complete models that exemplify the functions and detail this fundamentally different approach to office work. It is advantageous to include in the manual a quick reference card that summarizes all the procedural features.

The user's manual should make it very easy for a novice to set up a simple operation in less than an hour, while giving experts more than enough functions to chew on. It should be based on the procedures that most office employees use with classical equipment; it should explain the procedural differences where they exist; and it should provide the simplest answers to the implementation problems.

3 THE CARRIER PROBLEM

Webster's defines a network as any arrangement of fabric by wires, threads, and so on, crossed at regular intervals by others fastened to them so as to leave open spaces; netting; mesh. By extension, a network is a system of crossed roads, canals, and communications lines. Webster's specifies the networking capability as that of broadcasting simultaneously over all or most stations in the network.

Such a capacity in a network is fundamental to interconnecting workstations, giving the stations access to the text and database, and making feasible the exchange of messages. A company's communications network can be both local and global. The local portion connects workstations together so that they appear as part of the larger system. The interconnection is made by a physical medium: a coaxial cable, an optical fiber, a flat wire, or a twisted pair.

On any carrier, messages can be handled in either analog or digital form, but the trend is toward the digital (Fig. 3-1). With analog transmission, the basically digital information requires modulator-demodulator equipment, as we will see when we talk of modems. Digital transmission assures greater reliability (lower bit error rate), efficiency, and also the possibility of storing and forwarding information, including digitized voice.

The choice of local area network should be based on the requirements: modularity, reliability, expandability, common hardware, server software, and the range of services—electronic messaging, word processing, filing, retrieval, and so on. Assuming that the physical problem of the carrier facilities has been solved (and we will soon see how), typical attachments will be:

- Memory-to-memory communications
- Telephones

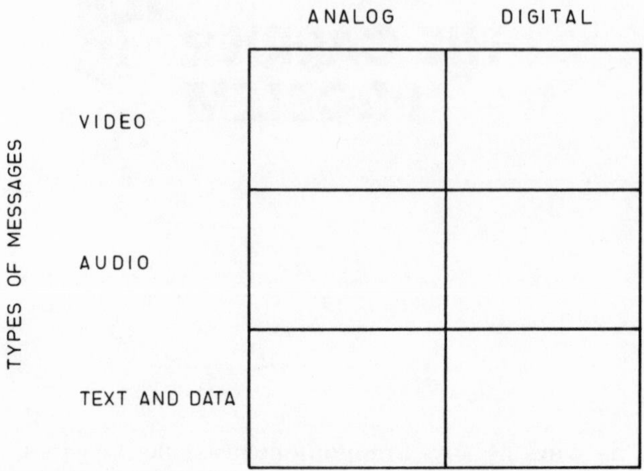

Figure 3-1. Types of messages and forms of handling information. The tendency is to move from analog to digital.

- Terminals or computer workstations
- Sensors to process control
- The imaging of workstations
- File transfer systems
- A host of messaging services
- Teleconferencing (from freeze frame to full motion)

These services will proceed simultaneously, and for their provision the word *channelize* has been coined. It means multiple simultaneous use of the same cable. That use is supported through logical approaches, but to start with there is a physical cable.

GOING COAXIAL

At the heart of every network is an efficient cable system capable of meeting virtually any information-handling need. Efficiency can be increased by installing a single coaxial cable on which we can channelize voice, text, data, and image. However, the coaxial cable is not the only possible network carrier. Alternatives are optical fibers, flat wire (8 or 16 channels), and twisted pairs. Optical fiber networks are typically broadband. (We will talk of bandwidths in the following chapter.) Coaxial cable, on the other hand, can be either broadband or

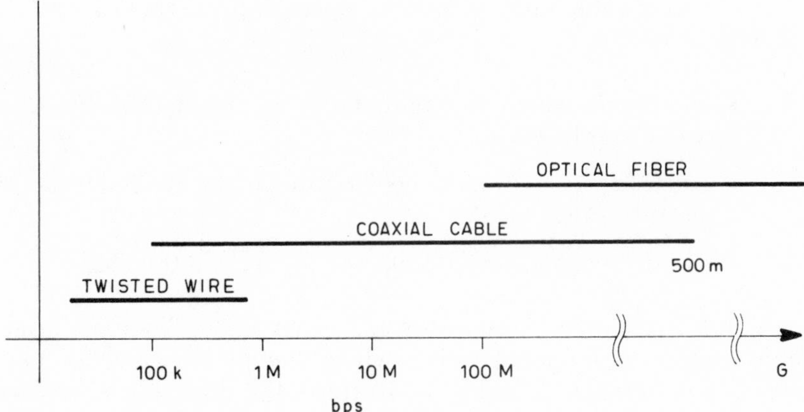

Figure 3-2. Data rates, in bits per second, supported by different types of carriers.

baseband. Flat and twisted wires support baseband data rates (Fig. 3-2).

A distinction should be made between available band and usable band. The available band of cable television (CATV) goes up to 400 MHz, but only part of it is usable for reasons of noise and other interference. Another problem is the modem, which becomes costly at high frequencies. When the modem is of lower quality (and lower cost), the interband ranges needed to avoid overlaps consume part of the band. For instance, of a 128-kbps band we may use only the central 64 kbps.

The choice of the medium should be based on three main factors:

1. The installation's projected growth
2. The interface cost
3. The noise in the environment

The cost of installation dwarfs that of the medium, so we should not try to economize when choosing the cable. If the WS interface cost is low and a study indicates that data rate requirements will grow well beyond the supported bandwidth, then a coaxial medium is preferable. Otherwise, flat wire is an attractive alternative.

This is written from the perspective of the early 1980s. By extrapolating from experience with semiconductors, we can guess that eventually the cost of the coaxial interface will come down so sharply that there will be no significant difference in cost up to 10 Mbps. By one estimate, an interface should cost less than $100 by 1986.

In a coaxial cable network we can typically distinguish three levels of reference:

- *The trunk*, which transports radio-frequency (RF) signals between amplifiers
- *The feeder*, which connects the trunk to the general location of the subscriber
- *The drop cable*, which links the feeder and the user outlet

Trunk lines vary in diameter and attenuation. They are usually constructed of protected cable, which includes a rigid aluminum shield with a bending radius of 10 times the diameter. A dielectric surrounds the central copper conductor and separates it from the shield. Optional components are a polyethylene jacket over the aluminum and a compound injected between the aluminum shield and the outer jacket as protection in underground installations. Cables which run outside buildings or are mounted on poles are usually jacketed.

The feeder cable is usually of smaller size than the trunk cable. Indoor applications suggest three selection criteria:

- The physical constraints of the building
- The signal level necessary for adequate distribution to all users of the network
- Local and national building codes

High-gain distribution amplifiers are used when multiple high-level feeder legs are needed for different floors of a building. Taps are placed along the feeder cable to provide for connection to the user outlets. Drop cables incorporate a foil-and-braid shield to minimize radiation leakage. Even the least costly coaxial cable has effective shielding and exhibits low loss in uses up to 400 MHz.

System design is based upon the operational characteristics of the amplifiers, many makes and models of which are available from CATV applications. Performance and cost are the two key factors to be considered when evaluating an amplifier. Performance is defined by the gain, output level ratings, noise figure, and distortion characteristics. Cost is directly related to the quality of performance: Amplifiers with low noise and distortion are more costly.

Standard offerings in amplifiers are of the modular type; they can be configured to satisfy a wide variety of cable attenuation, tilt, and temperature ranges. This permits picking modules appropriate to individual systems. Two formats are available: automatic gain control (AGC) and manual gain control (MGC). The AGC amplifier maintains a relatively constant output when input variations are ±6 dB and provides constant signal levels to user outlets. MGC amplifiers compensate for thermal variations only and are employed in broadband applications.

Directional couplers divide or combine inputs and outputs of RF signals while maintaining the system impedance and isolation characteristics. Each ensures that a fractional portion of the signal will be tapped off to a network branch or outlet, with low insertion loss between the input and output trunk connections. This sees to it that signals being transmitted from any network device will be transmitted only toward the head end.

With current technology, a key advantage of coaxial cable over optical fiber is the ability to support multitaps. The multitaps facilitate connection of drop cables to the distribution system. They are available with different levels of attenuation so that outlets can be similar at different locations on the distribution network.

With isolation provided, all outlets stand alone: the connection or disconnection of a user device does not affect the operation of the overall system. Manually programmable directional taps provide internally housed security traps; they demonstrate the continuous development taking place in CATV products.

Terminators are an important aspect of any system. They are of several types, and they are used in large and small networks. They limit reflections in the system and minimize undesired signals.

Another critical issue is the power supply. Distributing power over the coaxial cable eliminates the need for a power outlet at each amplifier location. As a result, the amplifiers can be located anywhere in the network. Grounding the system at every amplifier will assure greater reliability and long life.

The power is coupled to the coaxial cable through the use of power combiners, which permit the injection of power in either or both directions with minimal effect on the RF signals. Care must be taken not to inject alternating current (ac) through multitaps or couplers not capable of passing power.

A fundamental consideration in the design of the coaxial system is the *head end.* It is the point of origin of all RF signals and the collection point for all signals being generated in the network's interconnecting devices. It must be able to support multiple services. Therefore, it must be carefully considered and designed so it can be expanded without upsetting the system.

The network may employ a midsplit, subsplit, or dual cable system. In a dual system one cable forms the forward and the other cable the return path. In the midsplit and subsplit systems there is one cable and the frequency band available on it is divided. In CATV there is little need for a logical return wire, hence the largest part of the band is devoted to forward transmission. In a midsplit the division between forward and return frequencies is usually made equal.

From an engineering standpoint, the layout of the return path is more important than that of the forward path. All return amplifier output signals eventually converge at the head end, and the same is true of the noise. Hence, in the return direction, signals are subject to noise degradation.

Basic design considerations must include the topology of the network, the associated components, the passive loss from directional couplers, taps, splitters, and combiners, and the resulting signal distributed throughout the network. Network architecture is a key preoccupation. Most systems today are of the tree type. That structure is the most favored one when all information being transmitted is to be accessed at any point and intersubscriber switching is not required. Interfacing tree structures involves appropriate gateway devices between trunks. We will return to the subject of gateways.

DESIGN CHARACTERISTICS

Noise has always been a nasty problem in electronics. It is any unwanted input, and eliminating it demands both the right study and supporting components. Although it is most pronounced in a factory environment, it is so important that offices also should be studied for possible interferences.

Another characteristic of the communications system is homogeneity. When we look into the physical aspects of a network, we find that the use of coaxial cable as the transmission medium eliminates the need for the many wires in traditional installations. Physically, the cable is very durable: it does not require the use of conduit; it can be fastened directly to walls or ceiling; and it can be buried as is for connecting system elements in many different buildings. If it is accidentally broken, it can be repaired in a few minutes, which compares favorably with the hours needed to repair a multiple-pair cable.

A major advantage of a coaxial cable network is that all components are readily available CATV parts. Another is the ease of connecting workstations and file servers through multitap approaches. Adding terminal point to the system is very simple. All that is necessary is the addition of a tap and a section of cable to connect the terminal device. The tap is quickly installed, and its cost is minimal. This assures flexibility through the attachment of remote locations as necessary to fit the growing communications needs of the organization. The coaxial system will carry information in both directions simultaneously by means of widely separated matched RF channels.

We have said that the coaxial cable is the physical medium. Within a logical networking organization, it will constitute the *compatibility layer* between the free-standing workstations characterizing an office automation environment and the data processing resources which already exist in the organization (Fig. 3-3). The software of the LAN architecture will provide the drivers.

Closely related to this subject is the matter of vendors and implementation. Using only the products of a single vendor leads to a proprietary, *closed* design. This has been the IBM strategy for years. Working with several vendors leads to an *open* design. Xerox has indicated that it favors this strategy, and so do several other vendors. A third alternative is the hybrid approach. This is the way Wang has

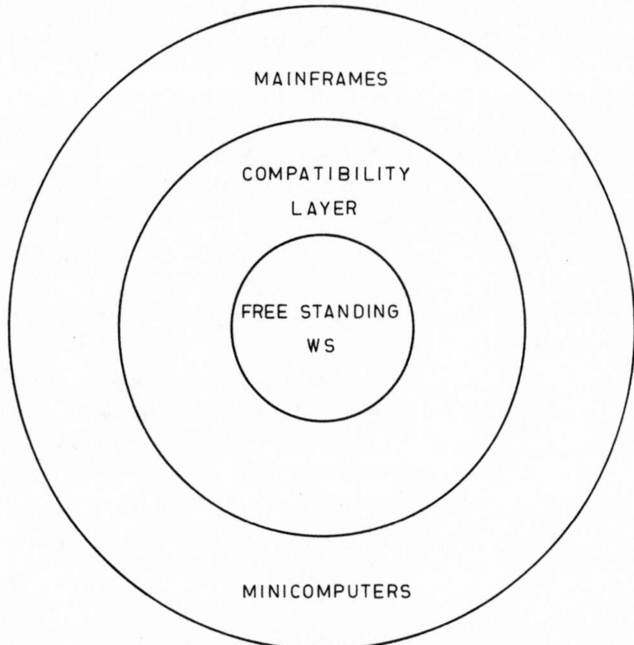

Figure 3-3. A logical compatibility layer connects the microprocessor-based workstations to the existing information systems environment of mainframes and minicomputers.

gone: it supports compatibility but also preserves a wide band for its own equipment on the Wangnet. The choice is not academic. It has much to do with control of the installation costs, flexibility in systems design, and the fact that no manufacturer today provides the whole range of components needed in an office automation environment.

The physical medium and the architecture will establish the limits and capabilities of the local area network. Typically, a coaxial cable will support wide bandwidth, high speed, multiple simultaneous uses of the same cable, and, when technology permits, replacement by fiber optics without upsetting the established system. The latter will be possible if proper design work has been done from the beginning.

Present-day coaxial cable systems tend to be divided into two basic parts: the workstations and the servers (gateways, databases, printers) with their bus interface units and the head end at a central location (Fig. 3-4). Most important in a communications environment is the definition of carrier function:

- The upper range of frequencies, the *forward channels*, used for transmission from the head end to the remote devices.
- The lower range of frequencies, the *reverse channels*, used for transmission from the remote devices back to the head end.

Modems transmit forward to the remote-device modem's receiver for that channel. The signal from the remote device back to the computer is received at the computer modem.

Increasing the number of attached workstations is merely a matter of tapping in new sections of cable for additional remote devices and adding the necessary modems. Flexibility is further enhanced, because all RF signals are transmitted throughout the network and any terminal device can be moved to any location to fit the requirements of the workplace.

The laying of the physical cable is not a subject of this section but the possible transmission schemes should be touched on. There are two types: frequency division multiplexing (FDM), and time division multiplexing (TDM). In FMD, a specific frequency is assigned to each channel supported by the physical cable. This approach is useful when transmission rates vary widely between the head end and remote device. It is also useful with a variety of point-to-point or multidrop applications, which are typical of an office environment. A specific radio frequency (channel) may be assiged to each unit or group of devices. The range is wide. Whereas the standard telephone wire has a frequency range of only about 3 MHz, a coaxial cable can effectively carry up to 400 MHz.

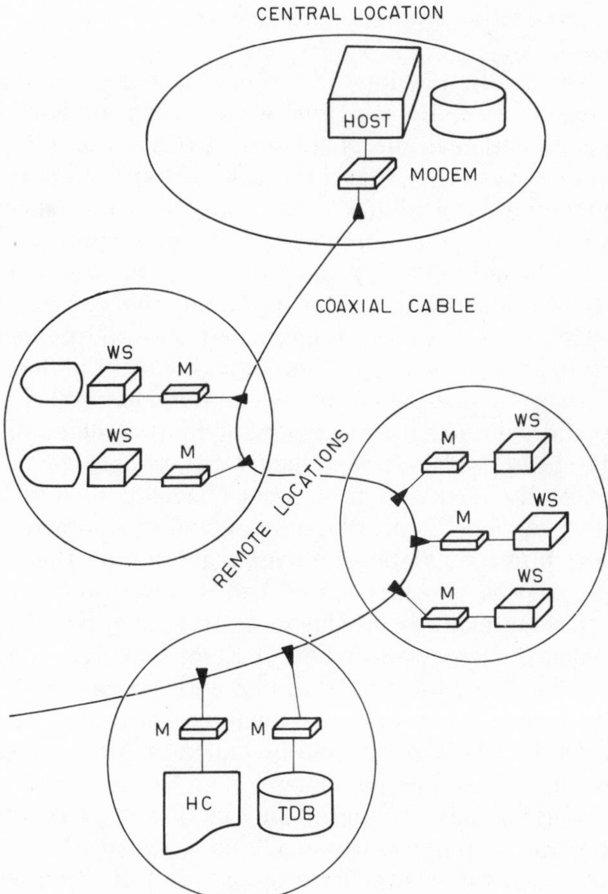

Figure 3-4. Central and remote locations connected through a coaxial cable LAN.

The frequency range of the broadband spectrum sees to it that noise and other electrical interference from the working environment does not affect transmissions, as it does in a conventional communication system. These are some of the positive characteristics of modern cable-based carriers.

Time division multiplexing permits a number of remote digital devices to use the same channel assignment by timesharing the physical resource. This can take place up to a specified rate of kilobits per second. The basic concept being to divide time, and therefore line capacity, the division can be fixed through slots or be dynamic. With TDM, there is a high fragmentation of the band's data rate, the delay is deterministic, and the process permits a high level of bandwidth usage.

Originally developed for the transatlantic cable, time division has been successfully used where there are good band utilization prerequisites and realtime characteristics. An example is process control, and one variety is a reservation type application. In a TDM solution a number of workstations can share the same channel. This is quite useful for data acquisition and terminal control applications. It also calls for rather sophisticated modems to accommodate high rates of digital data transfer, thus reducing the communication load on a system computer by an estimated 30 to 50 percent and freeing the central processor to perform other critical missions.

In this sense, data from the computer can be selectively transmitted to addressable remote-device modems. A channel control modem at the head end receives data from remote-device modems during cyclically recurring time slots allocated to remote workstations or other devices. Typically, only one word is transferrred from a remote device to the computer during a given time slot, but it is possible to effect block transmission of data acquired from a remote source.

Let's recapitulate. The most attractive aspects of a coaxial cable system, regardless of whether FDM or TDM is used, are reliability, wideband capability, flexibility, and the ease with which the system can be expanded. Since expansion costs are low, users can begin with a starter installation system and add to it incrementally as their experience and needs dictate.

Applications are limited only by system perspectives. New communication drop points can be added as the need arises, and they can be located virtually anywhere along the cable. Internetworking will help extend the network over a larger geographical area as need dictates.

REQUIREMENTS FOR PHYSICAL PLANNING

The installation of the communications medium, like that of any information system, calls for good planning. The physical environment, transmission errors, and age effects are among the critical factors. To match the physical environment, we should make a correct choice of jacketed or armored cables. At joints, the connectors and the coupling adapter should be covered with shrink tubing to prevent accidental grounding and be mounted on shock-absorbing material if vibration is a problem. In damp environments the connectors should be waterproofed.

Transmission errors tend to be a function of the quality of the link components and their installation. Factors are externally induced noise and reflections due to poor connections. Significant distortion of the signal at the receiver would tend to indicate a link or connection fault. (Internally generated noise in the cable is probably negligible unless there is an imperfection in cable or material.)

The real problem may be external noise. The level of externally induced noise in the coaxial link increases with cable length, but it can be minimized by increasing the spacing between the coaxial link and the noise sources. The quality of the cable dielectric and the shielding used also will affect the noise characteristics.

Age effects are another important issue. Over a long period of time some deterioration of cable parameters may occur. It could result in increased attenuation and noise susceptibility. Hence, depending on the environment, an allowance of 10 to 20 percent of the total attenuation should be made at installation time. Contamination of the connectors also may result in increased attentuation and noise susceptibility at the joints.

Shielding is a helpful approach in the effort to control quality results. For lengths up to 1000 m, it may consist of a single copper braid. Above 1000 m, a foil, a foil and braid, or double braid giving 100 percent coverage should be used. The foil may be copper or aluminum. For indoor runs a polyethylene jacket is sufficient. For outdoor runs, whether exposed or buried, there should be a suitable armor. All cable jacket materials must be resistant to changes in electrical and physical characteristics caused by light and moisture. For links exceeding 2000 m in overall length, lower-loss cable is needed.

Coaxial cable should not be spliced. Sections can be joined by means of low-loss 75-Ω (ohm) connectors that physically match the cable. Intermediate connectors and coupling adapters should be covered with shrink tubing to prevent accidental grounding.

One of the basic precautions concerns lightning. Some installation areas are more susceptible than others to lightning activity. If the cable is to be buried in an area with low lightning exposure, it is advisable to bury it well below the frost line. If an aerial installation is planned, it is wise to use an overhead cable supported from a messenger grounded at both ends and also to provide pole protection wires on each nonmetallic pole. Routing either buried or aerial cables through the highest points of local terrain, which are those most likely to suffer lightning strikes, should be avoided.

A careful study should be made to determine which type of protection best meets the installation needs. This is most important for all high-priority carriers, because continuity of service is important and only the minimal out-of-service time can be tolerated. Examples are workstations during office hours and minicomputers or mainframe protectors in unattended central installations located in areas with a record of equipment failures caused by lightning or power fault current-induced surges.

Quite evidently, the preceding considerations lead to a number of clauses which should become an integral part of any installation contract. Another and most important requirement is that each cable should be permanently marked every 100 m with a unique number to facilitate maintenance. In addition, at the ends of each cable, the following information shall be attached:

- The device to which the end being labeled is connected
- The device to which the other end is connected
- The physical location of the other end of the cable (building, floor, column, or other positive locating information)
- The length of the cable run
- The cable group
- The extension number of a telephone near the other end of the cable

Cables must be supported as necessary but at least at every 20 m (if coaxial). Cable routing in buildings should be such that installation, maintenance, and future expansion are as easy as possible. It must take into account physical and environmental obstacles in areas where the building's framework does not provide protection; there a conduit must be provided to protect the cable. The conduit must be properly made to prevent damage to cables.

Furthermore, acceptance of the network by the owner should be conditioned by the results of a sequence of system measurements. The parameters to be measured should reveal:

- Open circuits in individual conductors or shields
- Short circuits between conductors and shields
- Grounds on individual conductors, either between a conductor and shield or between a conductor and a grounded object
- Short circuits between the shields of individual connectors (to test for ground loops)

As with all system projects, documentation must be submitted. It should include a construction schedule, layout proof of performance plan, test data for each reel of cable, the manufacturer's manuals for the cable, the complete *as-built* reproducible drawings of the cable system, and the troubleshooting procedure—a step-by-step routine to discover faults in the network.

USING MODEMS

The term *modem* comes from the primary function of the device, which is the *mo*dulation-*dem*odulation of a carrier signal so that digital information may be transmitted over an analog communications facility. Ordinarily, that facility is a conventional telephone line, but it may also be a private cable installation. All signals in a space division multiplexing (or SDM) analog network are converted to a radio frequency before transmission. The conversion is accomplished by the modulator-demodulator, and a modem is used for each attached device.

The modem functions as a receiver as well as a transmitter; it ensures that the converted signals are intelligible to the device at either end of an information transaction. In one sense, it encodes into RF; in the other, it decodes from RF into whatever form of signal is compatible with the receiving unit.

A whole industry has developed around the design, manufacture, and sale of modems. It is changing from being merely a provider of black boxes to becoming the supplier of complete systems for complex communications networks. The emerging leaders are the companies that can meet the increasingly sophisticated networking needs of users.

A modem has many technical characteristics, but recent trends make these five the outstanding ones:

1. Speed
2. Network analysis
3. Short haul
4. Agile type
5. Modem on a chip

Among the functions which characterize modem sophistication, *speed* is perhaps the most classical, and it is an important consideration for users. There is today a distinct trend toward higher speeds: a definite transition from 300 bps (bits per second) to 1.2 kbps (kilobits per second) and from there to 4.8, 9.6, and 56 kbps. The only sector in which 300-bps sales are increasing is the personal computer one.

Higher-speed modems are needed for high-speed networks. Still, the early 1980s expertise in RF modem technology was not comparable with that of digital modem technology. (Radio-frequency modem cards handle 100 kbps; they look very much like radio printed-circuit boards.) The first higher-speed modem has been working at up to 2 mbps (0.1 to 2 Mbps) and is in a printed-circuit-card format. It is currently sold by original equipment manufacturers (OEM) and can be incorporated into different equipment. Next came the 5-Mbps modem. Its most useful applications are in token passing and collision detection (see Chap. 5). The next step is the 10-Mbps modem.

Companies that are expert in this field suggest that it is pretty difficult to reduce the printed-circuit card with existing techniques and pricing. Very large scale integration (VLSI) was not, at the time of writing, answering the requirements for such a board, although frequency synthesizer chips were done with RF logic.

From the standpoint of technology, it is relatively easy to build logic arrays and reduce them on chips (flip-flops, and so on) for TDM systems. The reduction of digital components to VLSI is easy, although the economics of the operation is related to the number of boards needed. If we have to produce 1000 boards per year, there is no need for microcomputerization, but if the demand stands at 50,000 boards per year, the incentive is there to move immediately to the chip level.

Another significant development is that of modems that perform network analysis, where such features as the RS-232C interface and the (analog) line characteristics are monitored. Tests are carried on during normal data transmission by using out-of-band signaling. In this procedure, diagnostic information is transmitted within a second carrier frequency distinct from the forward channel.

Some modems include enough intelligence to enable users to do extensive networking and diagnosis. One of the most significant features is the ability to single out the cause of a failure so that reconfiguration and restoration can take place. Other features enable the user to keep track of the modems for inventory purposes by means of tracking configuration and inventory numbers.

Modems can monitor their own condition and that of connected communications lines and terminals and so become part of the overall network structure. Network testing does not halt communications. The modem commands and responses are handled by gateway software, which suspends normal data communication activity only for the time required to carry out the test. In this sense, network status is continually monitored at regular intervals based on traffic and error volume. As thresholds are exceeded, the sampling rate increases, so that rapidly deteriorating situations can be followed and corrected.

Also commercially available are devices that perform modem diagnostics rather than complete network diagnostics. With this type of unit, the user can look at the local and remote modems and the communications line between them and get a spot test on the line. Other, less sophisticated modems give status indication on the front panel, such as *clear to send*, or *request to send*. Still less complex is a device which only tells whether the modem is online. This type of modem is in demand for use with personal computers. The diagnostic features are not needed, and the users are looking for low-price, competitive modems.

The diagnostic features referred to are part of a range of network control equipment to help avoid system downtime and keep all users online most of the time. Proper network control devices provide the user organization with the capability of performing digital and analog testing and interactive data and line analysis. Typically, such devices gather statistics and generate quality reports. They assure the ability to reconfigure the network connections and switch in backup facilities or online spares, do monitoring, patching, switching, and testing, and generally assist in creating and integrating a data communications network.

A third technical distinction is between short- and long-haul modems. In the past, limited-distance devices have been used primarily for in-plant and in-building applications, but it now seems that both local area networks and tail ends of backbone satellite data communications networks stress attention on the short-haul modem within a total systems configuration. Within the short-haul market, the major trends are high speeds, lower costs, greater reliability, and, most important, the ability to cover greater distances and accommodate more conventional data lines, rather than just pure copper.

We stated that in a coaxial cable we can have both point-to-point and multipoint transmission and that with the latter we can have either a TDM or an FDM solution. The FDM solution calls for *frequency agile attachments*, because current technology does not offer low-cost taps which are tunable to the frequency band of the connected device and switchable to a new connection through software. An *agile modem* can be polyvalent when inserted in different fractions of the available band. If there is a permanent allocation, as in the case of the Wangnet's Wangband, we don't need the agile modem capability, but we do need it in any other FMD situation. Since the "other cases" are more general, and will be even more frequent in the future, the agile modem characteristics can be appreciated.

Among the technical developments concerning operation in a TDM mode is that the use of *channel control modems* eliminates the need for the head-end processor to query for data transfers. Such devices are also useful for handling data from many low-speed units simultaneously.

A fifth technical distinction is that between the traditional bulky black box and the modem on a chip. The incorporation of modems within the WS is well within our technology, but government regulations have not made clear where the terminal device ends and the lines start. Still, U.S. vendors are building more and more units with incorporated modems.

MULTIPLEXERS AND GATEWAYS

A modem is one of the vital components of a network, but it is not the only one. Another critical unit is the *multiplexer*, or *mux*. It combines traffic from several low-speed communications lines onto a single high-speed line. We have already referred to the two popular types of multiplexing: FDM and TDM.

Particularly important within a network environment are the *statistical multiplexers* (stat muxes). These are TDM-oriented units that dynamically allocate communications line time to each of the various attached workstations. The allocation is made according to whether a terminal is active at a particular moment, including buffering and queueing functions. Stat muxes get increasingly sophisticated. One early 1980s product, for example, was designed as the first step toward a nodal processor with alternate routing, X.25 gateways, and a software-based network management supervisory port. A variety of design approaches is available. Some products are intended for private networking with an X.25 option, mostly for use with single-vendor equipment. Others are projected for linking a multivendor environment to X.25 channels.

The handling of synchronous protocols is an important feature of many new stat muxes. New protocols are pushing this trend as vendors and users seek compatibility with established network architectures. One of the important characteristics of stat muxes is traffic balancing. In this they must be efficient; for they interface to a variety of equipment.

Also important are *concentrators*, which multiplex several low-speed communications lines onto a single high-speed trunk. They differ from multiplexers in that they are programmable. Often, the host computer software must be rewritten to accommodate them. With a concentrator the total capacity of the high-speed outgoing line, in bits per second, is generally less than or equal to the total capacity of the incoming low-speed lines. In contrast, the output capacity of a stat mux may exceed the total capacity of the incoming lines.

Other devices on a network with which we have experience from the long-haul solutions are the *front ends* and *message switches*. Their days may be numbered, however, because the *gateway processor* has started to replace both them and the concentrators and protocol converters. The conventional front-end processor is installed in front of a host to provide network communications power by relieving the latter of the data communication chores. The traditional message switch takes in many low-speed communications lines and routes the data streams to a central point, where the messages are concentrated for processing. Based on established processing criteria, the messages are routed over one or more lines connected to the system. Once they are processed and the destination data are acted upon, every WS can access every other WS in the system. Gateway processors go beyond those capabilities and are also instrumental in enabling computers of different vendors to talk to each other.

The basic purpose of a gateway processor is to connect two different network elements. Such devices are of three types:

- One connects a local area network to an X.25 packet-switched public network.
- Another connects a local area network to appropriate satellite links.
- A third can talk to a terminal network on one side and a host on the other.

Most manufacturers have decided to go along with the X.25 network interface for packet-switched networks, using higher-level data link control (HDLC) protocol. In the first class, one of the inputs to the gateway processor has to be X.25 to permit mixes of CPUs to communicate. If these mainframes and minicomputers are not otherwise compatible, the gateway processor's X.25 capability will make the linkups possible. The stated functions are mediated through software, and the specific hardware requirements will change as technology changes. Software design is based on the packet assembly-disassembly principle. Through gateway processors, CPUs and workstations can use the network and talk to each other, and the overall system can be kept dynamic without extensive logical changes.

4 BROADBAND AND BASEBAND

The increased importance of local area networks is due to the expectation that interconnections of computers, word processors, and graphics terminals and facilities such as voice mail will become common and that the ability to transport information between workstations will be fundamental. Such systems lead toward integrated communications, corporate networks in which data and word processing, document transfer, and other communications functions are combined in a single system.

Multifunctional networks will grow in importance during the 1980s, with the innovative industries such as insurance and banking leading the way. The networks will be more effective if a single carrier is used to combine the different services being offered—from voice to image, data, and text—and this introduces *broadband* requirements.

Broadband rests on CATV (community antenna television, or cable television) technology. The CATV industry started in the United States in the late 1950s with the creation of community antenna television as a way to overcome physical obstacles in TV transmission. Though the physical obstacles were overcome, other problems did develop in the early days, such as a low signal at the end of the cable and noise from defective sets installed upstream.

Even when a strong signal comes into the tap, for an application all we need is 1 mV (millivolt) at the TV end, but this has to be consistent throughout the attached devices. To correct the early problems, manufacturers developed directional taps and broadband amplifiers. Such devices allow the distribution of the signal in a nearly homogeneous way. They also assure that poor TV equipment attached to the cable does not introduce noise to the system.

The reasons for adopting CATV technology are economic. It gives a good communications path at low cost, and it is reasonably easy to split into channels. The basic channel in the United States is 6 MHz. With a 300-MHz cable this gives 50 channels of data communications quality.

Developments designed to enhance entertainment electronics eventually found their way into the information systems industry. Broadband provides a wide bandwidth for data transport, does so with little expense, is (by now) reasonably immune to noise, and supports clear signals in an able manner. A broadband solution is more complete than a baseband one and has better utilization potential. The major virtue of baseband systems is their simplicity. There is, however, a great deal of misunderstanding about their implementation.

In the literature the terminology itself is not always clear, particularly the difference between broadband and *wideband*. In this text, we will use "broadband" to identify the data rate up to the limits of the coaxial cable and "wideband" the speed all the way to light. That's why a reference to the latter will rarely be made.

In terms of application, local network architectures can be divided into two main groups depending on their bandwidth: (1) *broadband* (BRB) and (2) *baseband* (BAB). The difference is in speed of transmission and in the fact that a broadband carrrier supports many baseband channels. Figure 4-1 explains the range of bits per second supported by each alternative:

> Baseband will range between 0 and 10 Mbps, but the 1- to 2.5-Mbps range is more typical. Quite often, BAB transmits digital signals.
>
> Broadband transmits analog signals and operates at 0 to 400 MHz, although for reason of noise problems manufacturers prefer to implement their local network architecture from 5 to upwards of 10 MHz.

Prior to examining the baseband and broadband characteristics, let's turn to the fundamentals of LAN application. Both low and high bits per second provide the means for the interconnection services required for smooth, uninterruptable operation of a workstation. The difference is in capacity of the carrier to handle all required tasks. The key to the question of whether to use a broadband or baseband network is therefore a careful analysis of the tasks to be performed. Very closely related to that analysis is the change in the way of

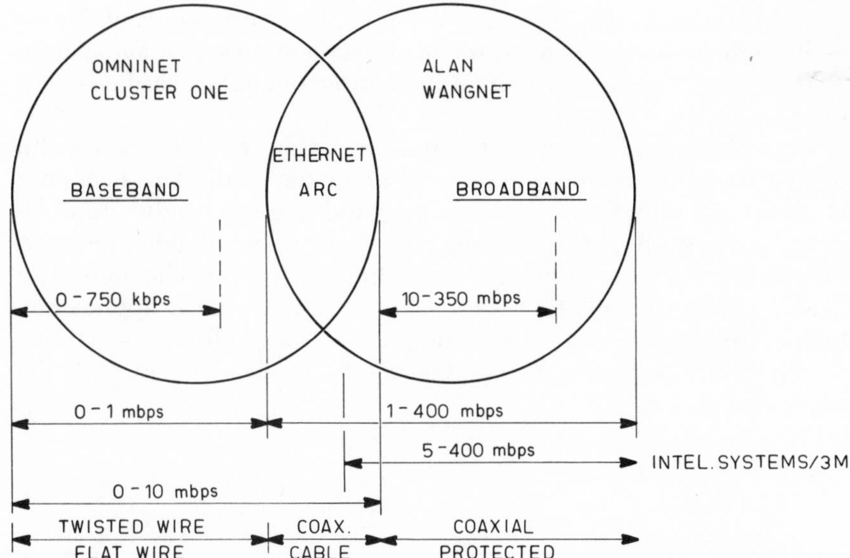

Figure 4-1. A comparison of the broadband-baseband range, in bits per second, and of the LAN possibilities in either class.

thinking of the people who will choose, design, and implement—from a mainframe-based concentration to a fully distributed environment. To investigate their thinking, General Electric in 1980, 1981, and 1982, held LAN meetings and seminars to which it invited all vendors to hear their solutions.

When we talk of high technology, where experience is still scanty, anything short of a generic approach borders on superficiality. It would be unprofessional to give in these pages "advice" on the type of LAN to select without knowing the *individual* problem. Only in the most general terms can it be stated that in a factory environment it is best to use broadband and in an office environment baseband with broadband running through the building to interconnect the baseband networks. That approach is suggested at the conclusion to this chapter.

BETTING ON BANDWIDTH

In principle, bandwidth is the key to high transmission speeds. As such, it has become a cornerstone in the design of office automation systems. Just as demand drove up the availability and lowered the cost of raw computing power in the 1960s and memory capacity in the 1970s, so in the 1980s the bandwidth need will exceed other system requirements. The more we have, the more we want. Bandwidth will be a dominant factor in implementing office automation systems and in making use of an increasing amount of hardware and software.

As we have said in this and in the preceding chapters, bandwidth defines the range of frequencies that can be transmitted on a communications channel. System designers would like the bandwidth to be as wide as possible, but maximum potential bandwidth depends upon the carrier and the equipment connecting the various channels. The need for greater bandwidth is therefore a function of the application, both current and projected. A basic premise for the future is that one workstation should meet every office need (Fig. 4-2). This imposes the requirements for:

- Compatibility
- Modularity
- Expandability
- Predictability
- Human engineering
- Wide bandwidth

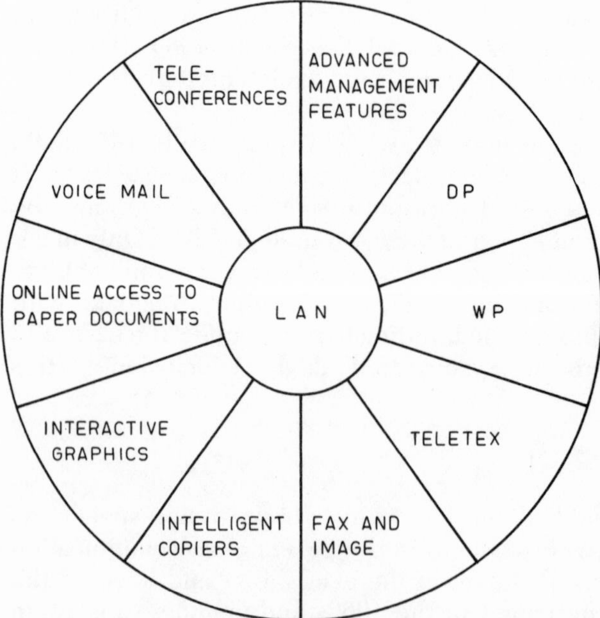

Figure 4-2. The range of services in an office environment which can be enhanced through a LAN solution.

At the center of the system is the local area network. As we have said in the preceding chapters, with a LAN the following features are critical:

1. *Distance is limited* to 10 km or less.
2. *Use is primarily internal*; the local area network is organized and installed inside the office premises or plant.
3. *Access is multipoint* and may reach hundreds or thousands of connections making use of available bandwidth.
4. *A careful study is prerequisite*; it should aim at the definition of protocols and connection costs.
5. *A choice of protocols is made.* The leading alternatives we will be discussing are the CSMA/CM and the token mechanism (IEEE 802 Committee).
6. *The network is owned by the user*; there is no public utility offering in this domain.
7. *Significant physical choices* of wire, modems, and so on, must be made.

The need for a local network is present in every office. The real question is not "Shall we develop a LAN?" but "Which LAN should we develop?" There are two succeeding decisions: broadband versus baseband, with the former having more long-term versatility than baseband and the capacity to include many basebands, and multipoint design. Products, markets, and timing have an impact on this second decision. We must look for products based on reliable approaches and for the manufacturers that are building equipment to meet workstation and databasing requirements.

As stated earlier, the key advantage of broadband is that it allows text, data, voice, and image to be *integrated* on the same carrier—for instance, a coaxial cable—by using RF technology, a capability that baseband does not yet have. But the need for wide bandwidth is not restricted to the local network structures; it is found in both the local and the long haul.

The market for broadband communications is expected to pass the $20 billion level by 1985. There is a projected further doubling of the market by 1991, with a battle developing between AT&T and the CATV industry led by Time Inc. and American Express. Market potential is reflected in Table 4-1 for LAN and attached devices and in Table 4-2 for broadband communications at large.

The availability of broadband channels is expected to stimulate the

TABLE 4-1 U.S. MARKET POTENTIAL FOR LAN* AND ATTACHED DEVICES† IN THE 1982-TO-1987 PERIOD

	1982	Est. 1987
Installed networks	8,200	40,000
Number of connected nodes	251,000	2,150,000

* The estimated average annual growth for LAN is 30%+.
† The growth in number of connected nodes is 50%.
The estimated market for LAN vs. all types of servers is about $7 billion.

use of video conferencing and accelerate the pace of office automation. Also predicted is the development of supernetworks, which will utilize satellite channels to link local area networks together. A Group IV facsimile transceiver being developed in 1983 is expected to operate at rates faster than one page per second.

Such projections are important in matching the capabilities of the gateway to the internal resources which will most likely be assured through a voice-data-image private branch exchange (PBX) (Fig. 4-3). To the local network which interfaces with the computer-based PBX will be attached multifunctional workstations able to support:

- Regular voice communications
- Dictation: voice store and forward
- Text editing
- Electronic mail, both video and hardcopy
- Television: broadcast and closed circuit
- Personal electronic filing
- Simple local processing and calculation
- Database access

Typically, such workstations will be microprocessor-supported; they will feature voice and key-driven input capabilities and have a

TABLE 4-2 PROJECTED BROADBAND COMMUNICATIONS MARKET

	1981 market, $ billion	Estimated increase over 1981, percent	
		1986	1991
Satellite and related media	0.3	700	1800
Enhanced TV, etc.	0.6	700	1500
Special electronic mail networks	0.8	350	430
Cable TV	2.9	300	480
Terrestrial communications plant	5	160	220

The 1981 total market was $9.6 billion; the estimated 1991 total market is $43 billion.

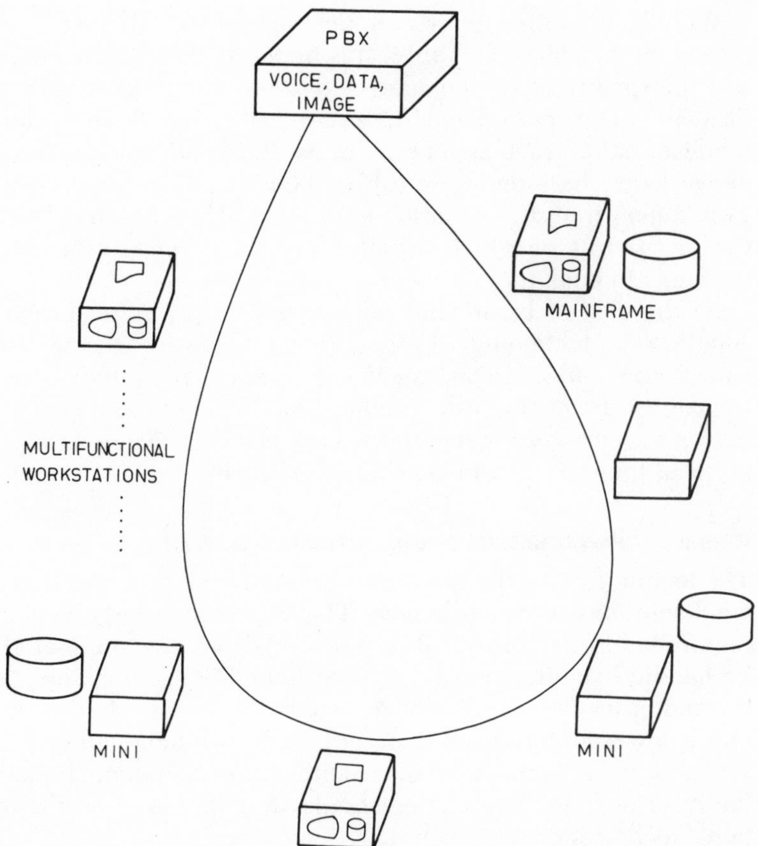

Figure 4-3. Possible role of a PBX in assuming a gateway between internal and external resources: voice, data, text, and image.

scanner and printer, microfiles, and other attachments. Short LAN-type applications will tend toward a utility-type approach. But to provide an information outlet on the wall, we have to reach a cost level fairly comparable with that of the power outlet. (The cost in the United States is $45 to $50, including labor, materials, and so on.) We do, however, know that this "information outlet" is a key to the office automation environment.

The point here is that broadband can provide the desired capability at about that cost, whereas baseband, which is a solution for a limited LAN, costs much more once the applications perspectives expand to broadband. Furthermore, with wide bands we can build far less efficient modems at substantially lower cost. The fact of having a lot of bandwidth available suggests that we can afford to be less efficient.

Wide bandwidth supports applications which can have a profound impact on the office. This subject is important because the bandwidth and the quality of the channel determine the maximum theoretical data rate, in bits per second. (Channel quality is defined by the signal-to-noise ratio.) Just as important is the tendency for broadband networks to share the same cable: their frequencies are compatible. This differs from the situation with most of the baseband networks, the proprietors of which usually don't allow even other baseband networks to hook in.

As the cost of broadband networking drops, more designers are adopting the technology. Using one manufacturer to piggyback text, data, image, and voice on broadband—and to get equipment as well—is a sound approach. Still, whether broadband or baseband, the local network is strictly a *communications medium*. As such, it must be protocol transparent and capable of expansion.

TECHNICAL CHARACTERISTICS OF BROADBAND AND BASEBAND

The technology for the implementation of both broadband and baseband solutions is available now. The choice rests largely on systems requirements, flexibility, bits per second capability, number of jobs to be handled simultaneously, service integration, error detection and correction features, and cost. As stated, the cost of the bus interface unit is lower for baseband than for broadband; but of all technologies available today to meet the office automation challenge, broadband is the most flexible. The choice should thus be based on the application's technical characteristics.

Let's again look carefully at the definitions:

> With broadband transmission, all signal information in the communication system is converted to radio frequency, and it is feasible to subdivide the frequency. Broadband multiplexes the coaxial cable carrier.
>
> With baseband, one signal (most often digital) can be sent through the system. Baseband uses the coaxial cable as one channel. The possible baseband problems are noise, lack of voice and image integration, and the number of workstations.

In either approach, the number of bits per seond depends on the physical and logical versatility we try to have, the devices we interface, the protocols used, and the analog or digital nature of the transmission. Of the three elements in Fig. 4-4 to be attached to the LAN, the one that consumes the most bits per second is database

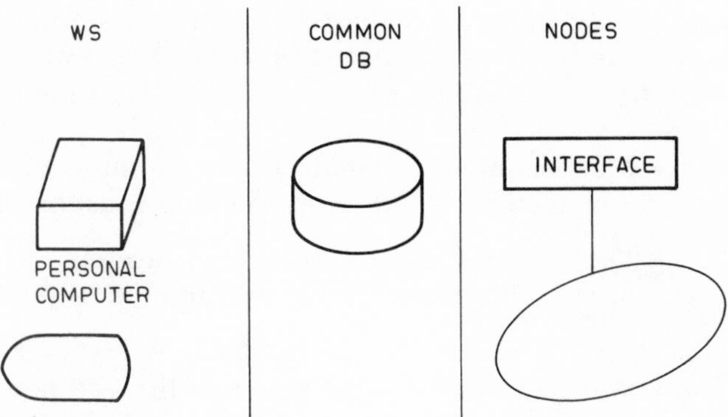

Figure 4-4. The most common elements to be attached to a LAN are the workstation (PCs and video units), the common database, and the bus interface units.

storage and retrieval. Can the speed of transmission supported by the architecture meet the databasing requirements of the workplace?

For short runs and a lower bits-per-second level of transmission, we can use twisted pair cable. Greater distances can be better handled with coaxial cable or fiber optics. The latter are also the means of supporting a multimillion bps capacity. Broadband provides most room for growth and high reliability; coaxial cable has been used since the 1970s in outside environments. Most of the available broadband architectures support a data handling capability of 350 to 400 Mbps with coaxial cable.

Fiber optics can support multiples of those rates, but the cost is still high, the reliability is rather low, and the multitap problems persist. Optical fiber can be used:

1. When there is an extreme amount of electromagnetic interference.
2. When there is very little space to run the bundle.
3. When a highly secure installation is needed.

The fiber itself is an inexpensive raw material, but tapping it makes the system expensive. Amplification also is expensive, but both tapping and amplification may be cheaper by the late 1980s.

As for applications, everything done on coaxial cable can be done on optical fiber, but the bandspread is much greater. It has been estimated that all the phone conversations taking place in the United States at one time could be multiplexed and sent through a single optical fiber cable. LANs based on optical fibers may take off by 1985 or 1986 and even overtake the broadband coaxial cable, but it is still too early for predictions. However, some facts merit attention:

- Most mainframe manufacturers are quite a bit behind in LAN architecture, whether baseband or broadband.
- Digital Equipment Corporation designed to 10-Mbps Ethernet specifications but has reexamined its position as to broadband.
- Wang and IBM bought Ethernet licenses but do not use them. Apparently the moves were taken to protect against accusations of patent infringement.
- Datapoint's attached resource computer (ARC) is 2.5-Mbps baseband; basically, it is a way to get into disk drives. (Its interface has become the standard link for the new announcements by Nestar and 3M/Interactive Systems).
- Datapoint's infrared transmission can be incorporated into broadband.

Light links and microwaves are very effective transmission channels, but their shared technical limitation is that of going point to point. Furthermore, in a number of important applications, the bottleneck today is not what we can transmit but what we can switch; we do not have the technology for switching all the way up to light. We can switch to little over a gigahertz and still control the signal, although we can detect up to about 40 GHz.

Let's return to the baseband approach. It works by directly impressing a digital signal, and that introduces the limitations of speed and distance. Technically, without a repeater, the higher the speed the shorter the distance. At 10 Mbps, the distance is limited to about 500 m. To reach 1.5 km, two repeaters are needed. Baseband transmission is basically TDM. There are no frequencies to be divided; there is no modulation; and there is no FDM. A third possible solution is space division multiplexing (SDM). However, SDM makes multiple WS communications impossible because only one signal can travel on the cable at any one time.

We have referred to the possibility of noise problems. In baseband the whole available range of bandwidth is used, whereas in broadband a portion is typically excluded for noise reasons (the 0 to 5-MHz in the Alan and the 0 to 10-MHz in the Wangnet). Arc welders in the factory and even office equipment such as some copiers emit noise.

Broadband manufacturers say that their bit error rate is better than 10^{-8}, whereas for baseband coaxial cable it is 10^{-6} and for twisted pair cable it is 10^{-5}. Also, broadband is a more secure system because it is more difficult to tap. The cable for broadband is shielded; that for baseband is flexible.

Nonetheless, when this was written, most available short-haul solutions were baseband. As Table 4-3 demonstrates, the art was still

TABLE 4-3 SHORT-HAUL SOLUTIONS

Firm	Offering	Carrier	Datarate
	BROADBAND		
Amdax*	Cablenet	Coaxial	7 to 14 Mbps (TDMA)
CDC	LCN	Coaxial	50 Mbps
Network Systems	HYPERchannel	Coaxial	50 Mbps
Sytek*	LocalNet 40	Coaxial	2.5 Mbps
Sytek*	LocalNet 20	Coaxial	128 kbps
Wang	Wangnet	Coaxial	340 MHz
3M/IS	Alan, Videodata	Coaxial	300 MHz
	BASEBAND		
Apollo Computer	Domain	Coaxial	12 Mbps
Computrol	Megalink	Coaxial	1 Mbps
Corvus	Omninet	Twisted pair	1 Mbps
Datapoint	ARC	Coaxial	2.5 Mbps
Hewlett-Packard	Optic Links	Optical fibers	dc to 10 Mbps
Hughes	Facilities Management System	Coaxial	1 Mbps
Intel	Ethernet chip	Coaxial	10 Mbps
ITT	Digital modules	Optical fiber	5 Mbps
Nestar	Cluster One	Flat wire (ribbon cable)	240 kbps
Nestar	Plan 4000	Coaxial	2.5 Mbps
Network Systems	HYPERbus	Coaxial Optical fiber	6.3 Mbps
Onyx	C8002	Coaxial	2 Mbps
Prime	Primenet	Coaxial	8 Mbps
Proteon	Pronet	Coaxial	10 Mbps
Scientific Data Systems	SDSnet	Coaxial	1 Mbps

TABLE 4-3 Continued

Firm	Offering	Carrier	Datarate
SD Systems	MARS/net	Twisted pair	800 kbps
Systems Technology	ES/4000	Coaxial	10 Mbps
Tandem	THL	Coaxial	300 kbps
3COM	Ethernet	Coaxial	10 Mbps
Three Rivers	Perq Ethernet	Coaxial	10 Mbps
Ungermann-Bass	Net/One	Coaxial	10 Mbps
Vector Graphics	Vnet	Coaxial	5 Mbps
Xerox	Ethernet	Coaxial	10 Mbps
Zilog	Z-Net	Coaxial	800 kbps
	MULTITHREAD (STAR TYPE)		
CMD (Can. Micro Distrib.)	Mupet		9 kbps
Corvus	Constellation		60 kbps
Digital Microsystems	Hinet		400 kbps
Televideo	808/816 Star		800 kbps
	PBX-BASED		
InteCom†	IBX	Twisted pair Optical fiber	56 kbps
Northern Telecom†	SL-1	Twisted pair	128 kbps
Rolm†	CBX	Twisted pair	19.2 kbps

* Cluster of channels on the coaxial cable, each at stated capacity.

† Integrated voice/data PBX. These are not proper LAN solutions and are added only as examples.

loaded with approaches adopted in the 1970s and carried over. Whether baseband or broadband, the number of the new, efficient offerings was still limited. Note that at the end of Table 4.3 three manufacturers—Rolm, InteCom, and Northern Telecom—feature PBX solutions. We will discuss the reasons later in this chapter.

Let's recapitulate. If we try to achieve data rates greater than those of the telephone line, either baseband or broadband will support them. The cost of installing either baseband or broadband is labor: pulling the wires. The cable cost is insignificant; both solutions help reduce the proliferation of cables.

DIVIDING THE BROADBAND

When we talk about a broad RF band and its division through FDM, we must necessarily refer to some established solution. The one chosen here is marketed by 3M/Interactive Systems (3M/IS). The broadband supported by 3M/IS is 300 MHz divided forward and reverse. There are, however, 440-MHz installations in operation, and the upper limit can be pushed further as more need for spectrum develops. Figure 4-5 presents a standard broadband coaxial cable RF configuration with:

1. Unidirectional RF
2. Low or subsplit RF
3. Midsplit RF solutions

Of the three sections of the midsplit RF, the *reverse* supports 17 channels of 6 MHz each, the *guard band* is unused and serves to separate the reverse from the forward and the *forward* supports 25 channels of 6 MHz each. This split is a development of the common entertainment applications in which four reverse channels are supported in the spectrum from 5 to 30 MHz, followed by a 24-MHz guard band and up to 37 forward channels of 6 MHz each. Still older installations have no reverse signals. Reverse signals are essential in workstation-to-CPU communication; to transmit back to the processor, we need a reverse channel.

Most of the early 3M/IS broadband applications involved just a few of the supported channels, typically at 4.8 kbps. The channel speed

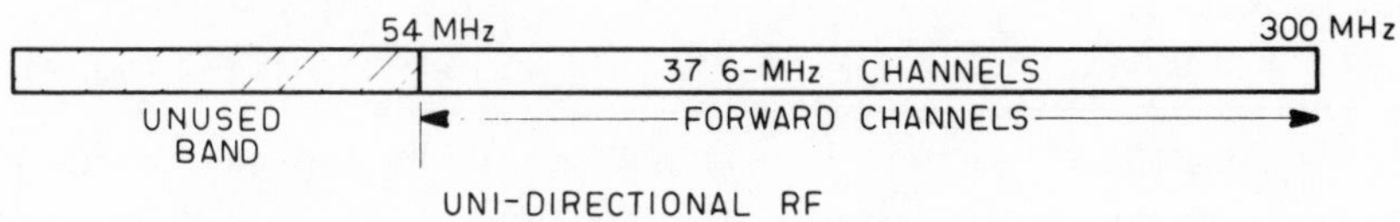

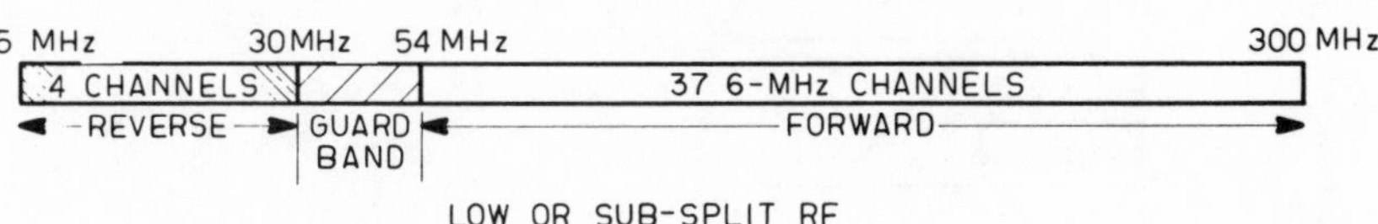

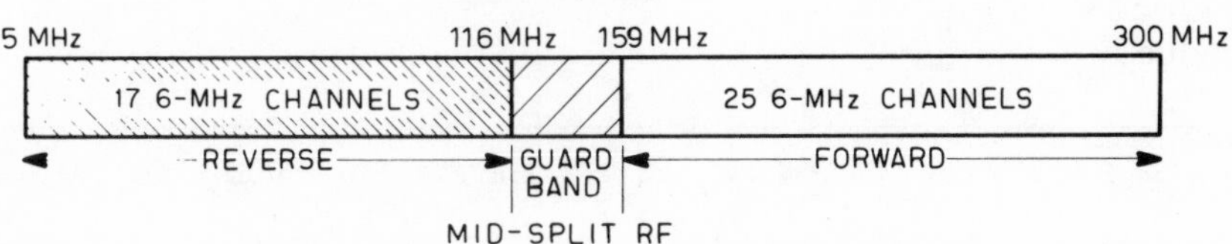

Figure 4-5. A standard broadband coaxial cable RF configuration.

was, however, increased and headed toward 1 Mbps. Clearly the 6-MHz band is not used with 4.8-kbps implementations, but until recently 9.6 kbps was the best we could obtain with modems for voice-grade lines.

Based on the 6-MHz CATV band allocation, Fig. 4-6 outlines the audio, data, and video channels supported by 3M/IS and the range of modems offered for each application area. As mentioned in another connection, environmental noise is more pronounced at the lower end (audio bands). The higher the frequency the less the susceptibility to noise: Above 18 MHz the range of bit error rate is 10^{-8} to 10^{-9}. Modems have been designed to match these frequency requirements. Design is typically based on technical suppositions by the individual manufacturer.

We have said that broadband systems are usually designed to travel miles and tap many users. We have also said that flexibility is important because experience with office and factory environments is that addition, subtraction, and alteration of devices, combined, amounts to about 20 percent per year.

Typical FDM and TDM configurations are shown in Figs. 4-7 and 4-8. A typical part of the setup is the *network monitor* (Fig. 4-9). It

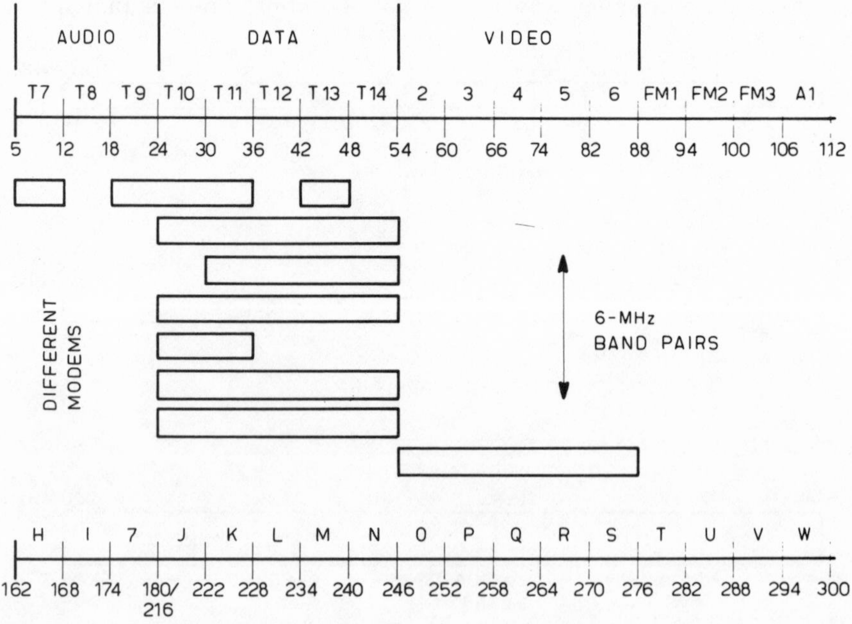

Figure 4-6. The audio, data, and video channels supported by 3M/Interactive Systems and the CATV offering of the same manufacturer.

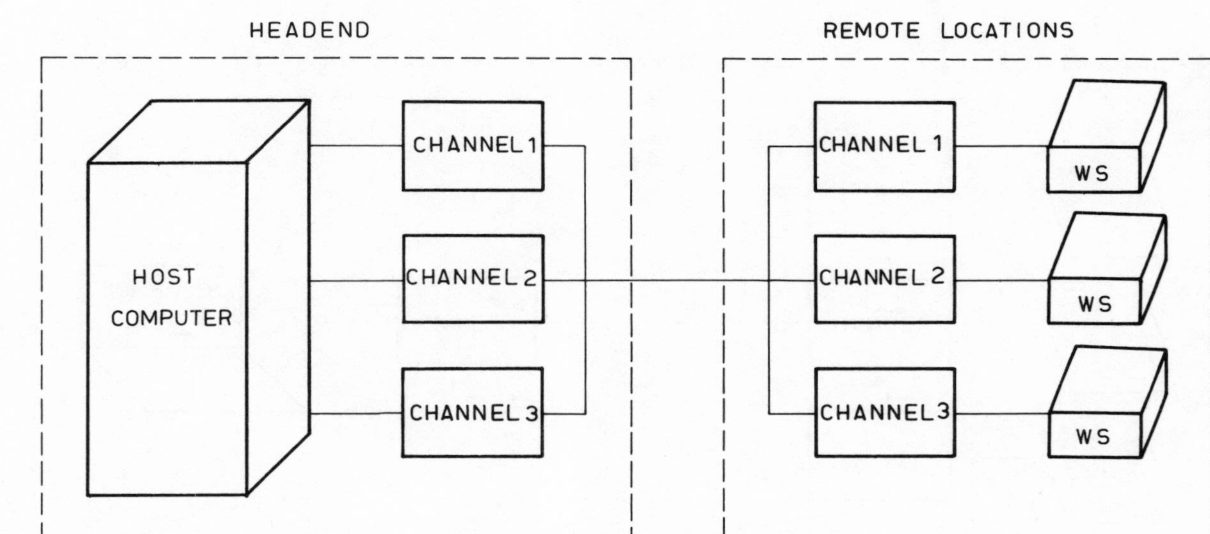

Figure 4-7. A typical FDM configuration involving host computer and workstations at remote locations.

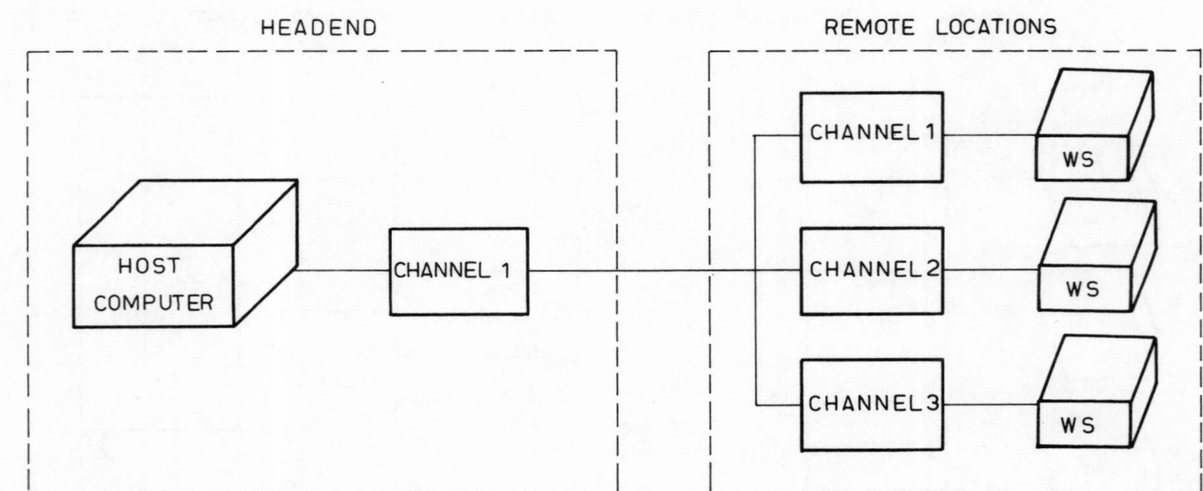

Figure 4-8. A TDM solution with host and remote workstations. Note the difference in number of channels as compared with FDM.

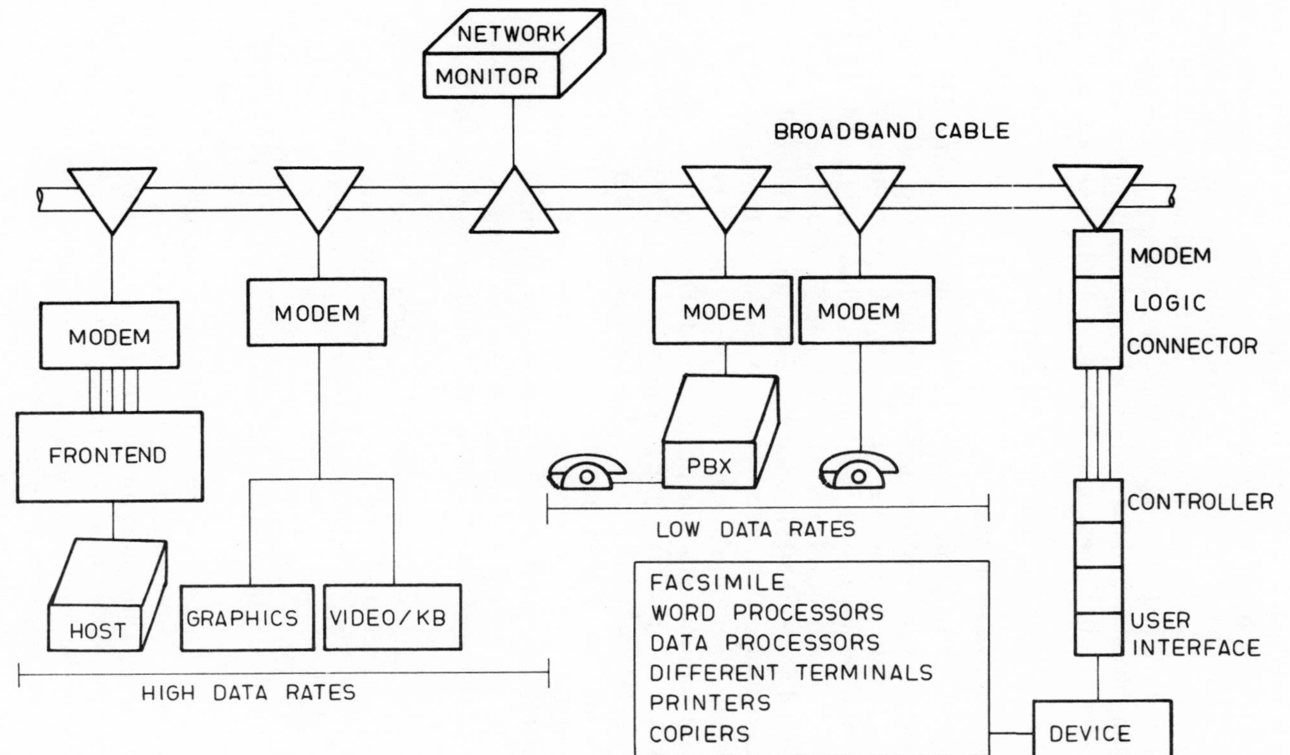

Figure 4-9. A network monitor in a broadband installation and the different classes of attachments.

supports the logical transport mechanism on the broadband coaxial cable and the high- and low-data-rate traffic. The host computer, graphics terminals, and video and keyboard units are high-data-rate devices. Low-data-rate devices are the individual PBX telephones attached directly to the cable. Figure 4-9 shows the interface units between the cable and the end device: modem, logic box, connector, controller, media access and higher-level protocol box, and user interface.

USING THE PBX AS A SHORT HAUL

We have seen in Table 4-2 that some companies, particularly PBX manufacturers, are advancing the computer-based private branch exchange as an alternative to a local network architecture. This comes within the framework of the Integrated Services Digital Network (ISDN), the topology of which is shown in Fig. 4-10. Quite recently in the United States the ISDN has become a topic of interest. Through the International Telecommunications Union the European countries are already developing technical standards to govern the interface between terminal equipment and the ISDN network, which they envision as a worldwide setup linking currently incompatible communications networks and a host of diverse services. IBM is pressing the FCC to take up ISDN-related issues.

Though an ISDN orientation does not necessarily oblige anyone to use the PBX as a pivot point, some people tend to think that way. They point out that there are advantages and disadvantages in a PBX-based solution, and they claim that the latter tend to outweigh the former:

- The major disadvantage is that the resulting system is starlike and centralized and therefore unbalanced; it is prone to lower reliability. Throughput problems also can arise.
- The major advantage is that, because we would be using a telephone orientation, the wiring is already in place.

The private branch exchange is becoming the gateway to telecommunications. Proponents of this solution claim that savings on voice features alone can economically justify the installation: lowest-cost routing, camp-on, billing control, call forwarding, and other features are add-ons. But such a claim actually misses the point, which is that the PBX can complement but is not the ideal alternative to a LAN. As a local transport system, the LAN offers fail-safe capability and can cover a fairly wide area: from 10 m to 10 km and, with interfaces, beyond.

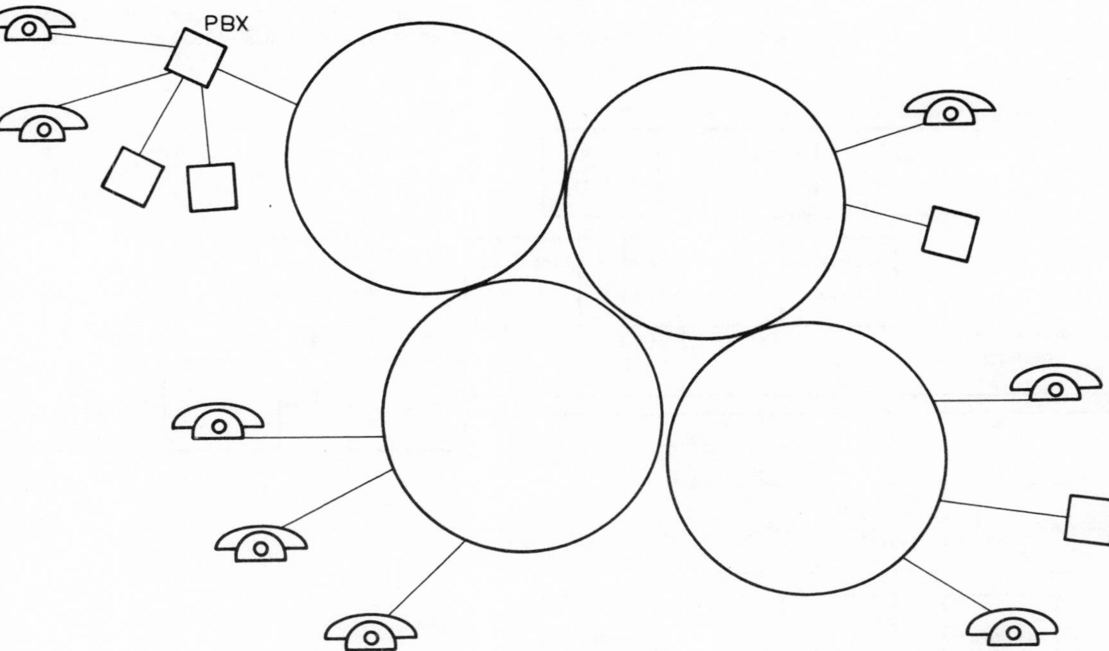

Figure 4-10. Overall aspect of voice and data services supported by an ISDN.

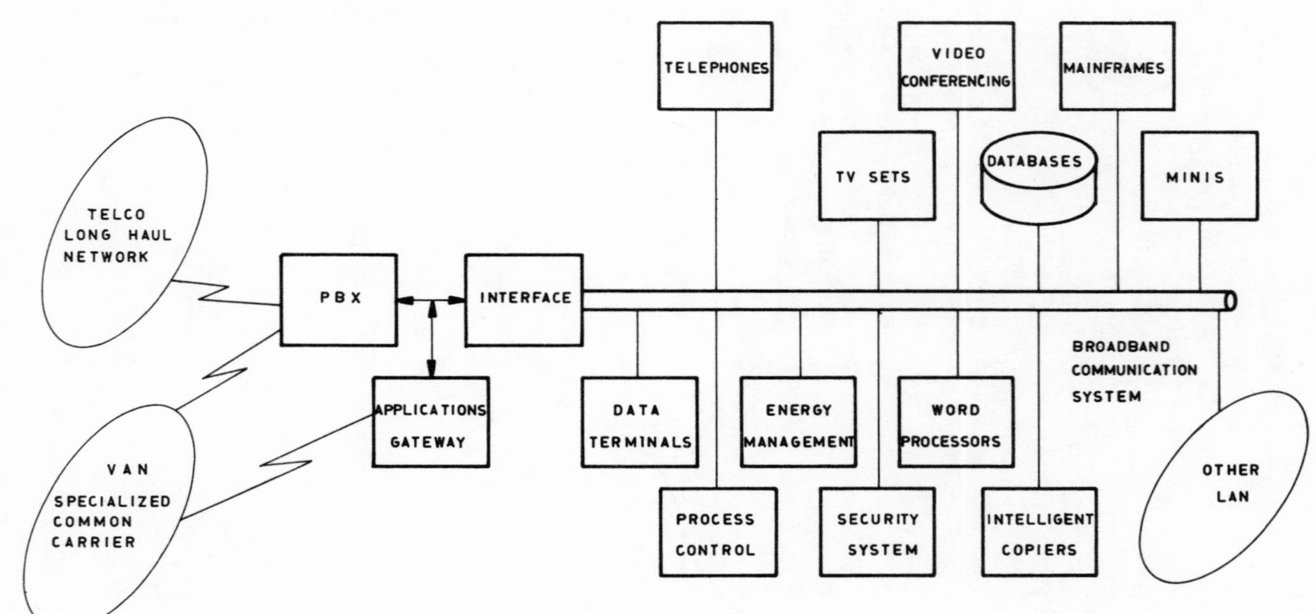

Figure 4-11. Using a dual gateway (PBX and dedicated computer) toward the specialized common carrier in connection with an internal broadband communications system.

The compatibility of the PBX and the interfacility network is shown in Fig. 4-11: The telecommunication long-haul network and value-added carriers interface through the PBX; eventually, the value-added network (VAN) can also link through an applications gateway. Subsequently, a broadband local area network supports a host of devices from mainframes and minicomputers to intelligent copiers, telephones, TV sets, word processors, and other LAN.

Undoubtedly, several manufacturers intend to exploit the uniqueness of simultaneous voice and data communications equipment while it lasts. But even the companies first out of the gate admit that their competitors are not far behind with systems that feature integrated data processing, word processing, and voice communications. And while several companies are aiming at the Fortune 500 or 1500 as the entry level to the market, at least one company, Prolink of Boulder, Colorado, designs its system for small- to medium-size offices of under 100 employees. For many of the user firms attracted to this system, the LAN will be something new. The manufacturer is quick to point out the benefits:

- Common supplier
- Common maintenance

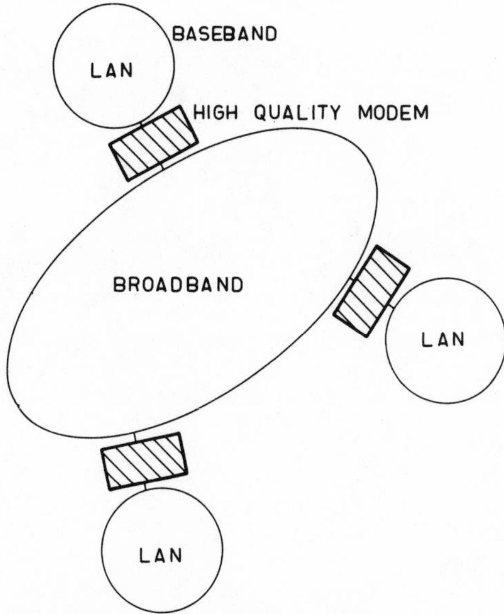

Figure 4-12. Employing a broadband network to interconnect different baseband LANs each of which is dedicated to office routines.

- Efficient interfaces
- Higher productivity
- Electronic filing
- Voice storage

In this, as in other offerings, all fundamental communications features (physical and logical) should be retained: frequency modems, the division of the band in different channels, the access mode to be implemented on each channel, and so on. Most offerings underlie the importance of the capacity to interconnect with other LANs, an issue particularly valid with larger networks (Fig. 4-12). Internetworking capability allows us to expand the area of application and also preserve investments already made on baseband by channeling the traffic between LANs. In turn, this permits us to start on baseband with reasonably small, contained, experimental models and then expand without loss of time, money, or effort.

5 PROTOCOLS AND TOPOLOGICAL LAYOUT

A protocol is *a set of conventions* that govern the format and control of information in transit through a communications network or stored in a text and database. The information may be voice, text, data, or image. Each type needs a well-defined procedure that is clearly understood by the users.

The protocol constitutes the logical connection to the physical lines of the carrier. Its existence and general acceptance make feasible an orderly exchange of information elements between private branch exchanges, computers, word processors, workstations, and communications devices. The protocol procedure constitutes a predetermined dialogue scrupulously maintained at all points of the communications link. "Protocol" is a relatively new concept, but it standardizes known and not new things.

In general, all protocols have two functions. One is *contact*, which includes identification and synchronization—for instance, the creation of a virtual channel. Synchronization concerns both source and destination. The other is *transfer*: It comprises not only the transmission function itself but also supporting features such as acknowledgment for assurance of delivery, error detection and correction, and synchronization.

Network architectures are layered, and so are protocols. In data communications we have protocols addressed to the data link, the routing, the virtual circuit, the session, and the presentation control, but we also need them for text or data access and memory management.

There are higher and lower layers of protocol. The latter may be transparent or virtual. A *transparent protocol* sends data through the system without particular constraints due to low-level details. The user cannot see it, but it is there. A *virtual protocol* obeys sequence and other constraints. Hence, it is handy, but not easy, to have transparent protocols.

Another protocol characteristic is *reliability*. A protocol is reliable if it provides end-to-end accountability for the functions, such as connection management, flow control, and delivery of messages, with which it is entrusted. Messages can be reliably delivered if a number of requirements, such as those of packet structure, header, trailer, sequencing, channeling, and acceptance, are met effectively. Implementation is that much more dependable when our choices are based on the proper study of the communications mechanism to be maintained.

Efficient protocol choices are characterized by both reliability and cost. Costs are directly related to the ability of one user to share resources with other users. A communications network shares resources which are allocated only when voice, text, data, or image is actually being sent. The importance of the implementation of local area networks lies precisely in this sharing of resources. LAN protocols must support:

- Cost-effective operations
- Low contention
- Modular design open to growth
- Common test and database access
- The shared resource principle
- A basis for an integrated electronic office
- The capacity to dynamically redefine and reconfigure the system

The four criteria of local network capabilities—type of topology, mass of transmission, the transmission technology itself, and the access method—do have an impact on protocol choice. We will now turn to this subject.

SYNCHRONOUS AND ASYNCHRONOUS TRANSMISSION

The terms *synchronous* and *asynchronous* are used in the literature to identify two totally different issues and consequently are confusing. In the classical data communications sense, an asynchronous transmission is one in which characters may be sent with random timing. It is also known as *start/stop*. In this procedure, the data bits of each character are introduced by a start bit and followed by a stop bit, which separates the characters. This protocol is inefficient, and the asynchronous mode is generally used only for low-speed transmissions: 1.2 kbps or lower.

In a synchronous transmission there is a constant time interval between characters. It is determined by a digital clock usually located in the modem. Thus, start and stop bits are not needed per character and data communication is more efficient. A synchronous communications protocol has a header and a trailer unit—the latter for error control purposes. We refer to the original (1960s) synchronous protocols as bisynch, or BSC, to distinguish the character level from the bit level (Fig. 5-1) used with packet switching.

The concept of packet switching, developed in the mid 1960s by Paul Baran of the Rand Corporation, increases the efficiency of synchronous transmission. Packets use a bit-oriented (not character-bound) protocol: flag sequences at the beginning and end of a frame effect synchronization. The frame includes a header, user information in the form of a bit string, and a trailer section dedicated to error control.

We said that in communications technology there is another meaning to synchronous and asynchronous operations. To understand it, we must visualize a distributed information system with hosts, workstations, and distributed text and databases. Processes (represented by applications programs, or AP) running on a WS may require information elements resident in a TDB other than its own, or it may need to communicate with other processes residing in a different WS or in a host. If the text and data communication operation can be *deferred*, then we are talking of an *asynchronous event*.

Online text and data entry is an example of an asynchronous operation. Though a controlled data entry may be involved, the information necessary for acceptance or rejection of the entered data may reside in the storage of the WS itself (on a microfile), whereas the updating of the local TDB (in a LAN sense) or of the central text and data warehouse can be done in a deferred mode.

Voice mail, teletex (electronic mail), and other types of correspondence are examples of asynchronous events. The fact of dissociating sender (WS) from receiver (whether WS, host, or TDB) permits a much better utilization of the available communications capacity. However, not all processes can work asynchronously.

A *synchronous event* is characterized by *realtime* update of the TDB, or it reflects a linkage between two processes operating on two

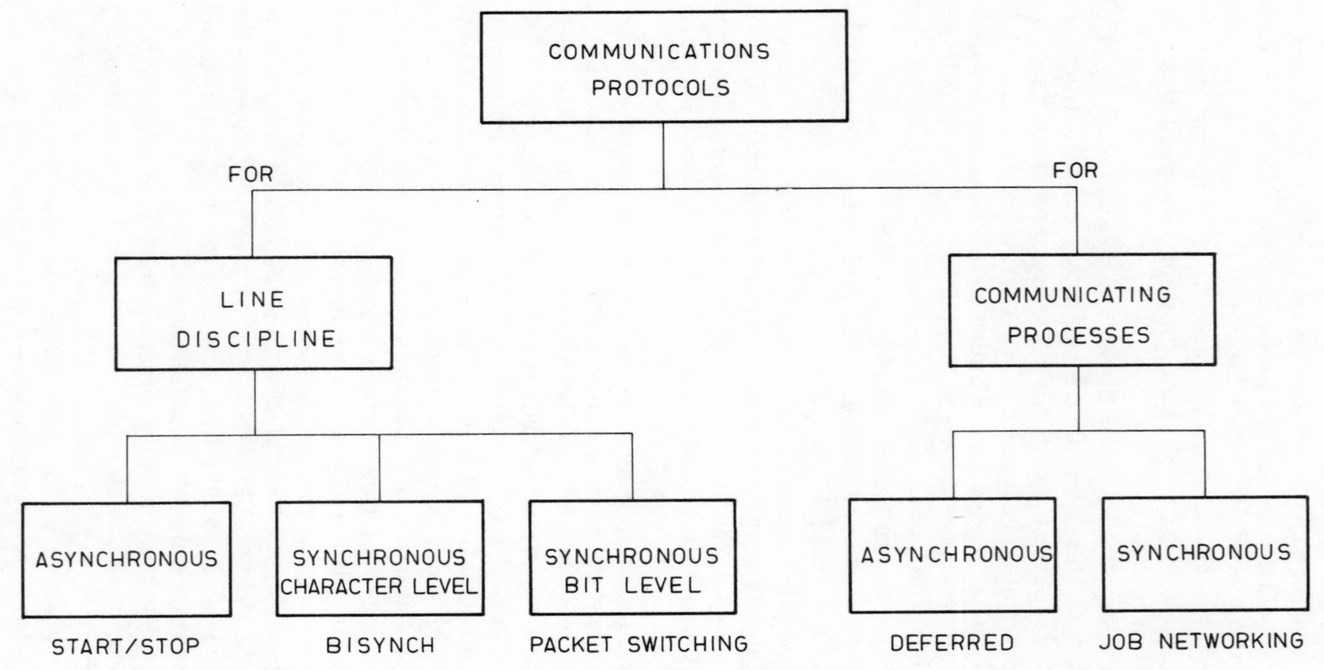

Figure 5-1. A taxonomical division of protocols by their use as a line discipline and for handshake between communicating processes.

different workstations such that the one cannot be completed without interaction with the other. This approach is also known as *job networking*. From a design standpoint, synchronous events should be given priority in the use of the communications resources, but the systems study should carefully establish which APs have *really* synchronous type requirements. A leading bank cut its communications costs by an impressive 60 percent through the implementation of distributed information systems (DIS) and the switching of some of the formerly realtime APs to deferred, thus filling the valleys of its private-line network.

Hence, synchronous and asynchronous protocols establish a well-defined interprocess communication mechanism. This makes possible process coordination to:

1. Carry out some cooperative task, as in the case of a group of processes working together on the same job
2. Avoid interference, as when unrelated processes need concurrent access to global resources

Having established the conventions, which is, after all, the role of the protocol, we must also establish ways of performing synchronization, mutual exclusion, and the mechanics of data exchange. These tasks should be carried out by the software of the architecture. Synchronization permits one AP to determine when another AP has completed some action. This is necessary whenever the first process reaches the point at which it cannot continue until that action has taken place (as in synchronous operations).

The mutual exclusion feature controls access to network resources and thereby assures that the different APs use them in a properly defined, orderly, and safe way. Mutual exclusion must be dynamic and parametrically controlled, because the exact nature of intervention by architectural software depends both upon the resources involved and the action taking place at that moment in a network-wide sense.

Analysis of the capabilities to be supported by the chosen protocols, and the network architecture within which they integrate, is necessary to determine (1) the kernel of essential features and (2) the value-added capabilities needed to support particular applications. Compromises have to be made, and the criteria for selecting the kernel and ranking the value-added features are basically cost-effectiveness, service versus implementation costs, level of demand, and sufficiency in a number of different applications.

Several of the technical features needed with a LAN have been part of mainframes. Interprocess communications mechanisms utilized with hosts usually fall into two classes: procedure calls and message passing. Processes are coordinated through the use of a shared object such as a semaphore, lock, event count, or monitor. Such objects are also known as *keys*. For any job, a process must obtain control of the appropriate key; therefore, it may have to wait until the key is released by another process.

By associating events in which processes must synchronize with keys, it is possible to obtain synchronization. Exclusion is accomplished by associating a key with the resource to which access is to be controlled. This will not permit a given AP to proceed until it is able to obtain the key. On the other hand, once a process has obtained the key, it manipulates the associated resource itself. This is a fundamental consideration in situations characterized by shared memory. Access is direct.

In the alternative situation of a system designed on a message-passing basis, the APs coordinate message exchange. Processes send messages and wait for the arrival of messages. If no AP is waiting for them when they are sent, the messages are queued. Since messages can be divided into classes, priorities and other features can be established through their classification. In a message-passing system, synchronization is assured by associating the occurrence of a given event with a message. Access is indirect: a given process typically acts as a server handling the resource on behalf of other processes. Data exchange is by passing rather than by direct sharing of memory.

Similar principles can be observed in local area network environments. An example is the family of network *interprocess communication protocols*. Originally, this term was used to refer to transport layer protocols with connection-oriented features. Although many of these protocols can be used to implement primitive forms of synchronization and mutual exclusion, their primary function is information exchange. Let's add that the similitude of communications primitives between mainframes and LANs is itself a very important feature. No company of good size should use personal computers and LANs without the possibility of access to the mainframe. Gateway routines can be considerably simplified when the software which drives the hardware is nearly compatible.

In a network environment, there is a tendency to apply message-passing mechanisms; they are considered to be better suited than procedural calls, and they are easier to build. Such a network interprocess communications mechanism integrates within the session control layer of the architecture.

To better understand the capabilities supported by a given network architecture, it is advisable to define the supported features. They logically fall into two main classes: service and protocol. Service features are those visible to the immediate user of the protocol. Such services are provided at the higher layers of an architecture. Protocol features are usually invisible to the immediate user and involve the architecture's internal operations. Hybrids, that is, features that have both service and protocol characteristics, also exist.

EXAMINING A PACKET STRUCTURE

Through the software driving it, a local area network provides data communications intelligence at each of its workstations. The software performs:

- Packet assembly and disassembly
- Buffering
- Error detection
- Flow control

These services permit the construction of packet-switched connections between correspondent workstations and shared resources (database, gateway, printer). Local intelligence manages sessions between the attached user devices. It provides economically the protocol and code conversion, speed matching, and data security. The LAN assumes responsibility for data communications functions through transmission management, including monitoring. Its functionality increases the processing capacity of the workstations by offloading them of substantial portions of communication handling.

The removal of network-dependent functions from user devices is achieved through the implementation of the proper protocols integrated at the bus interface unit (BIU) level by a microprocessor-based intelligent controller. As stated, the controller contains the circuitry that forms the physical and electrical connection to the network, made through a transceiver tap. In the BIU also resides the firmware supporting the data link control function.

An example of a physical packet structure, taken from the Desnet network, is shown in Fig. 5-2. The packet is delimited by a start and a stop byte. The start flag is followed by a 2-byte destination address and a 1-byte destination service access point, which is used for real or virtual internetworking message routing. That is true of the source address also.

The *header* includes a control byte. It is followed by the *informa-*

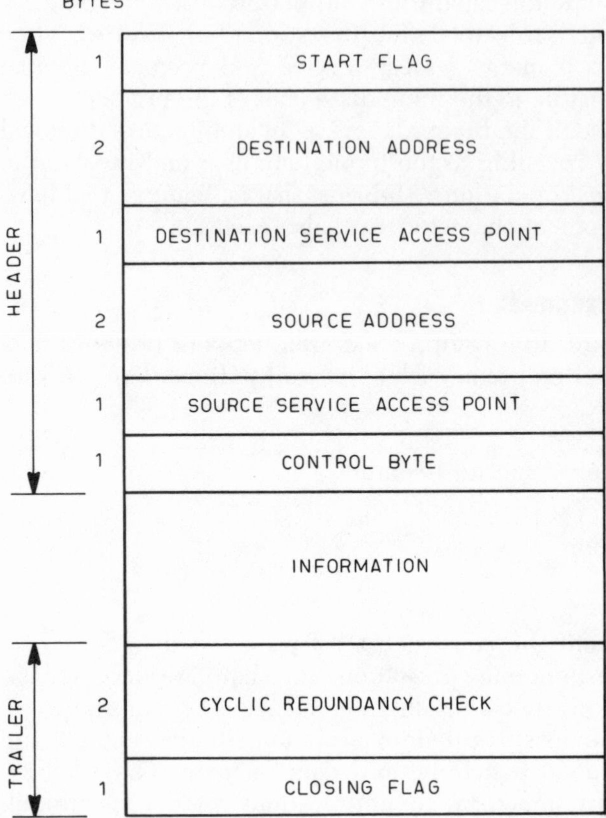

Figure 5-2. Packet structure for a local area network, including header, information field, and trailer.

tion field, the size of which is determined by higher-level protocols. A trailer follows the information field. It includes a 2-byte cyclic redundancy check and the closing flag.

The packet-switching standard is the Consultative Committee for International Telephone and Telegraph (CCITT) protocol. It includes:

1. A *link control header* containing a flag, address, and control
2. A *packet header*, composed of identification number (ID) defining a terminal or cluster controller, logical channel number, and control
3. The *information field*

4. The *link control trailer* with the frame check sequence cyclic redundancy check (CRC) and closing flag

Note that items 1 and 4 relate to data link control and item 2 is devoted to packet switching.

Through able use and interpretation of protocols, a distributed LAN environment manages the capabilities inherent in the computational and storage resources of the collective systems. It controls the sharing of the resources and assures secure properties to the LAN users.

Protocols are important both for databasing and for data communication. Their employment allows multiple processes and users to benefit from multiple tasking, shared memory, and virtual memory implementation. Processes residing in the network can hold the network and manipulate it because protocols are available. Common data communication protocols make it feasible to work under a variety of operating systems residing in the attached workstations. The same protocols can be implemented in different LAN architectures.

THE LAYERED APPROACH

Figure 5-3 shows the gateway structure of a LAN environment. It is composed of software and hardware entities, the aggregate being divided into layers. Such a local area network interface would typically be software-intensive and involve different layers each of which is assigned a specific function.

The lowest of the logical layers is addressed to the data link and therefore to error handling. The hardware part on which it rests comprises the link data pump (link driver) and the physical layer. The link data pump must be in hardware to maintain high-speed data rates. The physical layer will be conditioned by the design choices which are made. For instance, in a carrier sense–collision detection protocol it will involve collision detection, carrier sense, and modem, at the lowest level.

We will return to this subject, but at this point we note that with this piece coming in silicon, we can expect a cost similar to that of Universal Synchronous Asynchronous Receive/Transmit (USART), which in 1982 cost about $5 instead of the original $30. The functions of the USART are to serialize the bits for transmission and to provide bit stuffing in HDLC (data link of packet switching).

Figure 5-4 identifies the seven logical layers (plus a physical one) which constitute the standard of Open Systems Interconnection (OSI) of the International Standards Organization (ISO). Note that, from the

LAN link layer, both voice (toward the ISO/OSI physical level) and text and data (through the ISO/OSI applications layer) can be supported. Within the seven protocol levels, applications, presentation, and session control are characterized by information systems protocols.

The data link protocol for networks is the one which has so far received most attention. This layer defines how the information is formed into discrete data units. It includes:

- Rules for forming data packets
- Media access scheduling
- Addressing
- Error handling

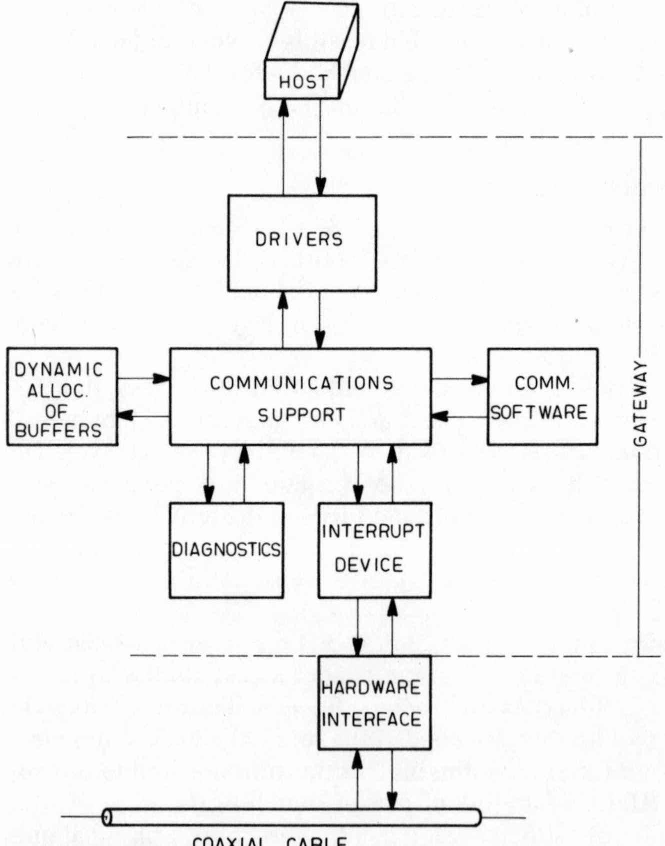

Figure 5-3. Component parts of a gateway in a layered approach within a LAN environment.

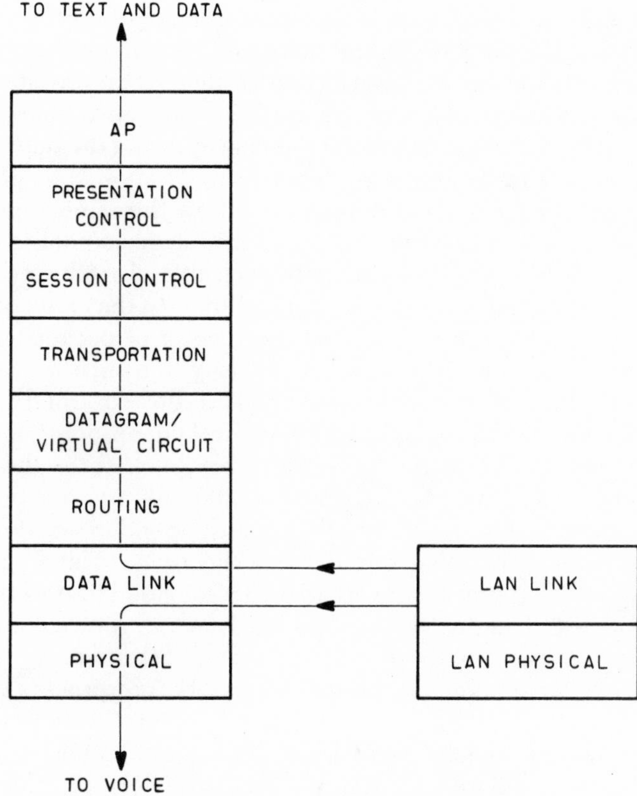

Figure 5-4. The seven layers of the ISO/OSI standard.

The data link layer protocol must be able to detect and possibly correct errors occurring in the physical layer, control the data flow to prevent overloading of the network, assume network access, and provide acknowledgment capabilities for the correct transmission and receipt of the packets.

Several LANs see to it that the physical and data link layers are implemented through a combination of hardware and firmware in the read-only memory in the interface device. The higher-up layers are implemented through software by using the facilities provided by the two lower layers.

Design functionality starts at the cable level. For instance, in Cluster One, which uses a flat wire, 8 of the wires in the 16-wire cable carry directional data, 4 convey handshakes and control information, and 4 function as grounds. The cable shield, if any, may provide an additional ground. The interface to the cable is through transceiver-multiplexers that permit the data being put on the cable to be read back at the same time. This *read-while-write facility* makes it possible for collisions to be detected when more than one station attempts to gain access to the network cable at the same time. The immediate read-back will be garbled if the data entering the network collide with transmissions already in transit.

Not all the LAN architectures follow the same approach. In Ethernet-type networks, for instance, the carrier signal is detected as the presence of data on the network cable. In Cluster One, carrier is implemented as a separate control line. In that way, other stations are kept off the network so that the receipt of packets can be acknowledged and a multiple-packet two-way transmission can take place.

In the Cluster One case, two of the control lines are used to synchronize byte transmission in an asynchronous mode of operation. To see to it that the network interface disturbs the host operating system as little as possible, local read-only memory (ROM) and random-access memory (RAM) are provided to store the network software. This also permits modifications to and upgrading of the network interface software to be downloaded to sites through the LAN without changing the system hardware or reprogramming the ROM. Packets are usually sent direct to the host memory.

We have been speaking of a network interprocess communications mechanism. This is one of a family of protocols being used by the National Bureau of Standards (NBS). The ISO/OSI reference model is the architectural prototype on which the design of this protocol family is based. The location of a protocol in an architectural model is usually defined by specifying the services required from the next lower layer and the services to be provided to the layer above. In the case of the interprocess communications mechanism, the only service which seems to be required from below is the reliable end-to-end delivery of data provided by the transport layer, whereas the network interprocess communications protocol is to be a session layer entity.

Message handling should be examined within the larger networking perspective which we are considering. An issue of particular importance is the addressing information, which is classically part of the header. The information is built into the names of objects, and names can be permanently bound to addresses. For instance, the name of a transport user in the protocol may be a socket that specifies the location of the transport user through a logical identification: network, host, or port.

If by examining a given name we cannot determine the address of the object named, the name is said to be *location-independent*. Interprocess communications using this approach must bind a location-independent object name to an address that specifies which object on which host is being referenced. The flexibility of the approach lies in the fact that the objects named can potentially migrate from host to host and from WS to WS without affecting the applications processes that make use of them.

A location-independent name space makes it feasible for an AP to send messages to another AP without needing to be aware of its location. Hence, the location can change without affecting the ability to communicate. In this sense, a location-independent name space helps create applications whose component processes can migrate from host to host and from WS to WS without affecting the users of that application. Benefits include increased availability and the capability of balancing process load across the local network.

A *global name* in a local area network is one that has the same interpretation in all hosts and workstations. Such a name refers to the same object regardless of the machine in which it is used. "Global" does not necessarily mean unique, because more than one global name may refer to the same object. Neither does "global" necessarily mean location-independent, just as a location-independent name does not absolutely imply "global." Procedurally, once we have decided on a location-independent name space, we must also decide whether that name space will be local or global.

A collection of objects is specified by a *generic name*, but the nature of the collections varies with the protocol. Collections that can be specified by generic names are of three kinds: services, patterns to match, and arbitrary sets of objects. In the case of a service, the generic name refers to the collection of all objects that provide a given service. In the case of a pattern to match, the generic name represents the collection of all objects whose names match the pattern. In the case of an arbitrary set of objects, LAN users can assign generic names to groups of objects of their own choosing.

The notion of *mailboxes*, supported by local network architectures, is based on name space. Mailboxes may be fixed or created dynamically by processes, but usually a mailbox has a lifetime that is independent of that of any process: It exists until it is explicitly deleted. An AP can read messages out of a given mailbox. The mailbox resides on a specific WS or host, and only authorized processes can read messages out of it. To provide greater flexibility, several architectures provide for sending messages for later processing to a process not currently in existence. Furthermore, multiple-server processes can read requests out of a single mailbox.

Mailboxes can be divided into bins. In this case, the mailbox names are global, whereas bin names are local to the mailbox. The number of bins in a mailbox is fixed at the time the mailbox is created, but bins can be dynamically added to and deleted from a mailbox. The function of bins is to provide a convenient way of grouping together a collection of related services. For instance, a single mailbox may have a separate bin to hold requests for each kind of attached device. Significantly, the use of bins can considerably reduce the size of the global name space (only mailbox names need to be global), and they provide a natural domain for segregating messages into priority groups.

Answers to the problems which we have been discussing are provided by the different LAN architectures within the layered structure we have considered. Understandably, all announced architectures have started supporting routines at the lower layers. The *locator function* is a typical area which has attracted attention. Among the core capabilities of a LAN are application shared names, name space management, global names, local names association with global names, name look-up, address-name table management, global-local communications assignment, and name and address recognition. Higher capabilities include interfacing, error control, transport proper, flow control, measurement, and reporting. We will return to these subjects after we have examined the topological options characterizing the structure of a LAN.

In principle, there is no one-to-one correspondence between the type of topology, the baseband-broadband choice, and the protocol which is chosen. For instance, Wangnet uses collision detection in one band and token passing in another. It is, however, also true that local area network designers, as they try to optimize their product, are led to certain choices which look *as if* there were a connection between the design elements mentioned.

Whether in literature, project rooms, or professional meetings, there is no wide agreement on which of the three factors—topology, band, and protocol—should come first. But the sequence in which they are written is not random; it reflects the author's personal choice in going about them.

TYPES OF TOPOLOGY

A network is a homogeneous aggregate composed of heterogeneous entities such as links, nodes and switches, and gateways. The links are the carriers of information: voice, text, data, image. In modern networks the switches are intelligent devices able to concentrate and route the traffic according to the characteristics of the communications media handled by the network (Table 5-1).

TABLE 5-1 TYPICAL CHARACTERISTICS OF COMMUNICATIONS MEDIA

Type of usage	Facility	Status	Correspondence
Voice	Telephone	Interactive	1 to 1
	Broadcast ratio	Passive	1 to many
Image	TV	Passive	1 to many
Text and data	Video terminals	Interactive	1 to 1
	Hardcopy (printers)	Passive	1 to 1 or 1 to many

A nonrestrictive topology is the product of hardware and software design. In turn, this is a function of the type of topology (which we will examine later) and the supported features. Examples of the latter are handshake and control-line receivers with, for instance, hysteresis inputs to minimize noise. From an application standpoint this is a welcome possibility even if the network is designed to tolerate a moderate amount of noise.

The ways in which the nodes and switches of a network are arranged are the pillars on which the whole application rests. As shown in Fig. 5-5, the predominant types of LAN topology are the centralized (star and hierarchical), bus or unrooted tree, spider, loop, and virtual ring.

Centralized: Star and Hierarchical

It is best to distinguish the star and the hierarchical topologies. Both are centralized, and both depend on a centrally located active resource, which is the master. But the star solution presupposes that the master is the one and only intelligence resource with command functions.

In different terms, a star topology connects end stations point to point to the master. There are no intermediate nodes, such as intelligent concentrators. The end points can be intelligent or unintelligent devices and can be data-, text-, or voice-oriented.

The hierarchical topology can be viewed as a variation of the centralized approach. Besides the central master resources, there are nodes—such as intelligent concentrators—which might themselves act as star structures. This approach leads to subnetworking but is always based on centralized principles.

Star and hierarchical are the oldest and least reliable types of topology; the central switch can be a minicomputer or PBX. Being the

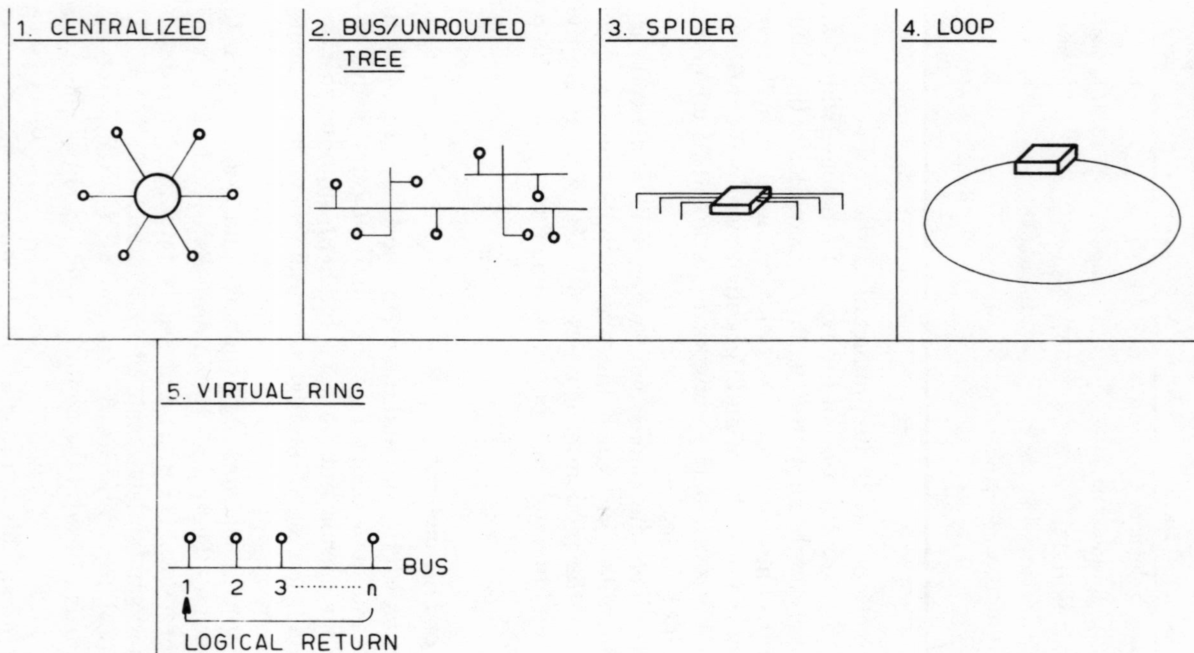

Figure 5-5. Predominant types of LAN topology and their structural characteristics.

poorest options, they need no further attention than to say that a twisted pair can be used as connecting wire.

Bus or Unrooted Tree

Another way to refer to the unrooted tree structure is as an ether (*ether* is the Greek word for "air"). It is neither centralized nor a loop. It is reconfigurable and has a distributed control capability. Its problem is maintenance. Ethernet, of Xerox; Network One, of Ungermann Bass; Localnet, of Sytec; and Solonet, of Olivetti are examples of ethers. In the years ahead we can expect many more.

Ethernet-type local networks utilize processor bus technology, which is typically coaxial-based. As of 1983, networks have cable segments up to 5000 m in length, and on a 500-m section 100 connnections can be tapped. Up to five segments can be linked together, with two repeaters in a path. The 100 devices per segment must be spaced 2.5 m, or multiples of 2.5 m, apart. The cable is marked, and a considerable amount of planning is needed for its usage.

The Ethernet protocol is contention mode and collision-based, as we will see in the next section.

Spider

In contrast to the centralized system, in which the central device is the most intelligent mode in the network, the spider interprocessor system defines an electronic pathway by means of a network of active and passive hubs. These link workstations together by connecting to the interprocessor bus. File processors and applications processors are attached to this pathway, which provides access to all resources. We will look at the mechanics in more detail when we examine Datapoint's ARC local area network.

Loop Structure

From an applications standpoint, the loop concept dates to the early 1970s. In its original version, which was a significant improvement over the then available multidrop line, it presupposed a hub-polling protocol and a node-host attachment which acted as central control (driver). The host injected signals going in one direction and picked up the signals as they returned to form the loop. Various network architectures can be based on the loop principle. They have in common that to move from one WS to the other requires passing on the information (token). The physical medium can be coaxial cable, twisted pair, triax, or flat wire.

One of the arguments to be found in the literature concerns the difference between loop and ring. A valid answer is that the loop was the original version and from it different *dialects* have developed. For instance, a 4-wire loop variation permits the creation of two 2-wire subloops around the driving station if the wire is cut along its path. The author prefers to use the word "ring" to identify a group of solutions which, though developed from the original loop concept, are different enough to justify a family of their own. Examples are the round robin and the Cambridge ring.

Virtual Ring

Also known as round robin, the virtual ring approach is based on token passing (a slot in the communications program) logically implemented on a bus. It is in contrast to the loop structure, which is a physical ring. The virtual ring is organized on the bus, and because it is software-based, it can support priority handling through algorithmic implementation.

Priority solutions also can be handled through hardware and software approaches. An example is the Cambridge ring, which is basically a physical medium with logical capabilities. A loop structure is subjected to a frame division in slots of 16, 32, or 64 bytes each. Each machine is assigned a slot and can speak only in its slot. This guarantees deterministic access, but it is rigid.

Another implementation is the star-shaped ring, on which an MIT project has concentrated. One of its goals is to combine the advantages of other methods. A bus solution, for example, has problems in the identification of failures, which is easier with a ring. However, the attachments are simple with bus, and so is priority control.

At the same time, significant effort is being made to assure network simplicity. Complex approaches are often counterproductive: they result in protocols which are not particularly efficient. The simpler approach is usually the best.

CABLE ACCESS PROTOCOLS

Each topology supports at least one type of access, but most topologies can support more than one type. The physical layout doesn't influence the protocol as much as one might think. There are, fundamentally, four cable access protocols, but each can have dialects and there are also hybrid possibilities.

The Slot Approach

The slot method is exemplified by the Cambridge ring. It is based on a type of time division multiplexing. A constant number of fixed-length slots continuously circulates around the ring, and a full/empty indicator within the slot header signals the real state.

In this solution, any station ready to transmit occupies the first empty slot by setting the full/empty indicator to full and placing its data in the slot. Sender and receiver workstations share the ring bandwidth until they have completely transmitted their packets. When the sender receives the occupied slot, it must change the full/empty indicator to empty. This guarantees equal sharing of the bandwidth among all stations. In a LAN the slots are usually short; a message may have to be transmitted within several slots.

Between two consecutive access possibilities of a certain WS, the slot travels exactly once around the ring in the empty state. All time periods of one cycle, during which the slot is empty, are put together in one contiguous empty slot interval.

Token Passing

The application of token passing is exemplified by ARC, round robin (token bus), and token rings. The token is an attribute of the session connection which defines unambiguously, dynamically, and possibly exclusively whether or not a particular WS has the right to access a given service. This is a necessary but not always a sufficient condition. Examples of tokens include send data, parameter reselection, terminate session, and synchronization. There are also user-defined tokens.

A token will always be in one of three states:

1. Assigned or not assigned to a WS
2. Assignable or not assignable
3. Available or not available

When a token is assigned to a WS, the user has the right to use the service. If it is not assigned, the user does not have the right to use the service at that particular time but may acquire the right without entering reselection. If a token is not assignable, the user does not have the right to use the service; reselection is required to change to the assigned or not assigned states. If the token is not available, the user does not have the right to use the service over the lifetime of the session connection.

It follows that the management of the token states must be guaranteed. The management activity consists of controlling the transmission channel by passing a permission token around the ring. When the system is initialized, a designated station generates a free token which travels until a station ready to transmit changes it to busy and puts its packet onto the ring. The packet can, in principle, be of arbitrary length.

In principle, the sending WS is responsible for removing its own packet from the ring. At the end of its transmission, it passes the access permission to the next station by generating a new free token. Possible queues are serviced in a cyclical manner as by a rotating switch which stands for the free token. Different strategies can be followed: a queue is serviced until it is empty or only a limited number of packets is serviced per access possibility. The former is known as the exhaustive and the latter as the nonexhaustive service.

In token passing there is no control station and no master-slave relationship, and it is possible to build a priority mechanism so that some stations have priority over others. Token-passing rings can be reliable. One installed at UCLA near a nuclear power reactor and motor activity was tested extensively and did not lose tokens. However, alternatives also can perform reliably, and choices must be made.

Contention

The favored protocol is carrier-sensing multiple access with collision detection (CSMA/CD); it is used with Ethernet and other LAN. The protocol is particularly suitable for baseband—collision detection seems to be very difficult on broadband. The capacity of the segment is important; at 10 Mbps a single bit has a length of about 25 m. [Other typical baseband solutions are frequency duplication, Manchester encoding, nonreturn to zero (NRZ), and differential Manchester.]

With the CSMA/CD protocol, every station wanting to transmit a packet must listen to the bus in order to establish whether any transmission is in progress. If it is, the station defers its transmission until the end of the current transmission. But packet collisions cannot be completely avoided because of the nonzero propagation delay on the bus. If a collision is detected, transmission is aborted and the station reschedules its packet. The retransmission interval is dynamically adjusted to the actual traffic load.

CSMA/CD can be applied with coaxial cable, flat wire, or twisted wire. Cluster One, for instance, uses a CSMA/CD protocol. The carrier line is activated whenever the cable is in use. Stations desiring to use the cable check for presence of the carrier signal and can access the cable only when it appears to be idle. As in the coaxial-based Ethernet, this is a noncentralized access control mechanism with the same priority for all stations. Let's add that an alternative possibility with CSMA is collision avoidance (CSMA/CA) used by some LANs such as Omninet.

In both Cluster One and Ethernet, collisions are detected by software during the first several bytes of packet transfer. In the Cluster One case collisions happening during retransmission are not checked in the same "early bytes" sense, but they are detected by bad check sums at the end of the colliding packets. Both colliding packets will be retransmitted.

To recapitulate, the carrier may be idle or busy. When it is allocated, the source station puts the destination address on the data line and, after a suitable delay, the carrier line is activated. The destination station address comparator will trigger the software in the destination interface and cause it to start receiving a packet which consists of four fields: type, length, data, and check sums. Cable allocation occurs when a station puts its source address on the data line.

A design criterion in any system of this kind is α (alpha), the *normalized propagation delay*. It is the ratio of the time a packet takes to travel throughout the network to the time necessary to transmit a packet. Therefore, it should be as low as possible and surely much less than 1. But as we increase the *cable length*, the propagation time increases and α increases. And if we increase the *signaling rate*, the packet transmission time decreases and α increases.

The catch is that, as α increases, the effective throughput of the system decreases: more time is taken up by collisions. Therefore, the standardization work by IEEE projects a minimum frame size so defined that α is never greater than 1.

CSMA/CD may lead to inefficient operation if the ratio of propagation delay to packet transmission time is too high. Also, overhead is a critical consideration. The header (address, etc.) in an Ethernet packet is about 150 bits. Although that might not seem a lot, it all depends on the application. Ideally, the attached devices should be exchanging rather large messages so the header becomes a relatively small portion of the total packet.

Ordered Access Bus

The protocol proper to the ordered access bus solution is known as multilevel multiple access (MLMA). It is frame-based and sees to it that information transmission occurs in variable length frames. A controller provides start flags at time intervals which signal the beginning of a frame. The frame is divided into two parts, a request slot and an arbitrary number of packets, with every station attached to the bus owning one bit within the request slot. By setting its private bit, a station indicates that it wants to transmit a packet within the frame. The transmission sequence is given by a priority assignment known to all stations.

In line with this protocol, the bus is modeled as a single-server facility. Packets from all stations, which have been newly generated and have not yet been scheduled, form a distributed queue: They cannot be transmitted within the current frame, but must instead wait until a new frame starts. However, to assure that all stations know the entries made in the request slot, the scheduling time may have to be significantly longer than the pure transmission time of the request slot.

The MLMA method is somewhat similar in concept to the contention resolution method for computer interrupt systems. There seem to be some basic assumptions in its use, the more restrictive one being that the distance between two stations transmitting in succession is uniformly distributed throughout the maximum bus length.

6 NORMALIZATION

The international normalization effort started at the beginning of this century with the creation of the Commission Electrotechnique Internationale (CEI) in 1906. This organization still studies all questions relative to international normalization in the domain of electrotechnology and electronics, though, as we will see, a number of other important bodies also contribute to the effort.

The members of the CEI are the national committees, which must be as representative as possible of all sectors of the electrical and electronics industry in their countries. This involves manufacturers, government authorities, and professional associations.

In 1947 the International Standard Organization was born. It works on both technical and nontechnical norms in all areas not under the authority of CEI. Since there are many overlapping areas, an accord has been established between ISO and CEI to create a system that covers the entire field of international normalization.

Most ISO members are government institutions or public law organizations (Fig. 6-1). The others are independent organizations in close collaboration with the public administrations of their countries. Today some 87 countries participate in a total of 1200 work groups on normalization; among them they involve more than 100,000 experts. This joint work has so far produced some 3500 norms in the ISO part alone.

Another normalization agency particularly important to networks is the Consultative Committee for International Telephone and Telegraph (CCITT). This is a consultant body of the Union Internationale des Telecommunications (UIT). The CCITT makes recommendations which are prepared by its study groups. Its work concerns exclusively

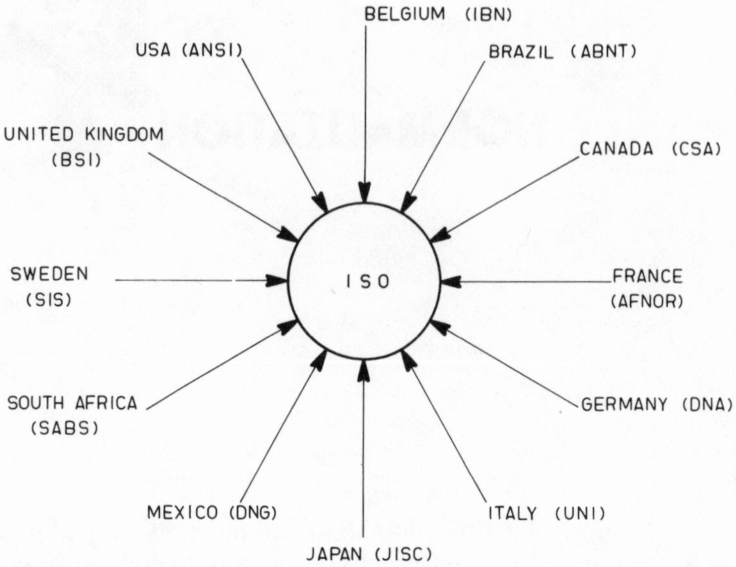

Figure 6-1. ISO member nations and national standards associations.

the norms of international telecommunications. In it 154 countries are represented, generally through their telecommunications administrations but also by private telecommunications agencies and industrial or scientific organizations.

The contributions by member countries can be significant. The international electronic mail service (teletex), for example, was proposed for the first time by a German commission of experts which had studied, over a long period of time, the issues related to telecommunications. The basic idea was to consider text transmission as an extended characteristic of text processing and editing with emphasis on:

- International compatibility among all users
- Guaranteed quality of service
- Complete character set, including all necessary special symbols
- Transmission speed of 2.4 or better
- Memory-to-memory communications capability
- Gateways

- Interactivity with the existing telex service
- The availability of international directories

In 1976, CCITT studied the international standardization of teletex. The resulting recommendations define the terminal characteristics necessary to obtain compatibility between all users of the service. Some four years passed till this subject reached maturity, and in 1980 the plenary assembly of CCITT formally approved the *Draft Recommendations* for teletex.

As an example of the effort needed for the institution of a new service, let's review the highlights: Draft Recommendation S60 concerns the teletex terminals, S61 the set of characters, S62 the control establishment, and S70 the transport service, which is independent of the teletex network. And since more time was needed for the recommendation to filter down through the telephone systems of the member countries, the first offering of an international telephone service was in 1982.

Significant standardization work is also done by country and on a regional basis. In the United States, the normalization effort is generally led by the National Bureau of Standards (NBS), but a major contributor to norms concerning computers and communications is the American National Standards Institute (ANSI). For instance, NBS has introduced a redundancy check at the transport level over and above the cyclic redundancy check at the bit level.

NBS is a new entity in information systems standards, a development from the weights and measures area which it originally regulated. One of its significant projects centers on transport and flow control. A similar contribution to normalization has been made by the committees established by major computer users to develop and implement specific norms such as Codasyl.

Other contributors are the committees which are currently attempting to develop an industrywide standard for LANs. For example, the Institute of Electrical and Electronics Engineers (IEEE) Computer Society Local Network Committee (Project 802) has been meeting to that end since 1980. The attempt has been to accommodate many diverse application areas and functional requirements.

A regional normalizations body is The European Computer Manufacturers Association (ECMA). Roughly equivalent to ANSI, ECMA was established in 1961 as a nonprofit organization by 20 computer companies, including American firms operating in Europe. Its objective is to develop norms which facilitate the use of computer hardware. Several norms established by ECMA have filtered through ISO, which includes representatives from ANSI and ECMA. ISO defines transport control, including flow control, congestion, windows, and packetizing to be assigned to session control. Current work on session control is oriented toward a logical connection basis.

In this chapter we will be concerned with two sets of norms: logical and physical. Starting with the latter, we will review the CCITT recommendations in the V series. Subsequently we will treat the recommendations relative to the X series, and that discussion will lead us into the ISO/OSI, where OSI is the Open System Interconnection.

THE PHYSICAL INTERFACE

It is important to realize that the physical level, which is the first of a layered data processing–data communication (DP/DC) architecture, must accomplish two functions simultaneously. The first is to interface between the data terminating equipment, which works in a digital form, and the telephone line, which is largely analog. In different terms, though digital lines are the generally accepted means of the future, analog lines will most likely still be in majority until the early 1990s and later. Digital-to-analog (D/A) and analog-to-digital (A/D) conversion by modems is the primary goal within the interface function, but not the only one.

The second function is to make up for unfortunate practices of the past: the use of different line disciplines from asynchronous to binary synchronous which must be interfaced for the data communication to take place in a modern, efficient network such as packet switching. This will also have logical aftermaths which will affect the higher-up communications layers in the ISO/OSI structure.

The significance of the preceding remarks will be better understood if we take a quick look at the development of data communication capabilities from the nineteenth century onward. Contrary to general impression, the earliest transmission, in the 1830s, was not voice but a digital one of sorts by telegraph. In fact, the telegraph was the first practical application of electricity. It used the Morse code for the transmission of text and data. Morse is basically an archaic binary code that uses only two digits, a long pulse, or dash, and a brief pulse, or dot, in combinations, to send alphanumeric characters and signs along a carrier.

The early use of telephone lines, modems, and true binary code led to the employment of nonintelligent teleprinter equipment (TTY). There are different ways to code a character with 6 bits to produce 56 usable signs; telex employs the 5-bit Baudot code. TTY protocols are start/stop. Each character has a start and a stop bit, the latter being 1.4 longer than the former.

In the synchronous transmission which later developed, the synchronization is accomplished by a clock and the synchronization bytes preceding the message. A further improvement is the parity (check digit) in the trailer to the message. With binary synchronous communication (BSC) this is addressed to the message only. With packet switching, the 2-byte CRC polynominal is addressed to both the header and the message. Packet switching utilizes bit level protocols and is a significant improvement over BSC.

Here it is important to note that data communication can utilize one of three technologies for transmission purposes. The oldest one is circuit switching, which is widely used for voice communications. The next, chronologically, is message switching; it was installed after World War II with the telex/TWX network. A development of the mid-to-late 1960s is packet switching; it integrates many message-switching concepts and improves upon them. Its object is reliability in communications and efficiency. Since packet switching slowly evolves to message switching, the standardization effort is directed toward the circuit and packet-switching technologies. They are the subject of CCITT recommendations.

In the 1970s, CCITT promoted a series of recommendations the intent of which was the standardization of data communications protocols.

- The standard for circuit switching was made X.21.
- The standard for packet switching was made X.25.
- The internetworking capability is assured through the rules inherent in X.75.

It is, however, important to understand X.21, X.25, and X.75 are recommendations formulated by CCITT and accepted by its members. Unlike the rules established by ISO, they are not international standards.

Behind the CCITT recommendations lies the fact that the telecommunications means used for data transmission between computer systems can be of various types and evolve quite rapidly. X.21 is vital if we consider that even older methods of switching and transmission can have a comeback because of the steady application of a more advanced technology to means which are already known.

Circuit switching, for example, which is defined by the X.21 proposal of CCITT, has been retained by at least two countries as a base of their newest data communication public network: the Nordic Public Data Network (NPDN) and DDX-C in Japan. Other countries may follow them.

Adopted in 1976, the X.25 protocol is undergoing some changes in framework. The result of the 1981 changes is that an estimated 15 percent of the X.25-compatible equipment will have to be retrofitted. Furthermore, after the fashion of computers and communications, the X.25 protocol is implemented differently from country to country.

Packet switching permits the multiplexing of many different communications on the same carrier without undue delays in the node switches. It also permits the efficient separation of functions between data transport and other facilities such as data processing, databasing, and end user services. With packet switching, information in binary form is delivered to the network as a packet which contains:

- The header with the address of the destination station and other data
- The information proper presented as a binary string
- A trailer for control purposes applicable to the whole packet

Certain implementations also involve an incarnation number that enables the reassembly and control of packet sequence at the other end of the connection. In terms of the transport activity, the intermediate nodes can forward the packets through alternate routes as soon as they are received. There is no reason to wait for the last packet of a long message to arrive before forwarding the one received.

The French Transpac, the American Telenet, the Canadian Datapac, the ECM Euronet, the German Datex-P, the Japanese DDX-P, the Swiss Telepac, the Dutch DN1, the Spanish RETD, the Argentinian Arpac, and the South-African Saponet are examples of X.25 implementation. It is, however, well to remember that the fact of following the X.25 recommendation does not assure internetworking compatibility. There are several dialects of X.25.

Internetworking (with a variety of transport standards) is the objective of X.75. Another factor is also important. There is no universal software package which would permit data terminating equipment (DTE) to interface with any other online system, even if both followed the X.21 or X.25 CCITT recommendation.

FUNCTION OF THE CCITT RECOMMENDATIONS

We have emphasized the possibilities and limitations of the recommendations made by the working groups of CCITT. To take a closer look at their function, let's consider the X.25. It specifies the interface between user terminals: the DTE and the physical layer at the end of the telephone line, i.e., the data communication equipment (modem DCE). With X.25, which is addressed to the networking layer (routing, virtual circuit), the terminal-to-terminal communication will be supported in a packet-switching–virtual circuit fashion.

CCITT has also developed recommendations for asynchronous terminals. The terminals are connected to a public packet-switching network through packet assembly-disassembly (PAD), which is furnished by the public network. PAD regroups the data transmitted start/stop by the terminal into packets for further handling on the network. Three CCITT recommendations are addressed to the PAD subject:

- X.3 describes the terminal characteristics of interest in PAD.
- X.28 specifies PAD handling from the terminal viewpoint, such as the identification of the computer with which the terminal wishes to communicate.
- X.29 specifies PAD handling from the viewpoint of the host, that is, the computer with which the terminal communicates.

It is important to note that the X.29 is an add-on to X.25. In the baseline, the converted data stream will be transmitted in X.25.

We have said that CCITT is primarily interested in the physical layer and the immediately following logical layers: the data link, routing, and virtual circuit. The protocol for the data link has been standardized by ISO. It is the higher-level data link control (HDLC), and it has two variations: line access protocol A (LAP A) for asymmetric networks and LAP B for symmetric networks.

Reference has been made to the CCITT X.25 for routing and virtual circuit. What has not been said is that an alternative to virtual circuit is datagram. Byte-oriented, it poses fewer demands on the network architecture and more on the DTE. The latter is responsible for ordering the received datagrams, controlling and searching for them if they entered an interminal loop.

Over and above the virtual circuit layer are other layers. The transport looks after flow control, and the session and presentation control reside at the DTE and are supported by its software. They have been the subject of the Open System Interconnection standard advanced by ISO.

A subject of interest in connection with network architectures is what the different computer manufacturers have adopted. We will take Digital Equipment Corporation (DEC) as an example. With the introduction of packet system interface (PSI), DEC made available a range of alternatives to support both public packet-switching networks and private data communication structures whether distributed or hierarchical.

- The Interactive Terminal Interface (ITI) connects DEC equipment through a public packet-switching network on the basis of X.3, X.28, and X.29.
- The Network File Transfer (NFT) facility permits a digital computer to access and transfer files from another DEC machine (in a manner compatible with Decnet).
- Network Talk makes it feasible for a terminal attached to a DEC machine to communicate with a terminal attached to another DEC machine at a remote site.

Such software has the goal of positioning the manufacturer within the framework of the developing packet-switching networks. DEC will support the following public networks: Telenet (United States), Datapac (Canada), Transpac (France), Datex-P (Germany), DN1 (Holland), and PSS (England). But the most important aspect is the support such software gives the international data communication standards and recommendations.

TECHNICAL CHARACTERISTICS

The number of protocols used for data communication purposes is multiplying at the same time users are pressing for greater compatibility. Typical American protocols are the 2741, 2780, and 3780, which were developed by IBM and are employed by practically everybody, but application of the X.21 and X.25 is spreading. IBM, for example, has announced its intention to provide for interconnection to public data networks supporting X.21 and X.25. This also is a reasonable approach, and it can have a significant impact. If we regard HDLC, LAP B, ADCCP, as frames (not packets, which are X.25), the BSCs tend to be replaced by the new data link standard.

The fact is that, for machines to communicate, we must establish and observe universal rules for transmitting information—the function supported by protocols. The alternative is to devise hardware or software translators that can enable companies to link multivendor sites. This is a costly and not particularly efficient solution which became necessary because equipment was incompatible.

But even if there were an announced, supported protocol, it might be ineffective because computer and communications manufacturers tend to alter control codes—one vendor's 3780 may not be compatible with everybody else's 3780. A dual approach may therefore be necessary: Adopt a universal protocol *and* develop inexpensive translation devices. It is doubtful that the protocol mess can be cleaned up during the 1980s. In the meantime, the lack of a good standard necessitates the writing of a lot of software that otherwise might not have been necessary. Also, every data communications user must develop the know-how to find his way through the manufacturer's maze and arrive at a valid system.

What we have just said underlines the need for clarifying codes and symbols. The adopted standards for public data networks are the following:

- V.21, CCITT for electric voltages
- V.24, physical interface for the telephone line
- X.21, bisynchronous protocols
- X.25, packet switching

The CCITT V series has to do with analog signals, just as the X series has to do with digital signals.

Three physical interfaces are very important in the analog domain. The governing standards and their applications are:

- V.10, connectors and pins.
- V.21, electric voltage. It affects the number of pins, and in the United States it is in the background for the recommended standard (RS) series.
- V.24, the functional level. (There is an X.24 counterpart, but its function is rather unclear.)

There is a lot of misunderstanding of what these CCITT recommendations are and are not and how the V and X series correspond. So also is there misunderstanding of the relation between the international and U.S. standards. For instance, it is often said that the U.S. counterpart of the V.24 is the RS-232C, but that is not exactly accurate. As for correspondence between the V and X series, an approximation is the following:

Analog	
V.10	X.10
V.21	X.11
V.24	X.21

There are other CCITT analog recommendations. DEC, for instance, is said to work with V.35 through an analog signal's virtual standard. The V.35 is good for data only. Table 6-1 contrasts the V.35 and RS-232 on the basis of distance, signals, and transmission capacity. (As we will see in the following discussion, however, the RS-232 is being supplanted by the RS-449.) The V.35 is a more advanced technical solution than its predecessor; it was adopted in the late 1970s.

Figure 6-2 shows a basic difference between RS-232 and V.35 and distinguishes V.35 and RS-449. The V.35 is addressed to data only; the RS-449 supports both data and control. As Fig. 6-2 indicates, the V.35 does not include a return wire to be used for control purposes. Its capacity standard is 48 kbps, but it is used all the way from 19.2 to 72 kbps and beyond. The electrical characteristics and the number of pins are important. The electrical underpinnings of RS-449 (considered by some people as roughly equivalent to X.11) are of two kinds. The RS-422 is a balanced approach, and the RS-423 is an unbalanced one.

How important the issue of right standards choice is can be seen in Fig. 6-2. Given its electrical characteristics, the RS-232C weights speed to distance. Performance is greatly improved with the new recommended standards, which are based on 56 kbps or more and a significantly greater distance supported by the device.

The RS-232C uses a 25-pin connector, and the RS-449 uses a 37-pin connector. The X-21 uses a 15-pin connector and employs a coding protocol. The V.35 has a 34-pin connector (Fig. 6-3). It can be appreciated, while we are talking of "standards," that here there is a rather notable lack of standardization which greatly hampers interconnection. It should be added that not all manufacturers follow the recommended standards in pin allocation, and the user is well advised to read the specifications of a given product carefully. Furthermore, there is no rush in adopting the RS-449 standard, but there does seem to be adoption of V.35.

Applications are the major reason why we need more pins, better electrical standards, and faster lines. For instance, graphics terminals

TABLE 6-1 A COMPARISON BETWEEN RS-232 AND V.35

	RS-232	V.35
Distance	17 m	330 m
Capacity	20 kbps	40 kbps, eventually 100 kbps
Signals	Single-ended, data only	Double-ended, data only

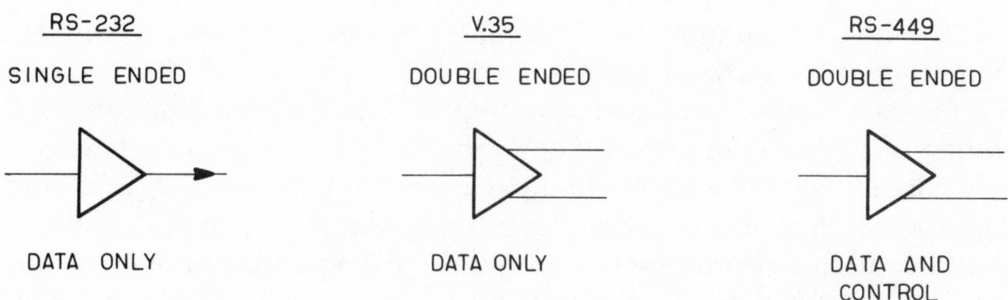

Figure 6-2. A comparison of RS-232, RS-449, and the V.35 of CCITT, RS-449 is the new U.S. standard; it divides into RS-422 (balanced) and RS-423 (unbalanced).

and fast refresh prerequisites require more kilobits per second (56 or 64) than the RS-232 can support. The same kind of statement can be made about the required distances. IBM, DEC, and other manufacturers are actively designing new equipment calling for lines running at 64 kbps. New approaches are therefore necessary. RS-232 can do the job at standard data rates up to 19.2, but not over that.

Now let us see what some organizations with an input to standards are doing in this area. AT&T manufactures the V.35 but not yet the RS-449. On the other hand, the Department of Defense has opted for the RS-449, which can be easily converted to MIL STAND 188. The interface at the speed level of 50 to 70 kbps is the Bell 301 standard. The boards will be driven at ≤72 kbps. A modem clock at 60 kbps, or conventionally 56 kbps, exists in the United States, and at 48 kbps in Europe.

This is important, because when the modem is clocking us, we are driven by it. We can drive faster if the modem lets us, but usually it does not. Figure 6-4 shows the electrical characteristics. However, for the BSC-type synchronous communications we only need 8 pins out

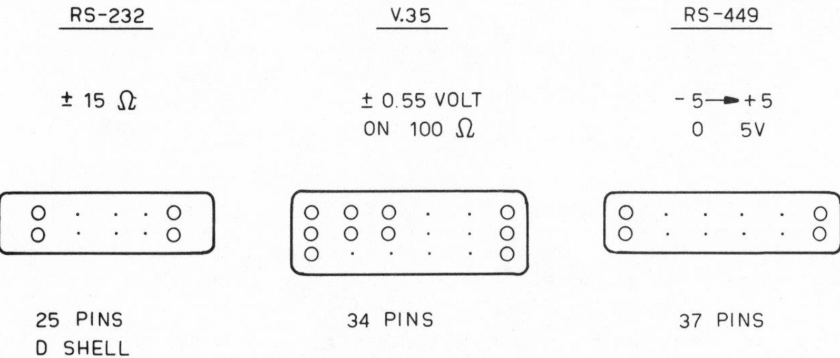

Figure 6-3. Number of connector pins in RS-232, V.35, and RS-449.

of 25, 34, or 37. An increase in number is necessary if we are to better the functioning of the system.

The fact is that the new recommended standards provide for much better electrical connection. They refer to different circuit sets which are not more costly but have higher capacity and better quality. On the other hand, it is also true that the new standards take time to settle in because of the magnitude of the current investment. Although adapters can be used to have coexistence on the same lines, a lot of machines cannot work together because their technical characteristics are not compatible.

The slow progress toward implementation is documented by Fig.

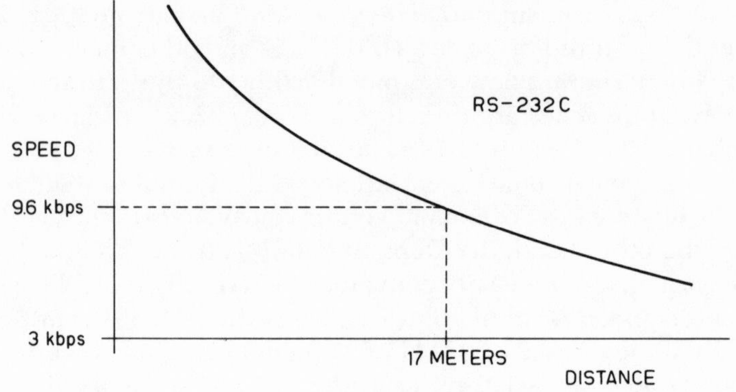

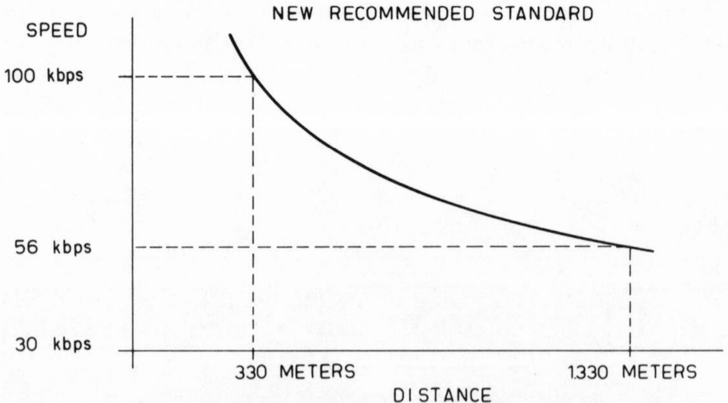

Figure 6-4. Characteristics of the RS-232C interface driving circuitry (without modem) and the new recommended standard: line speed versus distance.

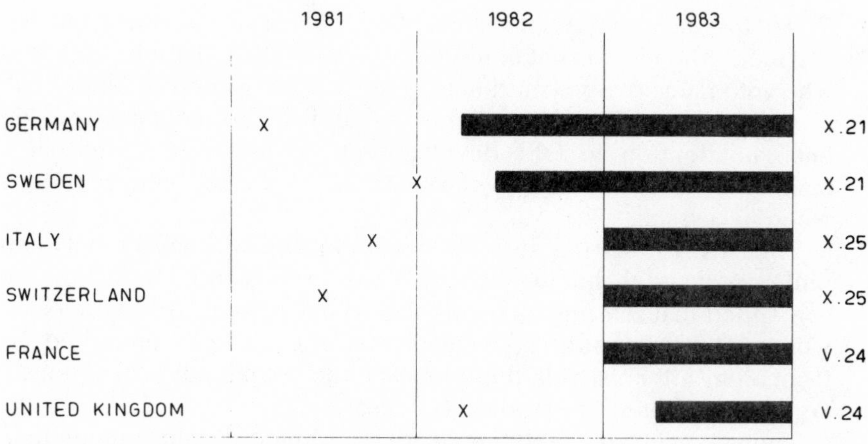

Figure 6-5. Timetables projected by the major European countries for the implementation of the X.21, X.24, and X.25 standards recommended by CCITT.

6-5, which presents demonstration and application timetables in a sample of six European countries. Significant also is the lack of a European standard: two countries have adopted X.21 as the basis, two X.24, and two X.25. This will make internetworking so much less efficient and more costly.

It is correct to say that, although there should be a standard and any effort toward standardization is welcome, the several contradictory and overlapping "standards" create a tower of Babel. This is another reason why the user should choose most carefully, plan ahead in system development, and be very inquisitive prior to making decisions.

Next we will examine at some depth the technical nature of the evolving Project 802 recommendations and their possible shortcomings.

Warning!

While this manuscript was being prepared for printing, the news broke that the American National Standards Institute (ANSI) had voted against the Open System Interconnection model of ISO. By voting against the OSI project, ANSI has seriously set back a universal attempt to achieve norms for interconnection among computers.

Standardization in data communications networks is not for tomorrow, and this prompted the founder of the Network Users Association

(NUA) to comment: "A vote against OSI is like a vote against apple pie and motherhood." Six out of nine members of the X3T5 subcommittee who voted negatively would not agree with that criticism. Their "no" seems to be centered on a feeling that ISO has not been paying enough attention to OSI development—or to the provision of a maintenance organization to make changes in the normalization rules when necessary.

The ANSI decision lies, in a certain sense, halfway between philosophy and technology. Organizations represented in X3T5 have contended that reference models should not be standards. Others are worried that it would take years to make changes propelled by technology after a standard is adopted. And yet nobody will seriously argue that, after all, a standard *is* necessary.

Though users do feel the need for standards much more than manufacturers do, users are not adequately represented in the ANSI committees, which are made up primarily of vendors' representatives. As a result, there is talk that users may turn to other organizations, such as the National Bureau of Standards (which voted yes for ISO/OSI) and the European Computer Manufacturers Association for guidance.

Finally, the aftermaths of the ANSI no vote are further complicated by the fact that the United States is the coordinating country for the OSI project. In a further negative reaction, the X3T5 subcommittee has also voted a conditional no to the latest version of the transport protocol, which would have been the first implementation based on the OSI work. This vote, however, will be changed to yes if the technical comments accompanying the X3T5 opinion are incorporated by ISO.

7

STANDARDIZATION PROJECT 802

We have been discussing standardization. Standards grow to accommodate applications just as languages grow in answer to new needs. The question, however, is whose standards?

Standards committees, by screening, tearing apart, and putting together again, refine the technical aspect of a given methodology or design. It is good to get reviews and to argue every point. That permits cross-fertilization, but there are also snags.

National and international bodies working on normalization have no direct authority over equipment manufacturers. As a result, they are obliged to limit themselves to recommendations which, if adopted, have a chance of becoming standard. Past experience is that acceptance of standards is not particularly characteristic of the computer manufacturers, who choose customer lock-in as a way to ensure profitability.

Throughout the short history of the industry, computer systems manufacturers have assembled unique products—both hardware and operating systems software—that discourage user defection, because the cost of conversion to a competitor's products is almost prohibitive. Indeed, given the increasing complexity of data processing systems, conversion has, to all intents and purposes, become unthinkable. Consequently, while competition for new applications and customers, has been intense, the profits have been made on upgrading the systems to support expansion. At that point, competition fades because the customer has few realistic alternatives to staying with the established supplier. Even within a particular product line, the challenge of upward migration to a system that will meet growing applications requirements often entails a painful switch in the general-purpose operating systems supplied by the manufacturer and required to run the system.

Computer users have successfully countered lock-in on several major fronts. In the large-system sector, the rising participation of plug compatible manufacturers (PCM) points to a standardization around IBM products. The concept was first applied by peripheral disk and tape manufacturers who provided subsystems with electronic interfaces that were compatible with mainframe processors. More recently, the Japanese manufacturers have led the charge by providing a computer system which runs with IBM software. Users have found that increased competition not only provides a price break but also often leads to improved service by IBM as well. Competition works.

The same thing may eventually be said of local area networks. The potential will be better realized and LANs will gain wider commercial acceptance only if the normalization problems can be solved in an able manner. Stated differently, despite the fact that several standardization bodies are working on the problem, there is no real prospect that a suitable and effective standard will be widely accepted in the near future. The consensus on possible solutions is still fragile; divergent views coexist; and compromises make proposed standards complex and involute.

Another question is whether the LAN standards under development will be applied in the near future. Experience in other areas suggests that standards take 5 to 6 years to filter down through the manufacturers' organization, but they move faster if the users contractually demand their application and stick to the demand. Furthermore, the standardization bodies are working mostly on the data link layer, but it is clear that no integrated multivendor systems can be based on such a low-level standard. The risk is one of producing a common wire without a common language to speak on it. It is also necessary to look at the higher-up layers, an issue on which we will elaborate as we review the work of Project 802.

Let's add that an original goal of the IEEE was to produce a standard in about 6 months time. When this text was written, 30 months had gone by and the standard was not yet in sight. Another goal was to establish a single standard and single medium. As the work progressed, it was decided to go into three types of protocols, which we will now examine.

LAN STANDARDS

The main issue in the normalization of LAN protocols is connectability. A protocol designed to assure it can be of high or low level, and each will support corresponding services. The high-level protocol can be designed as host-dependent or -independent. A host-independent protocol is preferable, and it can be further distinguished as resource-dependent or -independent (Fig. 7-1).

Protocol design is an important consideration, but it is well to understand that it is not a proper protocol which makes the communication per se. Its role is that of giving meaning to the corresponding layer, for instance, that of host independence. This is an additional reason why it should be properly defined.

Layering is characteristic of the latest computer designs and communications architectures, as we said in Chap. 5. Layers lead to the partitioning of all functions, which allows:

1. Clean department boundaries in terms of function
2. Easier fault isolation
3. The possibility of introducing VLSI
4. The establishment of effective rules for interfacing

The concept of partitioning is general enough to apply to both long- and short-haul networks, in properly projected network architectures, like the OSI model (which we will consider in the following chapter). The services provided by each layer are connection-oriented.

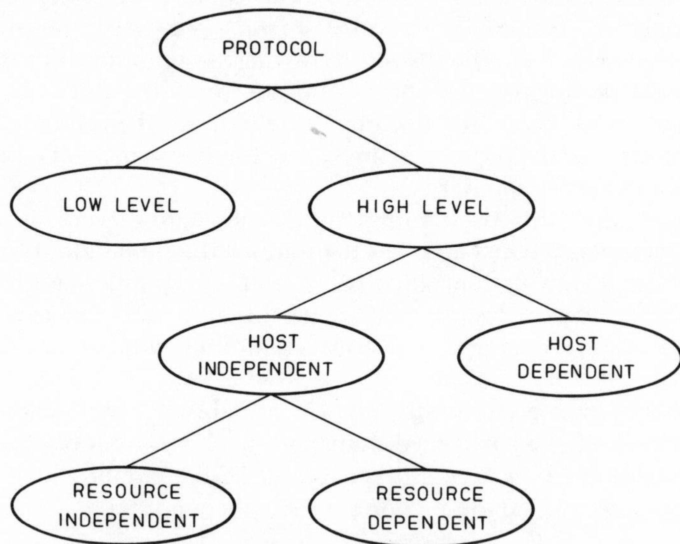

Figure 7-1. Protocols designed to assure connectability can be broadly divided between high and low level. The former are either dependent or independent of the resources employing them.

An important procedure in the development of a LAN architecture is protocol validation. This is a means of testing the rules which specify how coordination and communication among a number of processes will take place. Protocol validation can be used to test the system architecture completely in the sense that all possible permutations of event sequences within the region are examined. Testing is thus much more thorough than by the use of a script of test sequences applied to a particular implementation or simulation techniques that test randomly and are therefore likely to be incomplete.

Specifically, with LAN we have the ability to reach, at the same time, one or more or all of the workstations attached to the network. Process synchronization is, therefore, essential. This is quite different than the HDLC-implied environment projected by ISO for long-haul connections.

A double feat must therefore be achieved: Obtaining efficient protocols which correspond to the work to be done at the local area level and assuring standards general enough to provide for continuity. As cannot be repeated too often, standards are necessary for many reasons: one of the most important is that they help make products reliable and progressively cheaper. Also, they rid us of what is outmoded and pave the way for further progress.

Standards are necessary to help the manufacturers decide what they should put on silicon chips. But standards can also be double-edged. If they are too stiff, they may block progress or invite outright violation. Standards can also be misused, misrepresented, or employed to lead the buyer to wrong assumptions. It is handy, for instance, for the salesman to say the product "abides by standards." Yet we all know that it is one thing to make the standard apply to the product (as IBM de facto does) and another to make the product really abide by the standard.

Against this background the IEEE started work on Project 802. Correctly, the first task was to establish the right definition: "A LAN is a datacomm system allowing a number of independent devices to communicate directly with each other, within a moderately sized geographic area over a physical communications channel of moderate data rates."

The 802 group started work in February 1980 with the goal of standardizing a two-layer transport mechanism for digital information interchange that would meet both user and provider needs. The mission was divided among three subcommittees:

- Media
- Access control
- Higher-level interface

and smaller groups addressed the:

- Functional requirements
- Glossary
- Draft organization

The functional requirements for the transport mechanism were to support media and topology independence, a functional independence to be implemented as low as possible in the architecture, direct party-to-party communication, coexistence and interoperability, OSI standards cognizance, and fairness criteria.

Most important, the projected applicability of these standards was to involve not only classical data processing but also:

- File transfer
- Database access
- Graphics
- Word processing
- Teletex
- Digitized voice

Typical devices to be considered for LAN attachment were computers of all types and sizes, terminals, and plotters and printers. The scope was typically baseband: In the 1- to 20-Mbps range, accepting over 200 connected devices, at a lesser than or equal to 2-km distance, and featuring code independence, single and multiple delivery, and simultaneous servers. Between LAN and LHN an intermediate class, the "metropolitan area network," can be located, but we will not be concerned with it. Typically it covers a 25- to -35 km range.

It appears that the requirements of networks inside factories were omitted from Project 802, and there is another standards committee in the power engineering group of IEEE. That is, Project 802 mainly addressed the office system and left open such subjects as production control.

There are similar questions as to whether the evolving 802 standard will be suitable for voice and video communications. Yet voice is and will continue to be the best way of communication in the office. As it now appears, Draft C will not accommodate realtime voice. However, token ring does include a priority type of handling that might allow the servicing of realtime voice and other priority-type requirements. There is also the possibility of incorporating a PBX in the LAN to promote voice usage. But is this mature standardization?

THE LAN REFERENCE MODEL

The Project 802 LAN Reference Model is presented in Fig. 7-2. It will be seen that it differs significantly from the ISO/OSI structure. Specifically, the physical layer, which in open system interconnection is represented by the data communication equipment, is split into two sublayers:

- The lower sublayer is addressed to the cable; the cable is the medium.
- The upper sublayer is the media access unit (MAU).

The cable may be one of many kinds—twisted wire, flat wire, coaxial, or optical fiber. The objects of the MAU are signaling, encoding, and medium handling.

The ISO/OSI need for data link control (DLC) is met through HDLC; in Project 802 the DLC need is met by two sublayers:

- The lower sublayer is the media access control (MAC).
- The upper sublayer is the logical link control (LLC).

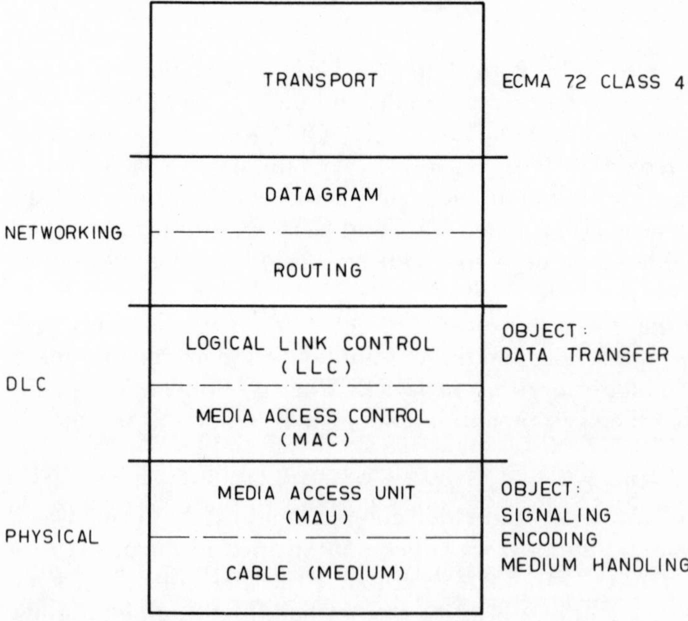

Figure 7-2. The 802 LAN reference model: subdivision of the physical and data link layers.

MAC interfaces between the logical link and the media access unit and thus assures continuity between the physical and logical functions. The object of the LLC is effective realization of data transfer.

In ISO/OSI, the networking layer is divided into two sublayers: routing (the lower one) and virtual circuit (the upper one). In Project 802, datagram is substituted for virtual circuit. ISO/OSI, X.25, and Project 802 employ packet-switching principles.

To identify the basic difference, note that in a virtual circuit organization, responsibility for the correct delivery of the information packets rests with the network. Out-of-sequence packets must be arranged at the network nodes prior to being forwarded to the destination host. That's how X.25 works. On the contrary, with a datagram approach, the destination workstation is responsible. That simplifies the network architecture and makes the approach to the design of the WS software more fundamental; it also presupposes intelligent workstations such as personal computers. This reflects a general orientation based on the LAN architectures announced so far. At the time of writing there was no standards work on the network layer, but its importance was recognized. Eventually some standard will be incorporated in the layered solution we have outlined.

There is the possibility of adding another sublayer, that of "enhancement," at level 3. The problem was being discussed but not yet seriously tackled at the time of writing. Therefore, it will not be treated in this book.

Finally, the transport layer, which is the highest in the data communication side, has not yet been studied by ISO/OSI nor is it within the current mission of Project 802. ECMA 72 Class 4 is addressed to it, but as yet there are no well-defined results to be discussed. Reference should also be made to two other ECMA committees:

- TC 24 deals with communications protocols.
- TC 29 handles text interchange between WS.

As the preceding discussion demonstrates, the communication protocol is a most critical element in the whole LAN system. It must guarantee a very safe high-speed data transmission with fault tolerance characteristics. Attention must be paid to protocol design and verification.

A careful study will necessarily involve analysis of the requirements and constraints imposed by the projected range of application, definition of the main functional features, logical consistency tests, protocol correctness, and fault tolerance verification. The latter cannot be done without the appropriate functional distribution of the control functions, a consideration of the ease of connecting different nodes to the network; assurance that different kinds of equipment can be connected to the network, and appropriate redundancy of the system's critical functions.

Synchronization and fault tolerance are typical goals of network protocols. The former arises when communication modules that reside on different nodes must interact through a common carrier. Fault tolerance is a critical feature of all good software, and it becomes essential in communication protocols because correct functioning must be guaranteed even in the presence of line errors and node failures.

These are problems a standards committee must face, and they directly impact on the media access control to be adopted. In turn, a chosen methodology helps define the traffic access characteristics of the network. As we will see in the following section, Project 802 adopted three different MAC solutions to meet this specific requirement.

The approach taken by a standards organization evidently reflects the types of loads to be expected. With LAN, the IEEE committee admitted that there are really two distinct areas of operation:

1. Light load, low delay, low throughput
2. Heavy load, long delay, and throughput going from higher to lower through a controlled degradation

This evidently required traffic analysis. It involved mean value studies (including time and speed balance and concurrency) and the analysis of fluctuations: distributions, correlations, and imbalances.

The basic concept of any transport mechanism is that, because of concurrency and parallelism, the network becomes congested as we add more stations on the LAN. Therefore, it is not at all true that a network working at double the speed can handle twice as many WS in the same environment. As a result, we must be very careful in handling multiple services such as voice and data. One service—for instance, voice—may monopolize the network and create imbalance. To start with, the transport requirements are different: Voice traffic can last 2 to 3 min, whereas data packets last for a few seconds. As a result, voice monopolizes the network, shuts off the data pipeline, and upsets the services the network should offer. Furthermore, in any network we must also account for the data load due to control signals.

To recapitulate: standards committees must assure that the projected network design can be balanced, preferably by handling homogeneous operations. Like a long-haul network, a LAN must be subjected to simulation and verification. This involves input parameters for traffic analysis and output statistics. The latter concern delays at each stage: mean and fluctuation in messages and link utilization concurrency.

IEEE STANDARD CONSIDERATIONS

Critics of the work accomplished by Project 802 are quick to point out that the committee's work on technical evaluations and standards is not conclusive. They forget that the foremost aims were to provide a balance among the proliferating incompatible local networks without limiting LAN work to only one type of protocol.

Project 802 defines three types of LAN technologies:

- Contention utilizing CSMA/CD
- A token bus
- A token ring

These are not only different but also incompatible media access technologies (Fig. 7-3). IEEE takes no position on their relative merits, but the logical link control protocol is common to all three.

Quite important is the Project 802 decision that a manufacturer implementing only a portion of the standard in a device may not claim compliance with the standard. A device in compliance with the standard must implement all the mandatory requirements. For instance, the media access unit (MAU) must provide all the functions of a standard MAU, operate at one or more of the standard data rates, have a standard access unit interface, and also have one of the standard media interfaces. If the device contains only the data terminating part of the access unit interface, then it must operate at one or more of the standard data rates, have the mandatory logical link control capabilities, and use one of the standard media access control methods.

As stated, the logical link control (LLC) sublayer is common to all the media access methods supported in this standard:

> The Interface Service Specification provides a description of the various services that the data link layer offers to the network layer, as viewed from the latter. This is in the form of primitives that represent the logical exchange of information and control

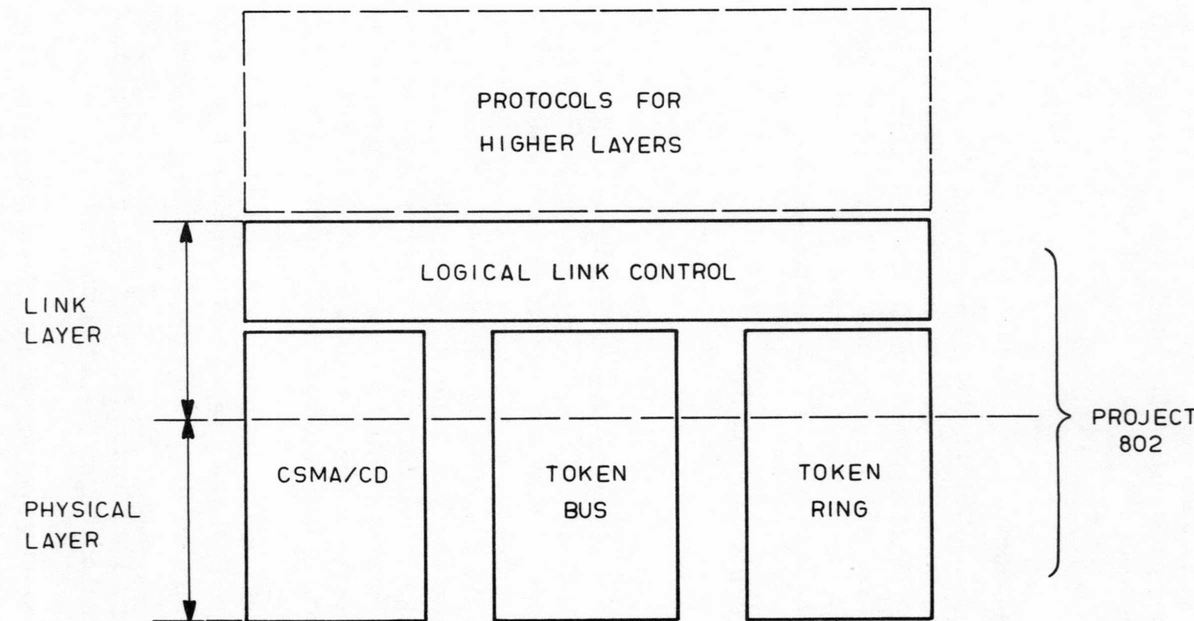

Figure 7-3. Scope of the IEEE Project 802 work: CSMA/CD, token bus, token ring, and logical link control.

between a network layer entity and its associated data link layer entity.

The Logical Link Control Procedures offer a description of the peer-to-peer protocol defined for the transfer of information and control between any pair of data link service access points on the local area network. A spectrum of features and capabilities is defined.

Logical link control procedures are independent of the type of media access method used in the particular local area network.

The LLC/MAC Interface Service Specification describes the services that the logical link control sublayer requires of the media access control sublayer in the data link layer. These services are so defined as to be independent of the form of the media access methodology, and of the nature of the medium itself.

The work by IEEE Project 802 was based on the valid assumption that a LAN is intended to have wide applicability in many applications environments and support file transfer and access protocols, remote database access, graphics, word processing, electronic mail, and even digital voice. Computers, terminals, mass storage units, printers and plotters, facsimile machines, photocopiers, monitoring and control equipment, and gateways to other networks are among the equipment and facilities supported. To have compatibility between communicating devices, standards must exist for each of the protocol layers. The 802 objective is only layers 1 and 2 of the ISO/OSI model. Higher-layer protocol standards may be applicable and should preferably follow the ISO model.

For layers 1 and 2, the goal of the IEEE standard is to ensure the compatibility of equipment made by different manufacturers so that data communication can take place between the devices with a minimum effort on the part of the equipment users or the builders of a system containing the equipment. To that end, Project 802 worked out specifications establishing common interfaces and protocols for local area networks.

One of the main purposes of the analysis by Project 802 was to look at LAN behavior under load. When the bus capacity is challenged by a requested data rate, the *real* capacity can degrade dramatically.

- In a contention environment, with 70 percent loading, collisions are *very* frequent.

- In contrast, token passing sustains the heavy load more easily, because queuing of requests creates an operational margin.

CSMA/CD presents advantages under lighter loads, say, 10 to 30 percent of bus capacity. There is less delay because there is no token passing overhead and no significant collisions are present.

Critics will say that the problem with these conclusions is the way in which they were reached: some by analysis and others by simulation, but no system cracking on a real-life basis—hence, no actual measurements. The problem with simulation, the same critics would say, is the great number of variables:

1. Statistical distribution of messages
2. Distribution of message lengths
3. Physical configuration (length of bus, location of taps)
4. And, with token, the topology of WS and servers

As this brief list demonstrates, the number of configurations and conditions varies greatly. A model must be realistic as to implementation and actual measurements.

Another problem to address is the probabilistic nature of solutions based on contention. Token passing is deterministic, and for some uses (plant safety, fire alarm, process control, weapons control) this is an overriding consideration. However, as we will see in the following section, *tree search access* is another deterministic approach and is perhaps more valid than token (though it has not been retained by Project 802). Still another consideration is the setting of priorities. Token passing is easier to prioritize than CSMA/CD, although priorities could be worked into the latter.

Technology also suggests the wisdom of creating in silicon the media access control software. We mentioned this in connection with the work done by Intel on Ethernet. In mid-1982 announcement was made of a similar project for token ring through the agreement of IBM and TI to develop sophisticated silicon chips (VLSI) for use in office networks linking computers and business machines.

Finally, critics object that the developing triple standard for media access does not consider a factory environment. (The same criticism was made of this book in its original version.) Wanting to be everything to everybody is one of the illnesses of our profession and one of the more common causes of failure. It is better to lower our sights.

The IEEE document describes the intended applications environment for the LAN as commercial and light industrial. Home and heavy industrial environments, although not precluded, are not considered to be within the scope of the standard development effort. This particularly concerns process control and other realtime, high-reliability applications.

ALTERNATIVE MEDIA ACCESS METHODS

The three methods which have been retained by IEEE Project 802 for media access are applicable to the MAC sublayer. However, the chosen IEEE standards cover only a part of a broader range of possibilities shown in Fig. 7-4. On baseband coaxial cable CSMA mainly works with collision detection (CD) capability. The alternative is collision avoidance (CA), as with Omninet. Broadband does not permit CD. CSMA/CD baseband can work up to 10 Mbps. Whether baseband or broadband, a random-delay mechanism can be implemented. For instance, in baseband that is the way Omninet works.

The token bus can work with baseband on coaxial cable or a

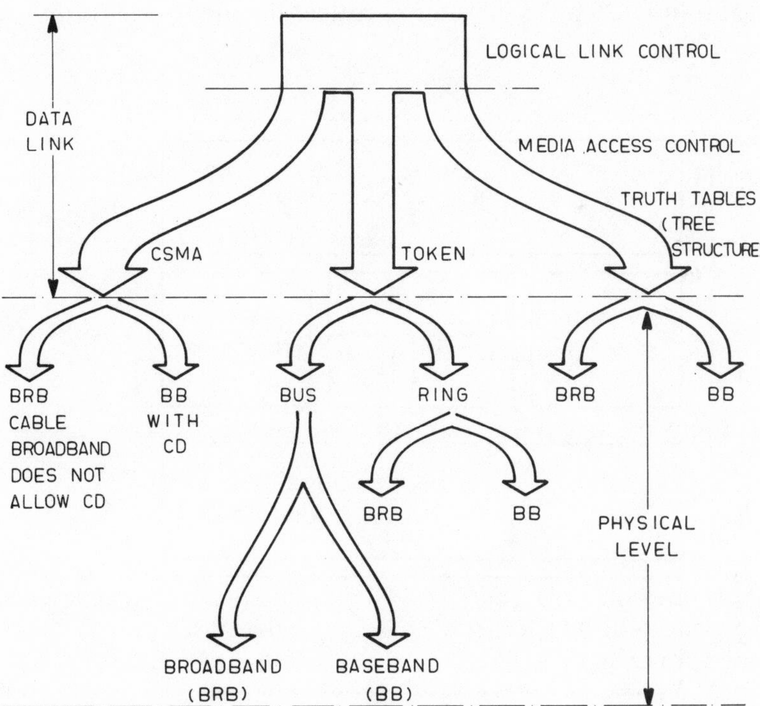

Figure 7-4. A broader range of possibilities in media access control involves alternatives for CSMA and token, but also truth tables.

different approach, frequency shift key (FSK), can be used. There can also be a broadband coaxial solution. The token ring can work with baseband on twisted pair or with baseband on coaxial cable. The latter seems to have a practical limit at 4 Mbps.

The slotted ring, which we considered in a preceding section, is not one of the ECMA, ANSI, or IEEE standards. The same is true of the tree structure, or truth tables, though there are rumors that AT&T is actively working on it. There is also the possibility of more MAC protocols such as "reservation" and other solutions that meet power engineering requirements.

As we will see in the appropriate discussion, a tree structure solution applies a binary identifier (0,1) to every station in the network. It is a distributed approach (unlike what "tree" may imply), and the truth table can be followed top to bottom and left to right by all workstations in the local network.

Figure 7-5 demonstrates that the type of access method plays a critical role in the definition of the data link layer. The logical link layer rests on the chosen MAC protocol and is evidently influenced by that solution. The same thing is true of the media access unit. Recall

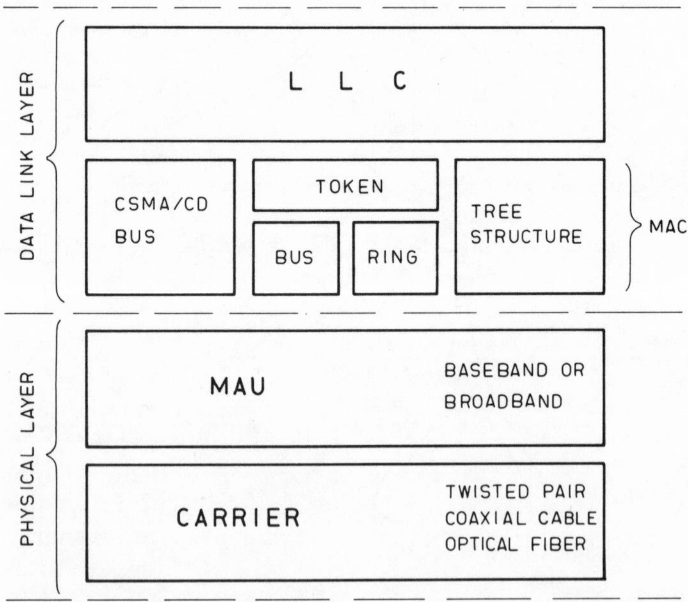

Figure 7-5. Explosion of the physical and data link layers into sublayers and alternatives existing in the sublayers.

that the design of the MAU is tuned to the load requirements: baseband or broadband.

As for the physical layer, we can add that the standards effort by Project 802 does not restrict hardware implementation but does include the rules the hardware people must observe in their choice of coaxial cable, twisted wire, or other medium. Among those rules is the bit error rate (BER). Here the guideline offered avoids pushing technology too much (as by projecting a BER of 10^{-13}), because extremes exceed the state of the art and open holes and gaps somewhere else. We must build our application not on hope but on facts. Similar comments can be made about the challenges encountered on the software side. As stated, the transport is effected through packet switching. However, bit stuffing widely used with X.25 is not permitted in the 802 standard.

Now let's look at some technical aspects of the three media access control methods which have been chosen, starting with CSMA/CD. The basic philosophy is simple: Each workstation on the bus listens to see if there is traffic; if there is, it waits; is there isn't, it transmits. That leaves open the possibility of collisions if two or more stations transmit at the same time, having sensed no traffic on the line.

With CSMA/CD, the channel can, at any time, be in one of three possible states: (1) idle, in (2) contention, or (3) transmission. In the idle state, the channel carries no signal. In the contention state the signals result from packets in collision or jamming. In the transmission state, the channel carries signals generated by a packet progressing toward a successful transmission. The duration of an idle state is referred to as an idle period; that of a contention state as a contention slot; and that of the transmission state as a transmission interval.

Thus, in carrier-sensing collision detection all stations sense the energy in the carrier associated with a successful message transmission and attempt to transmit when no carrier is sensed. They may fail because one or more other stations attempt transmission within a specified time interval. Hence, this collision must be detected and some appropriate action taken. Evidently, logical control approaches must be mapped onto physical devices by dealing with two distinct physical topologies. In a typical CSMA/CD bus solution every station transmits and receives from and to every other workstation.

The mechanism is fairly reliable, but the Project 802 viewpoint seems to be that CSMA falls apart over 25 km because of energy problems. Token buys independence of data rate and distance, but it has other problems. To cope with the traffic management requirements, a serially reusable data link must be scheduled to handle demands based on a performance policy for a given workload. The latter is defined by a set of arrival and message length statistics. To study it we can fix the number of messages per unit time that we attempt to transmit and the mean overhead per message. Then each design reaches an intrinsic limit: the "maximum mean throughput rate" of transmitting messages through the link.

If we fix the mean number of messages per unit time that we attempt to transmit and the mean overhead per message, while allowing the number of stations connected to the network link to become infinite, then certain designs can have a finite maximum mean throughput rate, but the mean delay to transmit a message can be infinite. Other designs can have both a finite maximum mean throughput rate and a finite mean delay to transmit a message. The choice of design implies careful study and simulation to cope with the projected traffic.

To conclude this discussion, let's add that, with CSMA/CD, the transceivers may transmit only when sensing the channel is idle; if collision occurs, transmission is aborted. The more collisions, the greater the bus saturation; as a result, idle time is wasted. In general, this system design is projected to function under relatively light load. The advantages are that control is distributed, immediate access is possible, and time to resolve conflicts is unbounded. Linear waiting is not enforced.

Now let's look at the token standard. The basic model is shown in Fig. 7-6. A physical or logical hub connects all nodes and workstations. One of them is working, and that one has the token. When it finishes transmitting, it passes control (the token) to another WS either serially or in accordance with a preestablished priority table.

In a typical ring confrontation with token discipline, every station transmits and receives from just one other station and control is either decentralized and passed from station to station or centralized, in which case one station determines the WS that will be allowed to transmit next.

There is a polling arbitration which requires a given amount of time to handle passing control and then message transmission. Polling is a special type of priority arbitration whereby control is passed from station to station around the network. Whatever station owns the token has highest priority, but there can be variations. One of the variations is the "passive hub." The hub plays no direct control role; it simply connects the workstations so that polling can be thought of as moving around a wheel. This approach, too, is fairly reliable, but errors are possible. The issue is: Where did the token go?

Token passing is rather simple-minded; it is not complicated to

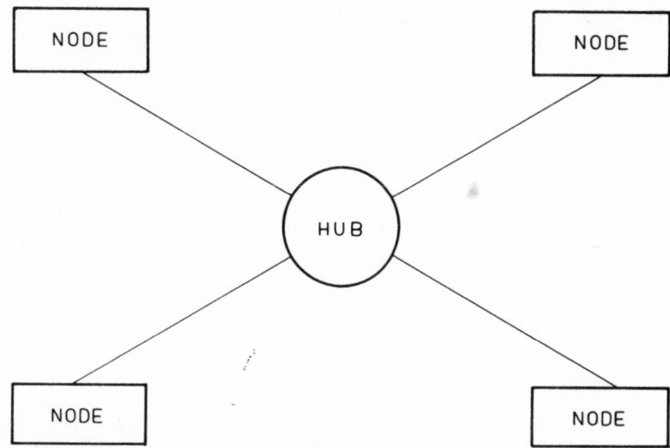

Figure 7-6. Model of a token-passing mechanism. The hub retransmits to all workstations.

implement. As stated, traffic can go in a loop or in a bus fashion. The token bus is deterministic and has advantages, but one of the problems with it is to define how to enter and exit the bus. Among the positive points of the passive hub are these: there is no central control; no collision can occur; overhead is a linear function of the number of transceivers; throughput is good under heavy load; a linear waiting time is achievable; and load balancing is possible. In a general sense, which may, however, not be applicable to all situations, CSMA/CD seems to perform best under light load and token polling under heavy load.

A non-802 alternative to protocol requirements at the MAC level is the tree structure or truth table. The two terms amount to the same thing, as Fig. 7-7 demonstrates. In essence, every station has a binary address, and this protocol assures controlled priority arbitration. The process is deterministic in search and also in back-off. Under heavy load, it looks like polling.

Transceivers are logically organized as a binary tree, and search proceeds first in depth and then from left to right. The system can be distributed or centralized. It can also accept priorities. To handle this protocol, MAC needs two counters (top and down, left and right) which must be updated with the going traffic every time a workstation in the LAN speaks up.

Among the advantages of tree search access is that this is a type of associative memories loop-up; hence, it can serve as a protocol both in front end and in rear end. Control is distributed; linear waiting is

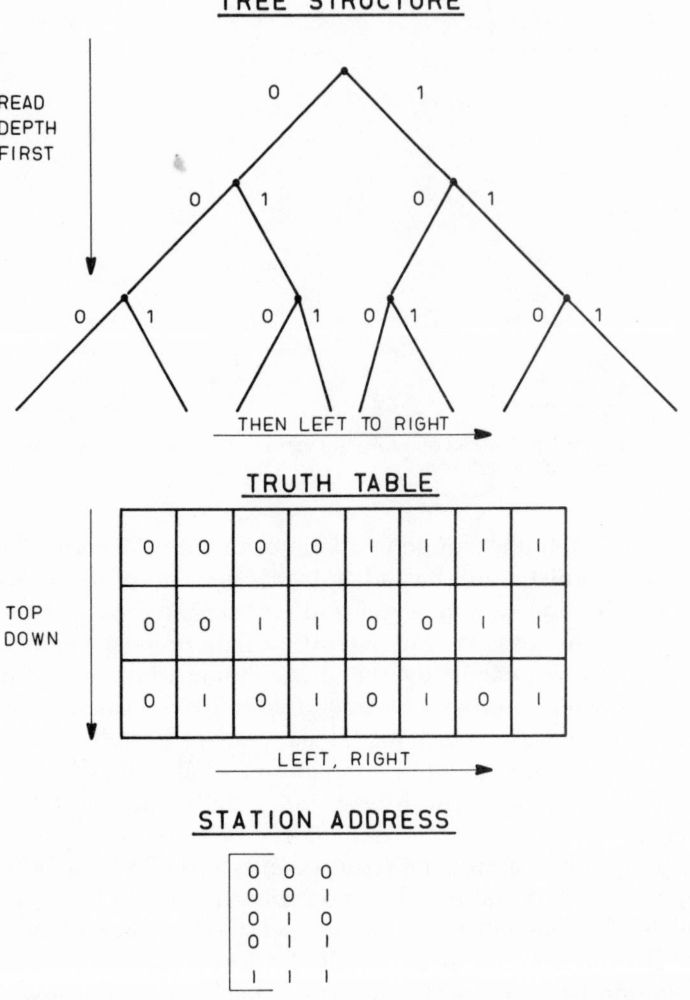

Figure 7-7. Tree structure (truth table) and station access under this non-802 protocol. The rule is: read depth first, then left to right.

enforced; and the time to resolve collisions is reasonable. But tree search access does not have the exposure of the other two techniques; hence, it is not yet sufficiently polished.

THE INTEGRATED SERVICES DIGITAL NETWORK

The Integrated Services Digital Network (ISDN) has not been studied by the IEEE, and its inclusion in this discussion may, at first glance, seem to be out of place. In reality it is not, because it is designed for international data communications perspective and hence the way local area networks integrate with the long haul.

The rules for ISDN are established by CCITT. Local area networks are an ambiguous problem to the Post, Telegraph, and Telephone (PTT) because the LANs are not part of their monopoly. On the other hand, value-added long-haul networks have an interest in common with the business LAN: internetworking. ECMA, too, is considering the internetworking issue but seems to differentiate between *internet* and *enhancement* protocols, thus permitting users to enhance or disenhance, as the environment requires.

Let's return to fundamentals. We said that ECMA actively works on the transport level (fourth layer of ISO/OSI), which is of interest to the public data networks. This fourth level affects the teletex (electronic mail) service and attracts considerable attention by ISO and CCITT. More specifically, the telephone utilities (AT&T and PTT) have already been engaged in the gradual implementation of the integrated digital network (IDN) and taken a step toward the total integration of services (ISDN).

Like ISO, AT&T and the PTT of Europe and Japan have every reason to make their public networks open systems. This favors a transition toward ISDN which may last until the end of the century. The PTT will therefore be very active, through CCITT and ISO, in early completion of the standardization connected with the OSI architecture in order to introduce the new services, which will have to be compatible with 64-kbps switched digital connections.

Yet, the public networks themselves, while gradually integrating the transmission and switching functions in digital form, have not shown much interest in local area networks. The latter have anticipated the telephone utilities and the value-added networks (VAN) in offering effective service down to the end-user level. The ability to interconnect impacts on this particular aspect and brings into perspective two issues: the interconnection strategy and the gateways.

The most fundamental property of a gateway is the level in the protocol hierarchy at which it operates. At the lowest level, it operates on globally addressed minipackets and routes them to their final destinations. The problem is preserving the low-level responses associated with these minipackets, since the gateway, rather than the final destination, would be marking the response bits. The same thing is true of committing global addresses to, say, ring hardware. Should a global address on the network consist of a ring number and a station number, or should a global address not include a site number?

At the next higher layer, gateways could route globally addressed basic blocks. The low-level responses are used to transmit basic blocks, but they need not be preserved for higher-level protocols. Above this level one could imagine the gateway being involved in more complex protocols as in a transport service. Rather than have a global address in each basic block, lightweight virtual circuits can be used to route basic blocks to their destinations. In this manner, instead of translating a global address to a next hop by using static tables, the gateway dynamically associates a next hop with each active port number. Let's note that the gateway routes a packet by performing a mapping from the port on which it receives the packet to the next station and port number.

Incidentally, an address is the data structure which defines any addressable object in a given domain. Its format can be recognized by all elements in the network, and therefore it must be meaningful throughout the domain. It must be drawn from some uniform address space. An example of a hierarchical address system is given by the telephone; another is the X.121 address format. In a network and/or internetworking environment:

A *name* identifies what we want.
An *address* identifies where it is.
A *route* is a way to get there.

Much of the problem of designing a gateway is concerned with the setting up of port mappings or routes. There are two different types of routes: (1) to ports which are dynamically allocated by client machines and (2) to ports which are always active. Routes to public ports can be set up statically on the gateway, in which case the name server would return a gateway port for any request naming a service on a different ring. Or routes to public ports could be set up by the name server as name look-up requests were received. The latter requires dealing with global addresses.

A given service may run at one or more nodes and may need to move from one node to another without losing its identity as a service. A given node may be connected to one or more ports and may need to move from one to another without losing its identity as a node. A given pair of ports may be connected by one or more paths, and those paths may need to change with time without affecting port identity.

A strategy for network interconnection must consider both the environment and the goals to be reached. In the case of the environment, it is necessary to study terminal traffic, file transfer, peripheral access, as to printer(s) or disk(s), and distributed computing. A usual goal is to join networks to make a bigger one obtaining higher bandwidth with low delay perspectives, and without change in protocols. In fact, the latter is a prerequisite.

Another prerequisite for a capability is that the user of the service(s) will not be aware of a connection. Two different solutions can be followed for this transparency; one involves LHN and the other LAN (Fig. 7-8).

The IDN/X.121 offers a good example of an address format for an

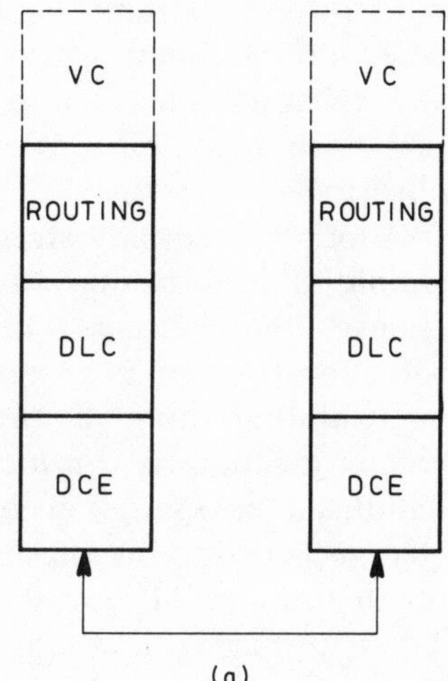

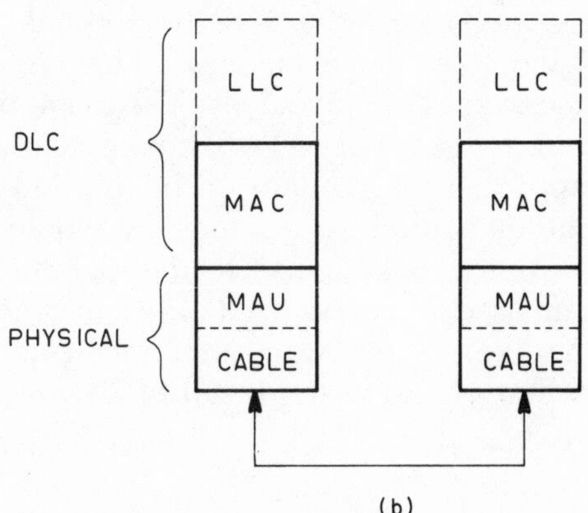

Figure 7-8. Alternative solutions for *(a)* long-haul and *(b)* local area network followed in implementing and internetworking capability.

international data network. It is composed as follows:

- Three digits for country code, with digits reserved for the United States. Up to 200 networks can be named.
- One digit for the network within a country.
- Five digits for the number within the data network.

Similar, but simpler schemes can be provided for Inter-LAN, where it is important that the gateway provide for port mapping. In a way, interconnection among LANs becomes quite simple if it is strictly limited to an interapplication exchange and if the principle that each LAN must be designed for one application is properly observed.

Another necessary strategy decision concerns local scheduling. A simple algorithm may suffice. Ports have priorities. The kernel chooses the message on the port with the higher priority if the selection conditions given by the processes are good.

Insulating the data processing from the database and the data communication requirements can also pay dividends. When a process handles a message, it accesses its internal data; but nothing has been changed outside the process—no message is sent. Hence, recovery is much simpler. All that is necessary is to repeat the internal process. The external world has not changed. Ruggedness and reliability can be achieved through data communication firmware. The software should possess checkpoints and rollback. Checkpoints can be applied at the journaling level. Rollback is in realtime.

Another solution is active redundancy, e.g., using two processes to handle the same message. The one acting as master will send the message. The slave doesn't send anything; but if the master fails, then it acts as master. Twin processes are a much more sophisticated approach that can always be applied not process by process, but at a more visible level such as the whole file server.

Yet, trying to push technology too far is not wise. Transpac got a rumored 75 percent reliability instead of the promised 99.99 percent. Another system was announced as having a mean time between failures of 10 years. It fell in 20 min.

8 OPEN SYSTEM INTERCONNECTION

We have spoken of the ISO/OSI standard and its seven-layer model. Table 8-1 specifies the object of each layer, the origin of standards, and the development of the protocol. It will be appreciated that protocol development in several layers (particularly applications and transport) is still in the works. What is important, however, is that so many normalization bodies currently concentrate on this subject.

Equally important for the future of computers and communications is that a layered approach has been adopted. A change in one of the layers does not upset the design and/or work of the other layers, even the adjoining ones. Successive layers are connected among themselves through interfaces. An interface is a set of rules covering the relations among dissimilar functions within the same node of an information processing system.

Interfacing is necessary because each layer executes different functions than the preceding or following layers. *Entities* in the same layer communicate with each other by using a peer protocol. A single entity must be both a sender and receiver, which makes it possible to describe the total interaction that constitutes the peer protocol by specifying the actions of the single entity.

Through a layered approach, we can more easily implement internetworking, the connecting of network configurations. With protocols corresponding to a layered structure, efficient bridges can be built between the logical components of the system without affecting other levels. For example, the network's transmission format could be changed from parallel to serial without impacting any but the lowest layers.

The layered reference model of the International Standards Organization (ISO) and the American National Standards Institute (ANSI) divides local network functions into seven hierarchical layers, or modules, as shown in Fig. 8-1. As with a LAN, the physical layer of the ISO/OSI protocol specifies the mechanical and electrical requirements and the procedures of the physical medium that connect the devices in the network.

The mechanical requirements have to do with the connectors chosen for the system, the electrical requirements with the transmitting and receiving signals necessitated by the particular medium being used. Included in the physical layer protocol is the set of procedures for exchanging data—also controlling and timing the networkwide data flow.

The data link, networking, transport control, session control, and presentation control layers are logical. Networking is divided into two sublayers: routing and virtual circuit (or datagram). Routing is the process of creating the route for messages to be transmitted in a given form and along an established path. This is done through software at the level of the node. With a virtual circuit, a specific path is set up from source to destination at the time a data communication call is made. A path once established is used for the transmission. If outage or noise occurs, an alternate path may be chosen.

In this chapter we will be concerned with some of the seven layers of the ISO reference, particularly with the protocol at layer 4 of the model, transport control. Like all other layers, this is composed of entities.

Just as important is the concept of sublayering. OSI provides for the division of a given layer into a number of sublayers, each a functional

TABLE 8–1 THE LAYERS OF OSI

Layer	Object	Origin of standards	Development of the protocol
7	Applications	Users	User protocols (for the time being)
6	Presentation control		
	File transfer	ECMA/ISO	In process of definition
	Virtual terminal	ECMA/ISO	In process of definition
5	Session control	ECMA	In process of authorization
		ISO	In process of definition
4	Transport control	ECMA	ECMA-72
		ISO	In process of definition
		CCITT	S.70
3	Networking	ISO	X.25-3
		CCITT	X.25-3
2	Data link	ECMA	ECMA 40, 49, 60, 61, 71
		CCITT	X.25-2
		ISO	ISO 3309, 4335
1	Physical connection	CCITT	V.11, X.21, V.24, and so on

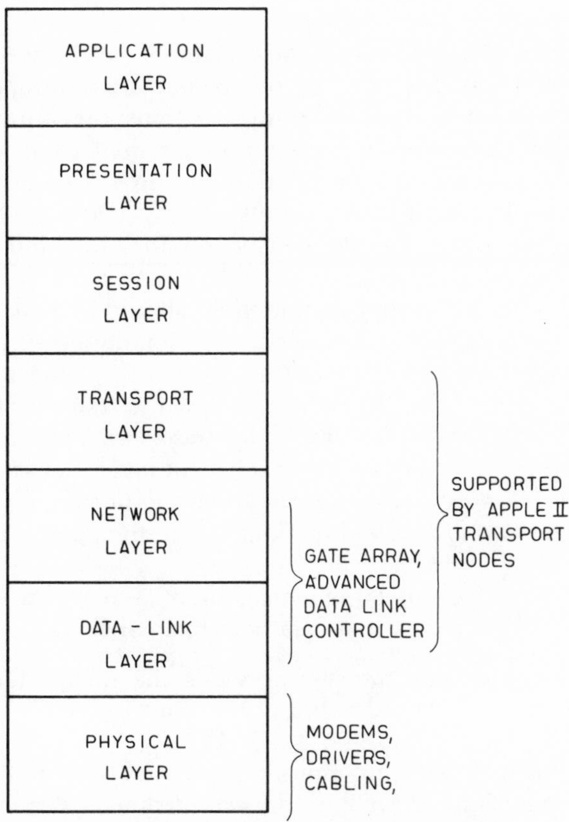

Figure 8-1. The seven layers of the ISO/OSI standard.

grouping within the layer in which it exists. Sublayers also help provide an upper and lower boundary of the transport machine toward the adjacent layers.

Services are specified by describing their primitives and parameters. A *named service* may have one or more related primitives which constitute its interface activity, and one or more parameters may be associated with a service primitive. Primitives exhibit a typical interrelationship. Furthermore, a primitive appears to occur instantaneously: It begins and completes at the same point in time.

THE TRANSPORT LAYER

The object of the transport layer is to provide transparent transfer of data between network users. For this purpose it must assure both connection-oriented and connectionless transfer as its basic service:

binding two transport users into a relationship. This is called *transport connection,* and the transfer of data between the users has end-to-end significance. The two characteristic properties of this setup are symmetrical and full duplex. A transport connection is symmetrical in the sense that the two correspondent users bound together by the connection are peers (there is no slave-master relation). It is full duplex in that data transfer may occur in both directions of the connection simultaneously. Another function of this layer is end-to-end flow control.

Basically, transport services should be looked at as independent of the communication medium which underlies the transport layer. The services provided by this layer relieve the transport user from any concern with the details of how the transfer of data is accomplished. To assure its services, the transport layer relies on the capacities provided it by its lower adjacent layer, networking.

Connection management and *data transfer* are the generic names for two groups of functions in the transport layer:

1. Connection management allows a transport user to create and maintain a data path to a correspondent transport user.
2. Data transfer provides the means for exchanging data between the pair of transport users.

Each of these functions is supported by specific services. Connection management involves the *establishment service* (connect and accept), which has to do with transport connections. The *close service* assures normal connection termination without possible loss of data. The *disconnect service* follows the abrupt termination of a transport connection with possible loss of data. The *status service* provides a way for the user to either inquire or be informed about the attributes and status of a transport connection.

These remarks may seem repetitious to the reader, since many of them have been made in connection with specific local network architectures. It is important, however, to remember that such LAN protocols characterize the particular architecture we have been discussing. The closer they are to the ISO/OSI the more closely the particular LAN conforms to international standards.

With OSI, data transfer is provided by three services. The *data service* permits a transport user to transfer data to a correspondent user. The *expedited data service* allows the user to transfer a limited amount of data outside the normal data stream. The *unit data* is a reliable means by which the transport user can transfer data to a correspondent user in a single access. ("Single access" means without the need for the connection establishment and termination necessary with more complex data transfers.)

Now let's get back to fundamentals. The establishment service is provided to initiate a transport connection. The quality of service can be negotiated during establishment, and this service also sees to it that transport users are given the means of reliably transferring a limited amount of transport user data in each direction. In OSI jargon, the set of parameters associated with the establishment service are T_CONNECT and T_ACCEPT. "To T" involves transport address, precedence, security level, compartment, class of service (basic, extended), and data. A similar list can be written "from T."

In all, four service primitives are associated with the establishment service: the T_CONNECT request, the T_CONNECT indication, the T_ACCEPT request, and the T_ACCEPT indication. The first primitive identifies the local transport entity attempting a transport connection establishment. The second signals that attempt to the correspondent transport user. The third primitive refers to the willingness to accept the establishment of the transport connection. The fourth signals that the correspondent transport user has accepted the establishment.

A number of parameters also are important to assure the duties of the transport mechanism:

Address parameters identify the origin and destination of transport users, which refer to each other by means of these transport addresses. A local transport entity can use the transport address to locate the transport user within the local host. Furthermore, transport addresses are mapped onto the addressing scheme of the supporting network service.

Precedence parameters indicate the relative priority to be associated with data transferred on the transport connection after successful establishment.

Security parameters establish the relative level of security associated with the transport connection establishment and which is to be associated with data transferred on the transport connection after successful establishment.

Compartment parameters indicate the user subgroup associated with the establishment attempt and may have a range of values.

Service parameters, at large, reflect the degree of enhancement

> that the transport layer is to perform on the service available from the supporting network layer.
>
> Data parameters specify a transport service data unit which is of limited length. (The maximum data unit size is dependent on the particular user-layer interface.)

A "graceful termination" service, T_CLOSE, is provided to end the transport connection without loss of user data which have been transferred. OSI has projected no formal parameters associated with T_CLOSE, but there are two service primitives: the T_CLOSE request and the T_CLOSE indication.

> A T_CLOSE request indicates to the transport layer that the user has completed sending data on the connection and will accept its termination.
>
> A T_CLOSE indication signals the transport user that the correspondent has no more data to transfer and is prepared to terminate the connection.

The "abrupt termination" service, T_DISCONNECT, reflects the refusal of transport connection establishment or the unilateral termination of a previously initiated transport connection. Such a termination is without regard to any data which may be pending transfer on the connection. T_DISCONNECT also provides for the unreliable transfer of a limited amount of data on behalf of the transport user.

In the OSI architecture, the status service, T_STATUS, is assured of obtaining, or being notified of, information concerning the condition or attribution of a transport connection. Status parameters are used as labels for some set of transport-related attributes; they are a function of the particular user layer interface.

The data service, T_DATA, is provided to transfer data on a previously established transport connection. Transfers by means of T_DATA constitute the normal data flow on the transport connection. Parameters specify an amount of user data, the *data unit.* It has a distinct beginning and end, and its integrity is maintained by the transport layer.

The OSI expedited data service: T_EXPEDITED DATA, assures the transfer of a limited amount of user data in a manner bypassing the end-to-end control of the normal data flow. Data transferred by this service is not synchronized with respect to data in the normal flow, and only one unit of expedited data may be outstanding at any given time in the transport mechanism.

The connectionless data transfer service, T_UNIT DATA, sees to it that data is transferred between correspondent transport users on a connectionless basis. It provides for single-access data transfer for correspondent users without the overhead of transport connection establishment and termination. The transport users refer to each other through transport addresses.

The protocols for communicating equipment making use of the OSI transport layer require the supporting system to offer a TIMER service. It must be provided to enable the specified protocol entities to schedule events. The parameters associated with the TIMER service are time, name, subscript, datum, and to and from; they indicate the time duration of the specified timer, and supply an identifying label associated with the timer by means of the name parameter.

CHALLENGES OF A GENERALIZED SERVICE

The establishment of international conventions in computers and communications is, in itself, an exciting task. It is also a complex one, particularly if we consider the variety of interconnected devices and the functions to be supported. Figure 8-2 outlines five basic facilities supported by office equipment at various degrees of involvement. Some of these units, such as typewriters and simple copiers, have no communications capability and are therefore of no concern here. But office equipment is increasingly communications-oriented, and that is true of units primarily designed to assure a text and data communications capability from the comfort of our livingroom, such as interactive videotex.

For all these units the support of an international standard such as the ISO/OSI logical mechanism should be a critical design (and selection) characteristic. The future giant steps of technology toward the provision of advanced user services will rest on two pillars:

1. The impact of semiconductors
2. Our ability to proceed with an international normalization to allow diverse equipments to communicate online.

The transport protocol mechanisms we are reviewing in this section are pedestal and base of pillar 2. To better appreciate that, we should take a system view of the *end* of the connection and focus on the forthcoming integration of voice, image, text, and data. This is done in Fig. 8-3.

Connected to the primarily digital local loop is a switch. It is followed, in the internal environment, by two boxes: the micro-PBX

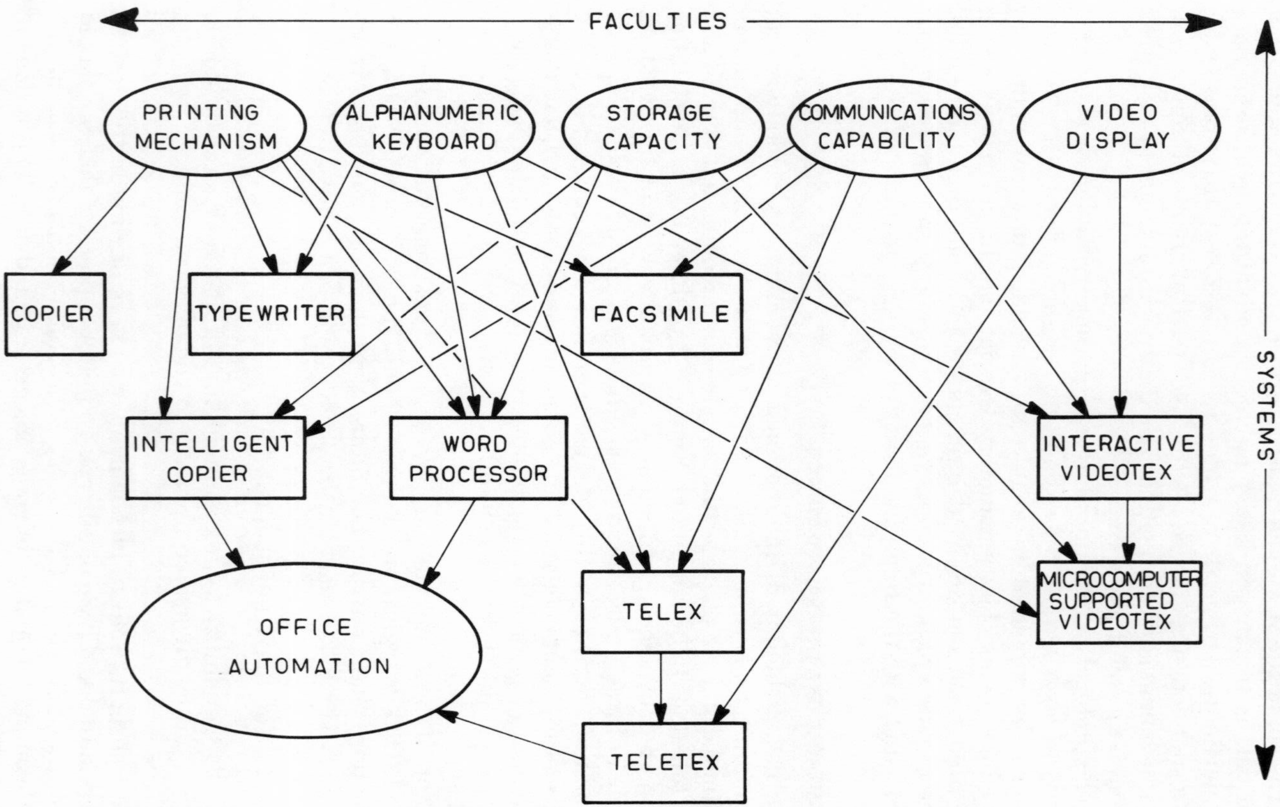

Figure 8-2. Basic facilities supported by office equipment at various levels of a system view.

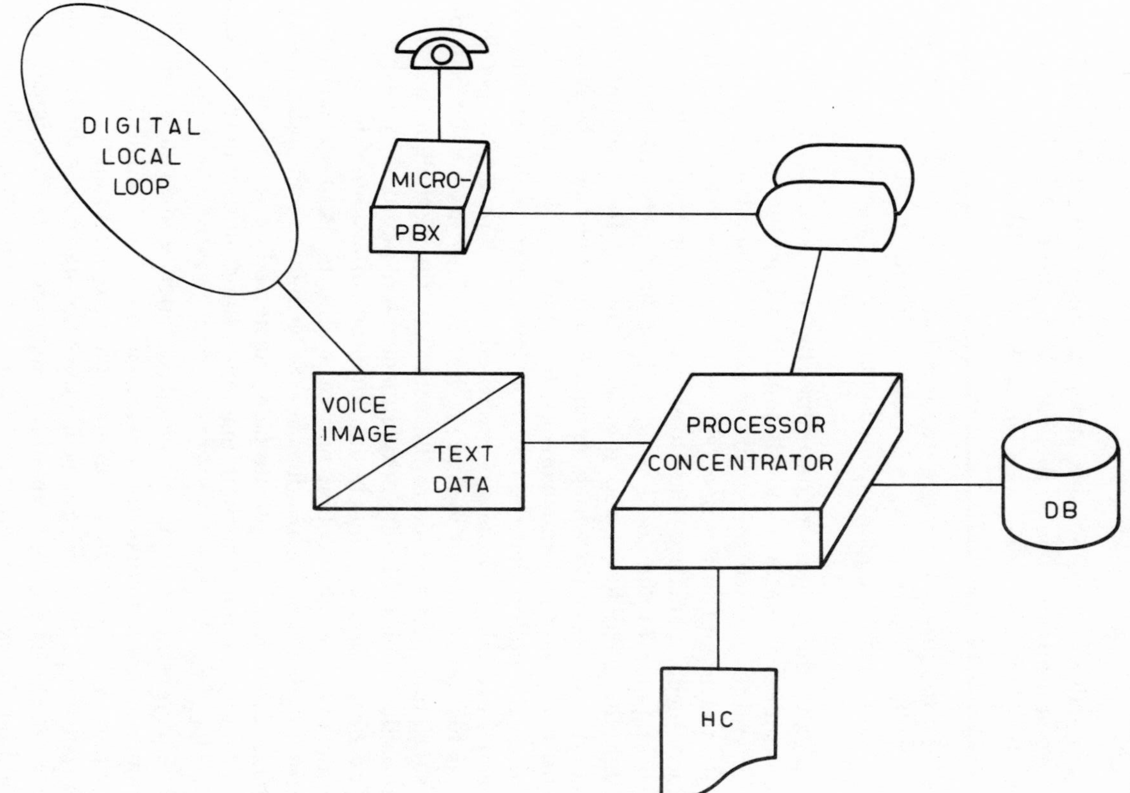

Figure 8-3. An approach to the integration of voice, image, text, and data within an office environment.

(private branch exchange) and the processor-concentrator. Actually, the two can be combined into one unit; they are separated for the sake of the example.

- To the micro-PBX are attached the voice station and the picturephone. These, too, can be combined and their capacities augmented by voice mail through disk storage and the proper software.
- To the processor-concentrator are attached a video (softcopy) unit, a hardcopy device, a keyboard (with or without graphics capabilities), and a personal database (or microfile).

Typically, the processor-concentrator will be a personal computer, which is another reason why it is separated from the PBX. When we talk of end-to-end, we specifically mean this microcomputer device and its attachment to the network. At the transport level, the major protocol mechanisms are made to support the interconnection of the microcomputer to the local area or long-haul network—the latter through the local loop—and through either of them to the other attached device(s) with which communication must be established.

The major protocol mechanisms, to which we just referred, are based on the notion that the transport layer operates in two classes: basic and extended. These are described in the formal OSI specification as two independent logical machines: They essentially provide the same transport service to the user, and the distinction between them is the amount of reliability enhancement afforded by each.

The *basic class* is a much simpler protocol machine designed to operate over communication networks able to assure a service as reliable as that desired by the user. Such network should not lose, damage, misorder, or duplicate data transferred on it without signaling the loss to the transport machine, something a modern X.25 network can do.

The *extended class* is projected to operate over less reliable communication networks, those which have an unacceptable residual error rate. As a result, they may lose, damage, misorder, or duplicate data transferred on them or have a failure not signaled to the transport machine. This is the meaning of the "extended class" designation. It should be prepared to detect and recover from network failures.

A key to both classes is connection identification. The transport connection exists between a pair of addresses, but there may be more than one transport connection between the same pair of users. Hence, a reference-numbering mechanism must exist to identify uniquely a transport connection and detect duplicate protocol messages as part of reliability improvement.

The OSI model also foresees a protocol version identification, with the version number included in the connection initiation message exchange to allow evolution of the protocol. Another vital feature is the establishment exchange:

- In the basic class, connection establishment uses a two-way handshake: the protocol data units are the connection request (CR) and the connection confirm (CC).
- In the extended class, connection establishment uses a three-way handshake: the protocol data units are the same as for the basic, except that a final acknowledgment (ACK) must be exchanged before the connection enters the established state.

With connection establishment initiated, the CR declares certain attributes which are to characterize the end-to-end interaction: protocol class, security level, compartment, precedence, maximum data unit size, and interactive options: connection, two-way transaction, or three-way transaction. Upon receipt of the CR, the receiver may accept or reject connection establishment based on the attributes of values declared. The receiver may negotiate only one of the values: the maximum data unit size, for instance, by specifying in its CC a maximum size which is smaller than that declared in the CR. This value will characterize the connection.

For security purposes, to prevent the unauthorized transfer of information, the transport protocol associates with each connection values of security level and compartment. The connection establishment exchange also specifies a precedence to be associated with the connection. Both classes of the protocol provide for upward multiplexing, supporting one or more transports on the same network connection.

In regard to data integrity, the basic protocol class includes no procedures, since it is assumed that the network will not damage the data. On the contrary, the extended protocol reflects on the integrity of control and data messages transferred between transport entities. This is accomplished by a check sum on all data units.

We have spoken of the acknowledgment procedure in the extended mode. An ACK bears the sequence number of the next data unit the receiving transport machine expects to receive. This automatically acknowledges receipt of all data units with sequence numbers less than that of the reference data unit. The ACK also contains a credit field which is used to calculate the flow control window.

- In the extended protocol class, a receiving transport machine may shrink its window.
- In both classes, cooperating transport entities exchange ACK to maintain correct synchronization of credit information and prevent deadlock in the face of a zero window.

An extended protocol class employs a timeout and retransmission scheme to recover from the loss of data units. After repeated retransmissions and an acknowledgment waiting period, a transport machine operating in the extended class will automatically terminate the connection. Connections may be voluntarily terminated by exchanging *disconnect request* and *disconnect confirm,* after which the supporting network connection is released. Such a procedure, however, abruptly terminates a transport connection and may cause data loss.

The *graceful close,* to which we made reference, permits connection termination without data loss. It is reached by successively half closing the connection. Each half close involves the transmission and acknowledgment of the graceful close request (GCR). The GCR occupies a position in the normal data sequence space and is acknowledged with a normal ACK. It also bears the number of the last unacknowledged data unit.

A transaction is supported by including the transaction data in a connection request marked to indicate that it is a transaction. The transaction is complete when the appropriate handshake takes place, unless the quantity of data is too large to put in the CR. If so, a short-lived connection is set up to send the transaction data.

EXTENDING THE LEVEL OF SUPPORT

The foregoing discussion makes it evident that a general-purpose transport protocol must satisfy requirements that vary with respect to the quality of the underlying network services and the nature of the user application. When the underlying network service meets the requirements of the user applications, little enhancement may be required from the transport layer. But when there is disparity, the transport layer must provide added services. Hence the transport protocol should be designed in a modular way by using the previously mentioned concepts of classes and options.

The ISO/OSI standard has been highly influenced by the work done by ECMA. The latter organization further defined five classes of transport; they range from class 0, as required for simple terminals such as teletex, to class 4, as required, for instance, by datagram networks. In principle, there is no difference between class 0 and the transport protocol adopted by CCITT for the teletex service. Yet all procedures are currently the subject of study, both by ECMA and by other standardization bodies. The intention is to ensure the maximum possible degree of compatibility. The main goals of this work, which to a substantial degree goes on in parallel in different parts of the world, can be stated as follows:

1. Be transparent; hence, do not restrict the content, format, or coding of the user information, whether data or control. There is never a need to understand its structure and meaning.
2. Assure error-free delivery. Only exceptional errors are to be visible to the transport service user.
3. Guarantee network independence. The transport service must be homogeneous while allowing a suitable variety of underlying communications media, protocols, and mechanisms.
4. Look into end-to-end significance; connect the end users irrespective of the number of individual communications links used.
5. Permit address decoupling by using a system of addressing which is mapped onto the addressing scheme of the supporting communications medium (transport addresses).
6. Be cost-effective by attempting to optimize the use of the available communication resources.

The software driving the transport entity should attain these goals through the use of the underlying services provided by the supporting layers. Where the notion of possible dialects comes in is in the admission by ECMA that in several implementations there will exist an equivalent set of interface primitives, which are considerably affected by the properties of the local operating system and language support. Even if such set of interface primitives includes strictly local functions, they can conceivably have an impact on the general message exchange and, through it, on the functioning of the transport mechanism.

Another fundamental concern, this one concerning the logical transport structure, is flow control. Its importance is evidenced by the fact that the behavior of the session influences and is influenced by the flow control behavior. A session entity that is authorized to place a data unit into the transport pipe cannot necessarily assume that the distant session entity has authorized the acceptance of data. On the other hand, the lack of authorization to place a data unit into the transport pipe does not necessarily imply that the distant session entity has not authorized its acceptance. A session entity may use the flow control mechanism to suspend the transfer of data for an extended period.

An equally vital facility is error notification. Only data that the receiving transport level believes to be error-free will be passed to the receiving session entity. If errors are detected and all possible recovery attempts (in accordance with the agreed quality of service) have failed, the connection is terminated and notification is given by a disconnect indication.

The *purge request* service is available only when a purge facility has been requested. Invocation of the purge service at one end of a transport connection causes the transport service to remove all data units in both directions of a transport connection. The corresponding session entity at the other end of the connection will be notified by means of a purge indication that this has occurred.

These examples help document that the functions in the transport layer are instrumental in bridging the gap between the services available from the networking layer and those to be offered by session control. Such functions are concerned with the enhancement of quality of service. For instance, in terms of connection establishment:

- Each transport entity is responsible for selecting the reference which the other end will use. The mechanism is symmetrical, and thus the need to assign a status of master or slave for collision detection purposes is avoided.

- The network service that best matches the user requirement can be selected by taking into account the charges for the various network services.

- Deciding whether to multiplex multiple transport connections onto a single network connection is facilitated, and so is establishing optimum data unit size.

- The mechanism is also responsible for mapping transport addresses onto network addresses.

Options help define additional functions which may be associated with any class. Classes and options within classes are negotiated during the connection establishment phase. The sender of the transport connection may indicate during the connection phase the set of options the sender is willing to support. The receiver will reply by specifying a set which is equal to or less than the set indicated, as we have already discussed. Default values can be defined for certain parameters. When a parameter is not specified in either the request or the confirmation, a default value is assumed.

We have also talked about the four classes advanced by ECMA. The objective of class 0 is to provide the simplest type of transport connection. As stated, it has been defined by CCITT and is being used to support teletex terminals connected to switched networks. The class itself has been designed to have minimum functionality; it provides only the facilities needed for connection establishment with negotiation, data transfer with segmenting, and protocol error reporting.

According to the available specifications, class 0 contains *no* facilities for multiplexing, disconnection, flow control, error detection, error recovery, purge, or expedited data transfer. There is no explicit transport connection clearing procedure. A clearing of the network connection, however, results in the clearing of the transport connection with the transport user informed via a *disconnect indication*.

The objective of class 1 is to assure a simple transport connection with minimal overhead connections. This class is suitable for permanent and switched network connections. It will be used by nonsophisticated terminals when no multiplexing onto network connections is required or for multiplexing in particular cases when the absence of individual connection flow control is acceptable.

In terms of function, class 1 provides the additional capacity to terminate a transport connection independently of the supporting network connection. But it does so without flow control, error detection, error recovery, purge, or expedited data transfer. If the network resets or clears, the transport connection is terminated without the transport clearing sequence and the transport user being informed.

In class 1, detection of a protocol error by a receiving transport entity signals the possibility of a malfunction of either the sending or the receiving entity. This calls for recovery action. In addition to the reporting of the error to the local error management function, the transport entity may freeze the state of the transport connection for diagnostic purposes, initiate a disconnect procedure in the expectation that the procedure will not be completed, transmit a data unit in the expectation that it may not be correctly received and therefore reported to the remote higher-level error management function. The action to follow is dependent on the receiving system management function.

Correspondingly, the objective of class 2 is to provide flow control to help avoid congestion at end points and on the network connection. This is vital when traffic is heavy and continuous or when there is intensive multiplexing. In terms of function, a credit mechanism allows the receiver to inform a sender of the exact amount of data it is willing to receive, with purge and expedited data transfer available.

Flow control is integral. Depending on the implementation, credit may reflect the availability of receiving buffers at either the transport level or the transport user level. The essential thing is to provide the user with a flow control mechanism, that is, with a means to stop receiving data.

Furthermore, for each transport connection and for each direction of data transmission a *transmit window* is defined. It constitutes the ordered set of consecutive data units authorized to be transmitted in a given direction. The lowest sequence number within the transmit window is referred to as the *lower window edge*, and the lowest sequence number above the transmit window is referred to as the *upper window edge*.

A procedure for expedited data transfer permits a transport entity to transmit data to a remote entity without following the flow control procedure of the normal data flow. This can apply only in the transfer phase. Purge is used to reinitialize a given transport connection. It removes all data in both directions of the transport connection and can apply only in the data transfer phase.

Finally, the objective of class 3 is to mask errors indicated by the network. Its selection is usually based upon reliability criteria reflecting the assumptions made concerning the network layer behavior with respect to error indication. It exceeds the functionality of class 2 through a capacity to recover after a failure signaled by the network layer without involving the user of the transport service.

It is further expected that class 4 will be fully compatible with the other classes and will be a superset of the latter in conformance with the general approach that has been adopted for the standards under consideration. More precisely, the objectives of class 4 additional to those of class 3 will be to meet the requirements of datagram and similar networks in which sequence integrity is not maintained.

SESSION SYNCHRONIZATION

A session connection facility enables two service users to establish a communications session between them. Simultaneous attempts by the users to establish the connection may result in two connections, leaving the users to decide which to accept or reject. No architectural restrictions are placed on the number of concurrent session connections. A user (or the session service itself) may always reject an unwanted connection.

Session connection establishment makes it feasible for the service users to exchange the values of session connection parameters. Typically, they must come to an agreement on a set of parameter values concerning the session layer. The interfaces which come into play are identified in Fig. 8-4.

Note that the providers of the transport service (including the layer itself) are data-communications-oriented, whereas the users are data-processing-oriented. A session protocol is applicable to layer 5. A session connection identifier uniquely specifies the session connection within the environment of the cooperating session entities.

To ensure a valid session connection service, the sender cannot initiate it until the response is received, except for requesting abnormal termination or resynchronization. The receiver cannot initiate any service after getting the indication of the major synchronization point service, except for the data transfer, resynchronization, and the user abort.

Expedited services initiated by the receiver after the response are not indicated before the confirmation to that response. It is, however, possible for the sender to flag (by appropriately setting a parameter in the request) that the receiving user has to stop sending normal data after he has given the response until he gets a subsequent indication.

The session connection provides two independent logical data paths for transparent data transfer: (1) The normal data path and (2) an expedited one. It also guarantees sequential delivery of data on each of the two paths without loss or duplication unless explicitly reported. An exception-reporting service is available in all phases of the session connection. It permits the users to be notified of unanticipated situations not covered by other services, such as unrecoverable session malfunctions. Normally the exception-reporting indication

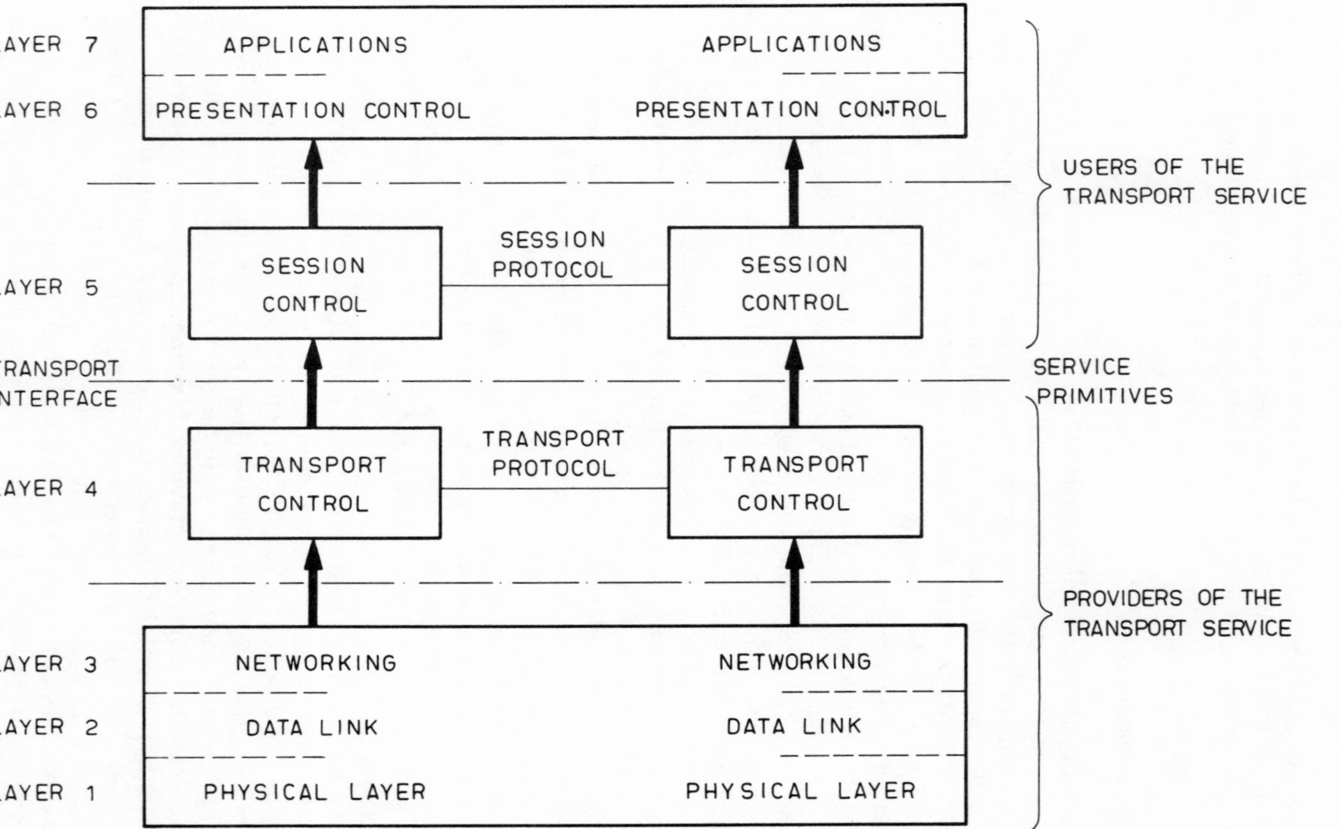

Figure 8-4. The seven ISO/OSI layers seen from the perspective of the providers of the transport service, the service primitives, and the users of the service.

would be followed by an attempt to reestablish synchronization to a previously defined synchronization point.

There are three session termination services:

- The orderly release service
- The user-initiated abort service (u-abort)
- The provider-initiated abort service (p-abort)

An orderly release allows either user associated with a given session connection to terminate it. The termination is accomplished cooperatively by the two service users without loss of data after the in-transit data have been delivered and accepted by both. The user invoking orderly release must have the means of determining whether the other user refuses the termination.

A user-abort service provides the means by which the users associated with a connection can instantaneously terminate the session and have the correspondent user informed of the termination. This, may, however, cause loss of data. A provider-initiated abort is a means by which the service provider can indicate the termination of the session connection for reasons internal to its operations or when the underlying transport service is not available. This, too, might cause loss of data.

A reselection facility provides the users with the means of selecting new values for each session parameter and determining the availability of certain services within the range defined during the session connection establishment:

> The *normal data exchange service* permits both service users associated with a session connection to exchange data units over the connection. In this case, the receiving session entity should deliver to the user at its access point each data unit as soon as possible, unless explicitly quarantined.
>
> The *expedited data exchange service* sees to it that both service users associated with a session connection can exchange expedited session service data units without being constrained by the right to send normal data or a quarantine service.

The quarantine service permits the sending session service user to designate that an integral number of data units is only meaningful when all of them are available. Such service is architecturally based on the assumption that quarantined data units are not delivered by the receiving session entity to the user, and the latter gets no indication that data has been quarantined.

It is, however, possible that the sending session user may request that all the data currently quarantined be canceled. Session connection parameters related to the quarantine service include the quarantine status and the maximum amount of data which can be quarantined. Such parameters are determined during session connection establishment.

A very important issue is the token management service. It provides the user with request tokens, give tokens, and release tokens. *Request tokens* are user bids for the ownership of specific tokens, which can be requested by a user only if they are not currently assigned to that user. *Give tokens* allow a session user to surrender one token or more. They can be given by a session user only if they have been previously assigned to that user. *Release tokens* permit the user to indicate that the implied service is no longer required but do not relinquish the right to request token assignment later on, when necessary.

More precisely, the role of a minor synchronization point is to define correlations between the flow of sequentially transmitted events in both directions, not any correlation with expedited events. The sender may create more complex synchronization structures by issuing further primitives before receiving the confirmation. Synchronization then consists of a series of concurrent units in the forms of a pipelined operation.

A major synchronization service is confirmed without reservations. As such, it allows the requesting entity to separate completely phases of the session connection. Furthermore, session control provides an automatically incremented serial number to identify synchronization points. Typically the increment is by 1, but certain primitives may cause the current value to be changed to a new value possibly chosen by the users.

When employing major synchronization point service, session service users might wish to structure their communication into separate dialogue units. For this (and also for nested or overlapping structures) the session layer offers the possibility of defining the beginning and the end of the data units used. The users may indicate which units are transferred transparently by the major synchronization service.

Note that the session service does not define any sequence numbering of events, nor does it provide any other event-identification or statistics-generating techniques. The value of a special counter will not be sent with any data transfer; the mechanism is negotiated and agreed upon at session establishment time. The overall characteristics are such that local actions could maintain synchronism between the counters at the two session entities, making it feasible that the same identifications are attached to the same events at both entities.

Session synchronization capabilities help the users at both ends of a connection synchronize their dialogue. They provide the user with the means for defining and identifying implicit synchronization points or setting either to a synchronization point or to a point known by the users. Semantics that users may give to their synchronization points are transparent to the session service.

Simultaneous requests for performing these services at both service access points must be resolved by the service provider. The synchronization point service may be minor or major. The two do have in common that, by requesting them, the users define synchronization points. Minor synchronization point service is a confirmed one, but the confirmation may be implicit or explicit. By means of a parameter, the requesting party may specify whether the response is explicitly requested or the confirmation will be implicitly given with the response to a subsequent explicit minor synchronization point.

The importance of these ISO/OSI session control definitions to local area networks should be self-evident. As previously emphasized, the more they are observed in the different architectures, the more likely it is that we will finally move toward a level of normalization which permits network interconnection without spoiling resources for conversion purposes and incurring consequent errors and delays.

In the last analysis, it all adds up to good management practice. The vendors of computers and communications gear, as well of LAN facilities, must realize that there will be no room for mediocre suppliers of products and services. Managements that hang on to weakness for whatever reason—tradition, inferiority or superiority complex, or just sentiment—won't be around in the 1990s. Neither will be their companies.

PART 2

LAN ARCHITECTURE

9 OMNINET

We have said that a local network architecture is composed of two parts:

- A *physical* part, which basically concerns the cable, taps, and modems.
- A *logical* part supported by protocols and software routines.

As Fig. 9-1 demonstrates, the logical and physical parts together determine the facilities of a given LAN architecture. From a design standpoint there is, however, an interaction among all three levels of reference: physical, logical, and supported facilities. Quite often the latter imply physical choices and logical provision either during a planning phase or as a historical fact.

For this reason, it is always important to look into the way a given company has developed and the products which it produced prior to launching a LAN. Corvus began operating in 1979. Its first product was a 10-MB hard-disk drive. Its second product was the Mirror, a backup medium for the information on the disk as an alternative to a second disk or tape drive. This is an interesting approach, because it can be used both as a poor-man's online backup and as everybody's *save* capability provided the device works correctly and in a reliable manner. (In its original release Corvus did not say that Mirror would improve performance, but in its 1983 release that claim was made.) The Mirror is an interface to a video or cassette recorder. The device takes digital data off the disk drive and transforms it into video signals to be stored on a video cassette recorder (VCR). The opposite process is followed in reading from the tape drive.

A third product is Constellation, an intelligent multiplexer that allows up to 64 devices to share a disk drive (Fig. 9-2). With the disk at the hub, this hierarchical type network can drive other Constellation multiplexers at a 17-m distance, with each multiplexer supporting personal computers. Among the technical specifications we distinguish flat 32-wire cable, up to 64 microcomputers, and up to 34 m distance from the central hub.

A Zilog Z-80 microprocessor is the heart of the Corvus controller. It features direct memory access hardware to control the Winchester disk(s), the Constellation multiplexers, and the Mirror Winchester backup. It also provides the software that controls data protection and communication. This hardware system allows each microcomputer to access the disk system as if it were the only computer attached. The software controlling the Constellation manages the shared medium and prevents the computers from unintentionally using the same area

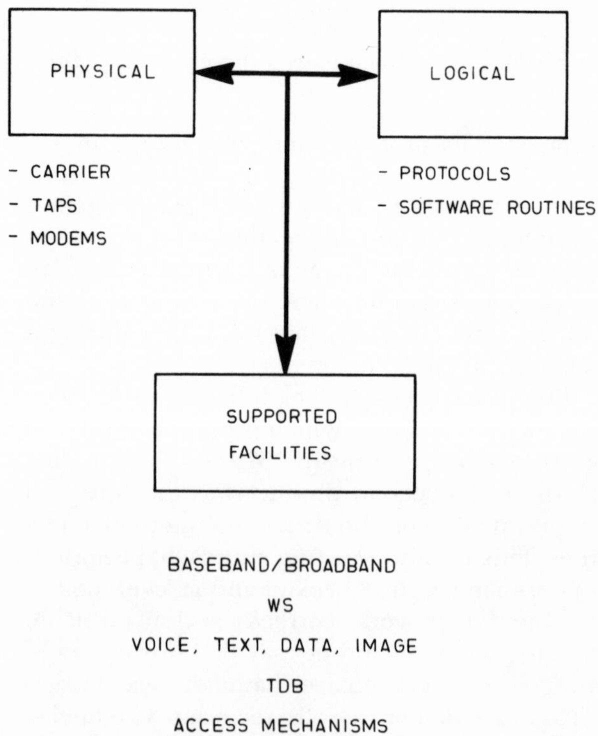

Figure 9-1. The logical and physical characteristics of a network define among themselves the supported facilities.

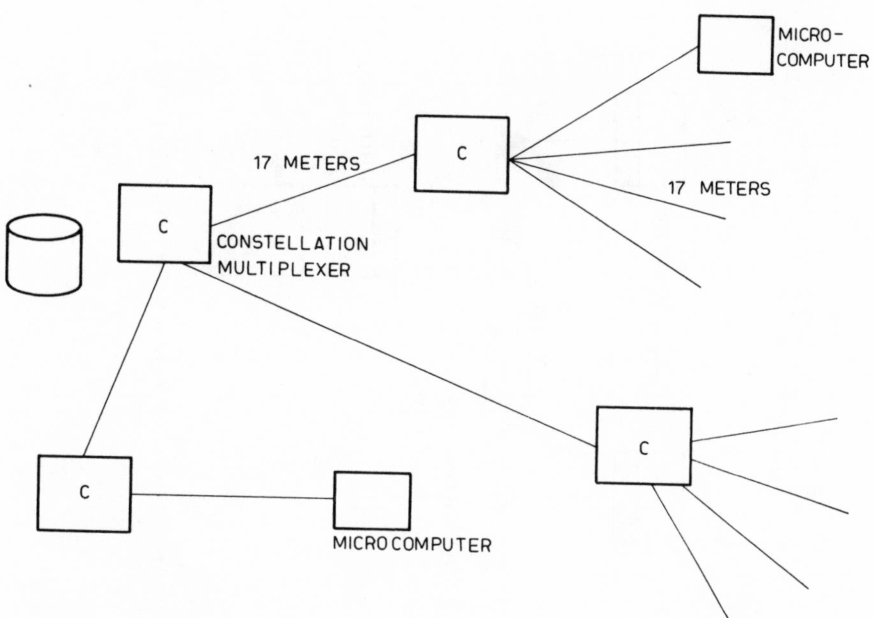

Figure 9-2. Constellation, by Corvus, is a star-type network that theoretically allows up to 64 devices to share a disk drive.

of the disk. The Omninet-distributed LAN architecture has made this solution obsolete.

A fourth Corvus product is a 20-MB disk drive (8-in Winchester) with three platters instead of two in the first offering. A fifth is a 6-MB drive offered as a very compact peripheral. A sixth is Omninet.

THE OMNINET ARCHITECTURE

The Omninet is a local network architecture that uses twisted wire (RS-422) in both protected and unprotected versions. The cable is composed of a pair of 20-gauge insulated conductors twisted together inside a common cover. The LAN allows up to 64 microcomputers and shared peripherals to be attached to it (Fig. 9-3). In its original release (1981) Omninet connected different personal computers from Apple II to DEC LSI-11. In the general case, compatibility required that the PC feature be a 100-pin connector, run on CP/M, and use the Z80 microprocessor. Apple II was one of the exceptions. Such constraints have, however, been relieved with Release 2 (1983).

According to the Omninet experts, there are three reasons why twisted pair was selected: its low cost, the fact that anyone can lay the

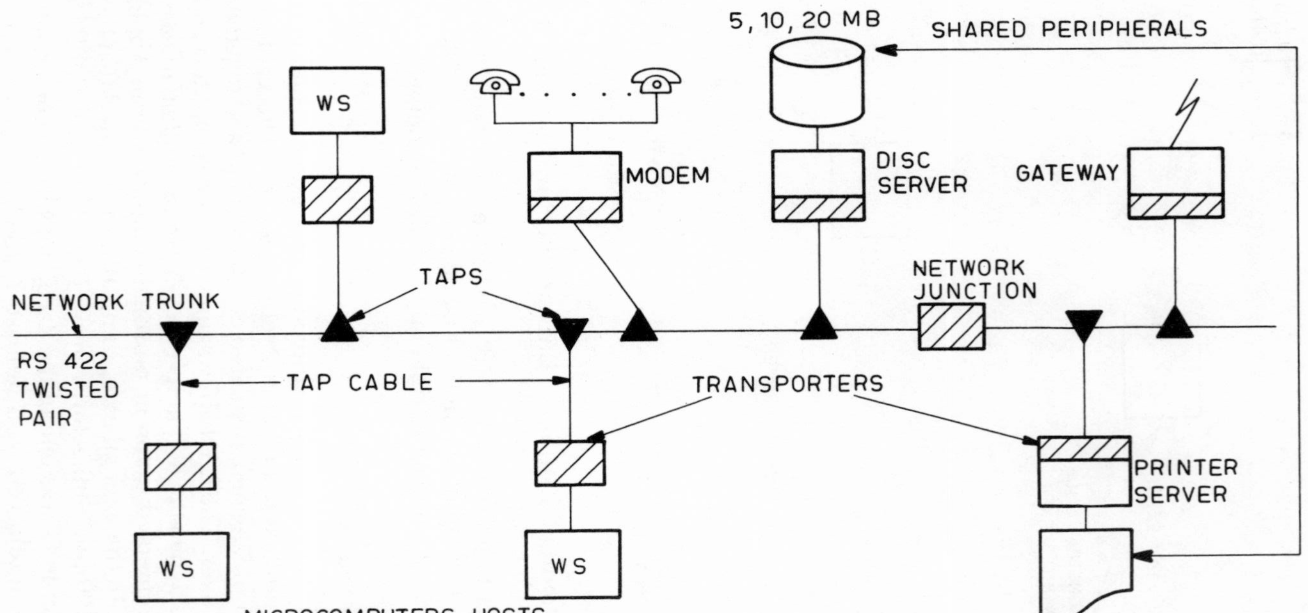

Figure 9-3. The Omninet bus with attached workstation, disk and printer server, gateway, and (to saturate the line) phone stations. Up to 64 attachments are possible.

cable and connect the transponders to it, and dependability. Shielded twisted-pair cable is no more susceptible to RF interference than coaxial cable is.

System performance is enhanced through a low-level acknowledgment protocol. If a message is received correctly, it is acknowledged by the receiving station. If it is not positively acknowledged within 15 to 20 ms (milliseconds), the sending station will retransmit it after waiting a random time interval. A message is retransmitted until it is acknowledged or until it has been retransmitted a maximum number of times specified by the user. This adds to flexibility. The transporter receiving a message sends the ACK immediately after the message has been validated.

The Omninet can have one or more trunk segments each of which is up to 330 m in length. When multiple segments are used, network junctions are required to join the network segments. Two personal computers can communicate provided they are no farther than 1300 m apart and the path between them does not exceed three network junctions.

Devices are attached through an intelligent network interface, the *transporter*. In the case of a microcomputer, an Omninet interface card is used. It contains both a transporter and a specific microcomputer-oriented circuitry. A network server is needed to attach a shared peripheral, such as a disk drive or printer, to Omninet. The server has a transporter and an interface to the specific shared device. An Omninet network tap is a passive junction connected to the network trunk. A tap cable connects the attached device—WS or shared peripheral—to it.

Now let's recapitulate:

- The *network trunk* is the Omninet common bus used to interconnect attached devices. The trunk can be composed of four junctions of 330 m each to a total of 1300 m.

- A *network junction* is active and joins network segments. Each segment is up to 330 m in length.

- A *network tap* is a passive junction used to connect network devices. A maximum of 64 network taps is allowed.

- The *tap cable* is a twisted pair, 5 m in maximum length, used to connect a network device to the network tap.

- A *network device* contains a transporter interface (card or network server).

Network tapping is straightforward by using tap boxes supplied by the firm. Each tap box contains five pairs of tighten-down screws to connect network wires; the pairs are labeled A1–B1 to A5–B5. The A and B sides of each pair are electrically connected. A simple network tap is shown in Fig. 9-4. The cable used for the Omninet network trunk is specified as unshielded twisted pair. If shielded wire is used, each network segment should not exceed 125 m. The shield drain wires are inserted into the A3–B3 tighten-down screws.

Two network devices can be attached by using a single network tap if the black wires of both tap cables are inserted into the B1 tighten-down screw and the red wires of both tap cables are inserted into the B2 tighten-down screw. It is, however, important that the total length of cable from any network device to the network trunk cable not exceed 3 m. The network terminator is another component: The network trunk must be terminated at both ends by installing a 100-Ω, ¼ W, ±5% resistor between the black wire and the red wire at each end of the network trunk.

In logical network management, each attached device must have a unique address that is set in a dip switch on the interface card or network servicer. The dip switch contains eight microswitches labeled 1 through 8.

- Microswitches 1 to 6 are used to set the device address, with up to 64 possible addresses.
- Switch 7 sets a network bias. Omninet recommends that the disk server be used as the device with the network bias set.

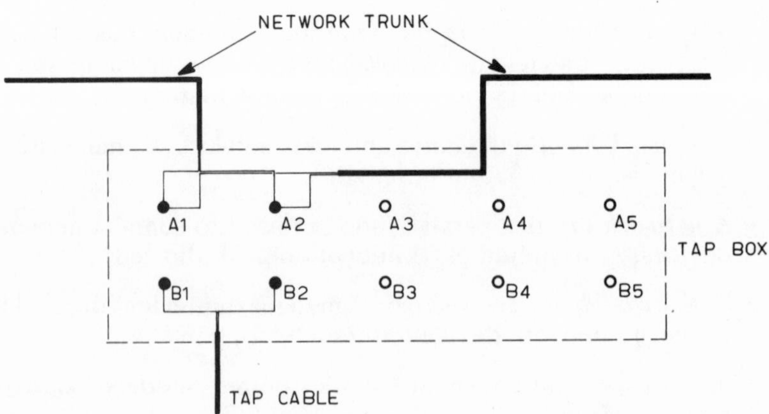

Figure 9-4. Example of a tap box connecting the network trunk and a tap cable.

- Switch 8 is reserved as a network terminator. A terminator is installed at each end of the network.

The disk server is attached to the network trunk by using a network tap and a 3-m tap cable in the same manner as with other Omninet network devices. A 5-ft flat cable is used to connect the disk server to the Corvus disk system. When Omninet is used with an existing Corvus multiplexer, the disk server flat cable is plugged into any computer port of the multiplexer instead of the disk drive.

Winchester disk systems can be installed on an Omninet network with the disk server transporter. This stand-alone device features an extended 6801 code and a Corvus disk system interface. All hosts (workstations) on the network can share the disk storage. The server eliminates the need for a computer to interface the disks with the network, thereby contributing to performance because no time is lost in transferring the disk data into and out of a dedicated computer.

Currently, one server can support up to four disk drives of 6, 11, or 20 MB each with a total of up to 80 MB of shared storage. Another unit, one that is similar to a server, is the Omninet gateway computer for interconnecting Omninets or linking them to other networks, including long-haul value-added networks. The disk server and gateway respectively support the databasing and data communication faculties. Device addressing sees to it that a message can be sent to any unit attached to the network or broadcast to all devices on the network.

THE TRANSPORTER FUNCTIONS

The reason why it's so important to examine the networking features not in a general, all-encompassing sense, but architecture by architecture is that local networks take many forms. Probably no single product can hope to dominate the market because of the diversity of user needs; and standardization is talked about only in the sense of a couple of layers.

The more sophisticated local network architectures to be expected for the mid-1980s will feature low-cost solutions capable of handling high-level languages and equipped with sophisticated operating systems, inexpensive mass storage, and high-performance communications facilities. These will allow data and expensive peripherals to be shared among many inexpensive terminals. Such systems will have broad bandwidth communication, serve workstations separated by kilometers, be easy to expand, and be able to incorporate many different machine types. The failure of one component should not affect the operation of others. Finally, the system should be easily hooked up to remote local area networks.

Component functions in an electronics circuitry can be served through logical and physical media. The transporter gear is divided into two parts: the transporter logic, to which is connected the RS-422 twisted pair, and the interface. The transporter implements the network protocol for the first four layers of ISO/OSI through the transport layer. Hence the name, *transporter*. It fundamentally consists of integrated circuits (Fig. 9-5).

The RS-422 physical layer protocol is governed by the gate array and uses no carrier signal. A function in the advanced data link control (ADLC) is, however, active at the data link layer and can tell if there has been a transition on the cable. This is activity on the network, and Omninet defines it as its carrier signal.

The transporter box corresponds to the lowest (physical) level of ISO/OSI. The RS-422 standard is a subset of RS-449 which is intended for modems. In the transporter design, the first component is a set of transceivers used to send and receive the differential pair.

The RS standard consists of two options: unbalanced RS-232 and balanced RS-449. Both are designed as modem interfaces. In the Corvus case, we talk of a balanced data line (differential pair). With unbalanced solutions, a noisy environment results in signal errors. With balanced solutions, variation due to noise will affect both mirror images, and error correction is thus possible. Balanced solutions permit higher speed and longer distance.

The transporter uses a Motorola ADLC chip based on the ISO HDLC protocol with the difference of the address bit. Through the HDLC protocol, the data link is supported. Another component is the 6801 microprocessor by Motorola. Its mission is to simplify the computer interconnection. A fourth component is the Omninet chip, which is oriented to the network layer. It uses the datagram approach and supports a 2-kB variable-length message.

Within the range of these facilities, the transporter circuitry permits a device to send messages and set up to receive. If a microcomputer wishes to send a message, it gives

1. The address of the sender (in memory)
2. The length of the message
3. The destination host number
4. The destination sockets
5. Status information

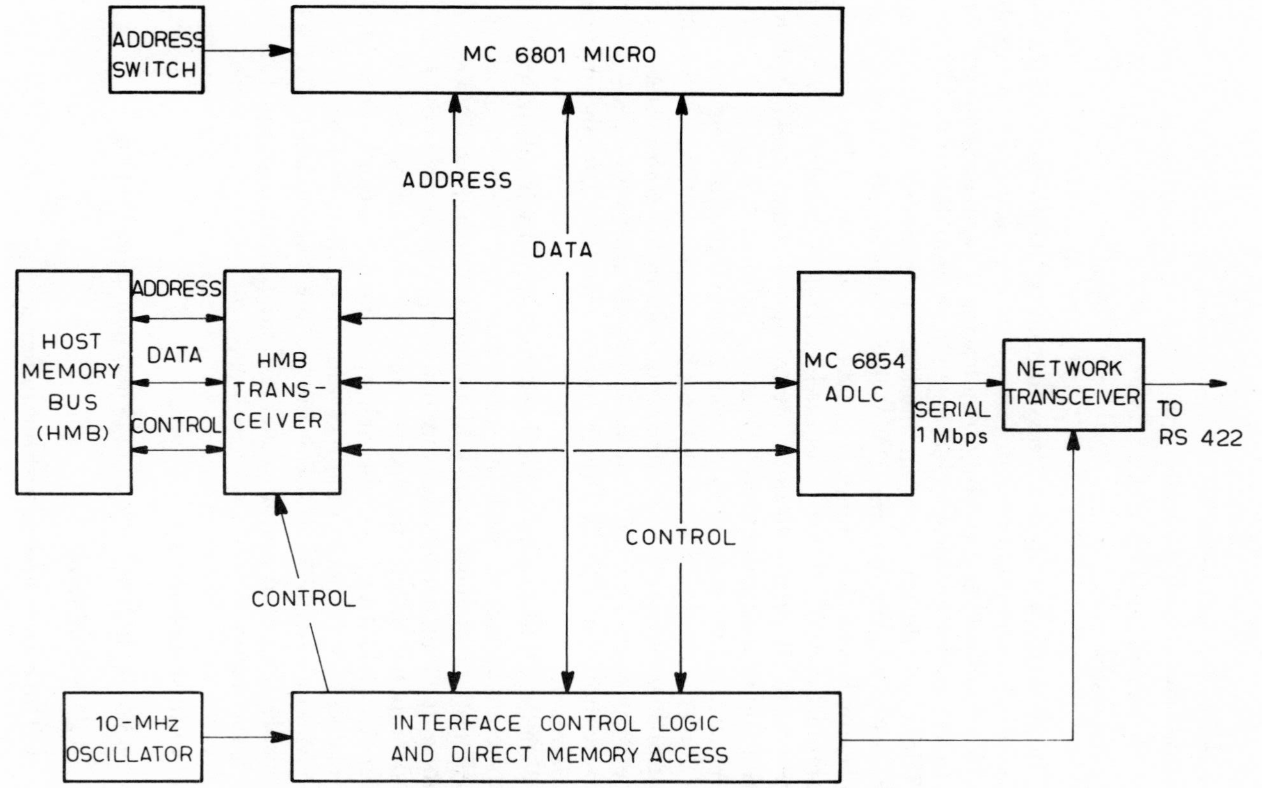

Figure 9-5. Components of the transporter unit: the address, data, and control lines and the microprocessor support.

The receiver must give:

1. Address in memory
2. Maximum length allowed
3. Socket number
4. Status

The socket is a unique address in memory. Omninet features four sockets to be set up until the device receives a message. A socket also provides addressing capability by allowing a message to be sent to a particular buffer in the selected host microcomputer.

The basic design uses an interface for directly accessing the memory of a host computer (DMA) that can be adapted to almost any processor bus with a minimal amount of additional hardware. For example, the Apple II computer can be accommodated by adding only five integrated circuits to the basic transporter gear. Packet splitting and demultiplexing are thereby made possible.

A gate array (one of three main chips) controls the interface between the transporter and the host bus or a peripheral device. This control logic requires no buffering of data in the transporter; it can access the host computer's memory directly with a 24-bit address. It also controls the RS-422 driver and receiver circuits, the network *transceiver.*

With the DMA interface, each cycle is explicitly invoked by a 6801 instruction. When needed, the gate array stops the 6801 processor's clock until a memory access of the host is completed. With this feature, the transporter's software has complete control of the transfer of data between the transporter and the host computer. In this manner, two DMA cycles, one right after the other, can be completely unrelated with respect to their location in the host memory.

A Motorola MC6854 ADLC is the low-level network interface with the cable. The chip performs many of the functions of the data link layer, including

- Bit serialization
- Cyclic redundancy code generation and checking
- Packet framing
- Three-byte first-in first-out buffering
- Implementation of the bit level protocol which uses nonreturn-to-zero inverted coding

Bit stuffing (zero insertion) is performed whenever the bit stream contains more than five 1 bits together. A Motorola MC6801 single-chip microcomputer oversees the two interfaces and manages the conversion and transfer of data and control information between the host computer or peripheral device and the network.

In terms of transition facility, carrier sensing takes place twice. When the ADLC senses that there has been no activity for 15 μs (microseconds), it tells the software in the microcomputer that it may proceed with a transmission. The software instructs the interface control logic to start a transmission. Because considerable time elapses during the execution of the software instructions (about 35 μs since the ADLC has reported no activity) a second level of carrier sensing is invoked. A special chip designed into the gate array provides a nanosecond reaction.

The transporter accepts two major categories of commands from the attached computer(s) to control the overall flow of messages within the local network: send message and receive message. The former command transmits a message up to 600 bytes in length to any destined host socket. It includes:

- Command code
- A result address
- Destination host socket number
- Message address and length
- An optional message header up to 255 bytes in length

The transporter transfers the message and optional message header without additional host software involvement. When the message is delivered, the result status code is set to reflect the status of the transmitted message. There are several possible results: message delivered successfully, message undelivered after x retries, receiving socket not set up, and message too long for receiving socket.

As we stated when we defined the concept of a socket, a *receive* message command prepares host sockets to receive incoming messages. It includes:

- Command code
- Result address
- Socket number
- Data buffer address
- Maximum message length

The optional message header length also is specified; the header and the actual message can be placed in different locations within the host's memory. The feature allows device drivers to place the message data directly into the user's buffer while storing the header information in the driver's buffer. This procedure eliminates the need for the driver to move the message data to the user's buffer and makes Omninet a modern logical structure that treats messages as files stored in the database.

CARRIER-SENSING CAPABILITIES

We said that the transporter registers the host's send request. That being done, it uses CSMA (carrier-sensing multiple access, but without collision detection) for possible overlay with data transmitted by another station and error control. When the network is available, the station transmits.

Topologically, the transporter in each node manages the network for that node and thereby serves as the common network interface for all nodes. Every transporter is the same except for a small part of its circuitry for interfacing with a particular host. No master network controller is required, because the individual transporters supply all the control needed for the chosen distributed network control scheme: CSMA.

To reduce the burden on the host, the transporter performs many high-level network tasks that are often the responsibility of the host computer in other networks:

- Generating and receiving acknowledgments
- Retransmitting messages
- Detecting duplicate messages

Collision statistics provided by Omninet are good. Collisions account for less than 1 percent, and the effective throughput stands at 100 kBps over a theoretical 125 kBps calculated for 512-byte packets. The collision avoidance scheme is implemented in the transporters by using a combination of two methods:

1. The CSMA mechanism is utilized to determine when the network is available.

2. The transporter computes a randomized transmit start time to minimize the probability of two devices trying to access an available network at the same time.

This approach seems to avoid the need for a collision detection mechanism. Also, it permits Omninet to be implemented on an RS-422 twisted pair of wires, thereby eliminating the cost associated with collision detection hardware. Error detection and retransmission activities are carried out by the transporters without software intervention.

Queuing occurs in CSMA networks when two or more stations are ready to transmit a packet while another is being sent. Every station must defer its transmission until the network becomes idle again. Since each station with a message to transmit will try to send as soon as the current transmission is completed, another collision would usually result, and that would necessitate further waiting. The queuing mechanism should be seen as an integral part of the overall text and data transport function. While the line speed of 1 Mbps (or 125 kbps) is impressive, collision may occur because of the long length of cable. Hence there is need to support collision avoidance.

As stated earlier, Omninet utilizes a positive acknowledgment method to ensure that a message has reached its destination without error. If acknowledgment of a message is not received, retransmission is automatically performed by the transporter until it is successful or until a user-specified number of retries have been performed. If transmission is unsuccessful, the sending host is informed of the nature of the error.

The positive ACK algorithm sees to it that the network is not released till ACK is received: this happens in 6 μs. Device handshake takes place in the following way:

1. The sender says: "I have a message to send."
2. When the network is available, the device can immediately send (and not wait for ACK).
3. If the receiver has a socket, the message is accepted. If not, it is aborted.
4. If accepted, the receiver sends ACK.

This is virtually point-to-point communication. We can also broadcast a message. In a broadcast everybody accepts the message but does not acknowledge it.

If the attached machine (for instance, DEC LSI-11 and S-100 bus units) supports it, interrupt can occur. Apple II does not support interrupt. Message transport within the layered ISO/OSI architecture necessarily involves processing beyond the data link and into the network layer. Two solutions can exist: virtual circuits and datagram. The virtual circuit (VC) is a sequenced and synchronized two-way conversation that involves the exchange of messages whose assurance is guaranteed by the network architecture. This minimizes the possibility that messages will be lost, duplicated, or received out of order. Datagram solutions, in contrast, imply that each protocol level requiring reliable data transfer must implement its own dependable delivery mechanism.

The way the designers look at it, providing virtual circuit service in the Omninet transporter would have required much more memory than that available in the 6801. Adding the necessary external memory and software would have increased the cost of the transporter. At the same time, many of the hosts used on Omninets are 8-BPW microcomputers with limited memory space and no highly sophisticated operating systems. They can neither hold enough software nor spare enough processing time to perform reliable communications by using a pure datagram approach.

A design compromise was then made for Omninet's transporter, which seems to be more reliable than datagrams are but is not as secure as virtual circuits. It is called micro VC. What it implies is that state information about message transfers is maintained for only microseconds and provides many of the features of a virtual circuit. Micro VC guarantees that a message sent through the network will be received correctly by the appropriate host. If it is not, the sender will be notified that the message was not delivered. Duplicate messages will be discarded, and messages will arrive in the order in which they were transmitted. Furthermore, the network's responsibility for routing data does not end when the packet arrives.

The transporter transfers the data into the host computer's memory at the location specified in special memory address sockets. (As we have said, each transporter contains four sockets, any of which may be activated at one time.) The socket number is specified in a separate file in the packet header, and the transporter automatically loads the incoming packets into the correct places on host memory.

Packet splitting is another function that uses the socket structure. Figure 9-6 shows the Omninet packet format. A packet includes two header fields. The "user header" is optional and can be employed to split the packet. If it is specified, the transporter will transfer it into a memory location different from the one used for the data portion of the packet, e.g., the user header into the system memory and the data portion into the user space. This solution eliminates the need for the host computer to move the data from one memory location to another each time a new packet is received. Indeed, the use of sockets is a

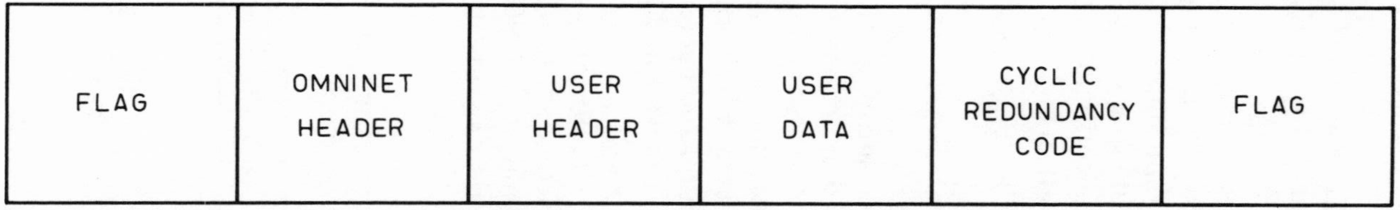

FLAG	OMNINET HEADER	USER HEADER	USER DATA	CYCLIC REDUNDANCY CODE	FLAG

Figure 9-6. The Omninet packet format: start and closing flags, network and user headers, information field, and CRC.

very important part of the Omninet architecture and should be given due attention.

In concluding this section, and prior to examining the socket mechanism, let's briefly restate why a LAN is so important. Until a few years ago, a computer-communications network generally meant a long-haul connection of a large number of terminals, geographically distributed across the country, to one or more central computers. Personal computer networks preserve the independence of each computer workstation while offering the possibility of sharing information and devices among the workstations on the network. A LAN is useful in almost all situations in which several people need to work together and share information.

THE USE OF SOCKETS

We have stated that four sockets are available and that they are evenly divided among the supported functions with and without control information (Fig. 9-7). The former contain the control address length and data group. Control information is very important. The Omninet software can split the data dynamically. The reason why this is vital is that the message includes control and data in the same packet. Given that each attached device has 4 sockets and the LAN accepts up to 64 of them, there can be 256 sockets in the system: 128 with control information and another 128 without. They are all uniquely defined. To set up a socket means to activate it to receive a message.

The disk server which handles the I/O for any device on the network needs more sockets; they are identified as B0, 80, 90, and A0

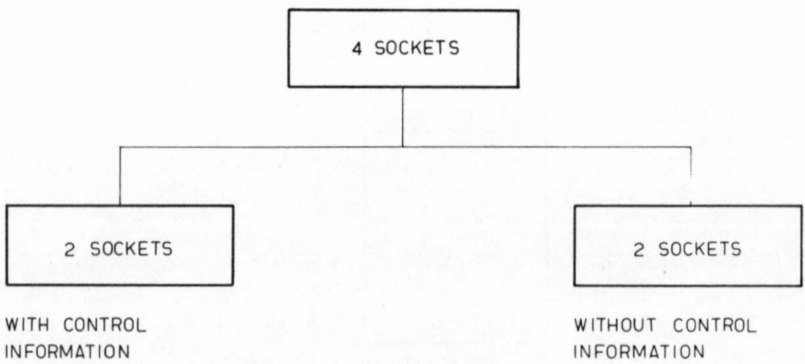

Figure 9-7. Omninet sockets with and without control information. Those with control information split the data dynamically.

(Fig. 9-8):

1. The B0 socket receives requests and queues them. It can handle up to 64 ID flashes.
2. The 80 socket is allocated to broadcasts. This facility makes it unnecessary to predetermine any transporter number for any device.
3. The A0 socket is dedicated to data.

To communicate processes AP 1, AP 2, . . ., AP *n*, respectively residing in WS 1, WS 2, . . ., WS *n*, must:

- Set up socket B0.
- Check socket B0.
- Check if a message is to be sent.
- If a message is to be sent, send it to socket B0.

If applications program (AP) 1 is compatible with AP 2 and both handle presentation on the screen, then any information on the one will be displayed on the other. Within this overall setup, the control is distributed. This enhances dependability, response time, and ease of access. In a star-type minicomputer structure (cluster) we have to go through the monitor to reach the information on the disk. This is not the case with LAN.

The approach has advantages; the critical question is to avoid updating the same record simultaneously by different devices. In the Omninet case, at this point the Constellation software comes into play by defining:

- *Users* who can log onto a terminal
- *Volumes*—areas of a disk
- An *access* mechanism which indicates the users and what they can access

The Constellation software allows multiple computers to share a Corvus disk system. A disk server is utilized when the Omninet local network is used. As stated, it contains both a transporter network interface and a Corvus disk system interface. Additional shared peripherals are added to Omninet in a similar manner. Compared with the distributed nature of Omninet, Constellation is a multiplexer

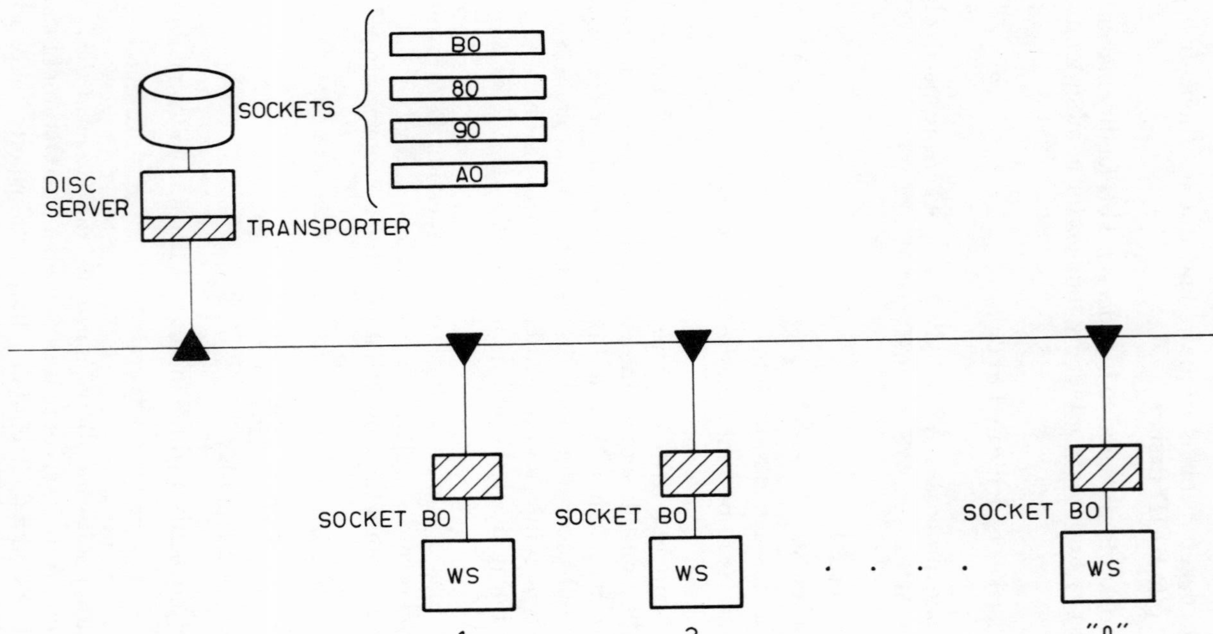

Figure 9-8. Implementing the Omninet four-socket approach at the level of the disk server and the workstations.

that interconnects up to 64 personal computers in an interactive multiuser network. Each PC enjoys high-speed access at 60 kBps to up to 80 MB of online Corvus hard disk capacity.

A multilevel security mechanism permits open or secured access to all or any portion of the database. It allows each computer to access the disk as if it were the only one connected, and the system incorporates sophisticated spooling techniques to permit printers and other peripherals to be shared. With both Constellation and Omninet, no computer needs to be allocated to network management, and each attached device can use its own single-user operating system.

The architectural approach of both systems leads to a hierarchy of access and usage rights:

1. System volumes (read only)
2. Private volumes (user only, read or write access)
3. Shared volume (multiple user, read or write access)

Control becomes most important in shared volume. It is achieved through *semaphores*, tables set up at disk level to tell who can use what. Technically, the semaphores are eight-character labels maintained at the system. The semaphores don't care what exactly we lock. We can lock records, files, printers, and so on. Also, there is no relation between semaphore and disk structure.

The described capabilities stop short of a rear-end machine (database, or DB, machine), though an independent supplier is offering rear-end capability as an add-on. Typically, a DB machine should handle all database requests and be able to monitor, journalize, and back up. Simple use, such as word processing, may not need the services of a DB machine, but DP-type applications might require such support. [The rear-end machine by Software Products International, of San Diego, California, runs on Omninet and uses semaphores. Not all micro-database management systems (DBMS) can take that approach.]

The capacities provided by a DBMS are best put to use by incorporating a second disk (or tape) facility for journaling. The Omninet design does not recommend duplicating all information elements (IE); also, the current LAN release does not support two sets of disk servers but handles daisy chains of four disks. It is, however, possible to have one machine and make it write twice.

A COMMUNICATIONS DISCIPLINE

When it comes to communications, the key to Omninet architecture is the use of gateways. The designers are working on modem servers

(MS) for five types of application:

1. IBM 2780/3780
2. A bridge through an (MS) to Omninet networks
3. Remote computer interconnection
4. X.25
5. IBM's System Network Architecture (SNA)

The MS for the 2780/3780 protocols is projected for 2.4- to 4.8-kbps lines, bisynchronous. The MS can handle up to eight modems of the remote point-to-point type. The MS works through spooling.

Regarding mainframe communications, primary emphasis is put on IBM compatibility, but other equipments also are served. The Omninet gateway, for instance, can be used for mainframes, minis, and microcomputers with supported communications protocols. For the SNA compatibility, the designers look to two different approaches: a connection which looks *as if* it were "local" and a remote batch approach. No video terminals are to be connected directly on the bus, because

- They need a transport and the cost is not justified.
- The simple video unit is slow and nonintelligent.
- The network is designed for communicating computers.

A combined DB/DC facility makes it possible for two networks to share a DB (Fig. 9-9). It is also possible to have a common printer which can print for both networks. That allows the use on either network of a "secure disk" dedicated to the applications while still sharing the common disk. This is also a solution to restricted access, without DBMS.

A product developed for the educational market is Apple Share; it makes possible the support of some 20 to 30 Apple IIs through a *network server* which is similar to the disk server. This setup accepts one to six floppy disks and a printer. Any one of the WS can use any one of the disks; the instructor can, through his or her station, put any message on the disk all users can share.

The importance of this application is that it constitutes a low-cost solution which can also help in data collection. The Omninet programmer's guide identifies the send-receive routines and diagnostics associated with applications and explains the network server and disk server requirements including pipes, semaphores, and mirror perspectives. Pipes permit spooling and intercommunication. Spooling

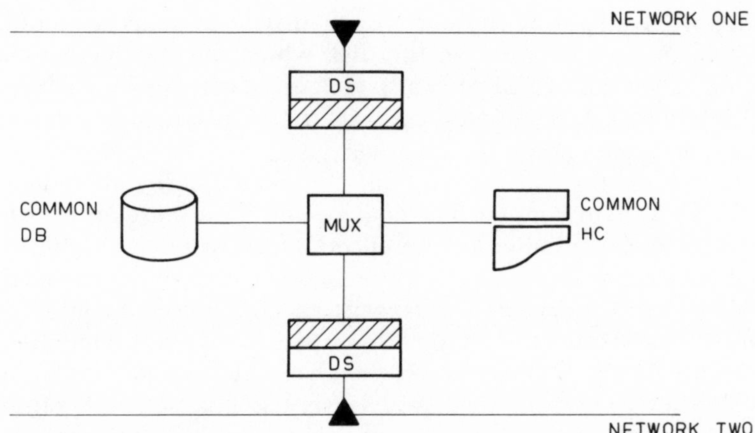

Figure 9-9. Common resources—database (DB) and hardcopy (HC) device—shared by Omninets through two disk servers (DS) and a multiplexer (MUX).

allows all computers in the network to share peripherals, such as printers. To provide a simple, yet effective, means of implementing spooling, the architecture assures data paths of pipes between the microcomputers.

A pipe is actually a first-in first-out (FIFO) buffer that is maintained in an assigned area of the disk and managed by the system controller. Since the data is stored on the disk, the two computers can proceed in a totally asynchronous manner. Pipes also permit computers to communicate with each other in a simple serial fashion. The sending computer transmits data into the input end of the pipe, and the receiving computer receives the data from the output end. This makes feasible the implementation of applications such as electronic mail.

Seen in a different way, the pipes are an area of a disk controlled by a disk controller. Say, Apple II and LSI-11 are on a given network. The LSI-11 does not communicate with the Apple II, but both can print on the same printer attached on the network. To assure an LSI-11–Apple communication we may either transfer data through a pipe on the disk (the software exists) or write the software for direct transfer. The code is not important; it can be ASCII or BCD.

Polyvalent approaches are feasible. Eventually, Omninet can have a disk with Pascal files and CP/M or other operating systems on it and support all of them. (Apple CP/M was not yet implemented at the time of writing but was expected soon.) Typical operating systems, such as CP/M, UCSD Pascal, and Basic, are single-user and file-oriented. To permit easy interface, the manufacturer provides I/O drivers for all supported operating systems. Each driver contains a mount table which designates areas on the disk which the specific computer is allowed to access. The table also contains a variable for each area that tells whether the computer can write to the area, read from the area, or is to be denied access to the area.

A volume that can be read but not written on by all computers is called a system volume. Personal volumes are those accessible only by a specific computer as referenced by its own mount table. Shared volumes are available in read-write mode to more than one computer. Multilevel security has several aspects. One is access control. Access in CP/M systems uses a floppy diskette drive at every computer. Each person wishing to access the system has a diskette to boot the system, which serves as a physical key. A user can give someone else access by handing over the key. Another access scheme (used in Apple DOS and Pascal) operates by providing passwords to modify the mount table. This assures a somewhat stricter security because it limits access to specific people and not just to specific computers.

The utilities can modify a user's mount table only after determining who the user is and whether the user knows the correct password. A special file lists which users can access which volumes. One user is designated the system manager and is the only person who can change the privileges of other users. When the computer boots, a log-in program checks the person's identity and supplies the mount table set by the system manager.

A further level of security for shared volumes is available in both read and write modes to more than one user, whose access is controlled by semaphores. Any WS can ask to lock a semaphore to limit or control access to the part of the file represented by the semaphore. The request is normally granted if no other computer has already locked it.

NEW DEVELOPMENTS WITH RELEASE 2

Reference has been made to Corvus preparation of an Omninet Release 2 for early 1983. One of the basic improvements with this release is the ability to handle a substantial variety of personal computers of 8, 16, and 32 BPW. Among them are the IBM PC and the Corvus Concept PC (32 BPW).

Another new development is the print server (spooler and despooler), which is available free of charge with every Corvus Omninet. The print server runs on Apple, but Corvus is also building a hardware box lower in cost than the PC that is able to support serial and parallel printers. More significant for network implementation is the development of a user-programmable communications server through Corvus hardware involving 64 kB, a Z-80, two serial ports, and a parallel port. To program it, the user may download through the LAN or employ a dedicated CRT.

Two LAN can be connected together through a *bridge,* which is an Apple II computer. The bridge reads pipe files from one disk and writes them on another. The solution helps sharing a printer, and it is good for small amounts of data.

The poor backup of the first release is also scheduled to be improved, first on the VCR itself. The National Panasonic NV 8200 model has an optional feature for connecting control signals. A program released in 1983 will first rewind tape and, if no tape is available, will say so, thus correcting a major shortcoming of the early release.

For this, as for all other networks, a much more secure database management is the double image on hard disk. Programming must assure that the update is on two different devices. This will not necessarily involve system software; it can be done through applications programs. A new release of Omninet will support multiple disk servers as a standard condition.

Still another solution is a daisy chain approach, which is easier to implement than the simultaneous double image. A routine must assure that each time a request goes to a disk drive it is modified to lead to a second request. If disk I fails, the server should address disk II and operate it as though it were disk I. (Figure 9-10 shows the two alternatives.)

Omninet also features an electronic mail service developed by Software Connections. The Mail Monitor uses a PC to provide the teletex functions. The software contains two programs:

- The "central post office," which runs on the dedicated PC
- The "local mailman," which runs on each user's PC

The post office program acts as the main distribution center. The mailman creates and sends letters and picks up mail distributed by the post office.

To send letters via the telephone company, the post office can, at a user-defined time, dial up another Mail Monitor to pass mail addressed to the remote site. The central post office always monitors a telephone line for any such incoming mail. From the local mail user's side, remote and local addresses are treated as if they are on a single integrated network. Without the dedicated PC, teletex operates as a

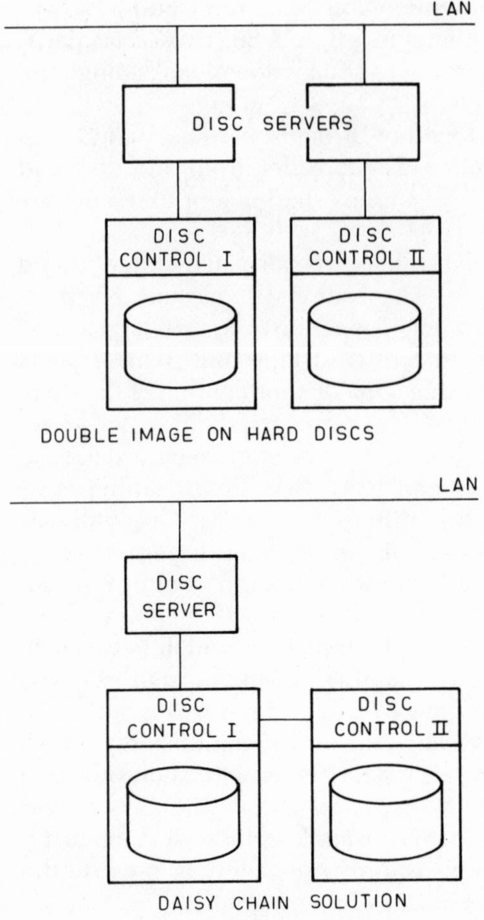

Figure 9-10. Two approaches to the creation of backup files on a LAN: double-image disks and a daisy chain solution.

batch-mode mail system: The local mailman program stores any mail on the network disk. This mail is not to be distributed and delivered until the post office program is executed.

There is also available a screen-oriented editor that the user can employ to create letters. A standard letter form is provided. One letter can be addressed to specific people or general distribution lists. Senders are notified when any letter has been received by everyone on the mail list. Data or text files may be sent along with the letter. A printer spooler utility is supplied as part of the software package.

10

CLUSTER ONE (Part 1)

Network Models and Technical Features

As with the Corvus systems and OMNINET architecture, we start this chapter on Cluster One with a brief description of the company behind the product. Nestar Systems was founded in 1978 with the objective of designing, manufacturing, and marketing a local area network: the Cluster One system. Cluster One Model A handles Apple II and III. (Discussions regarding the IBM personal computer were going on at the time of publication.)

In mid-1980, Nestar completed a financial agreement with Zynar Limited of London, a subsidiary of Rank Xerox. In addition to the financial ties between the two companies, Zynar and Nestar are engaged in ongoing joint development of hardware and software microcomputer products. Nestar's Cluster One Model A is marketed by Zynar in Western Europe under an exclusive arrangement. Rank believes Nestar should grow by more than 200 percent per year to reach a three-digit-million figure by 1985. The Nestar product line includes disks, multiplexers, and interfaces.

All Nestar products are based on personal computers for business use. The underlying philosophy is: "The larger the business, the better the customer. In the business world one needs more than the personal computer. It's a database world." The shared hard disk resolves a dilemma: a business can't have a copy of everything on floppy disks, yet it must have everybody interconnected. Through networks it is possible to:

- Specialize on different printers as required.
- Have better shared disk capacity. The bigger the disk, the lower the cost per byte.

Underlying facts of industrial life are adapted to by this approach. The business executives and their secretaries have no fear of personal computers because they play on them with the kids. And in the 1970s the power now on personal computers cost millions of dollars.

With local area networks, performance increases as delays shrink: Personal computers are dedicated to the single user. The reasons for movement away from time shared mainframes and minicomputers and toward personal computers are these:

- User-friendly approaches
- Price
- Reliability
- Performance
- Applications software

Personal computer software takes much less time to write, and off-the-shelf packages are much easier to find.

Today, however, it is estimated that only about 1 percent of some 2 million personal computers are networked. Nestar has some 400 installations worldwide, 100 of them in Europe. The number is growing and is expected to be 5 percent by 1985, together with a yearly population increase of 50 percent to 70 percent. The future is not with mainframes, but with personal computers and networks.

CLUSTER ONE MODEL A

Nestar's Cluster One Model A is a local area network based on the ether principle and optimized for the connection of low-cost Apple II and Apple III personal computers. The architecture was first announced in January 1980.

Model A supports up to 65 Apple IIs in a single network and offers:

- Direct station-to-station communication
- Online Nestar hard disk storage
- Shared printer
- Internetworking

The local area network features fairly sophisticated utilities and good reliability of data transmission. The attractive price/performance ratio has been an important motivating factor in applications.

Thanks to its modular design, Cluster One can be set up with as few as two stations and later be expanded:

- Through a communications server, multiple networks can be interconnected, both locally and at remote sites, to provide further growth potential.
- The file server function offers a range of storage capacities from an entry-level 1.2 MB floppy disk to over 4 gB (gigabytes) of hard disk storage (by using multiple file servers).
- A high-speed tape cartridge backup system allows up to 20 MB of hard disk storage to be backed up on a single tape cartridge in less than 12 min.
- Other specialized hardware and software functions can be integrated into the network without causing obsolescence.

The current product offering is based on the CSMA protocol, but Cluster One departs from the Ethernet standard:

1. The maximum data rate with Cluster One A (for Apple II) Ethernet goes to 10 Mbps but costs much more to implement.
2. No multiprogramming is supported on personal computers; hence, no multiplexing is necessary for I/O and processing.
3. Instead of coaxial cable, Cluster One uses 16-wire flat (ribbon) cable, which costs less than coaxial cable and is somewhat easier to install.

Of the 16 wires, 8 allow sending 8 bits in parallel. Hence, 250 kbps equal 31.25 kBps. The functional distribution of the wires is as follows:

- Eight for forward data
- Two currently unused; might be used for voice
- Six for control: three pairs with ground line

The other important parameters of the network are that the cable can be 330 m long and there are no repeaters yet supported. We will return to consider the technical characteristics in greater detail.

With Nestar software, stations can function as network servers and provide such direct services as shared disks and files, printers, and modems to all other stations. Cluster One offers unconstrained topologies, a modular design, and a range of server functions. Workstations are connected to the network through a Nestar network interface card and low-cost flat-wire cabling. Virtually any topology can be implemented to suit an individual user's environment. No modifications to the microcomputer are necessary to create a user or server station.

By adding the Nestar architecture, a stand-alone Apple computer becomes a network user or server station conforming to all protocols of the Apple operating systems: DOS 3.3 and Pascal 1.1. No reprogramming is necessary to use a range of programs written for the Apple. Local peripherals such as minidisks, lower-cost printers, and graphics tablets used by an individual Apple station can continue to be used without interference with or by the LAN.

Model A is evolutionary. Nestar's first generation product, the Cluster One Model 1, was designed with the educational customer in mind. It became an attractive alternative to having separate disks and other peripherals for each station. Still offered today, the Model 1 supports a combination of Commodore Pets, TRS-80s, and Apple IIs in the same local network. Design goals were met by providing four key benefits:

- Reliability of industrial-grade hardware
- Program library sharing
- Central management through a shared hard disk
- Expandability

As part of the network design of the Model One, a self-assigning address system was developed. Each device implements an identical interface, and this enables multiple devices to have separate and distinct addresses on a daisy-chained parallel bus. The problems of extra wires and address decoding are thereby avoided.

As Fig. 10-1 demonstrates, Cluster One supports a fully distributed control mechanism. There is no master-slave relationship among workstations, which communicate and cooperate with one another. Any number of stations—the servers—on a local network may provide services to other stations—the clients. (Note that this is a different terminology than that used with Omninet and with other LAN.)

Typical server functions are a mass-storage file system printer support, time-of-day clock translation of symbolic names into physical addresses, database management support, and gateways to other networks or computers. Servers may also be clients of other servers on the network. For example, the printer server may be a client of the file system server in the course of serving its own clients.

In general, servers are distinguished on the network by the software they run and any special hardware they contain. A station willing to listen to requests from other stations can use a higher-level protocol

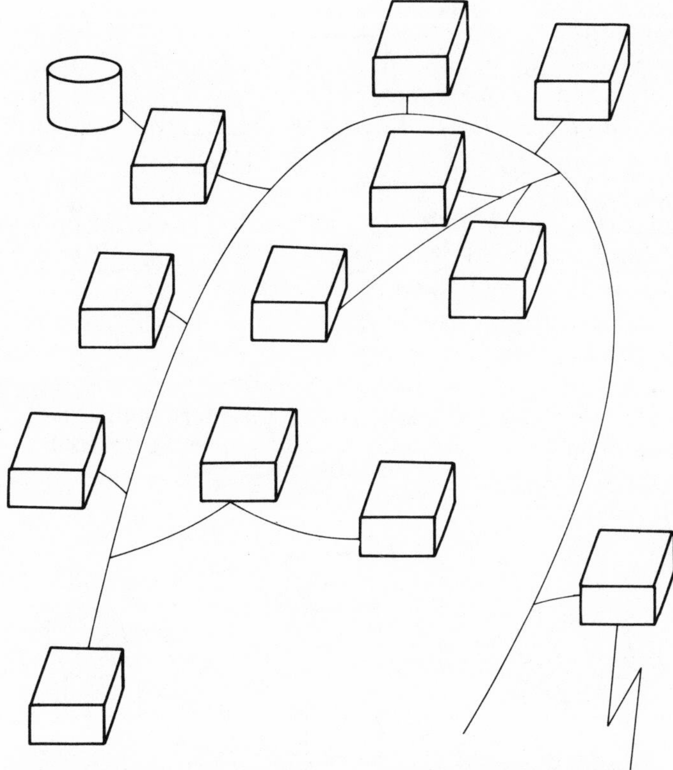

Figure 10-1. Cluster One supports a distributed environment of workstations, database and printer servers, and gateways. Workstations and control units are of the same make.

and perform a server function. To improve reliability, the logical functions of the servers are implemented through separate physical computers.

These references document that the network is fully distributed in terms of the functions supported. Alternatively, it would have been possible to merge all of the services into a larger centralized computer system with all its inconveniences (Fig. 10-2).

To recapitulate, experience with practical installations demonstrates the significant advantage of being able to communicate directly between user workstations without the need for a central controlling device. One or more of these stations can control mass storage devices which make data and software available to users of the network. By distributing control of the system over many components, the chances of a total network failure are reduced until they are

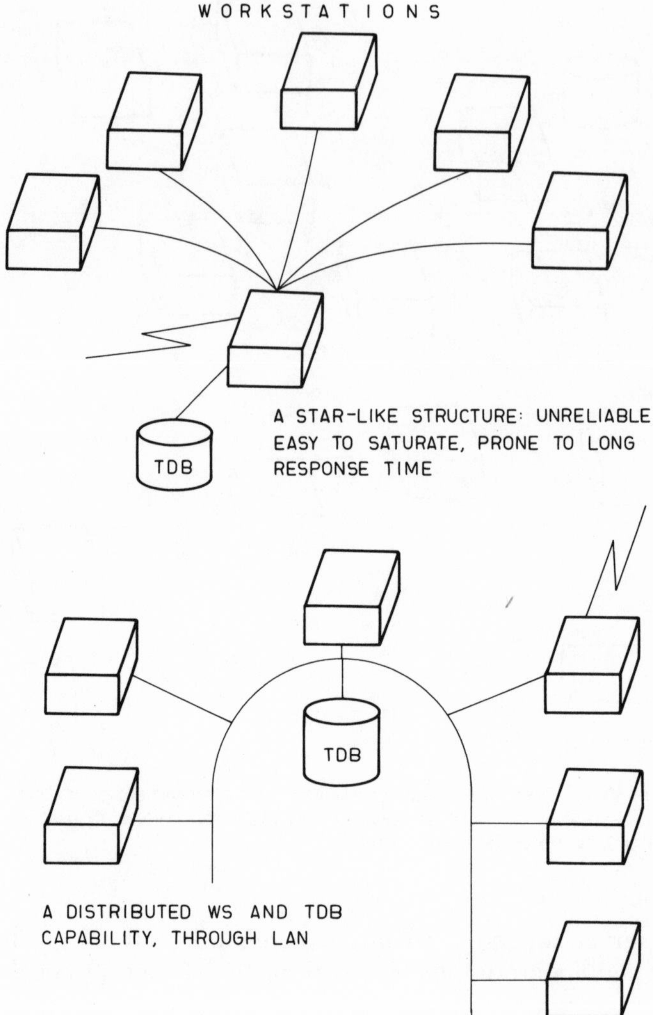

Figure 10-2. Comparison of a starlike system and workstations distributed through a LAN.

minimal. Computing in the 1980s will involve the pooling and sharing of storage and systems resources including databases. The cost-benefit advantages of sharing expensive resources among users are self-evident. Local area networks provide the opportunity of realizing them.

As for electrical noise, the worst environment encountered so far has been cabling run inside the main elevator shaft of a high-rise building, adjacent to major electrical wiring. No problems were experienced. For error-checking purposes, all packet transmissions between stations are fully controlled by the network routines, which automatically retransmit if there is any error in the data.

Environmental problems are eventually traced to the terminal devices, including personal computers. They may, for example, be subject to static problems. The network does not degrade reliability, but a proper study should always be made. If there are radiation problems that could impact the data on the wire, then the wire must be shielded.

In the general case, it is possible, through IBM-compatible protocols, to connect other than Apple microcomputers—a host for instance—but that will not be done interactively (Fig. 10-3). Nestar has stated that it will actually help the user to build software packages and add system features. It will also help exploit numerous possibilities of locally networked microcomputers, including communications to remote systems. For dealer and OEM agreements, it provides liberally discounted pricing, service and sales training seminars, full product documentation, customer software support, field service support, and leasing and rental programs.

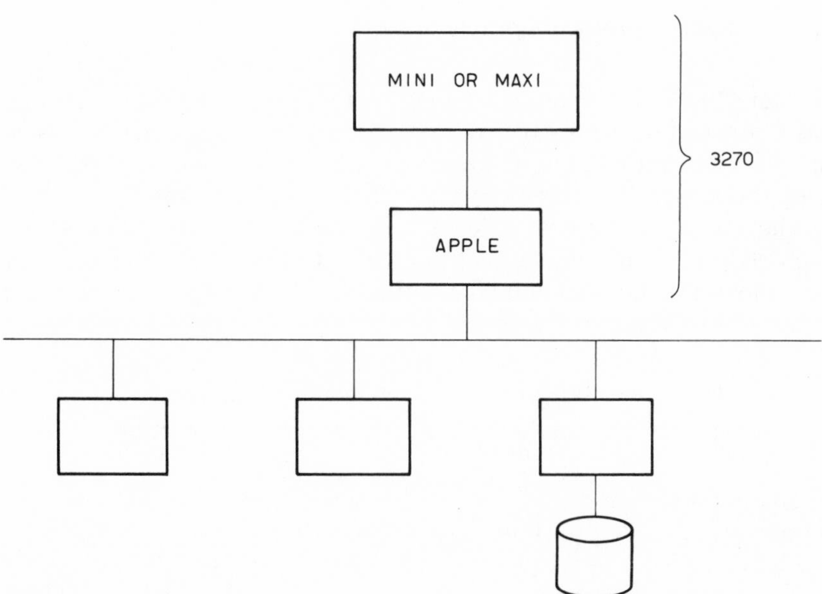

Figure 10-3. Possibility of connecting maxi- or minicomputers to a LAN through a PC interface.

SUPPORTED TECHNICAL FEATURES

The technical features supported by Cluster One or any other local area network should be viewed from the overall applications perspective. Microcomputer networks interconnect two major trends: the personal computer and the communications technology. The weaknesses of stand-alone personal computer use in business and industry are basically five in number. First, although the process cost has been greatly reduced, that is not true of the mechanical parts. Second, with stand-alone systems the information is not easily shared. Third, the software is not as sophisticated as that available with mainframes. Fourth, communications are not always encouraged. Fifth, there is a lack of standards. These weaknesses can be corrected by building and implementing a LAN.

The local area network improves system performance through its

- Interconnect channel
- Reasonable distance for WS attachments
- Topological independence
- Fast response time
- Modularity and extensibility
- Good reliability
- Layered protocol approaches

Cluster One is an example, as Fig. 10-4 shows. The design strategy has been to build on existing components (microcomputers, disks, printers), permit existing software modules to use the network, and keep the network architecture very close to the hardware.

The bus topology is simple: A long length of flat cable runs past each station, which is connected to it at the nearest point and can be removed without affecting any other WS. A station can be added in either of two ways:

- The bus can be split and a new station inserted.
- Taps can be installed while stations are transmitting.

Even temporary shorts will only garble some packets, and they will be retransmitted once the short is removed.

Figure 10-5 demonstrates the use of the clusterbus to interconnect workstations and servers. As previously stated, all attached devices have been standardized on Apple II microcomputers, including the interconnect units which serve as repeaters. The ether-type wiring is

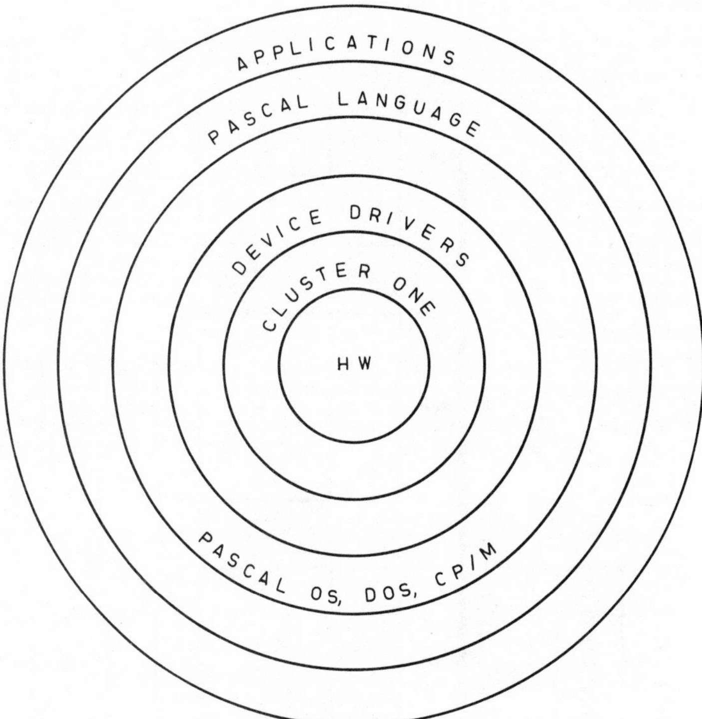

Figure 10-4. Successive support rings in and around a LAN: hardware device drivers (software), operating systems, languages, and applications.

divided into 330-m legs. There is no limit to the number of repeaters to guarantee intertalk.

The Cluster One 250-kbps data speed seems to be the highest rate that can be supported by a software-driven network interface running on a host personal computer and based on an 8-bit processor such as the 6502 in the Apple II, without large amounts of supporting hardware. According the Nestar, this speed allows normal network transaction traffic generated by Apple II computers to be handled easily.

The cable with 16 parallel wires (in either a flat form or packaged twisted pairs) requires only minimum-cost hardware drivers. It permits eight times the network throughput of a bit serial cable, since data is sent as 8 bits in parallel, or 1 byte at a time. The horizontal architecture sees to it that there can be no critical devices to impair either reliability or performance of the network. The Model A has no central controllers, polling multiplexers, or any other components that cannot be powered off while the network is running.

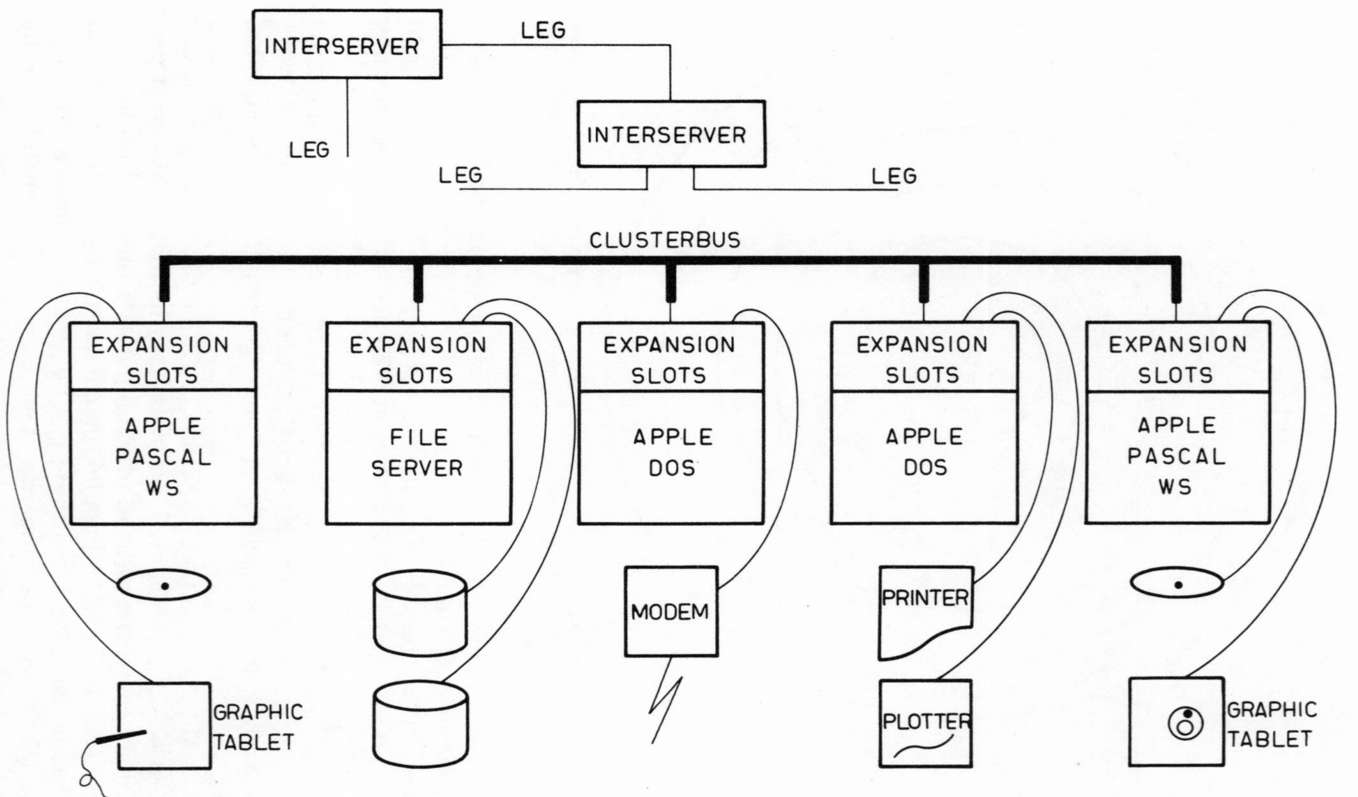

Figure 10-5. Interconnecting workstations, file server, modem, printer-plotter, and graphic tablets to a Cluster One bus.

Direct station-to-station communication is possible without the intervention of a central controller. There are passive connections, and the network interconnection scheme permits connections to be made and broken without affecting network operation. The network configuration is not constrained to straight-line, ring, or any other fixed configuration. Legs and WS can be added to the existing Model A network anywhere as they are needed.

We will be talking of software in a later section, but here we note that, according to Nestar, complete software is provided with the network so that large amounts of programming are not needed to use the system. The network software is just transparent to existing local operating systems, so that no operating system redesign is needed. The architectural routines look after synchronizing shared resources, interactive operation, electronic mail, and other applications. One example is The Messenger, an easy-to-use teletex program offered to users of the Cluster One Model A local network. It incorporates commands with user-friendly procedures, all of which facilitate the system's use by the novice and eliminate the need for special training. The Messenger integrates into standard office chores and enhances interoffice communications.

The Messenger can operate in conjunction with word processing, data collection, data management, and data processing packages to disseminate information effectively in the organization. It supports screen-based desktop workstations, operational hardcopy from shared printer resources, modular expansion with low incremental cost, electronic filing and recall, and time-shifted communications so there is no need to retry if the recipient is engaged. It handles color graphics, emulates the conventional in-tray, and provides the tools for instantly dealing with memoranda. Security is assured through password protection, automatic timestamps, and electronic receipts. Message switching to remote locations is realized by a communications server. Sample commands are help, send, read, check, answer, forward, display, list headings, write, and classify. Electronic messaging is a fundamental facility of a LAN. All LANs with gateways and teletex capability should be looked at as distributed information systems based on PCs.

As the system develops, the range of supported protocols is being enlarged in two ways: through Nestar's own development and by means of add-ons contributed by independent software firms. As Table 10-1 shows, the results are reasonably good but not perfect. For instance, there are several alternatives to Cluster One, each with a problem.

The 3780 protocol is officially supported by Nestar. The firm has

TABLE 10-1 LAN DATACOMMUNICATIONS PROTOCOL

Packet solution	Language	OS	Protocol	Remote Batch or interactive	Main problem	Vendor
Visiterm	Basic	DOS	S/S	Remote batch, Interactive	Can only transmit block equal to record length—one at a time	Personal Software (Calif.)
Linkline	Pascal	UCSD	S/S	Interactive, remote batch	Uses Apple II mem. as a buffer. The upper file limit is 22,000 bytes	Planning Consultancy (London)
Owlsync	Pascal	UCSD	BSC (3780)	Remote batch	There are several dialects of 3780	Owl (London)
Datalink	Pascal	UCSD	S/S	Still to be tested		Link systems (Calif.)

also helped two OEM customers with CDC and Burroughs mainframes to interconnect. The 3270 server will make a station user operate as a 3278 terminal, but this release will not support color graphics. What is important, however, is that the software will be offered off the shelf.

The limited-distance nature of local networks brings into perspective the need for internetwork links, or gateways. They may be high-speed links for networks that are close to each other, or they may depend on a telecommunications network for reliable transmission of data from city to city. Given the multiplicity of emerging network technology and the variety of communications protocols in use, gateways must be provided to permit stations on one type of network to exchange information with others on a different type or speed of network. Both electrical and software protocols must be converted when passing data through gateways.

The Cluster One architecture now supports Nestar-to-Nestar gateway capabilities; the next step is Nestar to mainframes. At the workplace itself, a number of devices such as banking terminals can be connected. For instance, passbook updating can be done the way the printer server now works: through an asynchronous connection.

Through an asynchronous 300-bps interconnection, the Cluster One to mini and mainframe data communication is already supported. Citibank is successfully using it in its London Forex installation. And as a cognizant executive remarked: "If one needs to double the capacity, he simply adds a second Apple computer. However, it will be a bad practice to do so: The LAN must work with the local DB; the communication to an eventual host should be the exception."

Cluster One versus Omninet

In the preceding two chapters we have considered the technical characteristics of Omninet and LAN. To help bring into perspective how the two networks compare with each other, Table 10-2 lists the features supported by each with reference to 18 basic criteria to be used in the study and the choice of a LAN.

The reference to the supported personal computers is important. Though the other 17 criteria seem to weigh toward the Cluster One LAN architecture, Omninet supports a variety of personal computers that work with the CP/M operating system, have a Z-80 microprocessor, and feature the S-100 bus.

This is the beginning of a de facto standardization. Hardware standards contribute to easy system assembly. The first microcomputer system, MIT's Altair, plugged into a 100-pin bus which came to be called the S-100 bus. Most of the early microcomputer manufacturers

TABLE 10-2 A CONTRAST: CLUSTER ONE AND OMNINET

	Cluster One	Omninet
Speed	240 kbps	1 Mbps
Protocol	CSMA/CD	CSMA
Carrier	Flat wire	Twisted pair (RS-422)
Stated maximum length	330 m	1330 m
Number of WS	65	64
Internetworking—no. of other nets	7	—
Storage facility	Disk and tape	Disk
Basic/Pascal DB	Dynamic division	Static division
Organization of data on DB	Directory/path name	—
File server	Up to 65	1 up to 40 MB
Security	Higher	Lower
Printer server	Up to 65	1
Printer per server	3	1
Spooling capability	Yes	No
Print in the night	Yes	No
Viewdata support	Yes	No
Supported personal computers	Apple II	Apple II, but also all Z-80 with S-100 bus
Specific AP	Micromoduler	—
	Messenger	—

developed their products around the bus to provide for ready availability of peripheral devices. Trade sources estimate that there are roughly 400,000 microcomputer systems that employ the S-100 bus even though none of the current leaders—Apple, Tandy, and so on—employs this bus structure.

NESTAR'S PLAN 4000

In early 1983, Nestar Systems announced a new local area network for personal computers called Plan (for PC, LAN) 4000. It is based both on Ethernet's Internet Transport Protocol, and on Datapoint's Arcnet. It uses hubs at the hardware level and implements the ISO/OSI layers 1 and 2 of the Arcnet. The access protocol is token passing. Internet is used for layers 3 and 4.

This is the first time two different network technologies have been incorporated in a single LAN. Introduced in 1977 by Datapoint as a proprietary network to interconnect its office equipment, the company in 1982 released its network for general use, putting it in competition with Ethernet. (See also Chaps. 12 and 13.) Plan 4000 supports a spider technology without loops.

The new LAN carries data at 2.5 Mbps on up to 4 miles of IBM 3270–compatible coaxial cable. In this setup, the data transmission capability of Ethernet has been integrated with the sender-receiver link of a token-passing system:

- Acceptable microcomputers are the IBM PC, Apple II, and Apple III.
- The Ethernet protocol will map out a token scheme at the first two layers of the seven-layer ISO/OSI reference model.
- The Arcnet hardware, which includes serial data transmitters and receivers, will harness the Ethernet preamble and filler frames to modify and pass on (read and accept) a system-generated token.
- Disk storage is available in 60- and 137-MB formatted capacity—up to four drives offering 548 MB per file server.

At the first two layers, Plan 4000 functions as if it were a ring while preserving the minimum frame length of the Ethernet statement and its ability to transmit over single-wire coaxial cable. At higher layers, the Ethernet protocol remains intact, allowing error-free identification of source and destination and also data messages of up to 1500 bytes.

In this design, the Ethernet frame provides 2.8 μs for the token to pass from station to station if no data are to be transmitted. In operation:

1. A token addresses the receiver and asks whether it has buffer memory available.
2. The receiver responds yes or no.
3. If no, the token passes to the next station along the line.
4. If yes, the sender waits for the appropriate check sum to verify that the message was received correctly.

The Ethernet protocol provides the formats for transmitting data over coaxial cable in addition to allowing treeing and branching of the system with modular additions or subtractions. Token passing takes care of busy carriers when contention risks create a bottleneck in text and data transmission. In this sense, the token-passing mechanism promotes network efficiency by requiring the receiver to state whether buffer memory is available. No time is wasted in trying to send data to an already loaded station, which may occur with a collision detection system.

However, this technical solution also involves some compromises. Unlike Ethernet, which employs carrier-sensing multiple access running at 10 Mbps for the physical and data link layers, Arcnet runs at 2.5 Mbps. On the other hand, Nestar maintains that PLAN 4000 can support up to 255 terminals. (The claim should, however, be taken with great reservation. It is wise to implement the network at a small fraction of what the manufacturer says it can accept.)

Nestar expects that most of the systems will go to the Fortune 2000 companies looking for extensive computing resources. To that end, the new LAN offers file servers that range in size: Hard disk storage capacities start at 60 MB and run up to 548 MB on a single server. The system can support multiple servers and, according to the manufacturer, permit virtual disks of unlimited size including multiple password, file protection schemes, and error checking and recovery.

A print server supports multiple printers and provides automatic print spooling. It offers user-selectable job priorities and queue inquiry. Gateways include:

- A 3270 emulator for interfacing network stations and mainframes
- A file transfer server (FTS) that permits the exchange of files between other Nestar networks or stand-alone workstations

- A gateway server that permits realtime packet transmission between networks
- An electronic mail service and a telephone company server

Interfaces will initially be available for the IBM PC at $595. Each PC requires a single interface card which plugs into an expansion slot in the IBM unit. Other beneficiaries of this combination are the Apple II and III personal computers, which can be linked in star and horizontal configurations. The interface cards include three custom chips for recognizing token-passing algorithms and for pulse shaping and modulation of baseband transmission. Also on board are power-up diagnostics and 2048 (4 times 512) bytes of buffer memory. A Motorola 68000 microprocessor is used with the file server. Plan 4000 supports a variety of personal computer operating systems, including UCSD Pascal IV and PC DOS 1.1.

11

CLUSTER ONE (PART 2)

Hardware, Software, File Access, and Response Time

HARDWARE OFFERING

We have spoken of servers, interservers, and connections to the network. Servers are any of the microcomputer stations which have been outfitted with a Nestar server function program; software permits them to provide direct services to all other stations on the LAN. Commonly used servers are:

1. The file server for shared disk files
2. The print server for spooled printing
3. The communications server for remote terminal and mainframe access
4. The database management server
5. The file transfer server which transfers files within and between networks
6. The internetworking server

As stated earlier, the servers and workstations are connected to the network's flat wire through taps. Servers are active elements; taps and connector bypasses (Fig. 11-1) are passive elements. Among the hardware products provided by Nestar to assure hook-up and enhance the databasing–data communication capability are network card A 2701, 2, 3, 4; disk drives; dual floppy units; tape drives, and network clock cards.

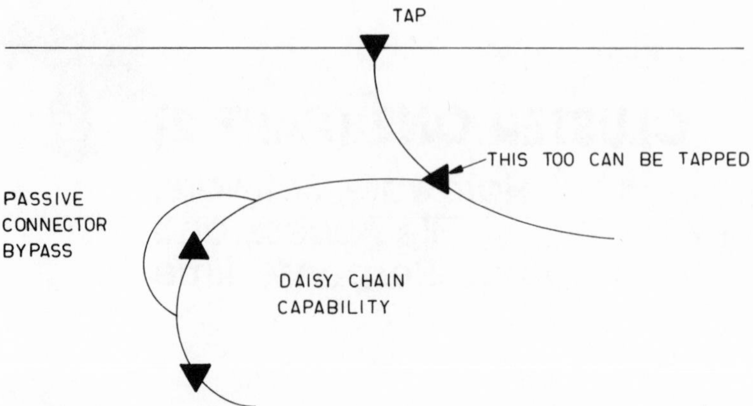

Figure 11-1. Tapping on the Cluster One flat wire: bypass and daisy chain solutions.

Network Card A 2701, 2, 3, 4

Network card A 2701, 2, 3, 4, available for just under $400, is designed for hook-up of two kinds of stations on the network: user and server. The latter relates to utilities, e.g., servers with programs to manage disk drives. Models A 2701, 2, 3, 4 are the same card, which can be customized. Any card on the network has a connection to Apple for power supply, but some (like the file server) need ROM capability.

The Nestar interface card includes an Apple II interface, a bus transceiver, protocols in 2K of ROM, 16K of buffer, an 8-bit address, and recognition logic. Each station is uniquely addressable through the network interface hardware and logic. User and service stations are connected in parallel along the 16-line unshielded bus that is tapped and connected to an interface card installed in an Apple II built-in expansion slot.

In addition to the network interface card, a station may have interface cards in other expansion slots. Any station, then, may tie to printers, plotters, modems, floppy disks, hard disks, graphics tablets, card readers, and the like, because each user station can control external devices for its own local use. When these external devices are network resources, special server software residing in the station is activated.

Local devices, such as printers, remain locally available until the server software takes over and controls printer allocation. When operated in the network environment, the Apple II has better response than when used as a stand-alone. Network printers, disk storage devices, and other resources perform much better than those normally attached to the stand-alone Apple II.

Disk Drives

Disk drives are of two types: A 2002, 16½ MB, and A 2003, 33 MB. The A 2002 central disk storage on Cluster One is the 14-in 16.5-MB Winchester. Software makes it look like a large set of virtual minidisks indistinguishable from the 5¼-in floppy disk employed at local Apple II stations.

The A 2003 allows users to store and to have fast easy access to large data files. It is the common medium for the delivery of application software to all users of the network; it facilitates security protection of applications and data and allows for central maintenance of software. The unit's formatted capacity of 33 MB comes equipped with all necessary interfaces, power supplies, cooling, and software. Two A 2003 units can be connected together to run from one server, and the same thing is true of the A 2002.

Dual Floppy Disk A 2001 Unit

The dual floppy disk A 2001 unit with 1.26 MB helps to connect to other computers. It is designed to provide inexpensive storage and utilizes dual double-sided 8-in flexible diskettes. In that way it provides 1.26 MB of online storage capacity. Its uses include offline software distribution and maintenance. The A 2001 is supplied complete with interface cards, cabling, power supplies, cooling, and the network file server software.

Tape Drive A 2401 (Streaming Tape)

IBM uses tape drive A 2401 and stores 300 kB on it. Nestar brought it up to 20 MB; the software will inform the server to automatically switch if the disk is 33 MB. Save and restore routines are available. The software save and restore capability comes with the tape drive.

From an applications standpoint, the Model A 2401 offers a low-cost, high-performance backup to users of Cluster One Model A. The high-speed cartridge tape drive uses ¼-in, 450-ft tape cartridges which hold formatted data. Operating in the "streaming" mode, it can record 8000 bits per inch at 30,000 Bps, making it possible to write 20 MB of data on one cartridge in under 12 min. The tape drive operates from Nestar's network file server, which requires less than 10 min to create or restore a backup tape for the Nestar 16.5-MB Winchester hard disk. The streaming drive incorporates two key features:

- An incremental backup and restore which permits the user to back up only the sections of the disk that have been modified since the previous backup.

- Error checking of data as it is being recorded on tape. This is accomplished by double tape heads. One writes the data; the second reads and verifies the newly written data.

If an error is detected, a signal is given to rewrite the block in question. This is accomplished through cyclic redundancy check (CRC) recording for error detection. Nestar says that the soft error rate is less than one in 10^8 bits (one bit in 12 MB) and hard error rates less than one in 10^{10} bits, or one bit in 1200 MB.

Network Clock Card A 2101

The network clock card A 2101 is installed in one of the file servers. Recall that customers can establish two file servers in order to have a duplicate online. Wiring connections with a distinction between data and address bits, host interface, and the network cable are shown in Fig. 11-2.

Figures 11-3 and 4 show basic technical characteristics of the Cluster One Model A local area network. Figure 11-3 shows the connection of two disk drives, a tape drive, and two floppy disks to the Apple-based server and the possible user-server interactions involving file, print, and interconnecting servers. Figure 11-4 shows the ability of the printer server to support multiple networks. Typically, the printer server listens to the network for "wake-up" messages, periodically interrogates print request queue (or file server), and finds and then prints the requested files. In this case LAN 1 and LAN 2 are connected through the same modem server. The latter also communicates with remote LAN 3, through the proper modem server interface, as well as with remote Apple II workstations. The supported line discipline is both synchronous and asynchronous.

SOFTWARE DEVELOPMENT

The ability of a microcomputer to sell itself to the user population lies in its applications library and that is true of a local area network also. Cluster One Model A network coordination is handled through a combination of mechanisms. Software supplied with the network allows for control of the network resources through rights controllers and network processes by synchronizing controllers. This software is run on an Apple II station, the file server, which also controls the disk drives. As described at the end of the preceding section, the shared resources of the network include the disk system, line printer, and modem. The file server implements rights controls to these resources

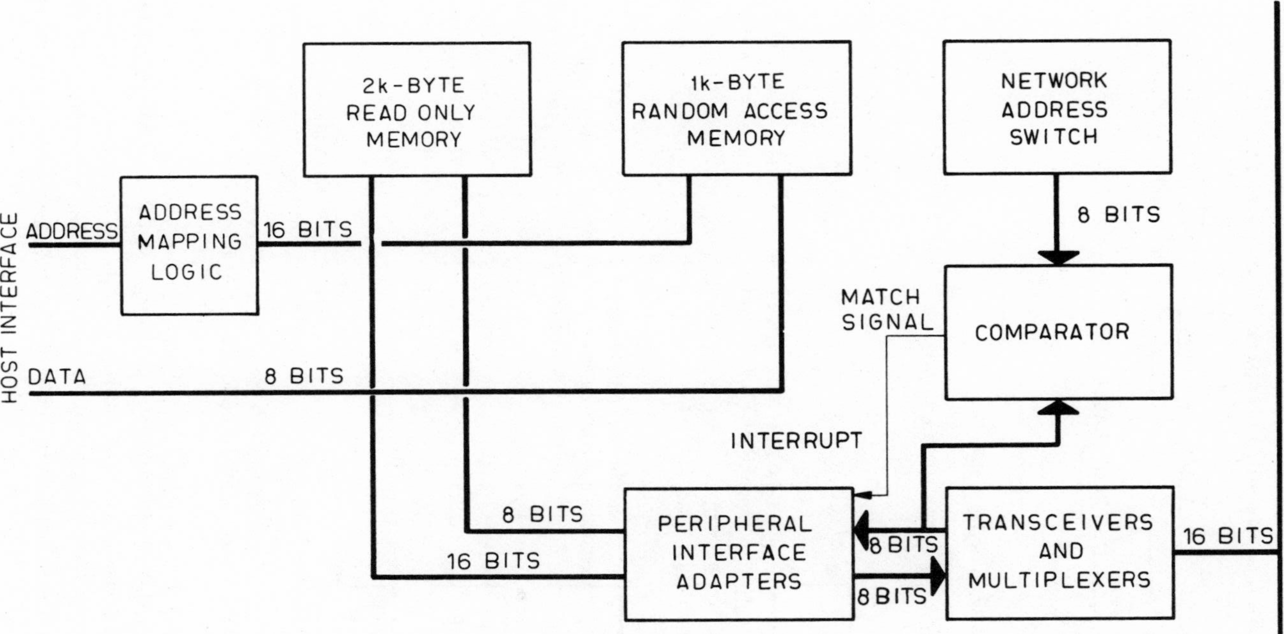

Figure 11-2. Wiring connections with a distinction between data and address bits, host interfaces, and the network cable.

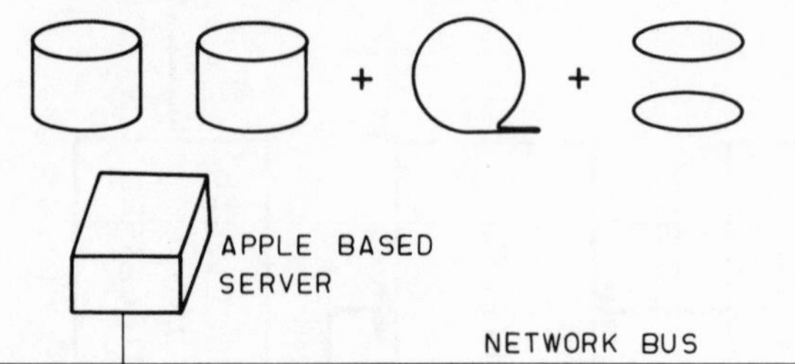

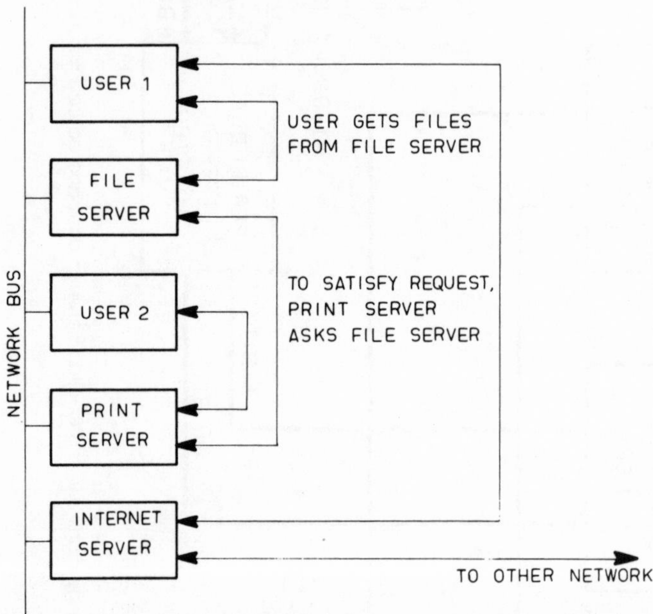

Figure 11-3. Connection of two disk drives, a tape drive, and two floppy disks and procedural reference to user-server interactions.

through the use of passwords, privilege control, and usage control. The first two rights controls apply strictly to disk files.

A password can be assigned to protect any disk file. Once it has been assigned, the file server will not allow a station to mount the file unless the password is presented. The right to create, read, write, insert, and delete files is governed by the privilege control software.

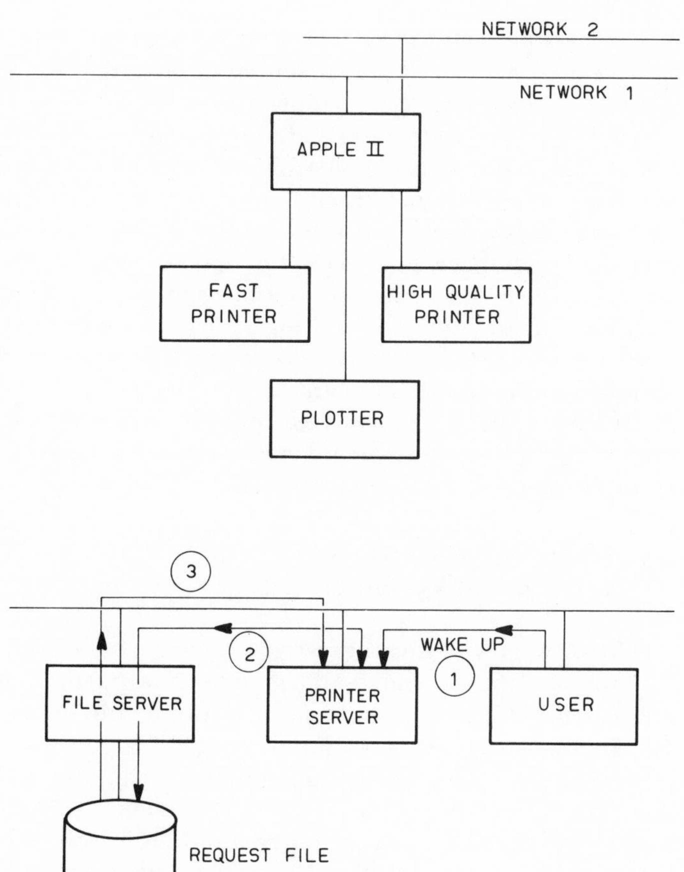

Figure 11-4. The print server supports multiple networks. It also drives two different printers and a plotter.

When a station first accesses a file, it can voluntarily limit the file privileges. Alternatively, the privileges can be assigned by the password. Some stations can be limited to read-only access rights; others may have both read and write access. Usage control permits a station to gain exclusive or shared rights to a file or lock to which no other station in the network is allowed access, thus assuring a security mechanism.

The lock command is the key to synchronizing controls on a network basis. It is needed when two or more of the workstations have the same access rights to a network resource, typically a disk file. Sequential access must be enforced. A shared resource such as a disk file or a printer can have a lock associated with it; this logical facility can be held by an individual station or shared with several stations through exclusive or shared rights.

To guarantee orderly sequential operation on the shared resource, the station requesting it must obtain the lock to the device before initiating a transaction. Once it holds the lock, access by other stations can be denied. Locks are used by the network software to control access to the shared database for updates and to regulate orderly access to the line printer and the modem. Rights privileges prevent stations from accidentally writing to a production file; they are also used for development work and production work to be carried out simultaneously on the network.

Hence, to the list of five basically physical products listed in the preceding section we should add a sixth and seventh which are software-based and run on Apple II computers:

- The network file server
- The network print server

The efficiency of this software is shown in the modularity, reliability, response time, and overall computer power which can be supported. As Fig. 11-5 demonstrates, gateways provide the necessary interface to remote workstations and other LAN servers. This is the eighth crucial facility. As a bridge to another Cluster One network, Nestar uses the file transfer server (FTS). This module was operating at the time of publication but was not generally released. It can be used to interconnect one or two other Nestar networks to make an aggregate of separate systems. This is a cabled-in connection.

The ninth necessary feature is the line access protocol. All communication between workstations and servers on the Cluster One network is direct, with a carrier-sensing algorithm in the ROM executing network-based protocols in each station interface. Such an interface is passive; hence, stations may be added to or removed from the network during operation. In the Model A network, the carrier-sensing function is implemented by using a *dedicated control line*, which indicates the bus is busy.

The devices attached to the network do not transmit until they see that the line is available. Hence, it is not necessary to perform full collision detection. The bus interface permits reading the data just written.

- At the start of a packet transmission the address of the station attempting to send is first put on the bus and then read back.

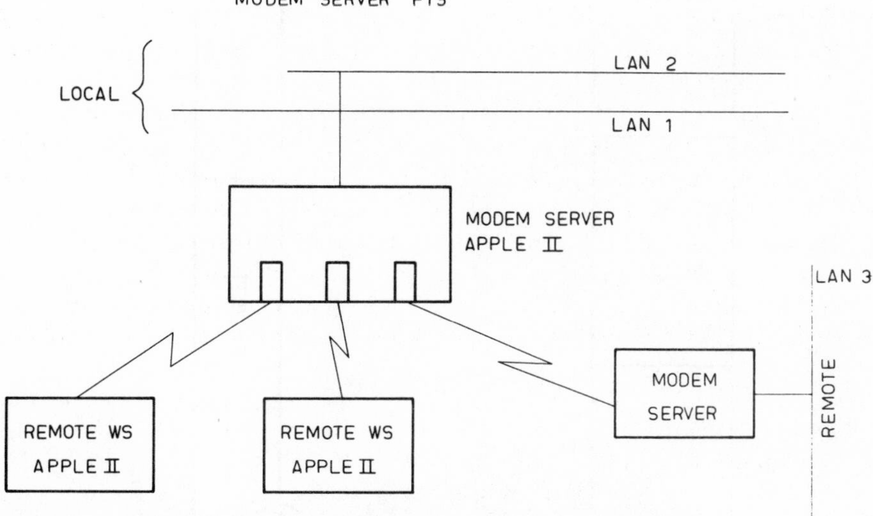

Figure 11-5. Role of the file transfer server (FTS) in interconnecting Cluster One networks. (This role has been extended to that of a gateway toward other systems.)

- When two stations do that simultaneously, at least one will not read back its own address and will detect a conflict.

This rarely happens, however, since each station has a random-waiting algorithm that helps avoid collisions that would occur at the end of a preceding transmission. Once the initial collision detection has occurred, the carrier signal is established and further collision detection is not necessary. The rest of the packet is sent, like Aloha, without collision detection. After the initial check, later collisions result mainly from erroneous stations.

Nestar has claimed that the data transfer rate in the network stands at 86 percent efficiency. The maximum burst rate (theoretical) is 30 kbps, and the maximum sustaining rate (per individual workstation) is 26 kbps.

Finally, the tenth vital feature of the LAN architecture is the packet format: a packet-switching datagram option has been chosen. Figure 11-6 presents the packet format. It works on an acknowledged datagram basis. The handshake assures acceptance. The CRC polynominals say whether the packet is correct. Note the ACK/NACK byte; before the bus is released, packet reception must be acknowledged.

Each packet of data being transmitted contains initial header information followed by up to 256 bytes of data and a 16-bit check sum. Once the packet is transmitted, the receiving station immediate-

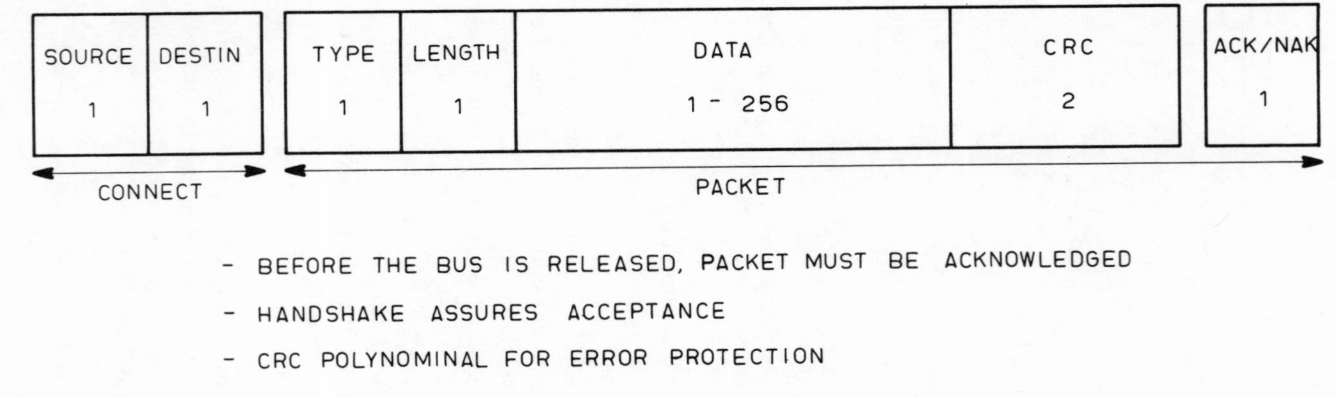

Figure 11-6. Packet-switching format for Cluster One, in bytes. The choice is datagram.

ly acknowledges the receipt of the packet if the CRC check sum matches the data. If not, it requests a retransmission.

The cyclic redundancy check error control algorithm is completely contained in the ROM-based protocols on the Nestar interface. It permits higher levels of software to work with reliable and correctly sequenced data. The ROM protocols are also responsible for taking messages longer than the 256-byte packet size and splitting them into network compatible sizes.

A single-packet transmission consists of the source and destination addresses and the packet identification, followed by data, check sum, and acknowledgment. Multiple packets can be sent between one set of connect and disconnect operations. In a broadcast environment there is no routing. In multiple-packet transmission packet 2 is never sent until packet 1 is acknowledged.

The data link layer protocol defines how the information is formed into discrete data units. There are rules for forming data packets, doing media access scheduling, addressing, and error handling. Important functions of the data link layer protocol are detecting and possibly correcting errors occurring in the physical layer, controlling the data flow to prevent overloading of the network, and providing network access and acknowledgment capabilities to ensure the correct transmission and receipt of the data units or packets. The physical and data link layer protocols are implemented through hardware and firmware (in ROM) memory on the network interface board.

The higher-level network layers are implemented with host software by using the facilities provided by the two lower levels. The next level of sophistication is to manage another network through telephone lines. This poses both software and data communication problems. At a rate of 31.250 kBps, we need 2 s to empty an Apple II on the local network. If we use a 300-baud telephone line, then it may take 2 h just to empty an Apple.

Transmission problems are much simpler on the bus: The interface to the flat wire of the network is assured through transceiver-multiplexers that allow the data being put on the cable to be read back at the same time. It is this read-while-write facility which makes it possible for collisions to be detected when more than one station attempts to gain access to the network cable at the same time: The immediate read-back will be garbled if the data entering the network collides with transmissions already in transit on the cable.

Flexibility results from the autostart facility in the network. The system can be so configured that specific stations, when turned on, automatically download specific programs to themselves or other stations from a network file server. The action makes possible no-operator server stations, turnkey applications, and publicly available stations. A good part of the error tolerance is due, in part, to negative acknowledgment of successful transmission to be sent back to the sender with no significant delay. If the packet must be retransmitted, this happens immediately.

Instantaneous acknowledgments considerably simplify the higher levels of the transmission protocol, since they assure that a packet that has been successfully transmitted has also been successfully received. Though datagram principles are followed, packets are never received out of order, and transmit-data buffers can thus be freed as soon as the packet is sent.

The simplest message on the network is a one-way, single-packet communication (datagram). Most communication between stations often requires a conversation consisting of several datagrams flowing in both directions. This virtual circuit type of connection can be accomplished without interruption over relatively long time spans by cooperating processes sending datagrams back and forth to each other. For short-term conversations, network overhead can be avoided by permitting multiple-packet two-way physical connections on the network.

The multiple-packet capability permits the construction of indivisible operations analogous to the standard read-modify-write memory cycle necessary for synchronization of multiple independent processes. Semaphores and test set flags can thus be implemented within the network. Another way to view the multiple-packet connection is as a short-duration nonmultiplexed virtual circuit established between two stations. Correspondingly, long-duration time-multiplexed virtual circuits must be implemented in a higher-level protocol. For instance, file transfers or program loads can be accomplished through a sequence of individual packet transmissions which are transparent to the ordinary user.

Collision coverage is necessary because two or more stations may try to access the cable at the same time, e.g., because of the nonzero transmission and detection time of a newly asserted carrier.

- Collisions are detected by software during the first several bytes of packet transfer.
- The colliding stations back off, jam the cable, and wait before retrying.
- Later collisions during transmission of the packet are unlikely because the carrier line is asserted.

To speed up the data transmission, later collisions are not checked, but they are detected by bad check sums at the end of the colliding packets. Both colliding packets must be retransmitted.

We have mentioned interface software and hardware resources supported by the network. The A 2801 Network File Server supports the IBM 2780/3780 standard, and at the time of publication there was in development a routine to assure compatibility with the IBM protocol 3270. The electronic mail program we made reference to is available under code A 2802, and the network printer server is the A 2803.

The Cluster One network interface software is automatically merged into the operating system of the personal computer when the station is started up. Packages include input/output (I/O) drivers that allow a station to access disk storage or use printers that are attached to other stations exactly as it would control a locally attached peripheral.

Particular attention should be paid to the OS facilities. A number of software companies offer shared multiuser systems based on a single microprocessor (though this is *not* an advisable practice). Digital Research's MP/M, for example, permits up to 16 users to share a common microprocessor and peripherals. MP/M is a derivative of the popular CP/M operating system that allows applications written for that environment to function for multiple users. Onyx's C8000 is a multiuser system based on the Zilog Z8000 microprocessor running the AT&T UNIX operating system.

Multiuser systems are fundamentally similar to timesharing systems of the past; hence, they are based on obsolete concepts.

In terms of functional performance, users may be happy as long as the demands on the single processor are low, but the systems have two of the great weaknesses of central computer systems, whether mainframe- or mini-based:

- If the processor should fail, everyone loses his work and the station has to wait until the system is repaired or restarted.
- Response time, particularly memory access, rapidly deteriorates with an increasing workload.

Because of the statistical nature of processor sharing, functions we take for granted in personal computers, such as realtime graphics and instantaneous response to keystrokes, are sacrificed. That's not the goal of implementing a LAN in the first place.

Within a properly designed monoprocessing environment, the CP/M is one of the best available basic operating systems for microcomputers working on Z-80 or 8080. In its standard form, it is not suitable for Apple II, but Microsoft produced a peripheral card with Z-80 which takes control of the Apple II. Microcomputer compatibility to the established OS has two parts: a hardware interface, which is relatively simple, and software, which is much more difficult and costly. The writing of CP/M is said to have taken three persons about one year, at a cost of $180,000. The result of the work was what is currently the most widespread microcomputer operating system in the United States. Its importance is a result of the many programs in AP libraries that depend on CP/M. As an OS, it relates to stand-alone units, not to the networking purposes to which they are put.

Finally, a critical consideration with any LAN is the assurance of network transparency. With Cluster One, a concept of virtual I/O makes the network transparent to most users and programs. The users need not change at all the way they think about the file system or I/O. Quite important, most existing software for personal computers runs on the network without modification, and anything necessary to adapt existing single-user software to simultaneous multiple-user applications in a distributed environment is easy to implement.

FILE ACCESS AND RESPONSE TIME

We have said that some stations on the network are designed to serve other stations and provide additional resources for all the attached personal computers. An example is the file server, which supplies shared disk storage, file system operations, and a realtime clock for the other stations and implements file protection and controlled file-sharing mechanisms.

The emphasis is on shared text and data. Through a unique system of controls, all information can be made available among users on the network. Stations can simultaneously update databases while ensuring that no other station is updating the same information. We have spoken of file security. By using the network password protection mechanism, one can protect the data so that only one designated user or group of users has access to specified files.

In terms of file structure, as Fig. 11-7 shows, the file server supports a hierarchical database. This is valid both for the directory and for the areas allocated to the user-data-system aggregate. Each data file is the image of a floppy disk (virtual diskette). At this level, the specific OS, e.g., the Pascal OS, takes over.

The Cluster One network file server runs on an Apple II microcom-

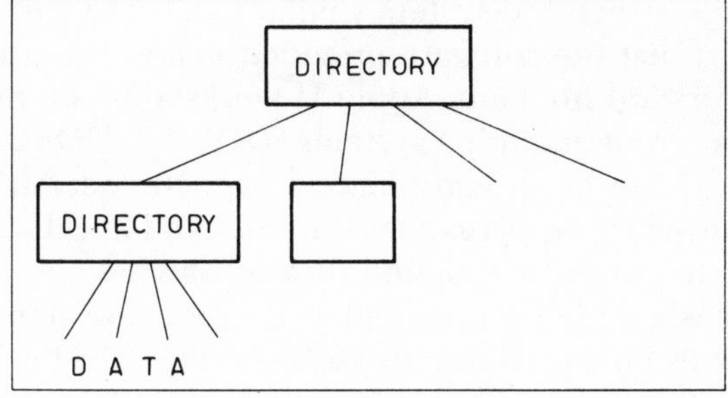

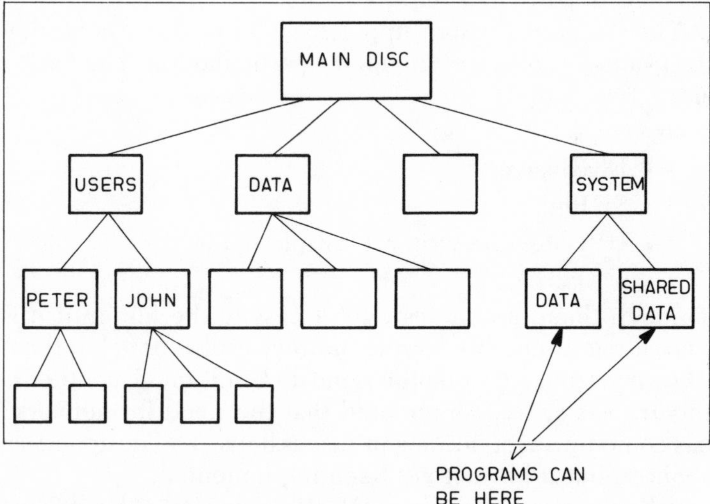

Figure 11-7. The way the Cluster One file server works: it supports a hierarchical database.

puter interfaced to the network. It can support a variety of devices ranging from two 8-in double-sided floppy disks to 66 MB of hard disk storage. Larger capacity is available by using more than one file server.

The network software allows multiple file servers on one local network, thus providing essentially unlimited online storage capacity. We have mentioned that the text and data on these sealed Winchester disks can be backed up by using a compact cartridge-type streamer drive which can write and check 20 MB of data in 12 min.

We have also mentioned the realtime clock which stations can interrogate. It time-stamps the creation, access, modification, and backup times of network files. Network-accessible files are organized with a tree-structured system similar to a UNIX directory. It has been explained that the software provided makes the use of text and data straightforward from any Apple II workstation on the network. All of Apple's current operating systems (DOS 3.2, DOS 3.3, Pascal 1.0, and Pascal 1.1) can be directly loaded over the network, with assurance given during this process that stations can logically connect to virtual disks on the network's shared disk resources.

Emphasis is put on shared files; they are one of the key competitive alternatives on which to build a LAN. The Cluster One network also provides the necessary software tools to utilize shared and updated database systems through either off-the-shelf packages or custom versions of particular requirements.

The standard version supports synchronization control, with which the available software can open a particular file. The basic commands are:

- EXClusive
- SHRed
- UPDate (one writer, multiple readers)

Through them, no one can get access to the file until it is released. Journaling is possible for any indirect application, but the AP must do its own journal either on the same disk or through another network file server. Nestar has commented that the need for network journaling has come up several times in discussions. The designers are thinking about it, but it has not yet been implemented.

A beginning approach to DBMS is the *DB Master*. Nestar worked with the program owner to release it for its network. The system is multikeyed, has primary and secondary keys, and can do sequential searches. The DB Master is not as diffused in usage as the Visicalc (the programs which built Apple), but database management systems are becoming increasingly important with microcomputer users.

The capability for shared communications should also be emphasized. The Nestar network communication server has just that. More specifically, it provides for data to be transmitted to another Nestar network, a mainframe which supports the IBM 2780, 3780, and 3270 protocols or a mainframe which features ASC II start/stop. Through data communication, the LAN considerably extends its file access range.

By bringing together the vital components of the end user requirements, the file access perspectives, and data communication, we bring into perspective the response time. Improvements in this respect depend on the reason for the bottleneck. Is the reason compute time or disk access? Chances are the latter is. A major financial institution in London, for instance, found a correlation with heavy disk access as individual traders wanted to look at prices. This bank has two kinds of transactions on the network:

1. Station to file server
2. Between stations communication

To overcome contention, it uses two LANs interconnected for tasks 1 and 2 (Fig. 11-8). The file transfer server works through a command file. Every 10 min it loads at network 1 files to transfer to network 2. (Both networks are local.) A transatlantic capability also is assured. Every night, at 3 a.m., the parent financial institution dials England from New York (through an automatic modem) and transfers files to and from London.

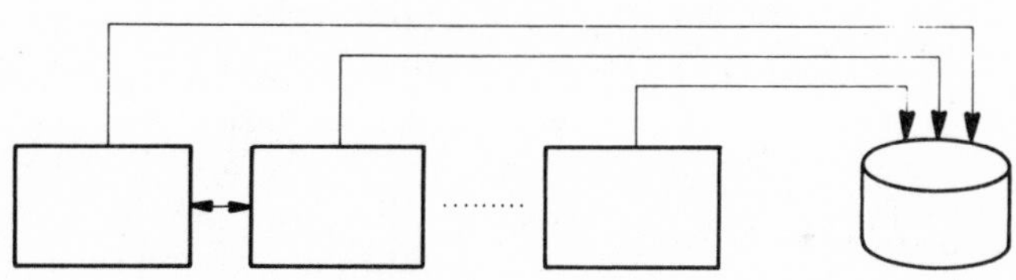

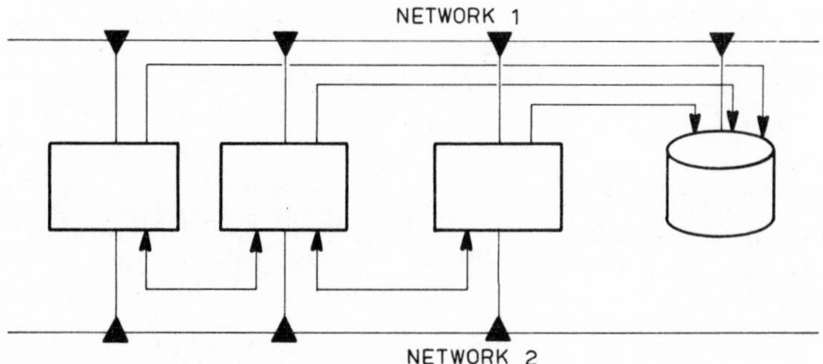

Figure 11-8. Interconnection of two LANs to improve response time at the workstation level.

At any other time, the network's data communication facility listens to the phone and accepts files as requests come in.

The handshake is fully acknowledged; check sums are used; automatic retry is featured; and, in general, the network software assures reliable transmission. As explained in the appropriate section, password protection is provided at the level of each of the files being handled. For each file, the user can specify public access rights (delete, file, replace), group access rights, and private access rights. Group access rights are assured through a group password. This provides significant flexibility with different access rights used for different files.

In absolute terms, if the application invites contention, then there may be no great difference between distributed (LAN) and timesharing (TS) solutions on minicomputers or mainframes. But applications can also be rewritten to allow for better use of the personal computer, the network, and the microfiles. A different way to make that statement is that if we only distribute computer power, there will be no bottleneck, but file access may create problems. On the contrary, if we can distribute the files, we position ourselves favorably for reducing contention.

We conclude by turning once again to the fundamentals. Low-cost LANs, such as Cluster One and Omninet, go well beyond distributed data processing and into distributed databases, data communication, and a user-friendly implementation. These are the background reasons why networks have attracted a lot more attention than a technological innovation might be expected to warrant. They are playing an important role in integrating the new computer-based tools intended for factory and office automation. And that's where the future lies.

DEVELOPMENTS IN FILE TRANSFER PROTOCOLS

In 1982 Cluster One had accumulated service in terms of applications and new developments in supporting software. Along this line, the file transfer server will be a standard product. Now it is offered off the shelf. The FTS will also serve the remote single-station site to help exchange files. With the 3780 protocol available for data communication toward the mainframe, this creates a uniform environment enhancing the WS interconnection capabilities (Fig. 11-9). For an interactive connection of LAN to minicomputer, Nestar suggests the 3270 server (Table 11-1).

FTS supports 3 "direct-connect" modems with automatic send and receive: DC Haze, Micromodem 2, Novation Applecat 2, and the British Owl modem. This service is important to the user because

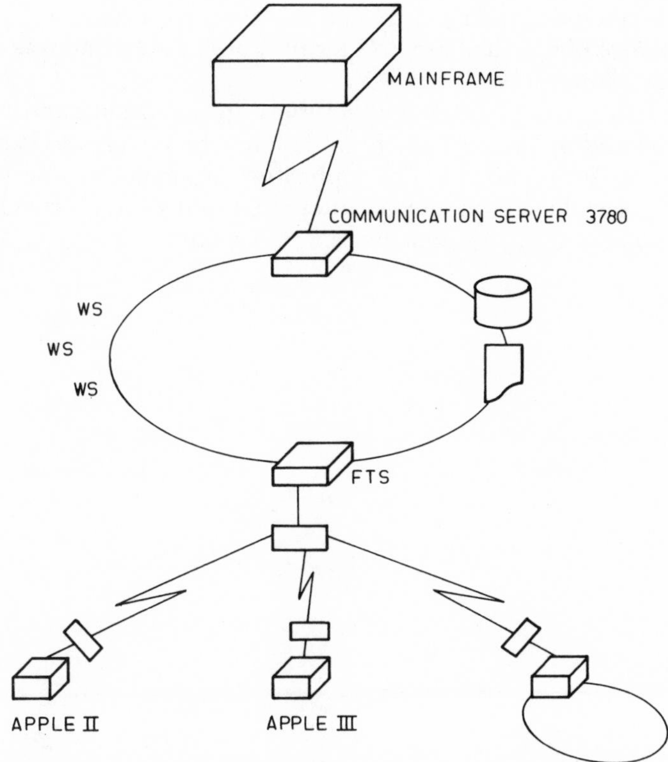

Figure 11-9. A communications server with 3780 protocol links Cluster One to the mainframe, and FTS connects to other Cluster Ones and to stand-alone personal computers.

automatic modems are much more convenient than, say, acoustic couplers, and permit night transmission. (It is, however, well to note that noisy lines don't help. They require manual supervision and the coupler will do a better job.)

Finally, it is proper to take note that with the offering by Nestar of a nonprocedural language (NPL) it will be possible to satisfy in an

TABLE 11-1 SUGGESTED DATA COMMUNICATION SOLUTIONS BY NESTAR

	Apple to Apple	LAN to LAN	LAN to mini	Apple to mini
File transmission	FTS or modem solution	FTS	3780 server	3780 stand-alone (Owlsync)
Interactive	Modem-level solutions	—	3270 server	User program (to be written)

easier manner data entry and reporting requirements for good maintenance of the database. (NPL runs under Pascal and was expected to be available in early 1983.)

In terms of language facilities, an important contribution may be offered by the package Foundation, which works in Pascal. Its goal is to ease the transition of application programs written for stand-alone PCs as the computers get integrated into a LAN through the parametric activation and deactivation of semaphores.

12 ATTACHED RESOURCE COMPUTER

Like all local area networks, Datapoint's attached resource computer (ARC) system comprises both hardware and software. Together they provide a baseband, token-passing, error-controlled, packet-switching solution for short-haul multiprocessor connection.

The hardware subsystem consists of resource interface module (RIM) adapters which attach to the standard I/O bus of Datapoint's and Tandy's processors and permit communication over coaxial cable. This hardware contains its own dedicated microprocessors which monitor and control the operation of the link, including

- Data transmission
- Buffer management
- Error detection
- Subsystem reconfiguration
- Related tasks

The computers to which the RIM adapters are attached require zero processor overhead for link control, which leaves the computers free for applications. The software component utilizes the interprocessor bus to assure transparent access to disks and their files and to the other workstations directly attached to the interprocessor bus.

The result is no different from results with the other LANs. It permits many processors to run independent tasks on a configuration of local disks, hardcopy devices, and communications equipment while accessing files which are concurrently being accessed by other processors in the local network. To appreciate the importance of this

LAN to the company's business policy, let's recall that Datapoint is a minimicro computer manufacturer. A new company in 1969, it made terminals. Then the use of the Intel 8080 microprocessor gave birth to its workhorse, the 2200. By 1975, it had moved into communications.

ARC was developed in the 1974 to 1975 timeframe. It was announced in 1977 after a one-year internal test as a minimum-entry level with a file system (common DB access) and two workstations. It has grown since in supporting configuration, but the basic philosophy remains: that of making the system user-friendly. That, after all, is the reason for existence common to all LANs.

Datapoint has been selling ARC since January 1978, and by the time of publication seemed to have about 2000 installations. Of those, 75 percent were in the United States. Three types of equipment can be attached to ARC: Datapoint, Tandy, and Inforex. These three and also, quite recently, Nestar and 3M/IS use the same RIM and the same protocol. Again, as with all local area networks, ARC use is growing under the propulsion of office automation.

Significantly, and more so for the personal computer field, only a few relatively inexpensive components are necessary to implement ARC with the new large-scale integration (LSI) network components. An interface card is required for each computer in the network. It fits into existing card slots in the rear, for instance, of the TRS-80 Model II. It is built by Texas Peripherals, a joint venture of Datapoint and Tandy and sells for about $400, but the price quoted by Datapoint for its equipment is much higher. The other necessary elements are inexpensive common coaxial cable and junction boxes, as we will see when we explain the architectural characteristics of the LAN.

STRATEGY BEHIND DATAPOINT'S DEVELOPMENT

The way Datapoint looks at the development of ARC is important in two ways. First, this is the earliest LAN still alive and is therefore one of the more mature ones. Second, and for the same reason, the way management looks at it helps to clarify strategic considerations. The strategy has been not to replace mainframes, but to help them answer end-user expectations while retaining the software investment. ARC itself has evolved since 1977–1978. Products and systems may be planned for 5 years, but often they are either scaled down or expanded as they materialize and take their place in the market. Expansion has characterized ARC.

At this point, however, another strategic consideration comes in perspective, the PBX. While basically its information switching exchange (ISX) is intended as a business telephone facility, the fact that it integrates the communicating functions of voice, text, data, facsimile, and graphics information should not be overlooked. Datapoint's ISX supports a combination of up to 20,000 telephones or workstations for data processing, word processing, and electronic messaging. As such, it complements and extends ARC's capabilities and also leads Datapoint toward a system structure with star characteristics, as in Fig. 12-1. Datapoint suggests there are three types of LAN—PBX-star type, baseband, and broadband—and the user has good reason, technical as well as operational, to avoid the star type.

Further, this argument has two other aspects. On the one hand, ARC and the ISX system enable Datapoint to offer considerable flexibility by combining coaxial-cable-based local networking and digital switching over telephone lines. In turn, this permits the structuring of integrated electronic office systems on a corporate-wide basis. On the other hand, the chances are rather high that the ARC architecture will lack the capacity, at some future time, to interconnect other manufacturers' equipment. Thus the user will be locked to Datapoint and Tandy. (Inforex is a fully owned Datapoint subsidiary.)

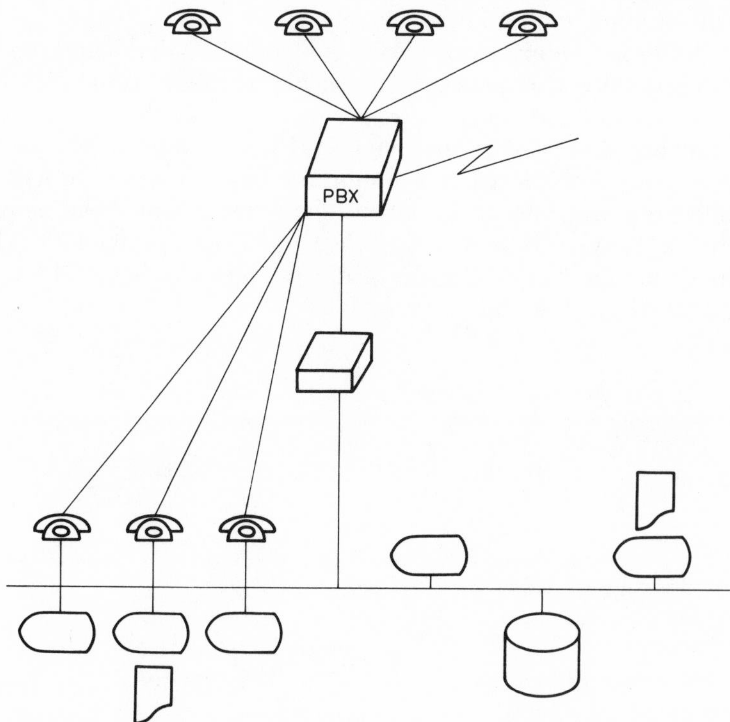

Figure 12-1. A system structure involving both a LAN and services provided through a PBX.

We have said that the ARC objective and Datapoint's goals coincide: to gain through small processors advantages usually available on bigger machines. To enable its attached processors to communicate, the ARC architecture rests on the token-passing approach, and not on contention.

We also referred to the resource interface module. A processor must have at least one RIM, which is transparent to the user. Its basic function is that of microprocessor control over traffic and security. RIMs are connected by a shielded, single-conductor coaxial cable. A minimum RIM link would be two RIMs connected by a single run of coaxial cable. A LAN including more than two RIMs requires one or more hubs. As we will see, they are of two basic types, active and passive.

There are no multiple processors on a RIM, but we can have multiple RIMs on a processor. Transceiving takes place at 2.5 Mbps (Fig. 12-2). Communicating between different ARC installations can be through switched (public) lines at 1.2 kbps for asynchronous transmission and 2.4 kbps for synchronous. Also by means of private lines, synchronous communications can be assured at 4.8, 9.6, 19.2, and 56 kbps (not 64 kbps).

As for hard-copy output, ARC can support a dedicated processor to run print jobs as necessary. This machine queues print jobs according to a user-defined procedure and makes use of the printing facilities available. As many printing stations can be established as necessary.

At the LAN level, an important characteristic of ARC is the interprocessor bus. It cannot run over 700 m, but it can be extended through active hubs. On the bus the RIMs are attached. The third fundamental component element is the hub. We have said that it is of two types, active and passive.

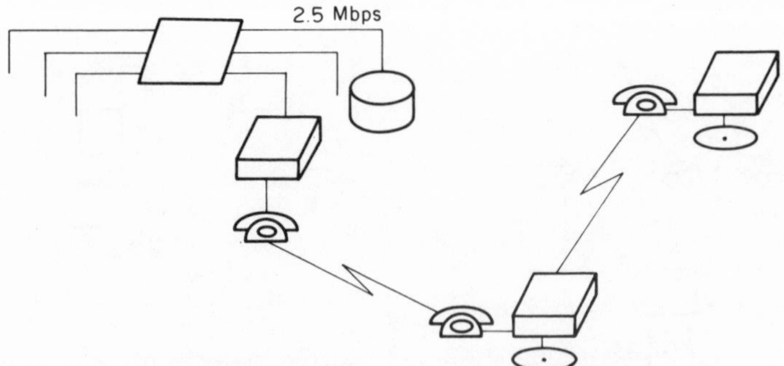

Figure 12-2. The approach taken by ARC in implementing gateways toward stand-alone computers.

The function of an active hub is to interconnect the RIMs within the ARC, link up to 16 RIMs or other hubs, provide signal amplification and conditioning, and allow ARC components to be linked up to 7 km apart at 700-m increments.

Active hubs are transparent to the user; hence, they permit interconnection of many RIMs to form larger systems. They perform signal conditioning functions for improved reliability of the interprocessor bus, and they provide the connecting points for 8 or optionally 16 lengths of coaxial cable.

Processors can be interconnected by running a length of coaxial cable from the first active hub to a second active hub, which will then allow attaching a total of up to 30 processors connecting the two hubs together. The interconnected restriction is a maximum of 10 active hubs along the longest path between RIMs. The maximum number of processors that can be directly attached to the same interprocessor bus is 255. However, multiple interprocessor buses can be attached to each computer, and therefore disjointed interprocessor buses can share common applications processors and file processors. We will return to the latter.

In this sense, the active hub is the vital element in the creation of an interprocess system with a "spider" configuration (Fig. 12-3). There are some fundamental characteristics, however, which should be kept in perspective; they distinguish the active hub from the RIM and see to it that ARC is basically not a star-type system:

- The RIM has a microprocessor and software.
- The active Hub has neither microprocessor nor software; it just connects and amplifies. This is a repeater function.

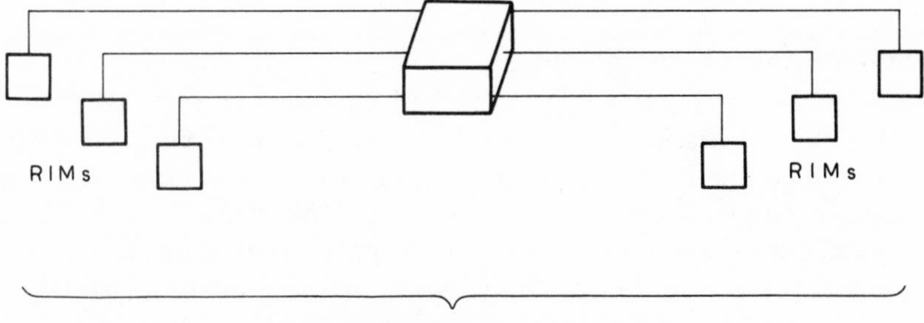

Figure 12-3. The technical solution followed by Datapoint with the hub as the focal point in creating an interprocess, spider-type configuration.

- There is one type of RIM with the stated 1:1 correspondence to the processor.
- The active hub comes in two versions; they handle 8 and 16 RIMs.

The PBX aside, there is one reason why ARC has a starlike nature. If the active hub dies, the network is out. But there are two good reasons for saying exactly the opposite:

- The active hub has no intelligence and cannot act as a master.
- Token passing creates a ring-type architecture.

Reference has also been made to the passive hub. It is a signal splitter typically employed when four or fewer computers are to be interconnected. Then its role resembles that of an active hub, except for the number of RIMs it can attach together and its not performing the signal conditioning functions of active hubs. Also, some special rules apply to passive hubs.

1. They may not be attached to the interprocessor bus.
2. They may not be attached to other passive hubs.
3. They may be directly connected only to RIMs.
4. The longest two cables attached to any given passive hub must total less than 700 m.

To summarize, passive hubs provide no reamplification, and the maximum distance they can handle is 700 m. Active and passive hubs are not compatible.

ARCHITECTURAL CHARACTERISTICS

We have said that the RIM is an LSI chip and is responsible for the DP/DB/DC communication to the coaxial cable. We have also said that the protocol of ARC is transparent to the user and that there is neither single master nor contention. The RIMs attached to the coaxial cable collectively monitor the entire operation. It is precisely the complete assemblage of RIMs, the interconnecting coaxial cable, and the associated hubs that is referred to as the interprocessor bus.

An important aspect of the bus is the addressing method employed within the system. Each RIM has two eight-bit addresses:

- The first is the I/O bus address the computer must send to give instructions to the RIM.
- The second is the RIM bus address, which determines which RIM receives a given packet transmitted through the interprocessor bus.

The two addresses are set by strapping options within the RIM; they can be changed in the field by a customer field engineer. They are completely internal to ARC software, and applications programs have no knowledge of them. All addressing requirements are taken care of automatically by ARC. The only time that a user must consider the address structure of the LAN is when addresses are chosen at the time the configuration is established. Once the installation is completed, operators and programmers of the attached resource computer do not need to know the actual addressing details.

Each RIM has an address set at installation time. When a new RIM is powered on, it disrupts the network. The token is passed by the machine which has control to the logical neighbor. As defined by ARC, a logical neighbor is the one to which the token is given. This is defined by tuning the network and establishing the RIM address. With this structure, and in spite of the physical impression the network gives, ARC tends to be a ring operating in a dynamically serial way. This is the logical characteristic of a spider solution.

In the ARC network there are no priorities in terms of signals, but there are priorities in the sense of servicing the WS. The structure, Datapoint states, makes it feasible to assign tasks and priority levels, though that is not implemented. Each WS can operate either online or stand-alone, but the RIMs are always online. In consequence, they receive the token and either use it or pass it along. Priorities are difficult to set. A RIM cannot ask for speedy reception of a token; it has to wait its turn.

The preceding discussion suggests that LAN efficiency is a function of how fast the ring works in passing the token station to station. That tends to put a limit on the number of workstations to be attached. Though Datapoint suggests that in San Antonio there is an ARC system with 800 processors on it, the prudent user will never exceed a lower two-digit number.

Datapoint also says that, to a considerable extent, ARC strategy and structure are influenced by the operating systems. Two alternatives have been suggested: DOS ARC and RMS ARC (Datapoint's own operating system); they are shown in Fig. 12-4. The RMS operating

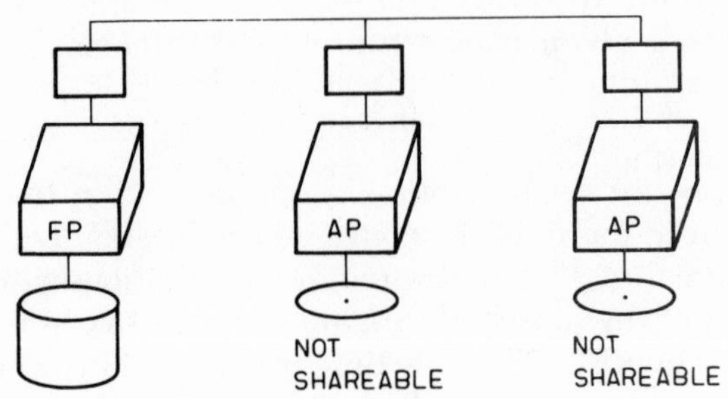

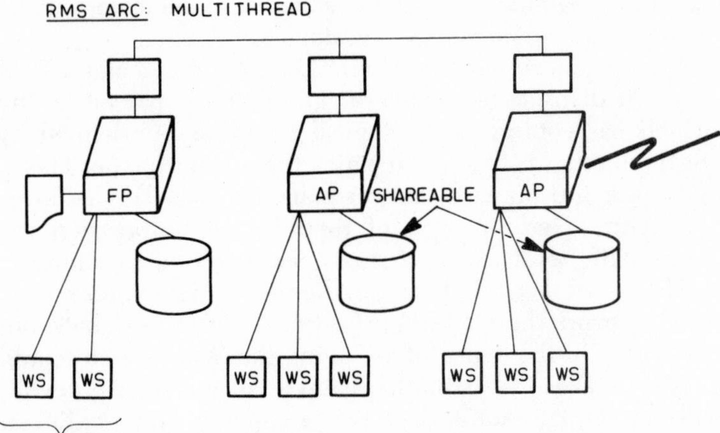

Figure 12-4. Single-task and multithread solutions promoted by Datapoint on ARC, with two different operating systems for its equipment.

system provides every workstation in a computing network with access to all the resources of the aggregate.

Once an ARC network is assembled, there are essentially three classes that define the status of each processor at any given instant:

- The *nonparticipating processor* is characterized by no change in operating procedures due to the processor's simply being attached to the ARC bus. Processors can be bootstrapped, powered down, powered up, serviced, or anything else, independent of the fact of their attachment. Active utilization of the RIM is complete, and programs that could be run on the configuration before RIM attachment can proceed in exactly the same way after the attachment.

- The *participating applications processor* possibility occurs when a processor logically mounts a remote volume and starts accessing it through the RIM. A local disk may or may not be present, depending upon the local configuration of the applications processor and the network structure.
- The *participating file processor* status occurs when a computer is serving as a shared file resource and making its disks available to the applications processors. File processors (FP) do not run application programs while in the FP capacity, since they are busy servicing the requests made on shared file resources by the applications processors. We will return to the file processor concept.

Applications processors are the machines actually processing the data under the control of the user applications programs, systems utilities, and so on. Such computers can be equipped with any complement of local I/O devices including disks, tapes, communications adapters, printers, and local and remote terminals. As stated earlier, the ARC architecture, although an early starter, is still developing and may reach maturity in about 1985. An evolutionary possibility is a tighter voice, text, and data orientation. No voice faculty was supported in 1983, but, given Datapoint's work on telephony, it may come. A possible future structure is the one shown in Fig. 12-5.

THE FILE PROCESSOR

A basic concept behind the ARC file processor approach is that, by performing actual computing related to data separately from where the data is stored, the only processing at the storage site is that required for storage and retrieval of data. This concept, which is common to most LANs, makes it feasible to increase total processing capability associated with a single file far more than would be practical within a minicomputer-based cluster. The file processor:

- Buffers data
- Optimizes the use of its shared disk resources
- Resolves access conflicts
- Coordinates the database transactions
- Provides data security
- Services incoming data requests

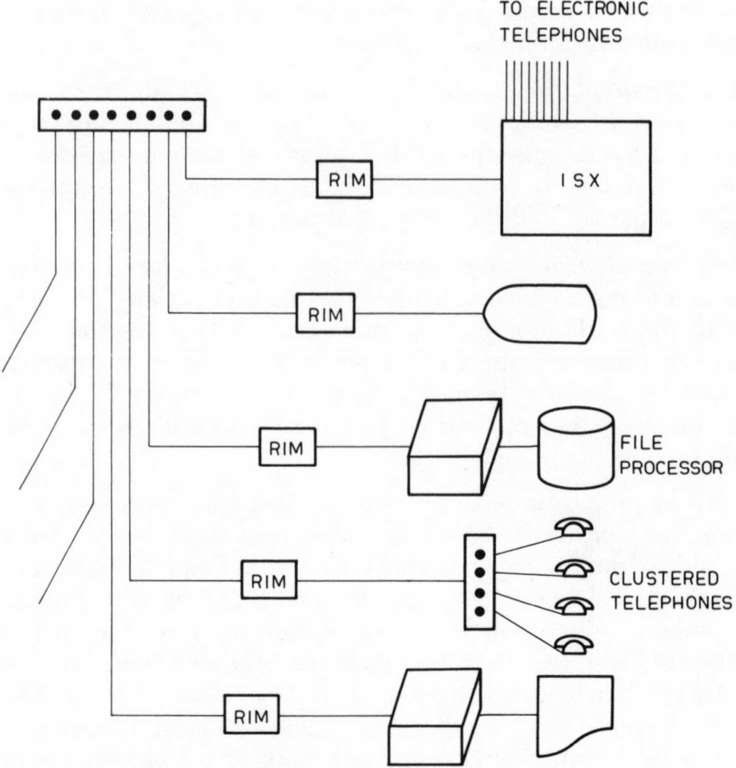

Figure 12-5. A future configuration suggested by Datapoint to integrate voice, text and data on the same network.

No applications programs run on a machine while it is serving as a file processor. Access to data is restricted according to user requirements; data residing on the common database may be subject to software constraints. Hardwired security can be provided through the use of local disks. This permits users to access the common database.

Security of a portion of the ARC database can be assured by using RIMs attached to ARC processors. In Fig. 12-6(*a*) the applications processors have access to all ARC system data, whereas the two B machines have access to only the database managed by the C equipment (the rightmost file processor). In Fig. 12-6(*b*) the four workstations clustered on the same processor have access to the local disk.

Hence, these are basic characteristics of the file processor: It is dedicated to data management; it provides high-speed access for

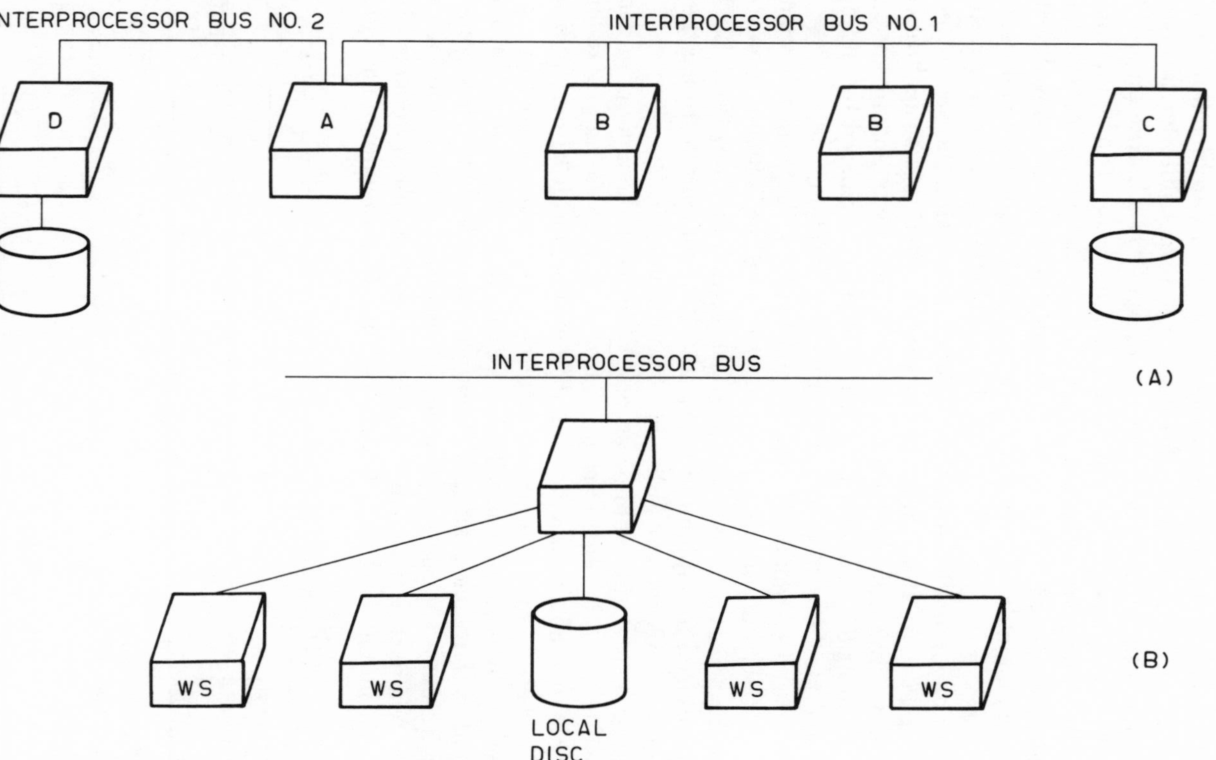

Figure 12-6. Access by the workstations to the ARC database and to the database of a different network.

multiple applications processors; it controls access of restricted information; and it is compatible with the OS. As a LAN architecture, ARC provides the file processor software and is responsible for the data management requirements. However, under DOS a maximum of 180 MB per file processor is feasible, but *n* file processors can be attached to an ARC. The system can be made to deliver faster data access times by adding another file processor to the existing system and reallocating the common database while all data remains common to all users.

Response time is a function of the application being run and the data volumes forced through the system. Increasing the size of the common database in a processor system is limited to the capabilities of the processor; either a larger or a second machine must be added. The notion of the common database of ARC is expanded by adding additional file processors and disk drives as necessary.

In a shared common database supported by a LAN, an important consideration is the *piping of messages*. A pipe is a software resource similar to a data file user for intertask communication (Fig. 12-7). Pipes are used to implement many advanced software features; they help give a LAN the capability of a mainframe.

Piping is related to volume access. With ARC, the amount of data accessible to an applications processor at any given time is determined by use of a command issued from the console of the applications processor. Volumes accessed through the interprocessor bus are referenced by volume name. The latter can be up to 8 bytes long, and they follow the same naming conventions as standard DOS file names.

Each time a volume is mounted, it is placed in one of the logical drives, where it remains until it is actively dismounted, replaced by another volume, or physically taken offline. Once a volume has been

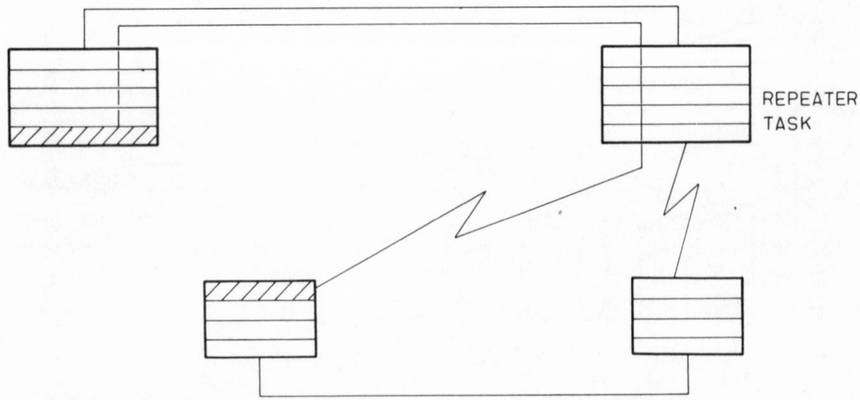

Figure 12-7 Synchronous and asynchronous communications processes, piping of messages, and the repeater task.

logically mounted, it can be accessed by specifying either the volume name or the logical drive number in which the volume is mounted. DOS assumes that local volume names are unique, that no two volumes directly online to an applications processor may have the same volume name.

If different file processors are used on the network, each has a directory to identify where the file is. That leads to the notion of directory assistance. On local disks directories can be created, renamed, or removed. The current directory can be changed, and files can be moved readily from directory to directory.

To prevent file-naming conflicts on shared disks, different users of a shared volume are assigned different directories at the time the volume is mounted. The directory into which the data placed is determined by the user name. Since each subdirectory has individual codeword protection, changing the current directory without going through the appropriate security procedures is inhibited.

Data security has been designed into the LAN. Local disks directly attached to an applications processor are absolutely private, and ARC access is limited to that processor. Access to remote disks at machines serving as file processors, as stated, requires

- A volume name
- A user name corresponding to a directory name on that volume
- The valid codeword associated with the volume and user name

Different volumes may have different combinations of valid user names if desired, and user names may use different codewords on different volumes. The degree of security can therefore be selected by appropriate assignment of users and files to various volumes and user name directories. Security across volumes is greater than that among different users within a single volume.

Passwords protect reading, writing, deletion, and change of security information. Through this approach security levels can be set up. If a file has protection level 5, a user with level 1 can't get access to the record. For floppy disk security, an encode/decode program gives an 8-bit password from the keyboard, and it helps scramble. To read, it is necessary to know the key. In scrambling, it provides 3 bytes of output file for each 2 of input file.

A relational DBMS is currently under development, but the following capacities can be provided in one way or the other.

1. *Restart, journaling, and recovery* to be assured by the DBMS. They are currently supported through applications routines.

2. *Rollbacks* through backup facilities provided by available utilities.

3. *Security*, as said above, based on "need to know" through names: named network, named nodes, named resources, named catalogs (subdivision of a disk), and passwords.

The following features of file organization are available with DOS: associative index method (AIM), index sequential access method (ISAM), relative, and sequential capabilities. Once an operator is certain that all remote access to a file processor's disks has completed, ARC/FP is taken down by simply rebooting the file processor machine, which returns it to stand-alone DOS operation. Subsequent applications processor access to its disks, if any, results in *drive offline* status being returned to the applications processor program requesting the access.

For downline loading purposes, all accesses, including DOS bootstrap, can be accomplished through the ARC routines, but a downline loaded applications processor cannot serve as a file processor.

DATA COMMUNICATION FACILITIES

Data communications facilities are important because much of the work a business does is communications-oriented. With the ARC architecture, an applications processor, or an additional one, can be dedicated to managing the communications requirements. Every applications processor in the ARC system can thus communicate through the common database with a remotely located computer or another ARC (Fig. 12-8). Communication to geographically dispersed locations is enhanced through a range of emulator packages and data communication software. RMS-type applications support communicating processors, synchronous operations, and multitasking.

ARC supports the possibility of using a mainframe as an applications processor. For instance, with the direct channel interface option (DCIO) an IBM computer may participate in the ARC system as an applications processor. The DCIO connects directly to the byte multiplexer channel and may be accessed by the IBM computer as unit record equipment. Programs may be written in standard IBM languages such as COBOL and RPG, and the system requires no modification of IBM operating system software.

RMS supports the 3780 and 2780 protocols, Hasp, and Datapool, through a transparent interface. The user communications facility (UCF) enables one to work through emulators. Dedicated communications processors can be justified by heavier data communication

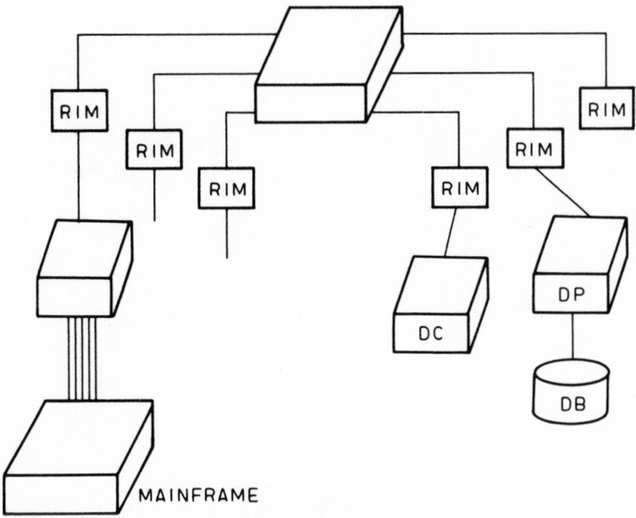

Figure 12-8. Communicating between the LAN and a mainframe, gateway, and database server.

loads, since any applications can be used for data communication purposes.

Supported modems and communications interfaces are the CCITT V.24 standard and the RS-232 for 300 bps to 9.6 or 19.2 kbps. Also supported is the RS-449, a standard similar to RS-232 but with improvements in signaling and distance. (See also Chap. 6, on normalization.)

13 ETHERNET

We have seen in the preceding chapters that numerous LAN products have already been announced. Furthermore, new entries are constantly being made. In many cases the manufacturers of computers and office equipment have developed their own hardware and software protocols, which are mutually incompatible. As a result, there is a rush toward the creation of de facto standards, provided the user community accepts them.

Along this line we have Ethernet, which uses coaxial cable and works on baseband. Ethernet's advantage lies in resilience: there is no one active component on which the network depends. Hence, other things being equal, it should demonstrate considerable dependability. Its disadvantages are these:

- The cost of the interfaces is high; hence, the overall LAN is very expensive.
- It is critical that it be installed properly, and LAN know-how is not yet widely available.
- Its baseband characteristic would prove a limitation. As experience increases so does the appetite for bandwidth.

The Xerox strategy with Ethernet is that of developing multivendor systems. This is fundamental for local networks, because in office automation it is unthinkable to have the same supplier for all equipment. The question is whether the technical specifications and cost of this LAN are such that the strategy can be effective.

In Europe, Olivetti, Siemens, and Nixdorf have adopted Ethernet, but given the cost of its interface—an order of magnitude greater than that of, say, Omninet—Olivetti does not plan to implement Ethernet for M20, its personal computer. In the United States, some initial commitments, like that made by Hewlett-Packard, seem to have been withdrawn.

Indeed, one of the most controversial LAN issues is the future of Ethernet. The position taken by some people is that Ethernet will have a healthy life, at least in the short run, but some cognizant executives think that the prospects are not bright. Still others believe that the brighter future is reserved for such Ethernet clones as 3 Com and Bridge Communications.

At least one report, written by the American consulting firm Strategic Incorporated, says that Ethernet will be Xerox's undoing. Many specialists emphasize the importance of more modern LAN architectures based on broadband techniques rather than baseband as in Ethernet. But as we said in the beginning, the basic problem with Ethernet is cost rather than capacity. It is true enough that Ethernet cannot be all things to all people. Even if simplicity could make it possible for a user to install Ethernet without great expertise, it would not be cheaper than the alternatives available in broadband, while it could easily be more expensive by an order of magnitude than other baseband solutions.

This is a pity, because on the technical side the Xerox effort has been pace-setting. In parallel with the work done by Datapoint on ARC, and independently of it, Xerox has taken one of the first steps toward developing the concept of an executive workstation. Ethernet is capable of handling electronic mail, electronic filing, some computing, and word processing.

A RETURN TO THE FUNDAMENTALS

Let's start with the fundamentals. Local area networks make it possible to move information between office machines: word processors, data processors, memories, and printers. They do so quickly, reliably, and rather cheaply. The Ethernet architecture depends on a single coaxial cable to carry messages from terminal to terminal. This is the network layer.

The user layer contains the office machines themselves. It is connected to the local area network by an interface, a transceiver, and a tap which code the data and transmit it to the network at the appropriate time. The routines supported by the architecture assure that messages get through to their destination—another terminal or a device in the server layer such as storage or printer.

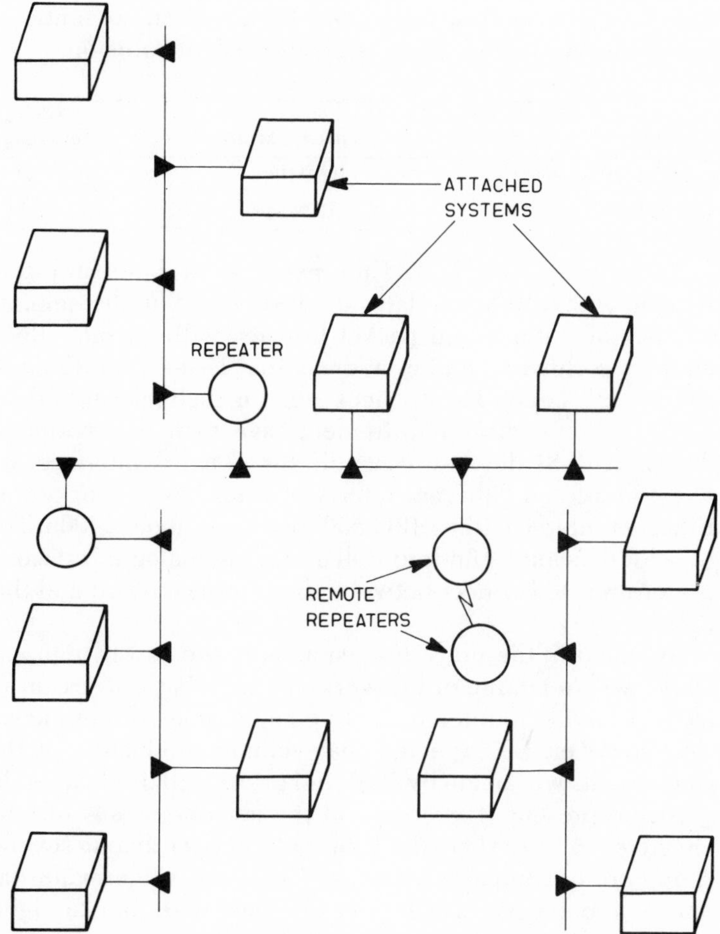

Figure 13-1. Typical configuration of an Ethernet with its attached systems, repeaters, and remote repeaters.

The Ethernet LAN is a baseband, broadcast, multiple-access system using carrier sensing and collision detection (Fig. 13-1). Its architectural concepts are based on years of experimentation, at Xerox, with a version of Ethernet communications. As in the case of all other LANs, not only were the details of the electrical and low-level protocols worked out, but attention was also paid to higher-up layers.

Among the different Ethernet versions which are now available, the first was developed through the Xerox experience and the second, also known as DIX, is the product of DEC, Intel, and Xerox collaboration. Both use coaxial cable, and both rest on contention: As more processors are added, there is greater risk of collision.

Version	Capacity, Mbps	Advisable throughput, %
Original Ethernet	3.5 Mbps	25
DIX Ethernet	10 Mbps	30

Technically, the DIX Ethernet uses a baseband transmission scheme with a 10-Mbps data rate. It provides for the employment of a number of stations and packet formats, with 48 bits allocated for a unique worldwide station address that is not duplicated anywhere, and it has a large (32-bit) check sum on each packet to detect errors.

The technological requirements see to it that without specially designed VLSI devices to handle the network interface, it is expensive to build an Ethernet interface. Intel has announced a multibus Ethernet interface (the iSBC-550) that costs about $4000. To that must be added several hundred dollars for an analog interface (the transceiver unit) to connect between the interface board and the physical cable.

As stated in the preceding paragraph, the cost is high, particularly when we are talking of PC workstations. That is a reason why Xerox looks primarily to interconnecting mainframes and minicomputers. It can, however, be expected that volume production of the needed components will begin by 1985 and prices will drop rather drastically.

At the present (1983) state of the art, one means of lowering the effective cost is to share the Ethernet interface among several stations. A number of companies, such as Zilog and Ungermann-Bass, offer a microcomputer-based Ethernet interface with four to eight ports for connecting terminals or other microcomputers.

The Z-net is an Ethernet alone at a 1-Mbps level and provides a gateway to Ethernet. Network One, from Ungermann-Bass, also has similarities to Ethernet at a lower transfer rate, and it is analog, not digital. With this and similar approaches, the effective cost per station can be reduced to about $1000 for a fully loaded system, which is twice as expensive as other baseband alternatives.

It is being said that, for personal computers, the Intel controller with VLSI is foreseen at $100 for the controller on a chip. It is known that Intel, Zilog, and AMD project microcontrollers on a chip. But it is also true that the current lack of VLSI support for the controller is an Ethernet disadvantage. Looking at both the economic and technical sides, we can list Ethernet's relative advantages and disadvantages:

1. Relative advantages. Reasonable simplicity, a certain range of compatibility (given the adoptions), low delay, stability, maintainability, and good transmission capability
2. Relative disadvantages. High cost of the interfaces, the baseband concept, and the list of things it does not support: priorities, an assured maximum time of transmission, higher-level error recovery, encryption capability, full duplex transmission, and a sophisticated security mechanism

It is true, however, that the latter are objectives of the higher-up ISO/OSI layers. (See also Chap. 8.)

Table 13-1 compares technical aspects of Ethernet and Cluster One. The comparison is meaningful because of the significant difference in the cost of the interfaces and because both employ the carrier-sensing method. We have spoken in detail of CSMA, so we need not return to the subject, but it is advantageous to look into the concepts which led to Ethernet.

Table 13-1 also compares the packet structures of Cluster One and Ethernet. Address size is a significant characteristic, because it

TABLE 13-1 A COMPARISON OF ETHERNET AND CLUSTER ONE

	Ethernet	Cluster One
	TECHNICAL ASPECTS	
Cable	Coaxial	8- or 16-wire
Topology	Linear bus	Unconstrained
Address size	48 bits	8 bits
Speed	10 Mbps	240 kbps
Carrier	Presence of signal	Separate line
Acknowledgment	Separate acknowledgments	Acknowledged datagrams
Multiple packets	Must release and reacquire	Without releasing cable
	PACKET STRUCTURE (COUNT IN BYTES)	
Destination address	6	1
Source address	6	1
Type	2	1
Length of field	46–1500	2–257
CRC	4	2
	64–1518	7–282

directly affects network performance. It is also proper to note that the shortest Cluster One packet is 7 bytes and in Ethernet the shortest packet is 64 bytes.

Details of the network's data link standards are transparent to the ordinary user. What users will eventually be aware of is the difference in how applications programs access such common system facilities such as file storage. Unlike the programming of a stand-alone minicomputer or mainframe, in a local area network such services will not be provided in the same physical machine.

When programming for a single machine, we typically set up a *request block* in the computer's memory and then ask the OS to perform the service. In a LAN, one personal computer will ask another, by using an agreed protocol, to perform a service. The way a programmer asks for a service to be performed is different, because groups of related services tend to be performed by a dedicated server device.

Finally, we might add that the successful use of a local area network depends on more than the specific carrier. It typically uses higher-level protocols, including an architecture for DB service and internetworking communications. We will now see how.

THE ETHER PRINCIPLE

The approach used in the Ethernet system traces its roots back to the radio-based Aloha packet-switching network developed at the University of Hawaii by Abrahamson. In this network, terminals equipped with packet radios share a common multiaccess radio channel. There is no central controller allocating access to the channel: a random-access procedure has been selected. In it each terminal independently decides when to transmit.

With the simplest Aloha solution, two terminals can transmit at the same time and produce a collision. After a collision is detected, each terminal has to wait for a random interval and then retransmit. This helps eliminate any central control; but as load increases, the maximum utilization of a pure Aloha channel is about 18 percent.

Stated differently, in its original application, the fundamental method used in Ethernet was employed by the Aloha scheme: a radio network which permitted effective communication among the islands of Hawaii. Significant developments have, however, been carried out at the Xerox Palo Alto Research Center as part of an experimental project which started in the mid-1970s.

Unlike the approach taken with the pure Aloha scheme, when an

Ethernet station wishes to send a packet, a carrier-sensing mechanism is first used. This forces the station to defer if any transmission is in progress.

- If no other station is transmitting, the sender can begin immediately, with zero latency.
- In any other case, the sender waits to transmit after the packet has passed.

The principal technical characteristics can be summarized as follows:

1. Transmission frequency: 10 Mbps
2. Topology: unrooted tree
3. Access method: CSMA/CD
4. Type of transmission: packet switching
5. Length of a packet: 64 to 1518 bytes
6. Level of ISO/OSI implementation: physical layer and data link layer
7. Maximum distance between stations: 2.5 km
8. Maximum length of one segment: 500 m
9. Maximum number of stations: 1024
10. Maximum number of stations per segment: 100

The name "Ethernet" is based on a little science history. It was once thought that a universal medium called luminiferous ether was the carrier of electromagnetic waves. Xerox decided to build its "ether" out of coaxial cable. The architecture so developed can detect a collision in progress by reading back the state of the cable as data are being transmitted. With that capability, a station senses when another station is sending data and stops transmitting, instead of continuing until the end of its packet. To assure that all stations know a collision has occurred, the transmission in progress is terminated with a burst of noise.

Furthermore, a randomized delay function has been added so that each station will wait a different amount of time instead of beginning to transmit immediately after a preceding transmission is complete.

This avoids causing a collision each time two or more stations have something to send. As stated, the delays get progressively longer as the channel becomes busier.

There are experts who say that Aloha never really worked from island to island, but the principles it established are valid from building to building. The underlying concept having been tested experimentally within a LAN environment, there is sufficient evidence that, as long as the fraction of available transmission time used is low, everyone gets a turn—eventually.

It is possible that two or more stations will simultaneously sense that the channel is idle and begin simultaneous transmissions and produce a collision. Each sender, however, continues to monitor the cable during transmission and can provide collision detection when the signal on the cable does not match its own output. When a station stops transmitting, it uses a collision consensus enforcement procedure to ensure that all colliding stations have seen the collision. A retransmission will then be scheduled.

If two stations have found the channel clear and start transmitting simultaneously, the two packets collide, and this collision scrambles the information. The error detection logic throws away the bad data. If the stations do not receive an acknowledgment by a certain time, they simply send the packet again.

- To avoid repeated collisions, each station waits for a random period of time before retransmitting.
- To avoid overloading the channel, and thus making it unstable, the range of this retransmission interval is increased at times of heavy load by using a binary exponential backoff algorithm.

Such mechanisms represent the Ethernet random-access procedure, which we have already considered as CSMA/CD. We have said that it can be applied to any suitable broadcast channel—radio, fiber optics, or infrared, and not only coaxial cable.

We have also spoken of attachments to the carrier. Individual stations connect to the cable by using a CATV-type tap. A small transceiver is attached at the tap and a cable is run down to the interface, which might be located in the station. The passive medium and the lack of any active elements in the shared portion help provide a reliable system. The tap, transceiver, interface, control, and station connection is shown in Fig. 13-2. This solution, devised for mainframes and midicomputers, involves server functions when addressed to nonintelligent or very small computers. In general, the server can

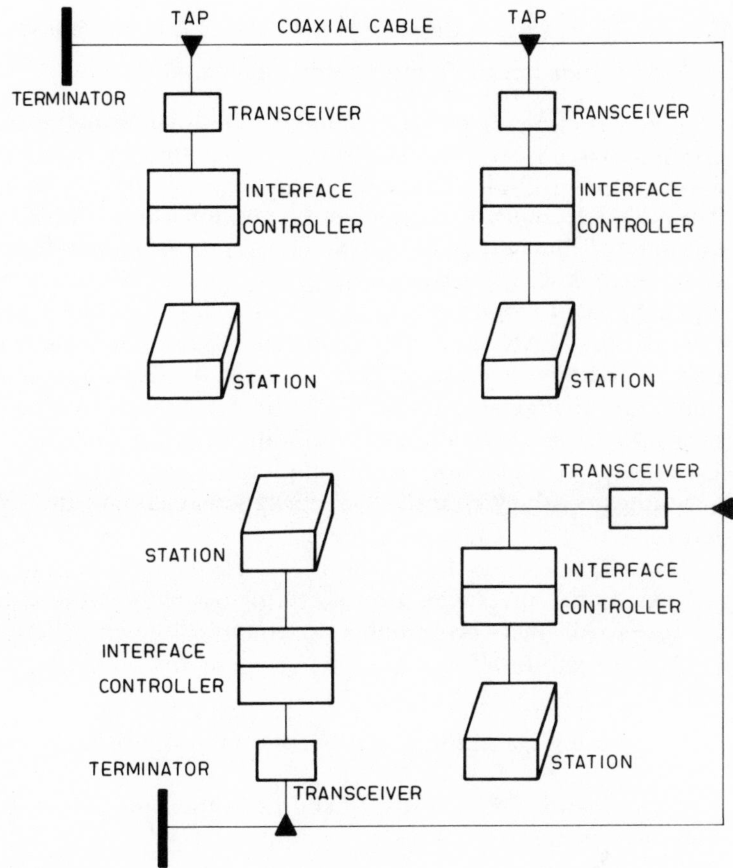

Figure 13-2. Transceivers, interfaces, controllers, and workstations connected to an Ethernet.

be a micro- or minicomputer with specialized functions: gateway, spooler, store and forward, and DB processor. Typically, the unit is dedicated to one function and capable of handling it intelligently. We can distinguish:

1. The *serial network interface message* processor (NIM) has 96 kB of RAM and ROM. It can interconnect nonintelligent serial-type machines to Ethernet.

2. The *general-purpose NIM* can handle up to 1.2 Mbps with 16-pair wire.

3. Load and monitoring.

4. *Store and forward NIM* can have a minifile server.
5. *Gateway* can connect telex, teletex, etc.
6. *DB NIM* permits the management of larger memory capabilities.

Through specialized servers, it is possible to better manage the equipment attached to the LAN. The server is an interface between the demands which arrive through the network, the local processes, and associated resources.

Like other LAN approaches, Ethernet assures an easy reconfiguration of stations. Equipment can be moved, disconnected from one point, and reattached at another without any need to take down the network. It is, however, good to keep in mind that no LAN—and Ethernet is no exception—can completely guarantee delivery.

Studies conducted in the early 1980s revealed a number of problems:

1. As the messages grow in number, many collide and only a small fraction of the true communications bandwidth is used for valid data.
2. If enough stations try to transmit, less and less data gets through, and the result is continuous collisions.

Experiments with a 3-Mbps Ethernet with some 100 units attached to it have demonstrated that:

- The busiest second has shown a 40 percent carrier saturation.
- The busiest minute was in the range of 15 to 20 percent saturation.
- The busiest hour was in the range of 3 to 5 percent saturation.
- The average use over 24 h was 0.8 to 1 percent.

But some users commented that simulation studies in their in-house environment exhibit a 75 percent saturation for the busiest minute (totally unacceptable), 30 percent saturation for the average hour, and between 2 and 3 percent saturation over a 24-h period. One Ethernet installation was said to handle 300 MB per day. This is within prescribed capacity. As defined by its manufacturer, a 3-Mbps Ethernet system, in normal use, carries about 2.2 million packets in a 24-h period, a total of almost 300 MB. That traffic roughly corresponds to about half of the volume carried through the Arpanet on an average day. But, of course, the load is not even, since it is light at night and heavier during the day.

The differential use accounts for the measures made in a Xerox experiment on utilization over a full 24-h day. They indicate that the traffic represents a modest but variable use of the network ranging from about 0.60 to as much as 0.84 percent. However, maximum utilization in the busiest interval has been much higher: about 3.6 percent in the busiest hour, 17 percent in the busiest minute, and 37 percent in the busiest second. Such results help to verify design assumptions: that computer communications applications tend to produce a *bursty* pattern of requests.

On the negative side is the fact that CSMA/CD shows instabilities when the loads get high. There are some quoted figures indicating that it is not wise to:

- Push the utilization beyond 30 percent usage
- Put video terminals directly on the network
- Plan to use at the extreme of available capabilities

The 30 percent limit sees to it that it is not advisable to use a 3-Mbps LAN for more than 1 Mbps, which corresponds to 125 kBps. In turn, a full CRT screen would be updated every 15 s, without considering access time and other delays.

Although this is just one example, a careful look at design characteristics helps reveal the following restrictions on Ethernet:

1. Full transmission specs have not yet been published.
2. Effective endpoint-to-endpoint distance seems to stand at 500 m (although DIX says 3 km).
3. If the effective range is increased, there is a corresponding constraint to tap on some intervals.

There should be no doubt that the three partners in Ethernet—Xerox, DEC, and Intel—will work to relieve these constraints. Some other companies, Olivetti, for instance, are looking into the technical feasibility of extending Ethernet's orientation by piggybacking services such as voice. Xerox has said it will do that also.

Among reasonable future developments is the projection that, when voice is transmitted via Ethernet (30 percent of bandwidth for data and the remainder for voice), 200 to 300 telephones may be served. Ethernet delays do not seem to be a problem for internal calls if no echo path is permitted, and the echo path can be avoided by using either four-wire telephones or a high-performance echo canceller (for echos of 50 to 100 ms).

Although such possibilities are evidently present, it is wise not to forget that the choice has to be made now, with present-day criteria dominant in a decision to go ahead with a first experimental installation. And it is also well to keep in mind, with all LAN implementations, that errors typically due to human failure should be carefully avoided from the beginning. To that end, the users are well advised to become familiar with the basic technical characteristics of a LAN, both hardware and software. That's another reason why the simpler the network the better. With Ethernet, an example of possible human failure is removing the terminator at the end of the cable. On at least one occasion, a lightning strike generated a large surge in the building ground and disabled a number of transceivers. The correct installation procedures can significantly improve lightning resistance.

THE PACKET PROTOCOL

We can organize the component parts of Ethernet described in the preceding section into a layered structure, as shown in Fig. 13-3. The way Xerox looks at its local network architecture, the levels are user, network, and server. We have said that the supported layers in the ISO/OSI sense are the physical and the data link. The Xerox specifications for data link cover datagrams and therefore go beyond the boundaries of the classical data link.

One way to look at the facilities supported by the physical and data link layers is to explode them into their component functional parts. The former includes transmit/receive and encode/decode (Fig. 13-4). The latter includes link management, encapsulation, and station-to-station interface.

In this packet-switching environment, packets sent through the system exhibit a bimodal distribution of length. Most of them are short ones containing terminal traffic, acknowledgments, and so on. The load is a function of both packet length and frequency. Therefore, the larger part of the total volume is carried in the large packets often containing file transfers. This distribution is supported by some of the measurements reported for the Arpanet but differs from the distributions frequently used in analytical models of networks. Almost all of the traffic consists of encapsulated internetwork packets, or pups.

The minimum-size packet with no data would usually include the Ethernet and pup headers, whereas acknowledgments and packets

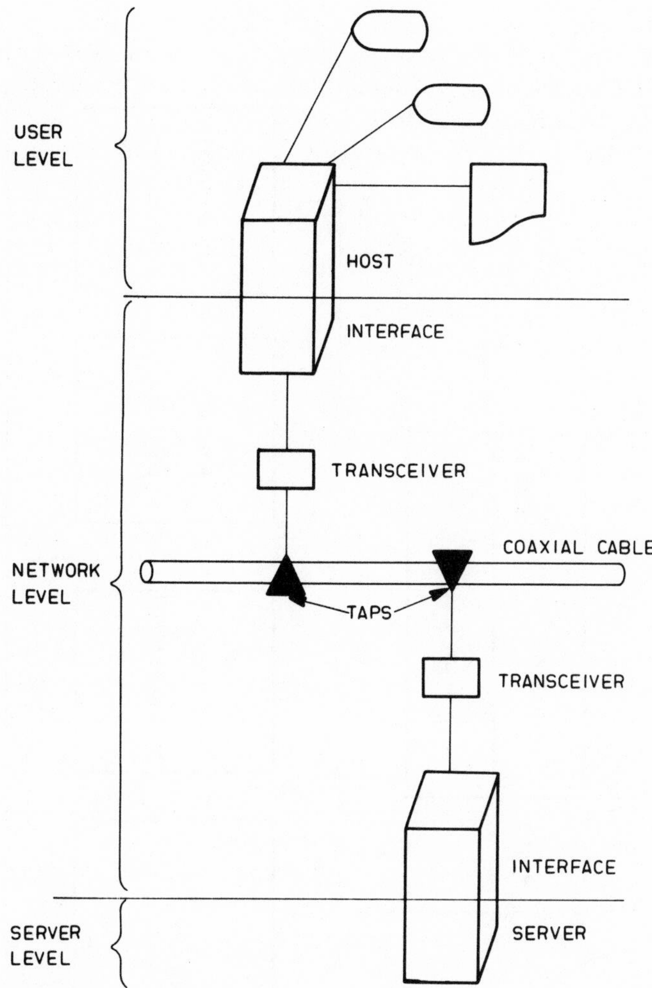

Figure 13-3. Logical parts of an Ethernet architecture: user, network, and server levels.

with only 1 or 2 bytes of data would be just a bit larger. At the other extreme, software considerations usually impose an effective upper limit on the size of a packet. Depending on the particular system, this ranges from about 200 to 540 bytes. Experiments made by Xerox demonstrate that the mean packet length is about 122 bytes and the median is about 32 bytes.

Figure 13-5 shows the structure of a packet. It's a string of bytes

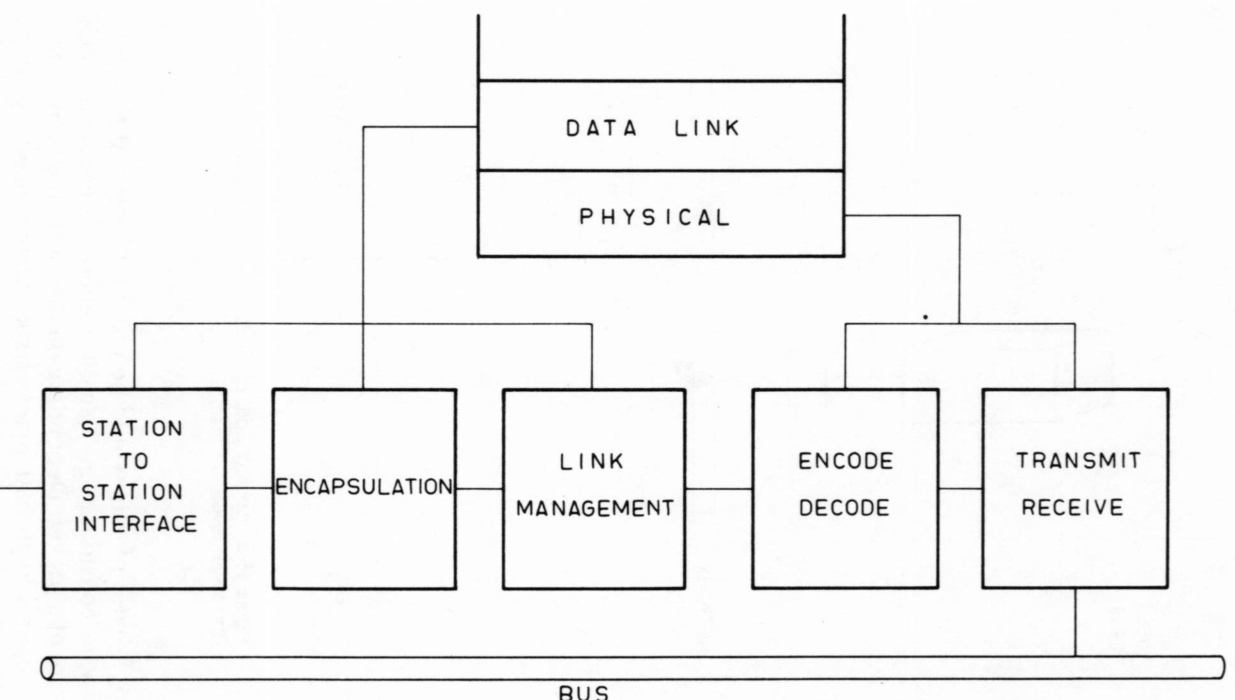

Figure 13-4. Functional components of the physical and data link layers of Ethernet.

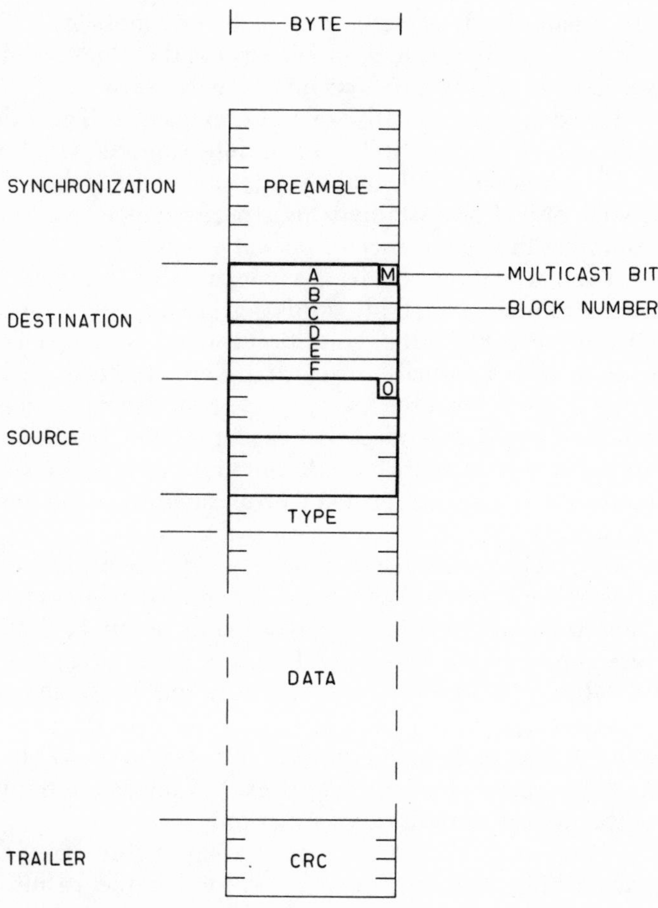

Figure 13-5. Structure of an Ethernet packet: preamble, destination, source, type, data, trailer.

broadly divided into six groups:

- Preamble
- Destination
- Source
- Type
- Data
- Trailer

The goal of the preamble is synchronization through a known waveform; it occupies 8 bytes. The *multicast bit* is the first bit after the preamble. It says: "I can receive a message." The destination address has 6 bytes; A,B, and C express the block number. The source section has 6 bytes; its first bit is always zero.

The data are typically an internet packet. The role of the cyclic redundancy check (CRC) is error detection. As with the X.25 protocol (which is, however, virtual circuit, bit-oriented) the role of the CRC is a vital one: For sustained high performance, we certainly want to minimize the occurrence of packet errors.

When a station receives a packet, the interface checks that an integral number of 16-bit words has been received and that the 16-bit CRC is correct. If either condition is not met, the packet is considered in error and is normally discarded. Xerox suggests that with a passive listener set to receive every packet on the net, there was initially reported one damaged packet in about 6000, but there was also wide variance among machines. Simulation with a revised interface has produced normalized packet error rates of about one in 2 million packets.

To conclude this discussion we review the technical characteristics already considered. With Ethernet, up to 1024 computer systems or stations can be connected to a cable of up to 2500 m in length. Interconnection is by relatively simple transceiver units operating at a 10 Mbps. Ethernet operates entirely with baseband phase-encoded signals. Each station wishing to transmit over the network first listens to the traffic on the cable until it detects that the cable is free. Then it quickly transmits a complete packet of information, including details of the packet's intended destination.

If two or more stations sense a gap at the same time and begin transmitting simultaneously, they detect the resulting collision of signals and back off for a length of time determined by a randomizing procedure. This is the manner in which carrier-sensing multiple access with collision detection works. The scheme has the advantage of requiring no overall network master to supervise the system.

Ethernet is said to have had, as of May 1982 or about a year after its announcement, some 75 installations worldwide. However, several of them are in one and the same site, as the cases of Intel and AMD document.

Access to mainframes and sharing of peripherals seem to be among the applications, but at the International Symposium on Local Networks held in Florence, Italy, in April 1982, Xerox itself said that the cost of the Ethernet controller is too high in comparison with Apple II. One of its specialists even suggested, "If the application is of the data entry type, better get Cluster One."

Ethernet can, however, be promoted through a consistent effort to bring interface costs down (an effort in which Intel is currently engaged) *and* by steady enhancement. Toward the latter goal, Xerox recently announced more Ethernet protocol layers for the seven-layer ISO/OSI model.

- One is the Internet Transport Protocol document, which specifies protocols for the network layer (Internet datagrams).
- The second comprises sequenced packet and packet-exchange protocols for the transport layer.
- The third is the courier document, which offers OSI model presentation layer functionality.

The new protocols will be helpful to vendors who want to make terminals that are usable on the Ethernet-compatible service. They will also promote the LAN's appeal if its costs can be reduced enough to make it competitive with other baseband solutions.

14 A LAN SOLUTION BY IBM

Whether motivated by free choice or by market forces, every computer manufacturing company feels it needs a local network architecture to sustain itself in an increasingly network-oriented environment. With its baseband token solution, IBM is no exception.

Network architectures like the System Network Architecture (SNA), designed for a long-haul application, are not fit for LANs. Choices have to be made for the short-haul applications. On the other hand, networks which have different operating characteristics also face addressing, routing, and protocol problems. IBM opted for a ring approach at the local area level; it is also reasonable to expect that it will provide gateways to SNA and, quite likely, to some of the leading value-added networks.

IBM chose a synchronous token ring for its LAN and implemented it at the IBM Zurich Research Laboratory. The key points necessary to comprehend the technology are the wiring concept, code selection, and ring synchronization by means of "phase lock" loops.

The wiring of a single ring is based on a two-level hierarchy with passive or active "distribution panels" at different locations in a building. Stations are connected to the distribution panels by means of relays (hence, a passive connection) or by means of other active panels in a star-type arrangement. The ring solution is no newcomer among the company's offerings. In more than one respect it looks like a highly upgraded 3600 setup, and there is also lots of similarity to the 2750 and 8100 approaches. As for upgrading, the twisted wire supports 4 Mbps, and one can do a lot with that band as opposed to what could be done with the old 3600 connection. (In fact, IBM is said to have tested up to 8-MHz transmission under laboratory conditions.)

Synchronous transmission was chosen because it permits operation at lower signal-to-noise ratios than asynchronous operation and thereby makes longer transmission distances feasible. Start/stop packet burst operation with preambles was rejected because of synchronization delay. Possible transmission codes were evaluated, and the two-level differential Manchester code was chosen because of its being simple, providing low jitter, and making frame delimiters feasible.

As is to be expected, IBM's LAN is intended to protect the company's own product line from plug compatible manufacturers (PCM). As a result, what the manufacturer presents as an asset is in reality a limitation. The hypothesis of an asset starts from the premise that, since all stations have identical hardware, stations can be interchangeable. The limitation arises from the lock-in strategy mentioned earlier in this book.

At the same time, other vendors who could see lots of opportunity in providing IBM-compatible LANs brought into the market local networks well before IBM could introduce its own. That is the case in the October 1982 announcement by 3Com of an Ethernet accepting the IBM PC and of the January 1983 introduction by Nestar of Plan 4000. Both LANs have distributed architecture.

In the current status of its own LAN design, IBM's LAN also seems to favor a sort of distributed control. The failures are detected when the token is lost; monitoring is effected through a question posed by the network to the devices attached: are you a monitor or a station? When necessary, switching from a station to a monitor level takes 100 ms. And although IBM talks of distributed approaches, its solution is basically hierarchical.

All told, there is nothing terribly new nor is there any magic in the announced IBM local area network.

- It does not represent a technological breakthrough.
- It is simply a beefed-up version of something already existent for 10 years.
- But it is quite interesting in that IBM has belatedly waked up to the need for LAN.

A manufacturer that cannot provide a local network is immediately at a disadvantage. But IBM has also been careful not only to maintain but also to enforce its lock-in. Users who might have hoped they will no longer be completely dependent on their "traditional supplier" are in for surprises, and that is true of the PCM. Yet while the competitive forces in the marketplace obliged IBM to follow the path traced by other firms, there is no denying that its LAN entry will have an impact. The company has to protect its flanks, and a local network is a good way to do it.

Japanese manufacturers are also trying to move into this important area. Wang, Data General, and Datapoint suggest that the technological transition may be taking place more rapidly than was imaginable even a year ago. Hewlett-Packard and DEC are moving aggressively to capitalize on the potential of the business in personal computers. The minicomputer manufacturers are showing increasing interest in LANs, following the leadership of the microcomputer makers. The mainframers cannot do otherwise than react.

IBM AND THE FIERCE COMPETITION

To understand the degree to which LAN architecture integrates with IBM's strategic plans, it is necessary to consider the strategy projected by its management for the 1980s. No company strategy is the subject of broadcasts and pronouncements. It has to be pieced together, like a mosaic, from available bits of information. That's what we will be doing in this section.

With mainframes in the doldrums—the 3083 included—and with software problems known to have hit both the 8100 and Series/1, the emerging IBM strategy is based on a major thrust along the PC line. The original IBM PC was introduced in August 1981, and since management supported it all the way—also through such novel approaches as software collaboration and the handling of plug compatibles—the product did much better than expected. In March 1983 it was joined by the XT, a data communications–oriented personal computer, and there is a rumored $650 PC in the works as well as a PC more powerful than the one first introduced that uses Intel's new chip (80186).

All this gives to the market confidence that the mainframer is out to maintain his position. A LAN strategy integrates nicely into this overall picture, the more so as IBM also has further-out plans for:

- Workstations with color graphics
- Advanced WP concepts through DP/WP integration
- Voice and image functions
- Relational database models

IBM must protect its customer base. The computer market share of mainframes is decreasing from 83 percent in the mid-1970s to a projected 36 percent in the mid-1980s. Small systems are increasing their market penetration. Desktop and personal computers, whose market share was negligible in the mid-1970s, are on their way to an estimated 22 percent of the market by 1985. The minicomputer share also is growing, but at a much slower rate.

The market trend is clearly toward the smaller intelligent machines installed in quantities. This is the result of the large market expansion made possible by low-cost systems which allow small organizations to buy computers and large organizations to implement distributed architectures. All this is part and parcel of a transition from the first-generation batch systems to the network of interconnected personal computers passing through timesharing realtime and distributed hierarchical networks.

If IBM readies logical and physical products for the 1980s market, it is also true that those products will face challengers. By early 1983, however, it was apparent that the IBM PC had taken a good hold of the market and carved out the largest share for itself.

The local area network IBM prepares cannot be seen as an entity apart from the mainframer's lower end of its product line. On the one hand, the successful push up the product line to larger systems may tie the sales more closely to the capital budgeting cycle in the future. The most recent data suggest that demand continues to track industrial production, which is a concurrent economic indicator and moves with the economy.

In the U.S. market there is a growing surge toward myriaprocessors: personal computers and LANs. They support a distributed environment which is highly competitive with the upper-cost class; they call for expenditures below the $50,000 mark for similar capabilities and put a microcomputer at every desk, where it really counts.

These are some of the highlights of the developing fierce market in data processing, data communication and databasing. Nor should we forget that AT&T is tooling up for its massive entry into the same arena. There are many reasons to believe that it will become a formidable competitor, one destined to survive. Positioning is always important in business, and IBM's LAN effort should be examined from that perspective.

MARKETING STRATEGY

To the still small number of LAN designers and manufacturers, selling a local area network is a means of placing at the customer site some hard disks and LSI interfaces, but the large computer and microcomputer manufacturers have other goals in mind. To understand that, we should note that the LAN hardware itself does not exceed in cost 1 to 2 percent of the local area budget.

For the computer manufacturer a LAN has a dual role: to integrate the microprocessor-based equipment—hard disks, printers, and so on—into one DP/DB/DC system and to protect its flanks. Both issues require a marketing strategy able to cover the whole product range with particular emphasis on the lower end of the line, where the explosive growth is expected to come (more than 50 percent per year) and a neat integration policy.

When we talk of the lower end of the product line, presently of microcomputers and before too long of nanocomputers (hand-held machines), we refer to three markets:

1. Large to medium-size businesses, where they will be integrated at a desk and connected through a LAN.
2. Small to very small business, where stand-alone might have a limited future but the LAN concept will infiltrate before too long.
3. Home computer market, where the stand-alone will dominate for some time but the LAN will eventually take root to integrating microprocessor-based appliances with a control unit.

Since the stand-alone microcomputer is a cutthroat business, its marketing cannot be through the salesman channel. What are the IBM alternatives? Dealers, chain stores, and eventually supermarkets can sell the manufacturer's personal computers, but those mass channels are not equipped to handle the system support necessary for LANs. There must, therefore, be a two-tier approach:

1. Massive marketing of personal and hand-held computers through general-purpose channels not necessarily under IBM control.
2. Selected marketing of local area networks supporting the same equipment and interconnecting IBM minicomputers and mainframes into office information systems, and from there to SNA and satellite business systems (SBS).

This strategy alone suggests hierarchical overtones in the IBM local network being designed. Success, however, hinges on issue number 1: mass marketing. Not only can microprocessor-based systems make money only if sold in large numbers, but also their sale will spread equipment to the four corners of the home and business worlds, eventually to be interconnected through local and long-haul networks.

Let's, therefore, take a closer look at IBM's marketing strategy for personal computers. The mainframer is lining up established service bureau companies, such as Comshare, to sell hardware systems on an OEM basis. The machines will be used as intelligent terminals to tie into the service bureau mainframes and eventually into IBM's information network. It's wise to take good note of that.

IBM also sells its personal computer off the shelf through its own computer shops, specialized chains like Computerland, and merchandising chains such as Sears. Banks also are interested in trying their hand in the sale of personal computers. Chase Manhattan, for instance, is experimenting in one of its branch offices with the sale of IBM personal computers.

Table 14-1 identifies the main market channels IBM is known to use, but also suggests some other good outlets not yet tested. Auto dealers, for instance, may be a perfect sales base, in fact much better than department stores. They have central locations, big display windows, salesmen trained on rather complex products, and a pressing need to find some other product line to complement the sluggish sale of cars.

Figure 14-1 outlines a possible IBM marketing strategy for moving from stand-alone sales to complete systems. The success of such a

TABLE 14-1 POSSIBLE MARKET OUTLETS FOR PERSONAL COMPUTERS

Channel	Estimated capacity
SPONSORED BY IBM	
IBM shops	Low
Sears	Medium
Comshare	Good
Computerland	Good*
Software houses and OEM	Medium
Bank branch offices	Low
OTHER POSSIBILITIES	
Auto dealers	Good
TV and mail order	Medium
Already established office equipment dealers	Low to medium
Supermarkets	Low

* However, results will be very price-sensitive.

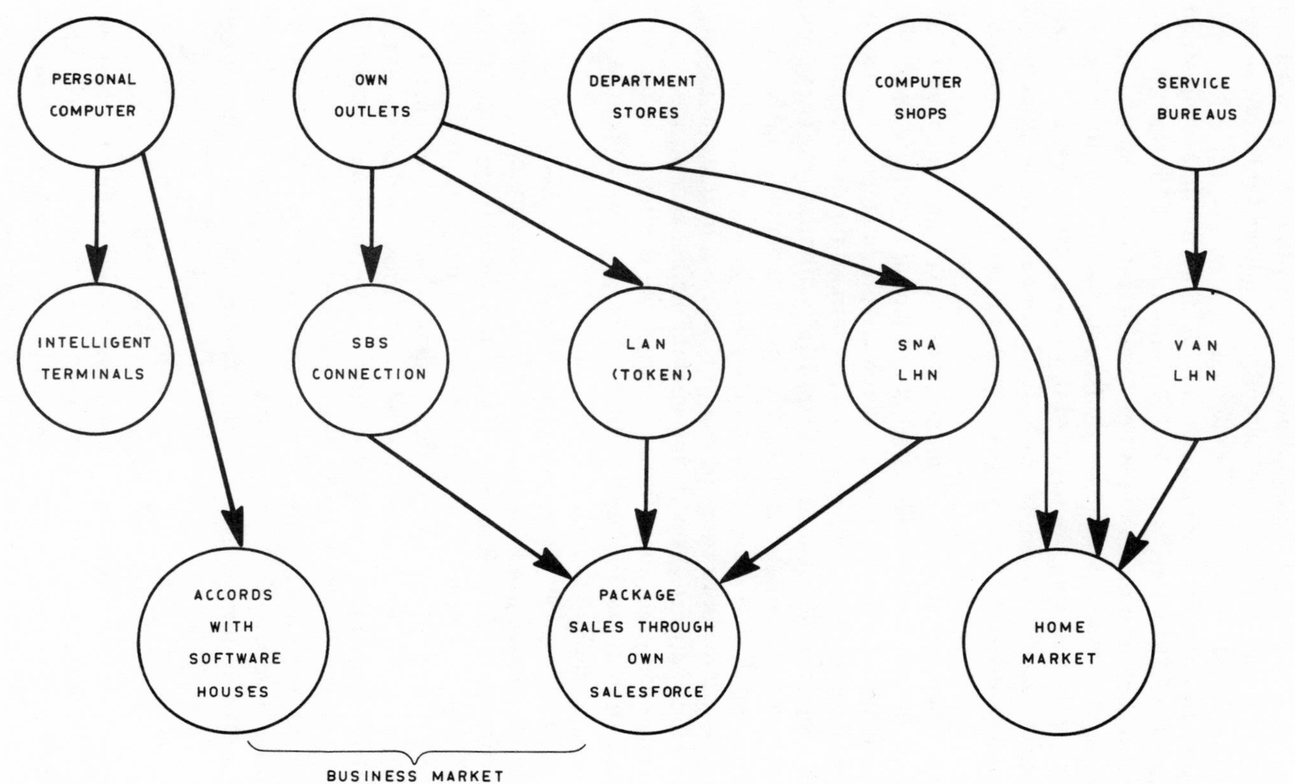

Figure 14-1. A possible IBM marketing strategy for moving from stand-alone sales to complete information systems.

strategy will rest on two pillars: how well it is prepared and what the competition may do. Other companies have followed different strategies to push their personal computers.

When Tandy Corporation unveiled its first 16-bit Model 16 in January 1982, it took its wares direct to the doors of data processing and management information system people through a special salesforce. Market analysts tend to think that the Model 16's biggest success will be among the larger of the small businesses, in the half million to $10 million range. As for LANs, Tandy made agreements with Datapoint to use the attached resource processor (ARC) architecture.

Apple may be following a similar strategy to enlarge the marketing horizons of its products. The strength of Apple largely rests on the large number of software houses which are producing an impressive stream of applications software. Apple is perhaps the one machine for which there are the greatest number of LAN alternatives. They have been developed not by Apple, but by independent LAN firms, although Apple has fully collaborated. But Apple, so far a market leader, may encounter some problems with Lisa, in terms of pricing, networking, software support, and general market acceptance.

As microcomputer manufacturers target the business market, still another strategy is the dealer blitz. Anyone who comes to the marketplace late needs much more imagination and thrust to carry the day. Remember that Tandy has 5000 distributors (Radio Shack) in the United States; Apple has properly focused on foreign operations. For instance, it has 300 distributors in Italy alone. One might think that electric typewriter and office equipment manufacturers, such as IBM, can easily follow up with their independent dealers. That is not so. Office equipment dealers have a different image of their wares and services. They are not easily converted to personal and hand-held computers, and they will be a failure with LANs.

With no established base of that kind, Apple has been wise in selecting its dealers, at least in the foreign countries. Its national representatives lured young, dynamic people from the computer and terminals manufacturers, including IBM, and helped them set up their own shops. They now sell hardware, software, and system assistance; thus nearly all shops are able outlets. In contrast, a manufacturer now converting an existing dealer chain to microcomputers estimated that only 10 to 20 percent of them are recoverable.

IBM has to react to this situation, and may well take a leaf from its own book of 30 years ago. A sound marketing strategy with personal computers will necessarily be based on three pillars:

1. Education
2. Applied science and applications software
3. Joint pilot projects

For latecomers, there is much wisdom in emulating the IBM experience of the early 1950s. Intensive education (internal and customer-oriented) was launched in 1953; applied science was supported in 1954; and imaginative joint pilot projects were started a year later—there were three in 1956–1957. The projects involved American Airlines for the online experience; Boeing for DBMS, and the DoD Sage for journaling systems. The difference is that in the 1980s the available time has shrunk and the three pillars must be erected in parallel within an orientation which integrates personal computers and local area networks.

There are two reasons why it was important to have these pages as a prelude to the discussion on the IBM LAN. First, IBM intends to market total systems. Second, as far as IBM is concerned, the ornaments which it will hang on the Christmas tree are as important as the tree itself.

TECHNICAL CHARACTERISTICS OF THE IBM LAN

Having examined the IBM LAN business perspectives, we can look at the technical aspects. As we stated, the LAN has a token ring and uses a packet-switching protocol. Such a protocol is analogous to an onion: by peeling off one skin—for instance, the header and trailer of one protocol level—we are left with a new skin, or protocol, beneath. This can be represented diagrammatically as in Fig. 14-2. Proper organization is necessary to see this process through. If a packet is transmitted from one station on the ring to another, without any controls, it can get lost or corrupted without the receiver knowing, and it has to compete at the receiving workstation with other packets from other transmitters to that station.

The problem of errors can be faced if each byte of data in the packet consists of, say, 7 bits and a parity bit, or 2 bytes are considered as 15 bits and a parity bit. However, neither of these schemes allows the transmission of data when all 8 of 16 bits are significant. If, however, a block protocol, such as supported by the Cambridge ring is introduced (the IBM LAN follows the Manchester approach), then a block of bytes can be transmitted from one workstation to another without competition from other transmitters to that station.

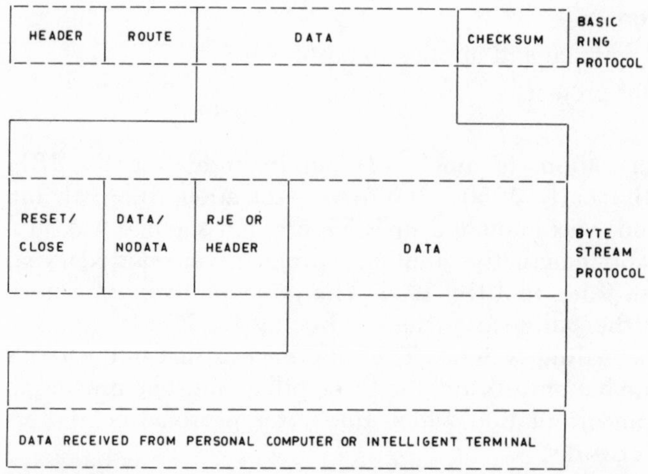

Figure 14-2. Basic ring and byte stream protocols. Note how the typical packet is built up or stripped down as it goes through successive layers.

On seeing a header, the receiving workstation looks to the transmitter by setting its source select register. Still, however, a packet can get lost and/or corrupted. Then the check sum at the end of the block will usually see to it that corruption is detected, and the whole block will be thrown away.

The header plays an important role. With, say, 12 bits we can handle about 4000 different users and processes. Each is identified by a station and port number, and the port number appears in the route field. This permits the transmission of blocks from one station to another, but with no specific guarantee of what will happen if an error occurs and the receiver throws the block away and with no rules about what will happen if, say, the receiver runs out of buffer space.

To correct these difficulties, it is necessary that another layer of protocol be used. There are two alternatives:

- A simple protocol for simple uses: making requests to the name server and downline loading or a connection between two ports on different stations
- A more sophisticated approach to be employed once an OPEN request has been issued and accepted

By a system of sequence numbers, timeouts, and control commands, the sophisticated approach can ensure that any data which is transmitted from one station to another will eventually arrive at the destination station error-free and in the correct sequence. Lack of buffer space can be taken care of by commands which indicate whether buffer space is available for the next transfer.

Within the command repertoire should be instructions for getting a link between two stations into a predefined state if something goes disastrously wrong or a machine attached to a station crashes. As more data communication layers are added, the supported services can be enhanced. If ever a transport layer is activated, it can provide the applications level with a set of network-independent primitives. The applications level will communicate with the transport service via these primitives, and the transport service will map them onto the underlying protocols. This supports transparency, because the applications level needs to know nothing of the underlying communications medium, and communications subnets may be replaced by subnets employing different communications techniques without modifications of the applications level.

This discussion has focused on the fundamentals of the ring technology, and the IBM token-passing procedure is implemented within a ring solution. The preceding paragraphs do not say what IBM should, would, or might do; they simply explain what it can do, given the LAN approach which it has chosen.

IBM is still in the beginning of implementation. Therefore, it finds itself some way from offering sophisticated approaches; hence, the emphasis on the basics. On the other hand, companies which have chosen token passing do suggest that CSMA cannot be used in process control applications, for example, because no one can be sure that data will pass through. Token passing, they emphasize, guarantees that data will pass through. But this only underscores the fundamentals.

The IBM LAN is structured in a two-level hierarchy:

- Token rings are used as subnetworks.
- The backbone network employs two different elements, bridges and block switch, for interconnecting rings.

IBM paid particular attention to assuring growth potential in large networks through interconnecting rings by bridges and a store-and-forward node, whose functions are provided by a block switch. Both the bridges and the block switch can be implemented in hardware. This solution employs the concept of a monitor function. A capacity seems to be incorporated to eventually provide synchronous channels for voice services, but it is doubtful that such services will be utilized.

Functions above network access and the basic transport mechanism are stated as being executed end to end. The block switch is able to perform such functions as link error control, address translation, and adaptive routing.

The smallest configuration consists of a single ring which can support up to 100 or a stated maximum of 200 workstations. According to IBM, this limit is of a practical and not architectural nature. It is suggested by traffic load, reliability, maintenance, and network management needs. Since in many firms the number of stations to be connected to a LAN may exceed the limit, a solution is provided to build larger networks by interconnecting several things through a backbone network.

As for layers, IBM speaks of end-to-end; the facts say otherwise. At current (1983) status the LAN developed by the mainframer supports:

1. Logical link control
2. Routing sublayers
3. Ring access
4. Physical connection

Transmission on the ring is in the form of variable length frames. A frame is delimited by "start" and "end" *delimiters* and consists of:

- A transport control (TC) field
- TO- and FROM-link addresses (AT, AF)
- The transport information (TI) field
- The frame-check-sequence (FCS) field

Delimiters consist of four-bit patterns representing violations of the differential Manchester code employed on the ring followed by two unused bits and two qualifier bits which serve to distinguish between start delimiter, end delimiter, and a shut-off delimiter. The latter is used to force any transmitting adapter into REPEAT mode.

The transport control field serves access control, multiplexing of asynchronous and synchronous traffic, ring supervision, and recovery. The first of its 8 bits serves to distinguish between a frame carrying asynchronous traffic and the synchronous communication (traffic mode indicator, TM). The second bit is the priority indicator (PI). It is needed to guarantee timely access of stations with synchronous traffic.

The third bit is very important: it is the token (TK). Access to the ring is controlled by the token, which can be in either of two states:

free (TK = O) or busy (TK = 1). The next serves as monitor count (MC). It is manipulated by the ring monitor for ring supervision and recovery purposes. Subsequently there are two bits whose meaning is not defined.

The seventh is a reserved bit. As implied by its name, its usage is reserved; it does not carry any information relevant to the ring access protocol. Finally, the last bit of the octet is a modifier (MO). It enables distinction between normal user frames and transport control frames.

The link addresses space is structured around the notion of a local network consisting of several interconnected rings. To simplify the routing function in the block switch, the IBM LAN employs structured TO- and FROM- addresses each four bytes long. The first two bytes of the link address denote the ring number; the second two bytes indicate the station number. The former are unique in the entire LAN. The latter are unique on one ring.

The transport information field contains higher-level data. It may involve any sequence of bits. In the HDLC it consists of a control and possibly an information field. Finally, the frame check sequence is composed of 2 bytes and is generated according to the standard CRC polynomial of degree 16. It protects the MO bit, the TO- and FROM-addresses, and the TI field.

As in all token-type approaches, access to the ring is exclusively controlled by the token. The supervisory functions are embedded in the protocol to invoke recovery actions when the token is corrupted. Token-related error situations can be of different types: lost token, busy token, and duplicate token. A token can be lost during a certain critical time interval when neither a free nor a busy token is transmitted over the ring. A circulating bus token situation develops when a TO-field with a busy token continuously circulates around the ring. It may be caused by noise hitting the free token bit.

Finally, a duplicate token situation arises when two or more stations are transmitting simultaneously because each has received a free token. Such an error can occur if a free token is generated, for example, by noise hitting a busy token. There are other ways also. For a lost token, integrity is assured by means of recovery through timeout. In the case of a circulating free token, recovery is through the monitor count field.

Automatic backup is enhanced by a monitor function in each ring adapter. IBM says that its LAN presents a guarantee of throughput and delay, and an interrupt mechanism is provided by a priority indicator in the control field.

There is one design shortcoming which must be emphasized. It has to do with the memory capacity to be supported at the LAN level. The hierarchical feature (and therefore the upstream storage) left aside, the IBM LAN puts disk memory at the WS level. It does not share hard disk. That's a mistaken strategy.

IS PROCESS SYNCHRONIZATION NECESSARY?

A LAN architecture must be addressed to many more issues than those we have considered. Depending on the projected applications, one of them is synchronization. With a token ring, there are three ways to achieve synchronous transmission.

The first is that no master clock is provided. The frequency is established by mutual phase-lock loop synchronization, and stability depends on ring length. The second is that each station uses its own quartz oscillator to send and is synchronized to the upstream station with a phase loop.

The frequency differences between stations are compensated for by inserting or deleting a bit from a special header field when buffer overflow or underflow occurs and using an elastic buffer at the receive side. Such a buffer, required at every station to compensate for quartz effects, can cause a delay, which degrades performance.

The third possible way to get synchronous control is to use a master clock requiring only one elastic buffer at that location. The ring adapter which provides this clock is identical with the one at which the active monitor function is located, the function guaranteeing integrity of the token operation. When another adapter has to assume the role of the active monitor, in case of monitor failure, then this adapter will provide the clock.

The third approach dominates the concept of the differential Manchester code IBM seems to follow with its LAN. Hence, even if the mainframer insists that his solution is flexible enough to be taken either on a centralized or on a distributed basis, chances are the basic characteristics will be centralized, no matter what else is being said.

IBM seems to have gone to great pains to demonstrate that synchronous channels with guaranteed delay and throughput can be provided on a token ring in addition to the asynchronous, packet-oriented, data operation. This was part of the effort to show that realtime and non-realtime voice services represent possible applications of the synchronous operation capability. The observation that a baseband solution like the IBM LAN cannot handle voice has already been made, and it is therefore pointless to pursue the subject.

In other words, process synchronization makes sense if a local area network is designed to support synchronous processes, which means working on a realtime basis and having processes that interlock with one another in the sense that the work of the one cannot proceed without activities performed by the other. That is poor policy with mainframes, and it has resulted in higher costs, spoiled capacity, delays, and unhappiness. It has been tried with minicomputers and has brought them to the maxi level without resolving the problem of long response time. It is better not to repeat the same errors with the LAN.

While talking about transmission in a synchronous token ring during the International Symposium in Florence, Italy, in April 1982, the IBM design engineers emphasized that to get a simple timing recovery circuit at the receiver, codes with high transition density are preferable. In addition, a zero direct-current (dc) component of the code is needed for alternating current (ac) coupling. A further important requirement in a token ring is a small delay per station to achieve high efficiency. This blocks out codes which are word-organized. As a result they left the IBM designers with basically two codes: the Manchester and the Miller. The latter was ruled out because it has a low-frequency component which results in additional jitter when ac coupling is used. The Manchester code fulfills the requirements mentioned.

The Manchester code, the IBM designers also emphasized, is well suited for optical transmission. The differential Manchester code allows for the interchange of A and B wires in a wire pair without leading to data errors. The transmission efficiency of a Manchester code can be further improved with no substantial increase in hardware complexity if predistortion is used. And ac stations permit the employment of different cables with different characteristic impedances in the various sections of the LAN ring. These are the highlights of the technical references.

The IBM solution calls for a unidirectional transmission with a two-level wiring hierarchy: backbone and local loop. Figure 14-3 documents what was just stated: IBM's LAN is basically hierarchical. In that arrangement, the backbone ring is passive, and so is the distribution panel.

Some other observations are significant. The ring cable can be coaxial, but the tap-to-bus interface units attached to the cable seem awfully complex when compared with those promoted by other LAN manufacturers. Complexity is unwarranted; it drives up both costs and needed expertise.

Regarding the use of cable, there is every reason to believe IBM will favor a mix of media: shielded twisted pair (Twinax), coaxial cable, and, later on, optical fiber. In the international symposium, the

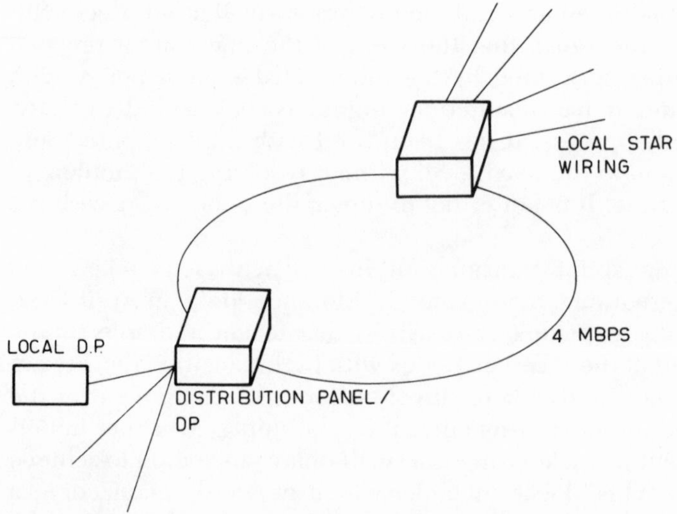

Figure 14-3. Topology of the IBM LAN: a basically hierarchical structure with the backbone ring and distribution panel passive.

design engineers made the statement that up to 100 or even 200 workstations per ring is feasible, because jitter was experimentally minimized by equalization at the receiver level. It remains to be seen, however, what is meant by "stations" in both the hierarchical and semidistributed versions of the LAN.

The designers also emphasized ring throughput and their opinion that token solutions are rather insensitive to an increase in distance (1 to 10 km). This, too, is something to be seen when the applications begin.

To recapitulate, the LAN solution advanced by IBM presupposes central control and hence lower flexibility, lower reliability, and higher costs than other solutions. It has to its advantage that it is reasonably open to fiber technology and, as its makers state, the system can be easily channeled.

The priority mechanism IBM uses only for the synchronous operations is one of the three alternatives that IEEE Project 802 is coming up with. That's good. The hierarchical approaches are, however, out of date, although they may serve the mainframer's product line. The IBM solution employs:

- Differential Manchester code
- Equalizer at sender or receiver to extend distance
- A transmission code which is dc-free

- AC coupling
- Common-mode suppression
- No ground loops

Once again on the negative side, the synchronization concept is centralized. An active monitor provides a master clock, and all other stations are slave. One station (the master) acts as an active monitor for token recovery, and all other stations are passive monitors.

All stations in the ring, IBM says, have the same hardware. The mainframer takes pride in that fact; users will be pardoned if they do not. Here once again we are in the lock-in: Competitive equipments are excluded. (See also the discussion in the preceding chapters.)

Finally, one is tempted to write on the negative side the choice made in cable transmission capacity and overall architectural concept. Baseband and ring meet the needs of the entry level user; even IBM with all its marketing skills can't change that fact.

AN ALTERNATIVE RING APPROACH

The approach taken by IBM is not the only one characterizing technical ring solutions. In fact, the first and more widely used implementation is the Cambridge ring. Like the IBM LAN, it consists of a set of nodes which are joined serially in the form of an endless loop. The nodes are of two types:

1. *Repeaters* used to regenerate the digital signals transmitting information round the ring
2. *Workstations*, which may be personal computers or small minicomputers

The two can be together, in which case a node consists of a repeater plus a station. Individual devices are connected to these stations by means of access boxes, as the Cambridge technology calls them.

Information is sent between stations in ring packets. The packet format includes:

- One start-of-packet bit
- One full-empty bit
- One bit used by the monitor station
- Eight destination bits
- Eight source bits

- Several data *bytes*
- Two control bits
- One parity bit

One user who chose the Cambridge ring LAN (Kent University) suggested that in 1978, when the decision was made, there were available three choices: this ring architecture, Ethernet, and an X.25 discipline through central switch. Ethernet was unpredictable in terms of cost; centralization was rejected; and the Cambridge ring approach was adopted. It gave the possibility of most facilities required, and it was cost-predictable.

The Cambridge ring works on the empty slot principle. When it is initialized, a specialized workstation, the monitor, sets up a framing structure on the ring so that at least one packet is in flight round it. The exact number of such packets is dependent upon the length of the ring and the number of nodes. Gap digits in the form of zeros precede the packet.

The monitor station is also used for monitoring the ring, clearing lost packets, and accumulating error statistics. When a station has a packet ready for transmission in its shift register, it waits until the next slot, that is the next empty packet on the ring.

- If the full/empty bit is a 0, the station transmits the packet.
- If the full/empty bit is a 1, the slot is already taken.

This procedure is repeated for the next packet, and thus the delay at each node is minimized. The transmitted packet goes around the ring to its destination, where the control bits are set on the fly to indicate busy, rejected, ignored, or accepted. In the latter case the data is copied into the destination station.

Eventually, the packet returns to the source, where the full/empty bit is set to zero. This empties the slot. The current content of the packet is compared with the original content, and that provides a consistency check. The Cambridge design has a built-in feature that prevents a station which has just transmitted a packet from immediately sending another. That is, one station cannot monopolize the available bandwidth.

At Kent University the ring is built to operate at 10 MHz with a maximum distance of about 100 m between repeaters. The signals are transmitted along twisted-pair wires. Transformers are employed throughout for common-mode rejection and isolation. The repeaters are powered from the ring. Facilities are provided to aid in maintenance and error recovery. For token-passing purposes, the typical delay within the adapter, per station, is one bit.

According to the user, the ring's reliability has been quite satisfactory: Only one error lasted as long as 3½ h; all others lasted less than 10 min. The total downtime has been 5 h over 4½ years of work, which essentially means that the Cambridge ring experienced two or three problems per year.

The parity bit at the end of the packet is used for localizing transient faults and ring breaks. Each station continually checks the parity of every passing packet and empty slot and wires it into the parity bit. If it does not match the old parity bit, a fault has occurred. Since the correct parity is inserted at each station, the fault must have occurred since the last active station. Thus the ring is steadily being monitored for errors, and any fault detected is located at the nearest active station. That information is transmitted to the monitor.

Starting from the available network software, Kent University has developed the following utilities:

- Booking server
- Name server
- Error logger
- Printer server
- TS server
- Compiler server
- Gateway to British telecommunications

Two of the servers on the Cambridge ring are based on Z-80 micros: the error logger server and the name server. The former immediately precedes the monitor station, has a hardcopy output, and is used to record error messages produced by the system from the other stations of the ring. It is feasible to send textual messages to the error logger server under program control.

The name server contains a look-up table, typically in programmable read only memory (PROM), with the names of ring devices in character string format including their ring addresses when presented with a name. It can also enable reconfiguration of the ring to be carried out in a transparent fashion to the other devices on the ring than those affected.

IBM has commented that the Cambridge approach increases overhead and leads to about 60 percent of possible performance. But Kent

University rejected the argument that there is a particularly heavy overhead and instead said that:

- The original objectives have largely been met.
- The Cambridge ring provides a good basis for the future.
- The constraints have been overcome, and they were quite useful.

Future development plans involve a booking server which would control access to the ports on the main hosts for defined purposes. An advantage of this solution is that the administrative load will not be on the hosts themselves. Another issue regards additional timesharing servers, a Spooler server to provide editing and filing facilities for users who process their work offsite, a file server on a distributed basis, and the selection of a 16-bit microcomputer as a long-term replacement for the Z-80.

15 WANGNET

Wangnet, which was officially announced in November 1981, is a good example of a broadband solution. It incorporates three separate layers: the Wang band, the interconnect band, and the utilities band. Combined, the three currently occupy only 35 percent of the total available bandwidth, which extends from 10 to 350 MHz per cable. The other 65 percent is reserved for additional capabilities to be announced as the architecture evolves, the Wang strategy develops in the WP and DP fields, and the user requirements in office automation become better defined and more concrete. However, Wangnet emphasizes that use of unassigned frequencies is not recommended without prior consultation with and written approval from the firm. The reason is that such use may adversely affect communications and operating equipment on Wang-assigned frequencies and therefore be counterproductive.

The *Wang band* enables users of office information systems and other Wang small business computers to communicate over the cable via a Z-80–based bus interface unit (BIU; Wang calls it cable interface unit, hence, CIU) with 128K of memory. The BIU sells for $4570 and it provides the interface between the cable and the system, packetizes data, detects errors, controls the flow of information, handles the carrier sense multiple access with collision detection (CSMA/CD) function, and is shared by all users on the system.

The *interconnect band* enables any non-Wang terminal to communicate with both Wang and non-Wang systems by using standard data communications protocols. Both dedicated and switched channels are provided by the interconnect band, which permits the simultaneous use of hundreds of different systems and provides dedicated channels for permanent transmission links between systems or terminals for point-to-point or multipoint operation.

The system supports 32 multipoint 9.6-kbps lines and 16 dedicated 64-kbps circuits. The new hardware employed is called the Wang *fixed-frequency* modem. The 9.6-kbps modems will sell for $850, and the 64-kbps modems for $1200. With *data switches* and *frequency-agile* modems, the switched interconnect band channels permit 512 devices compatible with RS-232 or RS-449 to be attached to the cable and the simultaneous operation of 256 circuits. Only one data switch is required to control all 512 devices; it sells for $12,000.

The *utilities band* permits the simultaneous operation of seven independent video channels able to handle a variety of additional functions, including both teleconferencing and security. The other new product from Wang, DVX, features digitization of voice and voice store and forward (voice mail).

We have mentioned the digital voice exchange (DVX) in a preceding chapter. We defined it as an automated, stand-alone voice-message solution which allows users to send and receive voice messages, *voicegrams*, via an *audio mailbox*. Capable of operating from any Touch Tone phone, DVX allows a user to send and receive voicegrams to or from any user on the system and to send to any phone (including dial) in the continental United States.

THE BROADBAND APPROACH

Wang looks at Wangnet as part of its overall strategy in the office automation market. As a senior company executive has commented, "A local area network is the tool that can help virtually everyone in the organization be more productive, because it makes information easier to access, distribute, and manage."

The way this company approaches the broadband choice is multifunctional. Combined with all the other Wang office automation products, Wangnet makes information, in all its forms, easier to communicate. By providing a common carrier for many different services, the company expects an integrational effect: Information has many different uses, but it also occurs in many different forms. At any given time, many information types are generated, communicated, interpreted, and acted upon throughout any organization. Such forms of information have many points of origin, different destinations and communications paths. Just one of them is data communications, and it is not the most novel.

Among the new developments adding their weight to data communication needs are voice mail, text merged with data, teletex, electronic filing, annotated reports, graphics, and image handling. The Wang thesis is that only broadband can effectively handle so many sorts of information that's spoken, displayed, heard, and seen on live video.

The way the designers of Wangnet look at the subjects, their LAN assures that all sorts of information can be concentrated at the local level. Organizational characteristics must evidently be considered, but certain studies demonstrate that an estimated 80 percent of the information transmitted between individuals and departments stays at the local level, usually within a single facility. By emphasizing this 80 percent ratio, such studies suggest that the remote computer communications facilities an organization already has generally serve only 20 percent of its overall communications needs. They also suggest that a cost-effective way to increase the total information-handling capabilities is to focus on communications at the local area rather than the long-haul perspectives.

On the basis of those statistics, the Wangnet designers argue that their product incorporates the fundamental view of information flow within an organization. Given its broadband capability, the argument goes, Wangnet can link virtually every office and every desk in a company into one highly efficient information-sharing resource. It can carry every type of information an individual now uses, including text, data, electronic mail, facsimile, and video, while there is the reserved capacity to handle an even greater diversity of forms of information in the future as the need arises.

An interesting feature promoted by Wang is the local area–long-haul connection: the remote Wangnet. It is a part of Wang's unified network product plan, and it allows its systems in geographically distributed locations to communicate with each other. For instance, a VS computer functioning as a host can be linked by multipoint communication lines to Wang VS, OIS, 2200, and Wangwriter systems at remote sites. In this sense, the remote Wangnet provides a mix of distributed and centralized processing: interactive data processing on the host VS can be performed from a remote site through a Wang workstation.

Wangnet can accommodate gateways for remote microwave and satellite connections. It handles communications bandwidth for video and teleconferencing, and it enables facilities management to dynamically control energy settings and also monitor security devices. The disadvantages start with Wang's tendency toward star-type solutions. The remote Wangnet, for example, uses a hierarchical network architecture incorporating a bit-oriented higher-level data link protocol.

With this structure, it provides multiple virtual circuits: messages are delivered in data packets framed by envelopes to assure good delivery.

At the local area level, Wangnet handles the Wang VS, OIS, and 2200 systems (Fig. 15-1). These can exchange text and data files and share processing resources, while non-Wang equipment can be conducted over Wangnet by using standard interfaces such as RS-232.

What the last claim does not mention is that the widest band is reserved to Wang equipment, and that's the second weak point if a company follows the policy of a multivendor environment. Indeed, Wangnet assures a 12-Mbps resource sharing link between Wang VS, OIS, and 2200 systems. With its 16-bit addressing capacity, the Wang band accommodates good-size network configurations.

Combining the last two points—star-type solutions at the workstation level and the 12-Mbps Wang band capacity—one would be tempted to think that hundreds of Wang systems, representing thousands of individual workstations and their concurrent data traffic, could be linked together on the Wangnet. Practically, however, such a vision ignores the applications environment and its data load.

Prior to seeing how users can implement file and document transfers between, say, their 220 Series connected on the band, it is advisable to examine what the file access and file transfer requirements are. The same is true of the needed estimate of the resulting collisions.

Another objection to clustering on a small mainframe in a way suggested by Fig. 15-2 is that, as far as a LAN approach is concerned, such solutions are self-defeating. The LAN is made so that the very low cost but reasonably powerful personal computer is attached to it. Not only is there no reason to go one degree remote through star interfaces, but also, because of them, the LAN advantages are lost.

Using agile software, such as Wang's Mailway, is a positive fact; getting into resource sharing between Wang VS, OIS, and 2200 systems is much less so. There are evident advantages in capitalizing on the peripherals and processing resources of any other Wang system connected to Wangnet. Just the same, for the reason mentioned, there are less evident disadvantages, and the latter may outweigh the advantages.

Let's, however, add to the advantages that, in the Wang line, Office Information System (OIS) and VS word processing users can remotely edit documents which reside on other OIS- or WP-equipped VS machines. Thus connecting Wang systems to the Wang band assures instantaneous access to information regardless of its physical location. As is the case with all LANs providing shared file capability, this

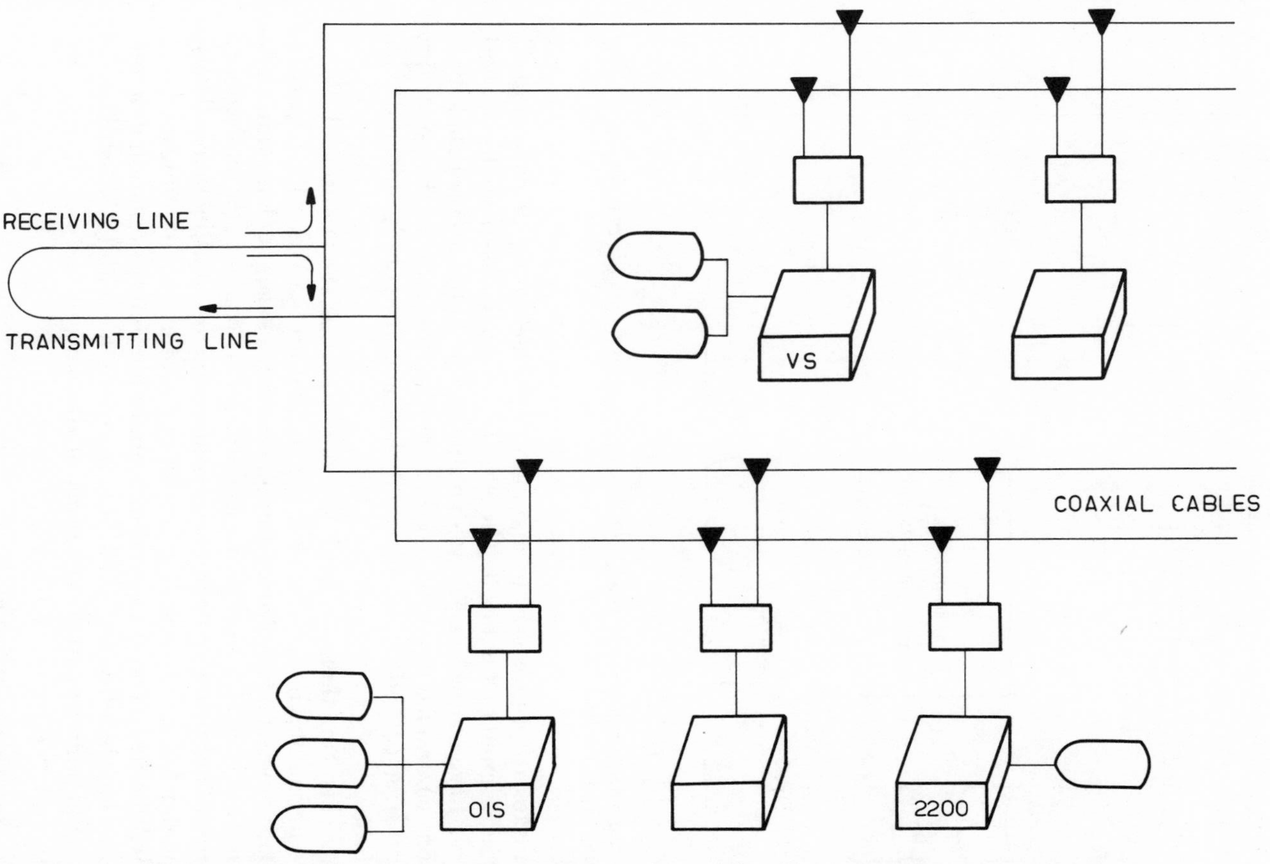

Figure 15-1. Wang equipment connected to the Wangnet. Note the use of separate receiving and transmitting lines.

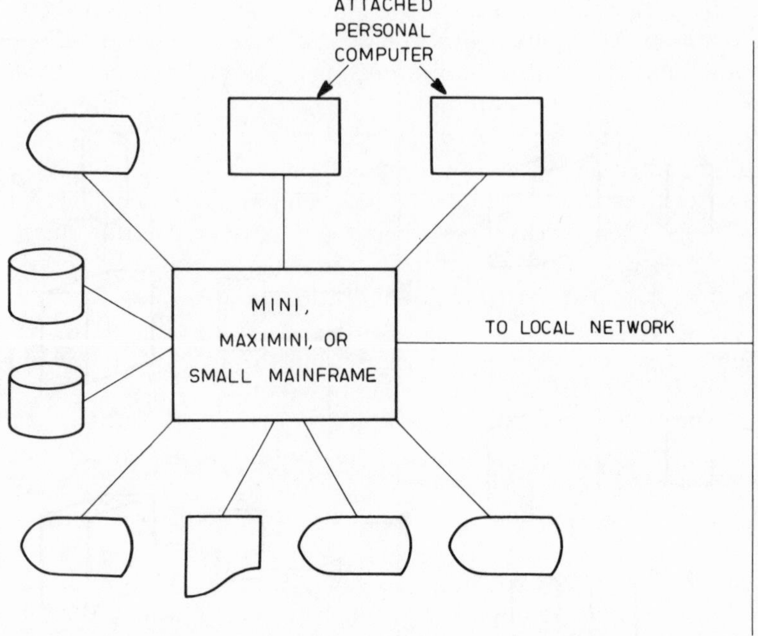

Figure 15-2. Multithread solutions that are suggested by some manufacturers but are to be avoided by the user.

makes it unnecessary to maintain duplicate copies of data in every department that needs it. The VS, OIS, and 2200 users on the network can have interactive access to a single copy of the text or data kept in one central facility. Among other benefits, this reduces the possibility of error caused by inconsistent data and irregularly updated databases.

This can then be said in conclusion: A heavy user of Wang equipment who has decided to keep within the Wang line—particularly one who has already implemented packages such as Mailway—has every reason to examine the broadband Wangnet for implementation. The system is a good LAN. But a company starting to feel its way with LAN, and which employs other mainframes and minicomputers, will be just as well advised to examine the implementation of a low-cost baseband system. After it gets experience with LAN—and proves the benefit—it can always think of alternatives.

THE THREE BANDS OF WANGNET

The Wangnet architecture uses a standard CATV coaxial cable as the transmission medium. The principal difference between Wangnet broadband solution and baseband systems is that Wangnet uses frequency division multiplexing to divide the total bandwidth of the cable into many separate communications channels representing hundreds of individual communications paths which can simultaneously carry various forms of information.

In a physical sense, Wangnet utilizes a dual coaxial cable link. One 350-MHz cable is used to transmit information; the second cable receives information. Access to Wangnet can be distributed throughout the business operations in a flexible and expandable tree structure which spans a distance of up to several kilometers depending upon the specific application.

A limitation on cable length derives from the interconnect band requirements. The distance along the transmit line from the data switch, through the network loop and along the receive line to any network outlet should not exceed 3.6 km in cable length. Wang thus proposes to evaluate the installations requiring cable runs in excess of those lengths upon a request for quotation and propose feasible solutions.

The Wangnet bus topology is treelike. A transmit-receive crossover located at the midpoint of the main coaxial trunk divides the cable into a *transmit* and *receive* half; the two are folded together. With this approach, which is typical of CATV, one cable tree is for transmission only. The other is a mirror image of the first and is for reception only. Data on the transmit line propagates toward the network loop. When it reaches it, it passes to the receive line and propagates back to all network user outlets.

Addressed physical or logical destinations capture information on the receive line. The main trunk and branches of the network distribution cable use sheathed coaxial cable, directional couplers, signal splitters, and unidirectional CATV-type line-extender amplifiers. Cable runs may be rooted through false ceilings, trench ducts, or elevated floor. Four port-tap devices connect sheathed distribution cable to flexible coaxial cable drops, which in turn terminate at network outlets. Any four-port tap can be interchanged with one having six or eight ports. All line-extender amplifiers used with the cable are ac-powered through the center conductor and shield of the broadband coaxial cable itself.

In its architectural design, Wangnet dedicates bandwidth areas to specific types of communication, thus permitting each band to be tailored to the equipment accessing it. Transmission speeds range from 300 bps to 64 kbps for non-Wang devices and to 12 Mbps for communications between Wang systems.

The broadband cable system design provides a 340-MHz frequency spectrum—10 to 350 MHz—with certain constraints as directed by the FCC. We did mention in the introduction that the spectrum is divided into distinct areas or bands (Fig. 15-3). The *Wang band* is dedicated to Wang system communications. It supports 12 Mbps, works CSMA/CD, and accepts attachment of any piece of Wang equipment.

The *interconnect band* is an important feature in that it allows the connection of other manufacturers' equipment. It has three parts. The first part is from 0 to 9.6 kbps, point-to-point or multipoint, and synchronous or S/S. It uses a V.24 interface. There are 32 of these channels, and Wang recommends looking at them as a leased telephone line.

The second part of the interconnect band is up to 64 kbps point-to-point or multipoint, and bisynchronous or S/S. It uses a V.35 interface. There are 16 of these channels. The third part is up to 9.6 kbps, bisynchronous or S/S, and point to point, but with switching capability. It follows the V.24 and V.35 standards. Fundamentally, the design of the interconnect band is based on industry-standard protocols—and rightly so.

The third spectrum band is the *utilities band* for cable television applications such as security and video conferencing. It supports seven channels in the United States, primarily for TV. It uses a free bandwidth, like any RF device, and it can answer teleconferencing, environmental, educational, and other purposes. Both freeze-frame and full-motion video signals can utilize these channels. The user can also implement facility-wide television monitoring systems.

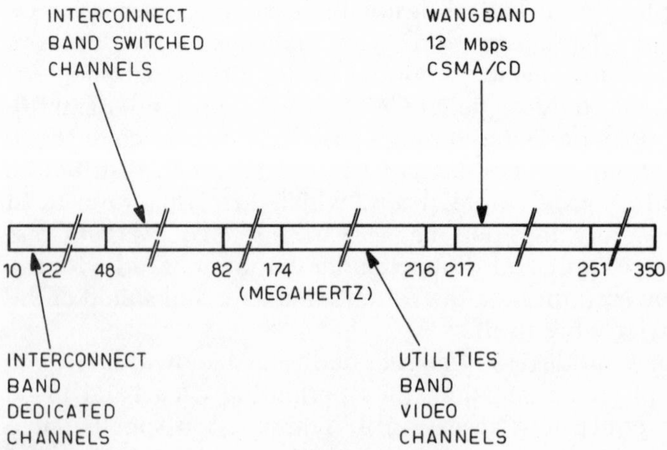

Figure 15-3. Partition of the 340 Mbps of Wangnet into the interconnect band (dedicated and switched channels), the utilities band, and the Wangband.

We have said that the first attachment to the bus is an interface unit (BIU or CIU). Sufficient BIU addressing exists for 65,535 attachments, but the actual number of machines supported depends on the nature of individual applications and traffic for the Wang band. The BIU is an intelligent controller that assembles information to be transmitted into variable-length packets.

By using the HDLC data link standard, the BIU transmits the information packet at the appropriate carrier signal. It also receives, buffers, and disassembles received packets, which are presented to the Wang equipment attached to the network. One of the major functions of the BIU in the Wangnet is that it performs the CSMA/CD functions. As we saw, with CSMA/CD only one signal is present on the band at any time. The interface unit listens to the cable and initiates a packet transmission only when no signal is heard.

The same problems we encountered in Ethernet and the other CSMA-based solutions are evidently present with the Wang band. Because of propagation delay, it is possible that two or more BIUs could initiate transmissions at the same time, so the BIUs also listen while transmitting. If the message heard differs from the message sent, a collision has taken place.

In the event of a collision, the sender and all other BIUs immediately stop transmission. Each BIU is programmed to delay a random amount of time before reinitiating the packet transfer. This naturally leads to the need to perform complete error recovery on all transmissions. The Wang designers also emphasize reinforced system reliability by distributing control, so that the failure of any single BIU on the network will not cause the entire network to close down.

Among the supported software faculties we distinguish

1. General-purpose file transfer
2. Support of teletex (Mailway)
3. Virtual terminal capabilities

Resident software permits the performance of VS data processing tasks from any Wang workstation suitably equipped, editing of a document resident on an OIS or VS system from any Wang OIS workstation, initiating document or file transfers to another equipment, and requesting document or file transfers from another machine. For file transfers between dissimilar systems (such as OIS and VS, VS and 2200, 2200 and OIS), certain types of received files require conversion on the receiving machine.

At this time (1983), the beneficiary is the Wang equipment itself, because it is the only equipment which attaches to the Wang band. A reason given by the designers is that no other manufacturer is ready to develop the needed facilities for a Wangnet implementation. If so, as the number of this network's installations increases, we are going to see much in PCM effort.

In the interconnect band, which as we said has been designed to support standard communications protocols, Wangnet handles concurrent full-duplex connections between systems or terminals regardless of manufacturer. This means the user does not have to change current communications software to migrate to Wangnet. As briefly described, the interconnect band provides 16 dedicated circuits for multipoint and nonswitched point-to-point communications at rates of up to 9.6 kbps. Both Wang and non-Wang units that support standard communications protocols in multipoint environments can be attached to these channels by means of Wang modems that operate on a fixed frequency.

The interconnect band also supports 256 switched circuits for point-to-point transmissions at rates of up to 9.6 kbps. Up to 512 Wang and non-Wang RS-232-equipped devices can establish communications sessions on these switched circuits by means of a Wang data switch and associated Wang modem. The function of the data switch is to monitor the switched circuits allocated within the Wangnet Interconnect band and implement frequency division multiplexing.

When a connected system initiates a point-to-point transmission to another system, its frequency-agile modem issues a request for services by autodialing the extension of the system it wishes to communicate with or by allowing the user to manually dial the desired extension. The data switch checks to see if the dialed system is available. If it is, it notifies both units' modems of which frequency to use, and data communication ensues. This presumes the implementation of a common protocol.

GATEWAYS FOR INTERNETWORKING

Wangnet has the gateway capability for communication over leased line or switched line networks, satellite links, and microwaves to other Wangnet local networks and Wang and non-Wang computers. The Wang data switch both controls multiple communications sessions within a single facility and can handle gateways for communications beyond the physical limits of the cable.

This makes it feasible to establish communications with systems at the local level with Wangnet or remotely via the communications lines a company is currently employing. Data rates, communication modes, and gateway-to-gateway link integrity depend on bandwidth and other critical parameters of the external transmission media.

Currently supported internetworking functions include the following areas:

1. Wangnet-to-Wangnet local networks
2. Wangnet-to-Wangnet long-haul networks
3. Wangnet-to-*X* local networks
4. Wangnet-to-*X* long-haul networks

In class 1 the Wang band supports 12 Mbps, the interconnect band 9.6 to 64 kbps, and the non-Wangnet Wang intersystem exchange (WISE) a 64-kbps communications band. Class 2 is served by the remote Wang facility (RWF) through the 3780 and 2780 protocols and Mailway. Mailway is primarily intended for electronic mail, but it also provides the gateway to other products.

The Wangnet interconnect band is being used for the Wangnet-to-*X* local networking. The TTY, 3270, 2780, 3780, SDLC, X.25, and Mailway teletex serve the Wangnet-to-*X* long-haul communications purposes, and that can be true of a PBX connection also.

Remote DP, WP, and file transfer are initiated by issuing commands through a series of menus processed—as in the case of the VS—by a user program. On any system except the Wangwriter, both remote interactive processing and document transfer can be performed concurrently with local processing. The remote Wangnet software includes provisions for intersystem security and transfer queue monitoring and control. Though a single task on each machine performs actual document transfers, documents and files can be submitted for transmission by a user at any time.

Requests are queued and processed in order by the file transfer manager. Each file is associated with transfer characteristics that define its received name, security access, and owner. System operators can monitor and manipulate the queues at each site. Equipments connected through remote Wangnet use Wang communications line controllers attached to full duplex modems.

Transfer rates of 2.4 to 9.6 kbps are supported. Each line controller includes 64K of memory, a dedicated microprocessor, restart diagnostics with internal memory and loopback tests, and an external status indicator (Fig. 15-4). Note, however, that the system is distributed at the midicomputer level and clustered in respect to the workstations.

Wang has been very keen to emphasize that, unlike fixed-architecture local networks, Wangnet offers various options for local and long-

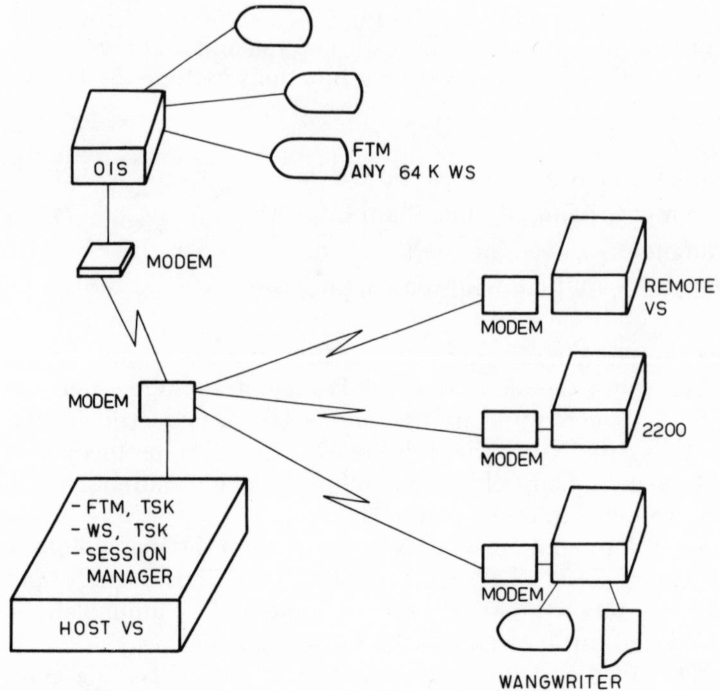

Figure 15-4. A virtual-circuit-based communications discipline through telephone company lines operating in the 2.4- to 9.6-kbps range.

haul network control, multiplexing, contention, and gateway implementation. The implication is that networking configurations may be custom-tailored for any organization.

Finally, to the remote communications messages it will be proper to add Wang's digital voice exchange. With DVX, the company claims to have overcome the problems of time zone differences, telephone lag, and unavailability of the called party because of time window. As with document transfer, for user convenience, the voicegram can be reviewed, recorded, canceled, or sent. One message can be sent to as many as 16 locations. Recipients can replay voicegrams immediately after listening to them and can reply to the sender, save the message, or forward the message, along with an explanatory header notation, to a third party.

The basic DVX, which accommodates 200 users and sells for $125,000, contains a central processor with disk drive, a four-line input/output message processor, a 10-MB operating system disk, a 275-MB message disk, and a system management workstation. The high-end DVX has 1.1 GB (gigabytes) of storage and supports 800 users. It costs about $320,000. However, neither the basic nor the high-end DVX yet has a tie to Wangnet.

By the end of 1982 Wangnet had some 50 operating networks and another 100 in development spanning three continents from the United States to Singapore via Germany and France. Given Wangnet's late 1981 announcement, these numbers look good. Other broadband networks, however, have a wider distribution. For instance, Sytek has been said to have some 150 systems operating in the United States and Europe.

16 3M/IS: ALAN

Designed for industrial applications and based on CATV technology, Videodata has been launched by 3M/Interactive Systems as a broadband network. But Videodata has no software to support a LAN architecture. An architectural solution is scheduled for a May 1983 announcement with betatests at Ford, GM, and Westinghouse immediately thereafter.

The product is still in search of a name. Videodata is not applicable to this five-channel broadband LAN operating at 2.5 Mbps. Meganet was originally retained, but 3M cannot publicly use it because another company has that trademark. ALAN (for advanced local area network) has been one of the options. There is no trademark on it, but it happens to be the name of a senior executive at 3M/IS, and it has therefore been discarded. In this book ALAN is retained to identify this still anonymous network.

Being a relatively new LAN design, this 3M/IS architectural effort brought in perspective (as of early 1983) three lessons to be learned by aspiring network designers:

1. LANs made according to the IEEE Project 802 standard are much more expensive in terms of interfaces than those which can use off-the-shelf RF modems.

2. If window testing and acknowledgment disciplines are included (as with ALAN), then only 40 percent of the stated bus speed can be taken as the real speed of the LAN.

3. There is *always* a significant time delay in ISO/OSI layer implementation and functioning between the existing and the new LAN.

In regard to item 1, though there are 250 identification numbers on an ALAN channel (plus 6 in reserve) there are no priorities on this LAN. Priorities are asked by the 802 standard and a second release of ALAN will provide them, but at roughly double the cost per BIU because special RF modems and more interface logic will have to be provided. In fact, 3M/IS properly states that, in its current status, the network is best suited for terminal-to-mainframe rather than PC-to-PC communications.

Window (buffer) testing and acknowledgment is a good feature of ALAN. The facility works as follows. Before talking, the transmitting device:

- Will ask the receiving unit if buffer space is available.
- If affirmative, it will transmit.
- If transmission takes place, then an ACK must be sent by the receiver.

This procedure adds up to three transmissions, and to this overhead should be added that which is specific to the token-passing mechanism.

As for the third lesson for network designers, the May 1983 BRB announcement by 3M/IS includes neither file server nor print server, and the first gateway to be supported will be a simple bridge linking the five channels on the cable. "People at Nestar have more facilities on the LAN than we do," said a senior 3M/IS executive.

It takes time to build the necessary facilities, and no manufacturer has infinite resources to throw into any and every product effort. Development can come faster if a product of advanced information technology—PC and LAN—attracts the attention of the user community in a big way so that add-on software is developed by many vendors and attachments are also.

In its current state of development, the 3M/IS local area network features:

- Token passing
- Physical bus, logical ring
- Transparent communications facilities
- A very low error rate
- Remote loading of the bus interface unit

- 4-kB buffer for each port on the BIU
- Network monitoring capabilities for statistics only (not for control)

The 3M/IS local area network divides the broadband cable by taking the 53.75- to 83.75-MHz band in the reverse direction, thereby creating the stated five channels (Nos. 2′, 3′, 4′, 4A′, 5′) of 2.5 Mbps each. In the forward direction these correspond to channels O, P, Q, R, and S. There is a 192.25-MHz offset band between the two. (The 53.75 MHz in the reverse direction has been chosen to line up properly with the O channel forward, because the 192.25 MHz is fixed.)

The broadband medium is a standard CATV-type system with a 10-km radius from translator to most remote BIU (called NIU, for network interface unit, by 3M/IS). Each BIU is designed to support two, four, or 8 ports. The communications discipline is asynchronous or specified synchronous protocols.

VIDEODATA

Designed and implemented by 3M/Interactive Systems, Videodata is a coaxial cable broadband network originally installed in factory environments. The motor industry in Detroit is its best client, but a notable office application is the Seattle First National Bank.

In its original release, Videodata particularly addressed the physical layer. Though the original implementation did not involve microcomputer use, being broadband, it can eventually carry a number of baseband architectures matched to the various speeds of the personal computers that make up the user and server stations in an office or factory environment.

Either network-supported or user routines can see to it that the network and file server respond quickly to I/O requests. The overall system time spent to satisfy each task is divided into transmission over the network, disk-seek and transfer time by the file server, and processing time by the server and user stations.

Videodata assigns a separate radio frequency or a different time slot to each communicating device or message, depending on whether FDM or TDM principles are followed. This permits thousands of messages to be exchanged simultaneously within a single coaxial cable over distances of up to 80 km. High data rates are easily accommodated with very little or no disturbance by noise and interference problems.

Being broadband, the network can handle simultaneous two-way voice, video, and digital data transmissions by using CATV technology that has been proved for decades. Recognizing that the facility most in demand is the rapidly developing microcomputer, the manufacturer plans to implement architectural support, as we have already noted.

As with the Wangnet, different networking options can be established. Their utilization should necessitate little change in work habits, provided the systems are designed to be easy to learn and the software is aimed at enhancing productivity through combined computing and communication capabilities.

The point about LAN architectures which we have made on several occasions is that isolated computer technology will not improve communications. From an organizational viewpoint, a LAN promotes a new style of computing: communication enhanced by flexible, personalized computer power. If the network can change dynamically to match an organization's changing structure, it can also promote the upscaling of computers and communications disciplines as the organization grows.

The preceding paragraph reflects the viewpoint of the manufacturer and of all those who bet on broadband as the way of the future: The business world needs rich functions to share business files, text, data, and programs. This is the core of the arguments advanced both by Wang and by 3M/Interactive Systems.

USING RADIO FREQUENCY

Communications technology splits fundamentally at the frequencies used on coaxial cable. We can think of coaxial cable as a simple wire used to send information by the voltage in it being left at zero or raised to some nonzero value. A station along the wire can detect the voltage changes and decode the information.

RF coaxial cable used for broadband transmission resembles CATV. Typical frequencies for television transmission are 50 to 100 MHz.

- A central carrier frequency is modulated up and down to transmit the information.
- The cable has far less attenuation than in the baseband region.
- A transmitter can broadcast over kilometers of cable instead of being limited to a few hundred meters.

Although baseband is typically digital, it can also be analog (as in Network One by Ungermann-Bass). Broadband is typically analog, but it is moving into digital solutions. ALAN design takes the latter path. Both FDM and TDM approaches can be used. Figure 16-1 shows the two alternatives. The first is frequency division multiplexing with point-to-point modems. The second is time division multiplexing with multidrop capabilities. Note the easy connection of an interface to permit cable extension (channel 2).

The information transferred between network stations can be in the

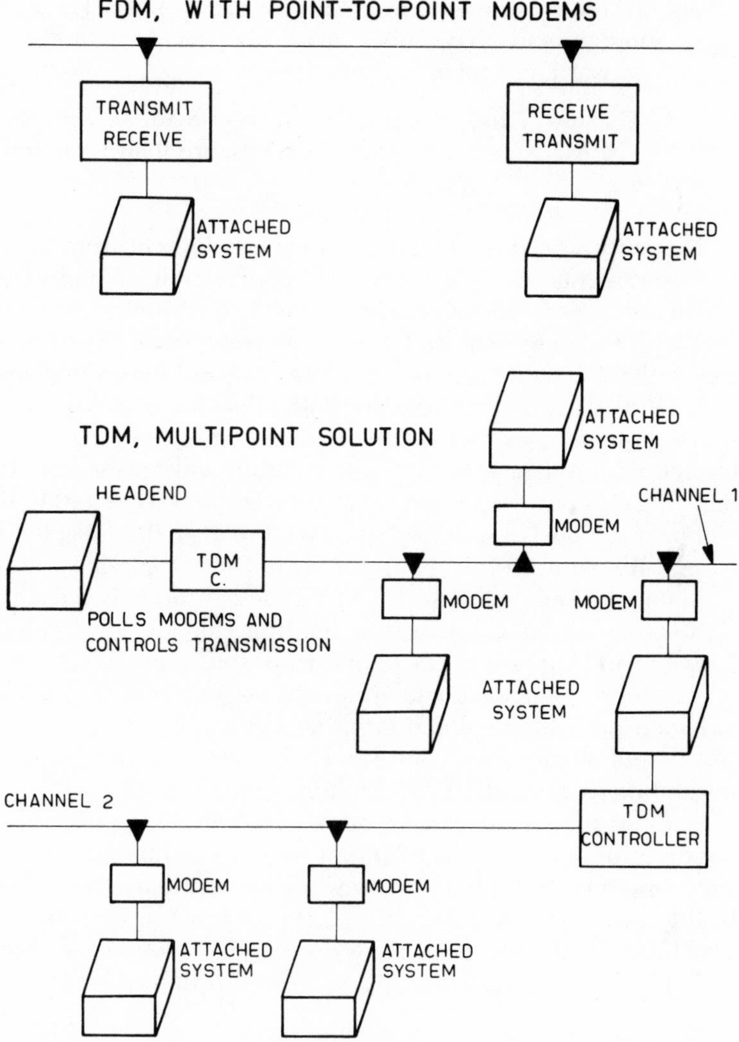

Figure 16-1. FDM and TDM solutions with ALAN.

form of computer-generated data, voice, image, or facsimile. Indeed, one of the key points with broadband is piggybacking: putting voice facilities on the cable along with image, text, and data. ALAN works in the 5- to 300-MHz frequency band.

1. The higher range of frequencies, 159 to 300 MHz, is reserved for transmission of signals from the head end of the system to the remote devices.
2. In the midrange of frequencies, 116 to 159 MHz, no channel assignments have been made to provide a buffer between forward and reverse signals.
3. The lower frequency range in the broadband spectrum, 5 to 116 MHz, is reserved for signals originating at remote devices.

This and other broadband architectures benefit from the fact that the components, shared as they are with the cable TV industry, can be produced at low cost because of the large volumes necessary for standard TV reception. Radio-frequency-modulated systems can also assure that the cable can, in principle, transmit both voice and video.

As with all systems, there are both advantages and disadvantages. An example of the latter is the requirement of a central retransmitter to receive the data sent from each station and rebroadcast it, amplified, at a different frequency that each station is expected to listen on. Not only can such a unit be expensive but also, if it fails, the network is unavailable until the retransmitter is back in service.

Among the advantages of CATV-type solutions is that the single-conductor coaxial cable is the medium for signal communication between all load points, the operator console, and the system computer. Radio-frequency signals eliminate the need for dedicated wiring between each load collection point and the control center, and the broadband circuitry sorts out signals in both directions while providing the equivalent of 10,000 pairs on a single wire.

With ALAN, loads can be added by merely connecting into the coaxial pipeline at any convenient point by using taps. Since expansion amounts to tapping in new cable sections, the transmission facility can be implemented in phases at low incremental cost. This enables a number of users to study the efficiency of a system before making a larger investment. System capabilities include:

- Cable engineering
- Communication interfacing for all kinds of signal needs

- Modems and multiplexers
- Design of computers and communications systems
- Preparation of software for user applications

A basic consideration is systems reliability. The cable and the amplifiers are the most reliable; manufacturers claim that amplifier reliability exceeds 200,000 h. Lower reliability characterizes the modems, and still less reliable are the computers and the terminals. Situational constraints must be considered in the design phase. For instance, when there is risk of cuts in the cable (generally because of construction) it is advisable to go to dual cable.

Care in installation is a paramount concern. If a cable is not cleaned well before a connection is made, the signal will not pass. Passive and active elements, along with some representative prices, are shown in Fig. 16-2.

- The cable itself (about 12 mm in diameter) costs about $1.20 per meter.
- The tap and splitter are passive elements; their cost is in the $12 to $14 range.

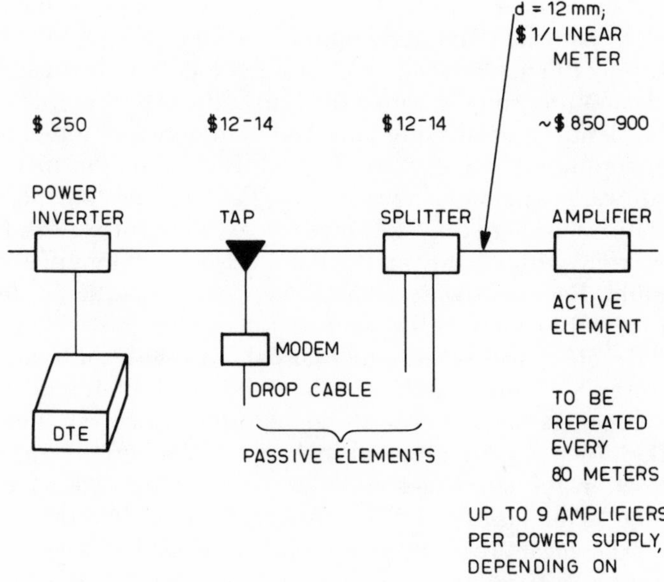

Figure 16-2. Passive and active elements on ALAN, along with indicated costs.

- The amplifier, which costs $850 to $900, is an active element that is needed every 800 m.
- Depending on line losses, up to nine amplifiers can be connected with one power supply. Thereafter, a new power supply is necessary. Each power supply costs about $250.

COMMUNICATING DATABASES

Since the early chapters we have emphasized that local area networks make sense if we employ, at the WS level, the most cost-effective devices technology can offer, and that means microcomputers. In a PC network all stations can have access to shared facilities such as local databases and printer servers to get hardcopy output. This is typically done by employing a dot matrix printer for high-speed work and a daisywheel printer for letter-quality printing.

In both cases, the objective is economic: to share expensive mechanical resources. That exemplifies an important principle of local area networks: The easiest way to add a function to the system is to add a server. Adding functions to the same minicomputer operating system is unwise. As with all levels of computer gear (mini, midi, mainframe), the bigger the operating software becomes, the more the overall operation is slowed down.

Let's also emphasize how unwise it is to assume that the provider of a sophisticated operating system for microcomputers will necessarily supply the networking functions needed. Very few vendors of personal computer software are willing to address the complex tasks inherent in blending databasing and data communication technologies into a coherent system design. Digital Research, for instance, provides software without a network. Its CP/NET system permits up to 16 stations to share the data and devices on a central host. But CP/NET is written without any particular network communication devices in mind. Each hardware vendor may select a particular technology and protocol to connect the workstations to the host.

In other words, although CP/NET provides a framework for multiuser software based on the familiar CP/M environment, many companies have chosen to develop their own variants of CP/M with their own sharing protocols because of the lack of support for applications in the languages and systems running under CP/NET. This is largely the task the LAN architecture should be undertaking.

The local area database is managed, as we have said, by the file server. It handles the DB service requests for I/O to and from disk files at the WS on the network. In a network of stations each of which has its own disks, there may be no need for a dedicated file server, but the local DB concept has major advantages.

The typical storage medium for stand-alone personal computers is floppy disks. But compared with, say, 30 floppy disk drives required to provide the same storage capacity, a file server with hard disks is more convenient and less expensive. Also, from the end user's viewpoint, it is easier to implement and manage.

The local area network, if it is to take advantage of shared databases, requires a secure way to assure the file transfer responsibility. Files must move from and to individual workstations without any alteration of text and data. The single-user system acting as file server should be operating in a multiple-user environment supporting user passwords, access control, and multiprogram synchronization.

Typically, these aspects of implementing the file server require architectural routines. If the LAN basic software does not provide them, they must be provided by applications software. This is one of the problems with ALAN. In its current release it does not support communicating databases. This section, therefore, is a description of what *ought to be* provided.

In terms of LAN architecture, the facilities we are describing should be closely knit with those of the communications server. The latter is a generic term that can cover many different jobs to be assured by a station talking over a telephone line to a remote computer. The communications server could be transferring files from one network to another, as in the case of teletex. It could be acting as a remote concentrator to a mainframe or it could allow users to access the network remotely and operate *as if* they were a station on the network.

As distinguished from a typical communications server, an *internetwork gateway* is a link for transferring information between two networks. Transfer can be made in realtime at the packet level or in batch mode. Internetworking is a basic response to the growth of computing and of the databasing and data communication requirements at large.

Communicating and file handling call for security and protection. Particularly if we plan to use microfiles, such as floppy disks, at workstations, we must have the possibility of encrypting the disks. We can do so in different ways. For instance, reading a given disk may call for finding a key characterizing a sector, and it is feasible to encrypt the key character. We can use the space between tracks and leave the regular tracks open, or we can skip some tracks in recording.

Apart from the software-based facilities it is possible to implement encrypters available in VLSI. Protection chips are available at about $50; their code is so intelligent that the user can change it every day and not run out of code inventory.

Journaling and recovery are two other necessary facilities of communicating databases. ALAN does not support them with its current release; its stated "primary purpose is communicating media, with no journaling action." Yet, in a business environment the LAN must provide protocol detail rather than let the user supply the protocol.

Fundamental routines needed for message delivery are still another part of necessary LAN software. For many applications, reading messages in first-in first-out (FIFO) order is sufficient, but it is also sometimes useful to be able to read them in some other order. For instance, a disk server process may accept requests to read and write records on a disk. To minimize disk latency, the server will want to process requests in other than FIFO order. Another example is an application that consists of more than one functionally identical process reading multimessage requests from the same bin. Each process would like to read the messages in the bin that are part of the request it is processing and skip over those associated with some other request.

In a priority mode, the protocol allows the bins of a mailbox to be assigned priorities relative to one another; these are established at the time the mailbox is created. In a read request, a process can specify a list of bins from which it wishes to read messages. If a message is pending in more than one of the specified bins, the message in the bin of highest priority is read. In this sense, bins provide a convenient mechanism for dividing messages into classes.

Flow control is associated with this notion. When the queue at a message destination becomes full, a flow control mechanism must be invoked. Several options are feasible. The simplest one is to notify the sending process that the message was not delivered, leaving it free to take whatever action it wishes. Typically, the protocol would be to wait for some period of time and then try to send the message again.

Another mechanism is the ISO reference model: having the sending peer entity periodically retransmit the message until the queue unblocks and the message is accepted or a specified period of time elapses. If the time period elapses before the message is successfully delivered, the sending process is notified. Similarly, the peer entity may ask the sending peer entity to hold the message until the receiving peer asks for it. Alternatively, the sending process holds the message until it receives notification to send.

The protocol must allow a number of messages to be queued at a message destination if necessary. There is no standard approach to this; some protocols permit different queue sizes to be associated with different message destinations. If the queue of a given message destination is full, a flow control mechanism must be invoked.

Sequencing is a necessary feature. Proper protocols for communicating databases should be to deliver messages in sequence. A series of messages sent by a given process to a given destination should arrive at that destination in the order sent, although nothing can be said about the order of arrival of two messages sent by the same process to different destinations or two messages sent by different processes to the same destination. An alternative, usually taken with datagram solutions, is to have the receiving station do the sequencing.

Still another necessary facility is priority handling. Many protocols for communicating databases allow messages to be partitioned into priority classes by assigning priorities to messages themselves or assigning priorities to message receptacles. In the latter case, each message receptacle is assigned a priority relative to all others in some well-defined group. A process is allowed to specify a list of receptacles from which it wishes to read a message. If a message is pending in more than one of the specified receptacles, the message in the receptacle of highest priority is read. In that case, message priority is determined by the receiver, whereas in the first approach it is determined by the sender.

Alarms supported by the LAN software are necessary to indicate the occurrence of an exceptional event, although not necessarily an error. With some protocols the arrival of an alarm can interrupt a process; with others, it is simply considered to be the highest-priority message pending.

To make it possible for an alarm sent by a process to a given destination to be synchronized with the stream of ordinary messages sent by the same process to the same destination, some protocols provide a message stream marker. The marker can be either an attribute of the message or a special type of message.

A protocol may provide an alarm capability by equipping a mailbox with an alarm bin. Such a bin has higher priority than any other bin in the mailbox. Messages sent to it are interpreted as alarms and are delivered regardless of the flow control status of the other bins of the mailbox.

COMPONENT PARTS OF A COMPANYWIDE SYSTEM

The component parts of a companywide system will typically range from those necessary to support announced functional characteristics to common utilities. It is therefore necessary to identify the service prior to defining the component parts. In this section we will examine two areas of interest that are different but complementary: voice communications and DP-oriented compatibility.

As mentioned, Wangnet is not the only broadband architecture presently able to handle voice messages. ALAN may eventually provide the carrier for digital voice exchanges by capitalizing on the product of ECS, a Dallas-based company 3M acquired in the late 1970s. (IBM also is moving into the field with *Speechfile*.)

The interest in this particular area lies in the fact that these systems are in the vanguard not only of office automation but also the merger of data and word processing. Again we return to fundamentals. In business systems and throughout the communications field generally, the two most commonly used displays are the visual and the auditory. Auditory displays traditionally have been limited to tonal signaling: bells, buzzers, whistles. But more recently, the human factors engineers have designed interfaces in which the machine actually talks to its users.

A simple example of speech output is the prerecorded message. Its higher bandwidth makes speech superior to tonal signaling systems, provided the basic requirements of reliability, cost, and voice quality are met. Yet tape and other analog playback mechanisms have difficulty satisfying the need for voice because they have moving parts that wear out. A method for achieving voice output with solid-state devices is to encode the speech waveform and sequences digitally and transmit them on the coaxial cable. To regenerate the analog signal, a standard digital-to-analog converter followed by a smoothing, low-pass filter is used. However, even for voice response systems with medium-size vocabularies, this technique can require excessive amounts of storage.

For these technical reasons, both analog and direct digital playback systems have proved unsatisfactory for most applications. However, designers also use machines that synthesize speech by electronically simulating the human vocal mechanism. These speech synthesizers rely on encoding the frequency characteristics of the signal. Only the parameters that control the speech production device are handled. The results are a simplified device and important reductions in required storage space.

Advances in very reliable semiconductor technologies are greatly reducing the cost of complex digital processing, and the semiconductors involved in speech synthesis techniques offer improvements in voice quality. As a result, reliable, not so expensive, high-quality speech output is now available for further implementation, and this poses the problem of handling the carrier in an able manner. It also brings into perspective the broadened functions of the private branch exchange (PBX).

Figure 16-3 shows an ALAN implementation with a PBX unit which provides for trunk assignment and line protocol conversion. The PBX identifies the called number. If the number is busy, the voice message is put on store and forward. At the receiving end, the

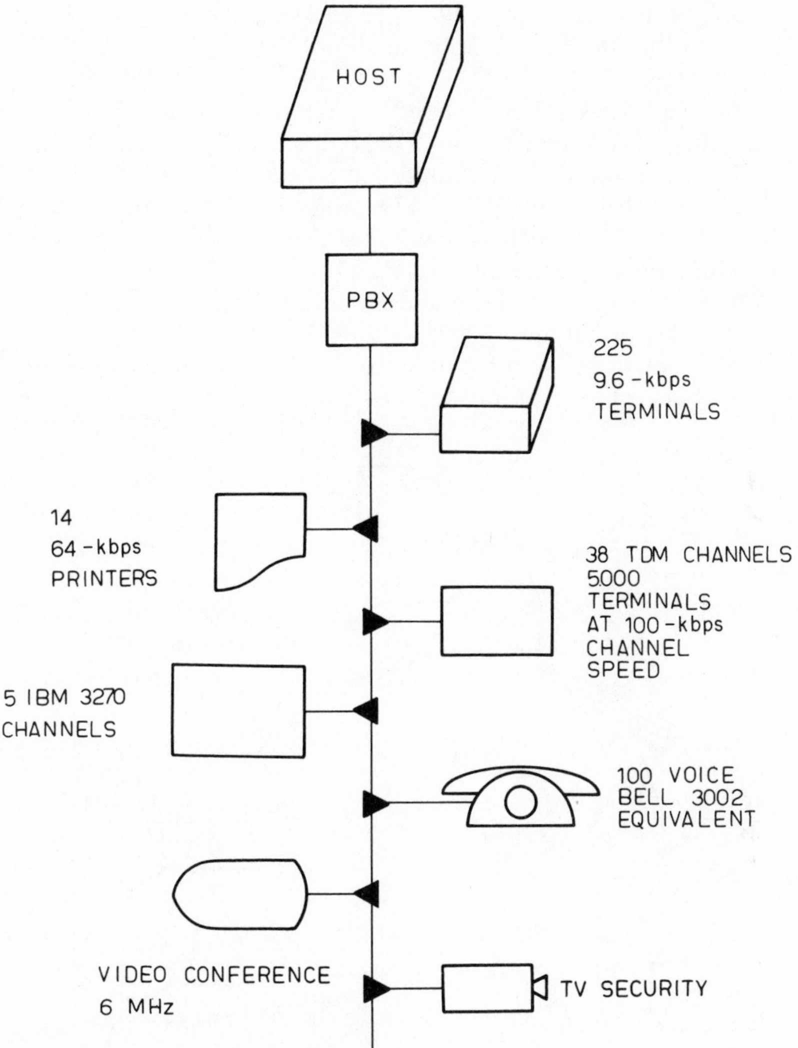

Figure 16-3. Implementing a broadband network with a PBX providing for trunk assignment and line protocol conversion.

station is equipped not only with voice facility but also with a modem at 9.5 kbps and data terminating equipment. The voice line works at 64 kbps. The 9.6 kbps for data transmission divide: 8 kbps for information and 1.6 kbps for addressing. It is also possible to make a frequency-assignable virtual connection.

The solution outlined merges voice and data. Because of it, from a single modem two types of information will operate: voice data and other data. They are not necessarily supported at every WS level, but they can be supported at specially designed devices with high intelligence.

Now let's look at the second area of interest mentioned at the beginning of this section: the DP-compatible approach. 3M/Interactive Systems originally announced that ALAN would operate five 6-MHz channels for the IBM 3270 protocol. Shortly thereafter eight channels were added to allow up to thirteen IBM 3270 controllers to operate on a single network (Fig. 16-4).

Modems assigned to a specific channel will transmit and receive on the same low frequency. This requires the use of a head-end frequency translator to convert the low-frequency signals from the modem transmitters into the proper high frequency for the modem receivers.

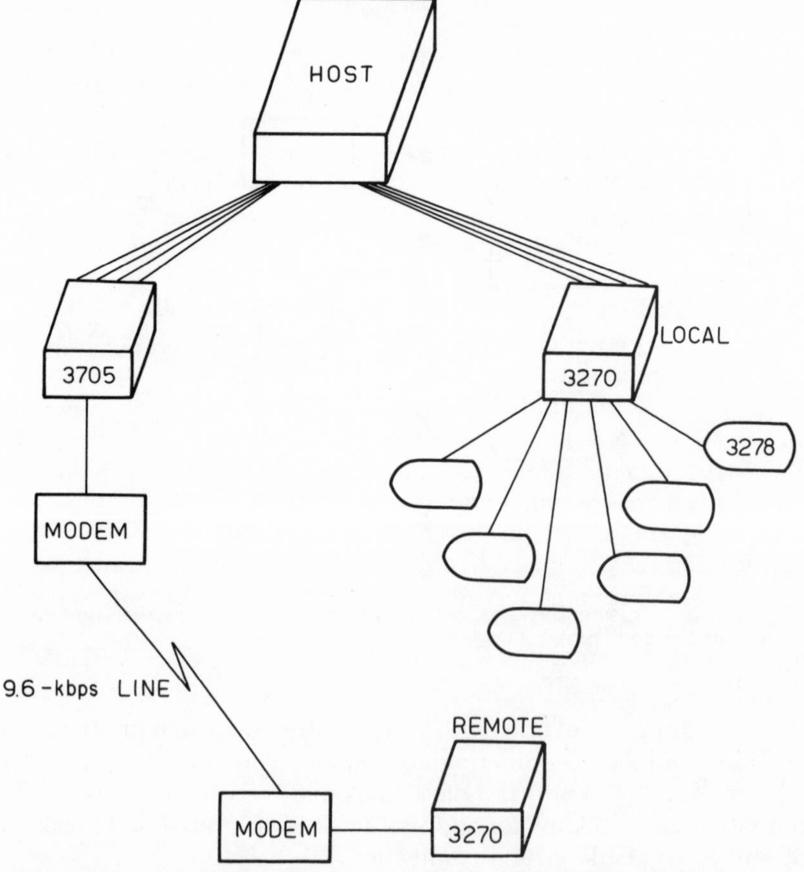

Figure 16-4. An Interactive Systems solution for the support of the IBM 3270 protocol for nearby terminals and long-haul communications.

When frequency translators are placed at the head end of the network, any modem connected to a given 3274 controller or its associated 3278 CRTs can communicate on a common set of low and high frequencies.

Typically, the signal is transmitted downstream to the head-end frequency translator, where it is raised to the proper high frequency. The latter is transmitted throughout the network upstream and reaches each modem-receiver. Each IBM attach modem consists of an enclosure with internal power supply and a minimum of three printed-circuit cards. The rear panel of the enclosure assures the connection of IBM equipment to the broadband network.

Other attachments to the network may be low-cost modems providing an easily interfaced, distributed data acquisition and control system operating on the broadband coaxial cable. Such modems operate in conjunction with the head-end RF modem. Any combination of up to 255 separately addressable modems may be used on one data channel.

Another device, the 2-Mbps serial synchronous broadband RF card, has been designed for high-speed OEM local network applications. It interfaces to the network via a single RF connnector and to the user's device via an eight-pin interface. Data speed ranges from 0.1 to 2.1 Mbps. Connection to the coaxial cable network is made through one or, optionally, two RF sockets that allow the card to be used with a single or dual coaxial cable system.

Still another device is the distributed multiplexer. It supports six asynchronous, full-duplex RS-232C data channels between a six-port head end and single-port remote units connected at any location on ALAN. This communications multiplexer interfaces with any processor equipped with a multiport or multiple single-port asynchronous RS-232C interface.

Remote multiplexers are used with any terminal, teletypewriter, or printer which has a serial, asynchronous RS-232C interface. Available bit rates are 74, 150, 300, 600 bps and 1.2, 2.4, 4.8, 9.6 kbps. Head-end multiplex units transmit in the range of 216 to 246 MHz and receive in the 24- to 54-MHz range. The remote modems operate in a reverse manner on the same CATV channels.

SOME KEY APPLICATIONS

A good idea of local area network capabilities can be gained through reference to significant applications realized to date. One of them, at the Seattle First National Bank, involves:

- Remote computer access
- Building security

- Branch bank communication
- Closed-circuit TV

All these are on the same cable. It is also possible to add emergency point-to-point intercom.

The Seattle First National local network project was initiated in 1979 on the occasion of the construction of a 34-story building. Management wanted to address, in an efficient manner, the interconnection of banking terminals, WP, security, voice faculties, and CCTV. The goal was to do so with the maximum possible flexibility. A microwave link at the top of the building was to be connected through a single cable to hosts, terminals, WP, and facsimile. Local area communications were to be based on broadband capabilities, with the local telephone company installing and operating the network.

Building construction, including the cable installation, was finished in March 1981. Operation started with 100 HIS and IBM terminals and a Bell Centrex PBX, while voice remained on twisted wire. Figure 16-5 presents the backbone of the ALAN (or, more precisely, of the Videodata) installation.

As happens in all installations, in the beginning Seattle First had its problems. With the architectural routines not yet available, the broadband cable was used multidrop and implementation problems did develop. According to 3M/IS, the reason for the trouble was that the attached devices used software which was not compatible with the 3M modems. (It was designed for IBM modems with special characteristics.) The vendor insists that when the software problems were subsequently weeded out, the installation worked as expected.

More information on ALAN implementation comes from factory installations. Plant wiring for such applications as energy management, for example, typically account for up to half the total cost of the system. With a coaxial cable network providing two-way communication capability from one end of a plant to the other, wiring cost can be greatly reduced. With such information utility in place for energy management, it is also practical to take advantage of the other broadband communications:

- Electrical and electronic signals
- Fire alarm and security
- Closed-circuit time and attendance reporting
- Inventory control
- Process control
- Word processing information

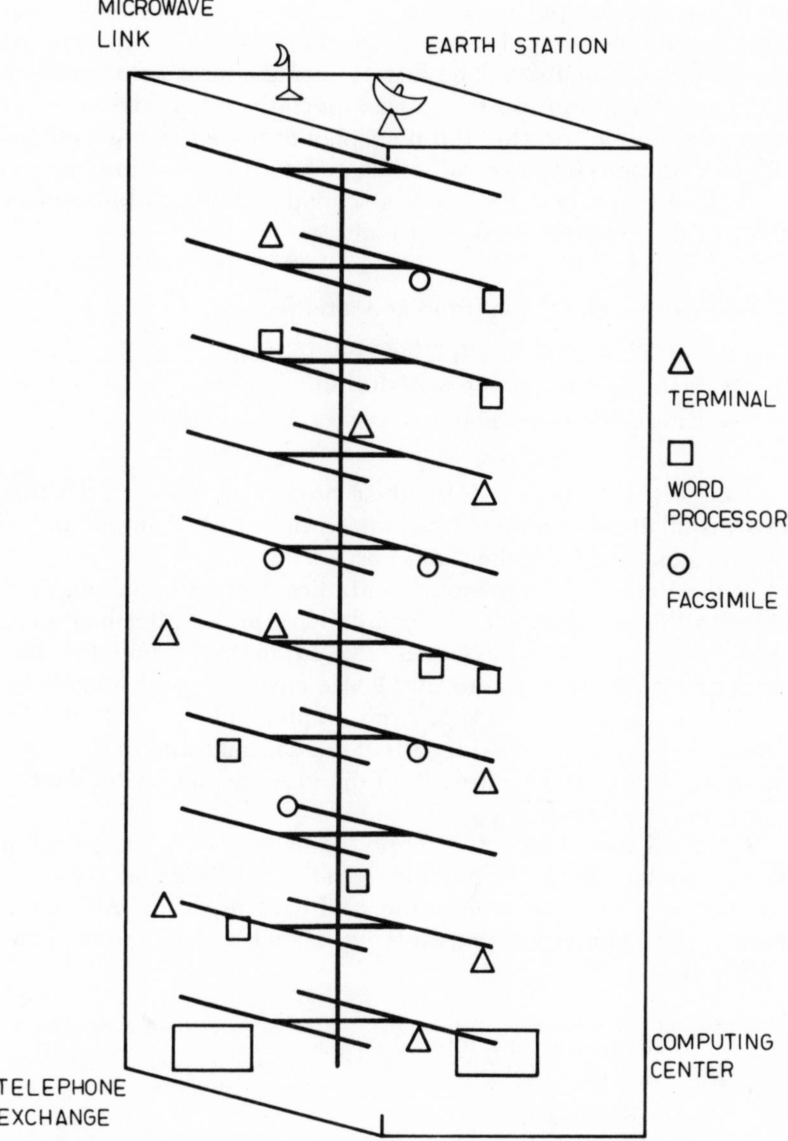

Figure 16-5. Example of building wiring with coaxial cable for data communication purposes. Both the BRB installation and the attached data terminals, word processors, and facsimile machines are indicated.

The processes may communicate over the network simultaneously with energy management signals, each of them assigned to a particular frequency band. Low-cost modems are available to accommodate such communication devices. Also available are multiplexers to allow up to six input/output ports of a computer to share a single channel. This is the type of application at the Ford factory in Batavia, which was completed in 1980. (The factory manufactures automobile transmissions.) Since in industrial, and especially automotive, locations it is not unlikely to revamp the floor plan at model change and cables can be cut, there is a dual cable installation. Furthermore, the coaxial cable is checked every tenth of a second. A 96-kbps link is secured through this implementation; it includes:

- Worker allocation (time and attendance)
- Inventory and in-process control
- MIS and production scheduling
- Energy management

Another example is a 3M/Univac project on office automation. In this installation, terminals transmit on the same channel, and about 100 terminals address the same host.

At the Veterans Administration Medical Center in Salem, Virginia, prior to the broadband LAN installation, the hospital had a coaxial cable installed for educational TV. From that came the idea of integrating WP, fire monitoring, EMS, facsimile, and nurse console. In still another case, the U.S. Army implementation at Fort Leavenworth (Fig. 16-6), the total length of the coaxial cable in the system is 13 miles. Much of it is directly in the ground; some is in duct work; and some is overhead.

A typical installation for energy management, an application we have emphasized, will provide basic capabilities of remote load control, peak demand monitoring, and load shedding. At the control end, a minicomputer commands each load and monitors such elements as:

- Coolant or oven temperatures
- Flow rates
- Electric current
- Air damper positions

Such a system automatically maintains less than peak electrical use by load shedding following established priorities. Should electrical demand approach the maximum allowable level, the system will turn off electrical loads, beginning with the very lowest priority items. The computer and communications system sets an alarm when conditions

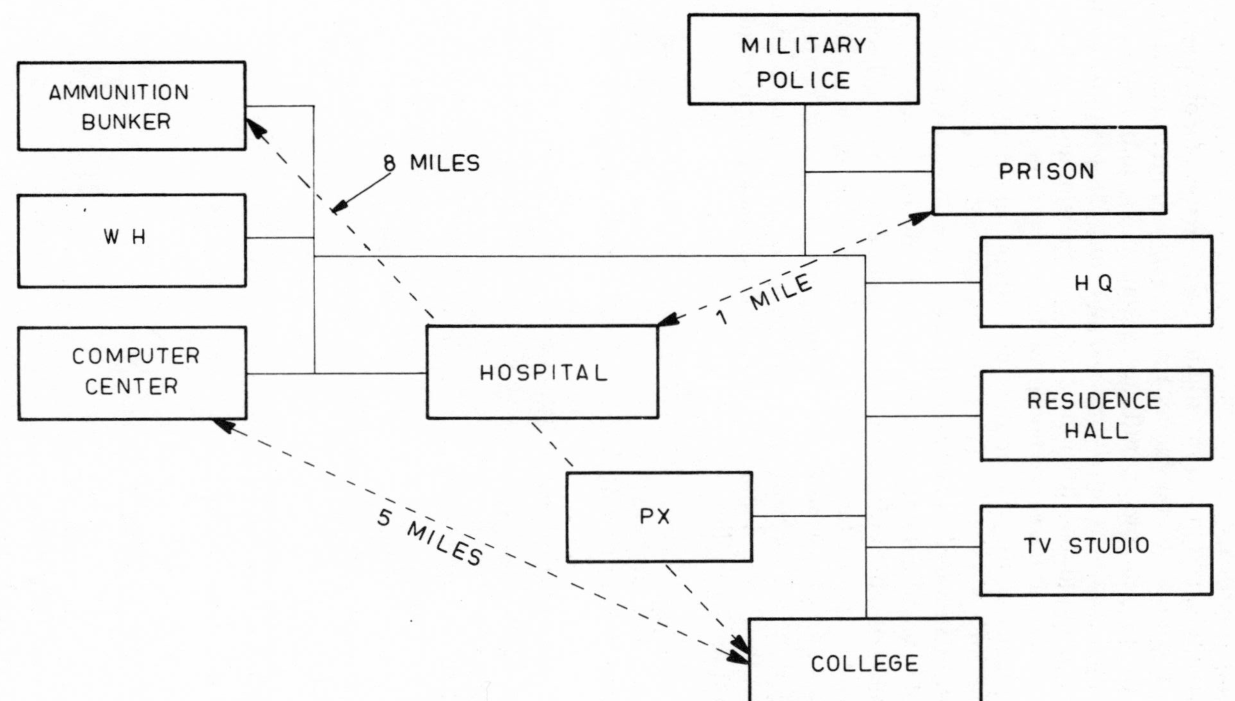

Figure 16-6. A campus-type BRB installation covering an 8-mi distance (U.S. Army, Fort Leavenworth).

warrant and prepares reports such as power use summaries by area within time periods.

We have returned to this installation because it is one of the earliest and most general to be found in office buildings, manufacturing plants, college campuses, military installations, and research and development facilities involving coaxial cable. Most companies have a continuing conflict between production requirements, which call for electric power, and energy conservation goals, which require minimizing electrical use. Computers and communications can help to reconcile this conflict by fast-response control of nonessential or lower-priority energy use when it is necessary to avoid peak demands.

Today's broadband technology permits us to design an entire coaxial network, including terminal and computer modems. Technical implementation assistance can be provided in an efficient manner. There is significant experience in projecting, designing, connecting, and installing the network, and the applications domain is growing fast. After the first and more obvious applications are implemented, a host of others will follow.

17

COMPETITIVE LAN ARCHITECTURES

We have mentioned a number of local area networks available from independent vendors. Also, we have covered the technical characteristics of the best-known systems such as Wangnet (Wang Labs) and ALAN (3M/Interactive Systems) in the broadband class and Ethernet (Xerox), ARC (Datapoint), IBM's Token Ring, Cluster One and Plan 4000 (Nestar, Zynar), and Omninet (Corvus) in the baseband class. All of these LANs offer cost and performance advantages beyond what is available from the telephone company.

From the beginning, the thesis has been that, as a closed network using special software and processors, the LAN is a valid internal communications architecture. It is tailored to transmit information among communicating workstations, local and long-haul databases, and other devices constituting the shared resources.

The strategy in using a myriaprocessor should be that of obtaining, at a much lower price, what a minicomputer or small mainframe can do. However, the user will also be well advised to remember that if, for instance, Visicalc costs $250 and not $60,000 as on the big machines, he must also give up the idea of making changes.

The PC software is a mass market of standard programs. The software manufacturer is not interested in making changes at any price, and the user who sticks his fingers into the logical mechanism and tries to change it on his own is likely to lose those fingers. The best advice that can be given to the user or prospective user of a LAN is to buy effective, low-cost solutions or devise his own from the beginning. That's a decision the user must make.

This chapter confronts several issues. First we will examine LocalNet by Sytek, the third broadband architecture at which we will look in some detail. This time we will further elaborate on the merits of broadband and its place in the market. Then we will briefly consider a number of other LANs to which the author personally assigns a smaller chance of success, although technically they are quite valid. The market gets saturated with too many offerings, and in the end there will be a shakedown:

- ALAN, LocalNet, and Wangnet are the most likely of the broadband class to survive.
- ARC is mature and has the greatest amount of installation experience.
- Ethernet has established a name.
- IBM's salesforce is there to propel its token ring.
- Cluster One is well established, particularly in the financial community.
- Omninet also is well established, and other manufacturers, such as Olivetti, Philips, and Honeywell, have adopted it or are about to do so.

That already makes eight alternatives, and quite likely they are three too many.

Finally, we will examine two software issues. One, on which we touched in the introduction, is the licensing of PC-oriented horizontal software for local networks. The other is the conversion of applied programming products written for stand-alone machines to software for myriaprocessors.

LOCALNET 20/40

Sytek, of Sunnyvale, California, has developed a high-speed, broadband, local network that links a variety of medium- and high-speed devices. Network nodes provide the required attachment to the bus. Its latest product, LocalNet 40, was preceded by LocalNet 20, which provides lower-cost communications for low-throughput units.

According to the manufacturer, over 100 LocalNet 20s with more than 6000 ports have been installed. Both LocalNet 20 and LocalNet 40 are based on CSMA/CD packet communication. Currently under study are token and TDM solutions.

Sytek bases its longer-range planning on in-house developments in collaboration with sister divisions. The network designer is part of General Instruments (40 percent owned) and benefits from the offerings of the other GI product lines. [Broadly, General Instruments divides into three groups: CATV, where the leading company is Jerrold (amplifiers, connectors); semiconductors, specializing in ROM, 16-BPW microprocessors, video games, LED, rectifiers, and modulators; and business data systems, including cash registers, points of sale, and some 200 service centers in the United States. Sytek is part of the latter division.]

In conformity with the broadband LAN strategy, the Sytek offerings blend two technologies: data communications and CATV services. Typically, data communication over long-haul lines requires much less bandwidth than TV signals. The major types of data communication units which have emerged are:

- Discrete-frequency point-to-point modems
- Frequency-agile packet communication units

Contrary to long-haul data communication supported by the telephone company, a vital component of the broadband LAN is bandwidth allocation. This involves concern over the number of signals transmitted and their bandwidth requirements. The latter are based on the current and projected services. Since requirements grow, channel allocations should be based not only on the needs at hand but also on future expansion. The design choices available with LocalNet center on the division of the up to 400 MHz of supported bandwidth. The choice made is FDM with:

- 120 channels at 128 kbps (300 kHz) each for LocalNet 20
- Five channels at 2 Mbps for LocalNet 40

However, instead of the 20 to 56 km (13 to 35 mi) to head end in the 128-kbps solution, the 2-Mbps channels run 8 km (5 mi) to head end. A senior Sytek executive has said that a basic design goal was supporting a broadband LAN in a competitive way at baseband prices. This helps bring video (graphics, image) to every location in a two-way communication system. With voice, it can provide a total communications package.

The technical argument Sytek advances is that a PBX, although it can integrate voice and data, can't handle video image with the exception of slow-scan television. And baseband doesn't integrate voice without the risk of totally saturating the system. On the contrary, broadband has the potential of integrating PBX. Ten years ago Collins built a broadband PBX by tuning analog channels to the same frequency. With multiple frequencies a variety of functions is possible. This is a cornerstone of the Sytek design. As stated, the company claims that its 120 channels at 128 kbps each can cover distances up to 56 km. One of the limitations of distance is the channel speed. The chosen speed provides greater distance and lower cost per interface.

A system overhead is imposed by the head end and interface box at each WS. LocalNet supports two user device addressing forms:

- A fully qualified address specifying a particular port on a packet communication unit (PCU)
- A partially qualified rotary address specifying any available port on a PCU or group of PCUs

The user device interface to the PCU, and therefore to the LocalNet, is controllable either locally by the user device or remotely by the network manager. This enhances the ports' overall network control and permits remote monitoring of a PCU from a network control center by the network manager. (We will return to this argument.)

The architecture permits user devices to communicate through sessions. Sessions provide the communication services to each port; they can be attached to and controlled from each port, and ports are attached to each user WS. Transactions between host and PCU are labeled either directly or indirectly. The label indicates the port and session numbers to which it applies. A *bridge* allows autorouting in channels, so that channel difference is transparent to the user. Every user must have a unique address, and 65,000 addresses are available.

Within this perspective LocalNet can be positioned as a packet-switched LAN providing communication functions through a broadband CATV system. Each channel (or subnetwork) provides data communication for hundreds of user devices. The latter are attached to the network via an intelligent interface device, the PCU.

Special network services, particularly support for network management, are provided by LocalNet server nodes. LocalNet subnetworks and associated PCUs, servers, and workstations, can be connected through the use of packet-switched bridges and gateways. The general architecture of the typical system has these components:

1. Packet communication units
2. Bridges and gateways for channel and network interconnection
3. Network management and control devices

A simple coaxial cable fitting in each area to be served assures access to the underlying analog broadband network and hence to LocalNet 20 and 40 service. The independence of the transmission system from the offered services makes connecting, disconnecting, and moving the PCU a simple process. The same thing is true of functional upgrades or the addition of new services such as voice and video teleconferencing.

A LocalNet 20 PCU assures a variable number of full duplex sessions based on switched virtual transport connections to other PCUs. Sessions can be formed to another port on the same PCU or between PCUs on different channels and cable systems, the latter through one or more interchannel bridges acting as gateways (Fig. 17-1). Flow control is maintained between PCUs to match the speed of user devices participating in a session.

A bridge is necessary in one of three situations. The first is when we have to go to more than one channel. If over 200 user workstations are on the channel, a second channel will be necessary. The second situation necessitating a bridge is when design choice is transparency in channel usage; the third is when more than 20 channels are employed.

Sytek, however, offers three types of interconnection: The bridge handles only channels on the same LocalNet; the *link* ties two different LANs, both Sytek, in different locations. Either a digital microwave or telephone line can be employed in connection to the link. The third type of interconnection, the *gateway*, connects a Sytek LAN to a non-Sytek network. For instance, a gateway to Ethernet is under development. For public telephone company networks and value-added carriers, the X.25 packet switching protocol is available. Sytek has said that several mainframers have asked it to develop broadband highways for them.

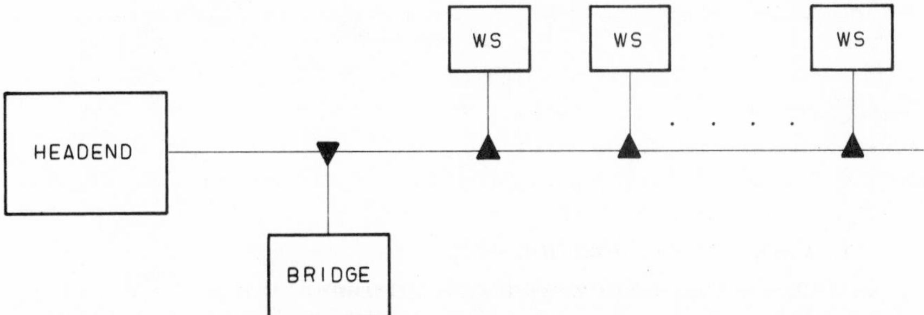

Figure 17-1. Connecting the LocalNet bridge between the head end and the workstations helps the latter talk to one another even if tuned to different 128-kbps channels.

Internetworking is a matter of particular interest, but there are some limitations. They particularly relate to the limited interfaces and serial connections available with RS-232, which is obligatory with LocalNet. Standard interface products (the PCU) come with two or eight ports. With them a LocalNet channel can be used to link different baseband systems (Fig. 17-2).

Sytek thinks that one of the LocalNet 128-kbps channels can be used to connect to, say, a Cluster One baseband network. Another 128-kbps channel connects to an Omninet. Then Cluster One and Omninet can talk to each other through the bridge. The same thing is true of attaching stand-alone PCs to a LocalNet channel. Yet, even if technically the connection through a bridge may present no particular problems, such problems may well develop in terms of transport control and contention. Even at 19.2 kbps per port, the Cluster One 240-kbps capacity may create queues, and that can be even more true with the 1 Mbps of Omninet. Possible bottlenecks are, however, situational, and this possibility should not be discarded outright.

One of LocalNet's competitive features is Sytek's development of a network control center capable of:

1. Directory services
2. Access control for security and privacy

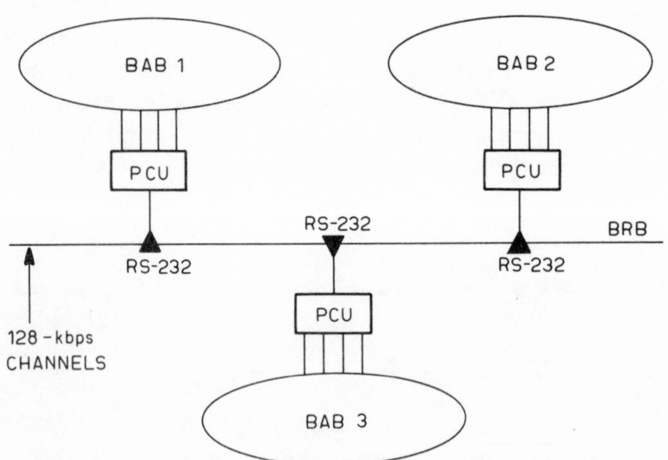

Figure 17-2. The LocalNet broadband cable can serve as an interconnect between different baseband LANs attached to it through standard PCUs.

3. Network monitoring for possible collisions, packet traffic, uptime, etc.

4. Encryption

With this offering, ports can be encrypted; so only the user having the right interface can access the port. Through an encryption algorithm, the control center can act as a "key server." Sytek also suggests making the database transparent to the user. From the standpoint of identification, the network control center can help by handling the specific names and addresses.

Costs are reasonable. Interface units for personal computers and, in general, devices working at less than 56 kbps cost about $600 per port. An interface handling two ports will cost $1200 and eight ports, $4200. Cost can, however, be reduced significantly with VLSI integration, and that is expected to happen by early 1984.

The Sytek costs for mainframe attachments are significantly higher. For host-to-host file transfer the price of the interface stands at about $10,000. Here again, with chip technology available by late 1984, the manufacturer expects that the cost will drop to $1000.

OTHER LOCAL AREA NETWORKS

Other LAN architectures that are currently available include Hyperchannel, Hyperbus, Cablenet, Z-Net, ConTelNet, Primenet, and Optonet. It is evident that this discussion of them will not be exhaustive, nor will it include all the offerings. Following it we will take a quick look at transmission media which could one day become favorites not for LAN, but for metropolitan area networks. A good example is infrared bridges. They provide efficient solutions but have the disadvantage that, when a new building is erected between transmitting and receiving points, the bridge is interrupted.

Hyperchannel is a LAN offering of Network Systems. The carrier is a baseband coaxial cable transmitting data at channel speeds up to 50 Mbps over 1000- to 5000-ft (330- to 1700-m) channels, depending on system configuration. Network Systems offers a link adapter capable of interconnecting Hyperchannel local networks over greater distances by using microwave or satellite transmission facilities.

The channel is a single multidrop coaxial cable for data distribution. Equipment can be attached anywhere along the cable and share, on a demand basis, the trunk capacity for communications between stations on the link.

Hyperchannel employs a CSMA/CD contention system. Devices are interfaced to the coaxial data trunk by Hyperchannel network adapters. Various models provide an electrical and logical interface to specific types of attached equipment. Each adapter can be attached to as many as four independent network trunks.

Basic prices are about $40,000 per network adapter. Four devices can be attached to each node. Netex software provides a universal access method for computer systems interconnected by a Hyperchannel network. Driver level and Netex software are available under license for $250 to $960 per month for one computer at a single site.

The *Hyperbus*, which is based on the same networking technology as Hyperchannel, assures interconnection between terminals, minicomputers, and RS-232C synchronous and asynchronous devices at transfer rates up to 6.3 Mbps.

Cablenet, by Amdax, is a broadband LAN offering a switched service, a dedicated service, and a general service operating simultaneously over a single, two-way, midsplit broadband coaxial cable. The broadband cable allows interbuilding and intrabuilding communications. Data, text, image, and voice are supported.

The Cablenet switched service permits up to 16,000 devices to share 14 Mbps by using two channels of the broadband system in each direction. The protocol offers each user a choice of two types of connections: switched virtual calls (SVC) and permanent virtual circuits (PVC). The SVC connection allows any device to communicate with any other device on the network. Alternatively, two user devices can always talk to each other by using a PVC connection.

A data exchange (DAX) unit provides the interface between the user's terminal and the broadband cable. Each DAX is an intelligent communications controller that supports four user devices. The physical interface is RS-232C operating at up to 19.2 kbps. The communications protocol of the user device may be asynchronous start/stop, bisynchronous, SDLC, or HDLC. All four protocols can coexist on the same DAX.

Cablenet software employs a reservation technique to control contention for the medium. Whenever a user's transmission needs exceed a specified level, DAX automatically reserves a portion of the cable's capacity for the user's exclusive use. When the demand subsides, the DAX surrenders the reservation and returns to standard contention mode. The DAX can be positioned anywhere along the cable, up to 25 mi (40 km) for the controller in any direction. It continuously self-calibrates its transmit signal levels to ensure good performance.

The *Z-Net* system architecture was introduced by Zilog in 1980. Applications for Z-Net range from electronic mail to office automation.

- Up to 255 stations can be connected to as much as 6000 ft (2000 m) of TV-type coaxial cable.
- Data transmission along the cable is at speeds of up to 800 kbps.
- Z-Net is especially designed for use with Zilog's 8-BPW microcomputers.

The Z-Net announcement was followed in 1982 by including a communications controller board, network transceiver, and an extended version of the U-Net software developed by 3Com. The U-Net package (the higher-level protocol portion of the Z-Net II software) allows Unix-based machines to communicate with each other over the Z-Net LAN architecture.

ConTelNet is a coaxial cable LAN using CSMA/CD and operating at 2 Mbps (with a 10-Mbps option) under the proprietary TICOS operating system. The system comes with a choice of modules for: an X.25 environment, a TTY solution, or a transparent environment for point-to-point connection among any family of like hosts and terminals while supporting all synchronous protocols such as bisynch, HDLC, and SDLC.

ConTelNet supports interactive terminal-to-host communications; distributed data processing; word processing; closed-circuit TV for training, teleconferencing, and surveillance; in-house distribution of commercial TV; host-to-host, high-speed file transfer; and, eventually, voice communications. It uses a three-board BIU with four ports, and with modular, add-on capabilities of a capacity up to 16 ports; protocol conversion; and concentrator, multiplexer, and statistical multiplexing functions.

ConTel assures having readied bridges to other cable-based local networks such as Ethernet; gateways to external communications systems such as X.25 networks, T1 carrier, and satellite networks; and a network control center (NCC) with status reporting and command processing. Modular, add-on functions offer diagnostics, display control and network statistics, downline loading and recovery of BIU, upline dumps from BIU, and alarms.

Primenet is a LAN developed by Prime Computer. It offers the capability of operating up to 16 prime systems in a baseband local ring fashion. Cable distance between any two nodes can be up to 750 ft

(250 m). The interface between each computer and the network is a $5000 Primenet node controller (PNC). Messages can be sent as one or several packets, with a data field of up to 2 kB. Data-transmission rates along the cable are up to 8 Mbps.

A Primenet can communicate with any other vendor's system that uses the X.25 standard. Primenet currently supports Telenet and Tymnet in the United States. Prime computers using Primenet can interface with a number of mainframes from other manufacturers through remote job entry emulation packages and protocols used by IBM 3271/3277 displays.

Optonet is a Nippon Electric (NEC) product. It has been marketed in Japan since early 1981 and is now sold worldwide. This LAN is designed to aid the integration of nonhomogeneous equipment into either stand-alone networks or interconnected systems.

Optonet is a token-passing, ring-type LAN that can link mainframes from different manufacturers including IBM and NEC. Its maximum cable length is 100 km (70 mi) per loop. The available configurations are loop models 6510, 6530, 6770, 6830, branch model 4800, and star models 2200, 2600, 2700. Branch and star subsystems include phone line connection capabilities. A different way to make that statement is that Optonet features star, branch, and loop networks easily interconnected directly or through gateways.

The star subnetwork is a low-speed system based on a PBX and twisted-pair wires. Its advantage is that it can be quite simply introduced into an existing building wiring, that is, a bunch of pair cables. This subnetwork is a traditional but adequate application when the major requirement is voice communication.

The branch subnetwork is medium-speed, based on coaxial cable, and shaped as a branching tree. It can offer a good communication facility to workstations at a reasonable cost. The loop subnetwork is a high-speed fiber optics loop particularly suitable for computer-to-computer mass data transmission. NEC also advises the loop for process control applications, because fiber optics technology is resistant to corrosive gas and noise and has a very low transmission loss.

For instance, Loop 6770 consists of up to 126 loop interface units (LIU), optical fiber cables connecting the LIU in loop topology, and a network monitor. With this fiber optics communication, the transfer rate at 32 Mbps is an achievement resulting from application of fiber optics technology. Message transmission on the loop is controlled by a token.

Loop 6770 offers virtual circuits through a unified general-purpose serial interface. Thus a computer node can communicate with any number of other nodes without additional hardware attachment, such as communication line adapters or a centralized control station. The message length on the loop is variable up to 4 kB. Given the 32-Mbps speed, a large volume of data can be sent in a very short time at good efficiency.

Reliability features of the *basic* network include a dual cable that provides alternate path and loop-back capability. Failed nodes can be bypassed. A frame check sequence in the transmitted packet checks for correct data transfer. A supervisory monitor is used to perform checks for diagnostic and maintenance purposes. With the fiber features, network availability is upheld through battery backup for optical modules and bypass.

An answer by U.S. technology is the fiber optics version of Net/One, the first fiber optic Ethernet-compatible LAN demonstrated during the International Fiber Optics and Communications exhibit of late 1982. This network is the result of a joint technology development effort of:

- Ungermann-Bass, which made the Ethernet-compatible Net/One network interface units and the communications software
- Codenoll Technology, which designed the fiber optic Ethernet transceivers
- Siecor/FiberLAN, which supplied the fiber optic transmission system, including a transmissive star coupler

An also significant late 1982 announcement is the 3Com new series of products designed to create a local network of IBM PC on Ethernet. Etherlink, Ethershare, Etherprint, and Ethermail (all trademarks) form the basis of 3Com personal computer Ethernet products.

The Etherlink chip and software offer both an Ethernet connection via a standard transceiver and a nonstandard direct Ethernet connection via connectors mounted on the Etherlink cards. Ethershare is a file server that provides virtual disk services. Etherprint is a print server, and Ethermail is an electronic mail package.

Finally, infrared transmission technology is particularly effective in high-density situations. Transmissions can be relayed as many times as desired to obtain greater distances or avoid obstacles in the line of sight. Repeater stations regenerate the signal and thereby eliminate any attenuation due to distance. The infrared systems are transparent to the computer and to software. Any equipment with published interfaces, except frequency division multiplexers, can be linked by using this equipment.

Statistical multiplexers, time division multiplexers, computers, and terminals can all be linked via the infrared path. Networking is accomplished through a multiplexer arrangement at the open end of the infrared link. The majority of today's LANs can be expected to be upwardly compatible with the advances that are anticipated in fiber optics and infrared technology.

APPLICATIONS SOFTWARE PORTABILITY

Although there is a proliferation of hardware in the LAN market, precious little systems thought is being given to solving applications software problems particularly connected with the portability of the vast choice of horizontal and vertical programs now available for stand-alone PCs. The overriding demand here is for portability.

At root of this issue is the growing number of companies now going to LAN-supported multiple-user environments rather than stand-alone PCs. Until the new generation of applications programs which are LAN-compatible and offered off the shelf becomes available, it is important to have a means of converting existing software to LAN usage.

The problem is how to tackle the subject in an able manner. As with all system problems, the best advice is to understand what's to be done and how to do it. The answer to the first question is reasonably simple: merge in the programs multiple-access facilities so that more than one WS can handle them. The "how to go about it" has two aspects: a technical one and a commercial one. The second is the easier, since it amounts to the establishment of a new pricing policy. PC applications software comes at a very low price—but for the single machine. If more than one WS is on the LAN, which is the typical case, either the price must be increased or a fee system must be established, with the LAN vendor a good candidate to collect the fees.

An evident problem is protected software. Here, for the time being, the policies are divergent. Personal Software decided on a license agreement. Microsoft and Apple also entered into an agreement. Visicorp has not agreed so far to let its programs be on hard disk. Hence, there is the Multicalc version of Visicalc purchased and converted by Nestar. But policies are changing, as the Visicorp case helps document. At the time of publication, the issue of putting an unprotected copy on the disk was under study, and agreements were about to be finalized on ways and means for collecting user licenses.

The technical issues are more complex. Network support must be so designed that stand-alone applications programs can be used in a local network environment. The key is to learn how to use semaphores, the lock, and the exclusive update, which is the way to multiuser programs. That kind of development is new and challenging, and in a certain way it is already taking place with the additions of hard disk to the PC. Among the requirements are:

1. Making access transparent
2. Patching into the OS
3. Intercepting system calls
4. Mapping system calls to the network

If we really wish to enhance software portability, there are two different approaches to be kept in mind. The best approach is applicable only with new programs and calls for the use of rules imbedded in packages such as Foundation (developed in England for Cluster One of Nestar). By observing these rules, conversion to a LAN environment becomes a matter of course. This approach can also be taken through the use of the Data Machine, which is essentially a database manager. The package uses semaphores and supports multiple-computer environments. It is designed by Pascal Systems (Menlo Park, California). If such tools are used from the original projection of the program, there is no need to modify the software; but TDM must be resident in every machine.

It is correct to add that the portability of applications programs will, during the coming years, become a major advantage for LAN offering. Nobody has the resources to start rewriting all of the programming support, and the local network that makes it possible to benefit from large libraries of horizontal software will attract much more attention than the networks that do not.

The second approach to stand-alone software conversion to a LAN environment is to create an interface between the existing application and the local area network OS. Note that this solution, shown in Fig. 17-3, is equally applicable to moving from floppy-disk-based programs to hard disk to benefit from larger memory and faster access, particularly in a multithread environment. The extensions suggested by this approach center around the creation of a set of abstract changes: open, close, and read or write data. This calls for more fundamental approaches to the OS functions of the LAN than specially written software may require. It also presupposes the integration of facilities such as locking and unlocking and the observance of network functionality to avoid processes sitting on the server(s) and the workstations.

To a considerable extent, modifications to be made to stand-alone programs will relate to the rewriting of the input/output part to use

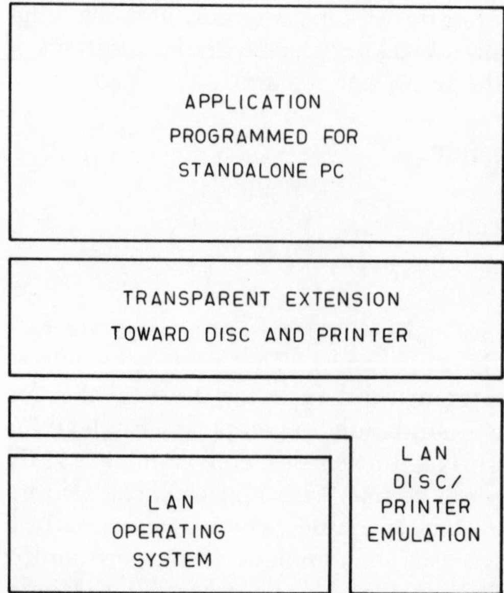

Figure 17-3. A strategy for conversion from stand-alone PC applications software to a LAN operating environment with disk and printer servers.

semaphores so that two computers can share the disk area while providing an efficient *lock* mechanism. The programmer must set the semaphore and then control read block, update, and unlock semaphore. The role of the semaphore is to show whether a resource is free or occupied.

Still another alternative is the dedicated "record server" interfacing between the WS and the file server. It knows *only* one file structure, handles the requests, addresses the file server, and returns to the appropriate WS. On the other hand, it weakens the system and increases the waiting period. In other words, although with this approach the semaphores are not needed, the penalty paid can be severe. If this solution is chosen, it is unwise to use Apple II; it is the slowest of machines to handle the record server requirements. Experts are, however, quite cool to the record server idea.

This can be said in conclusion: We have been considering different alternatives to obtain a certain portability of stand-alone programs. This strategy will provide some of the answers attending the problem of a conversion to LAN. But to take full advantage of LAN capabilities, the best way is to rewrite the applications. A number of software vendors are ready to do just that. Their problem is to identify the winners in the LAN arena, including

1. Protocol level
2. Layers of implementation
3. Makes and makers of products

Visicorp, for one, answered the latter challenge by supporting different PC makes in different environments through rewriting of its horizontal software. For this it uses the C language.

18

ENLARGING THE APPLICATIONS HORIZON

The development of powerful microcomputers makes possible a totally new approach to distributed information systems. Instead of many users sharing one machine, it has become practical to build a computer as a network of PCs to access shared databases and tap other common resources. Since each user can have a personal computer, the complexity of supporting multiple users is removed. If a computer breaks down, only one WS is affected. The whole computing process becomes very reliable.

To benefit from the advances of technology, a myriaprocessor (PC and LAN services) should make it possible for each user to access the shared text, data, and images to meet current needs. Whether local or long-haul, the network must function as an interconnected system in which a request for information may be placed by any workstation and the system will locate the information and return it in the proper format.

The PC offers an incredible amount of packaged computer power, even on an 8-bit, 64K basis. But by now the 16- and 32-BPW, 256K to 1-MB are becoming commonplace. Through the LAN, the personal computer addresses itself to interactive environments with big (though not colossal) text and data requirements. Two groups of people stand to benefit from the myriaprocessor capabilities: those with simple and those with sophisticated questions.

People with simple questions think of the LAN as nothing more than distributed switching, a kind of low-cost PBX for text and data purposes. Currently available software addresses itself to this situation. But people with sophisticated questions wish to obtain solid, technical, documented answers on how to interconnect, how to provide interchanges, how to provide a secure access to databases, and how to do other things which are tough even with mainframes. Sophisticated people expect a LAN to provide resource sharing, to minimize response time, and assure increasing computer power per workstation—while taking a peer level system approach.

Equipment independence is one of the sophisticated goals. Attention focuses on myriaprocessors as they allow computers from different manufacturers to connect together to form a network. Hardware difficulties have been dealt with fairly effectively, but software compatibility has been a more serious problem requiring standardization.

A good distributed system should provide a machine-independent standard for information exchange. Each user WS should be looked at as an independent system capable of running its own programs:

- It contacts any data center and exchanges information if security requirements are met.
- It communicates with other workstations through the LAN and the sharing of the local database.

Through a personal computer, each user has sufficient processing capability to handle data and produce the necessary reports and updates. By its nature, the system enforces good design in applications software by forcing a vigorous partitioning of the problem.

The required amount of data transmission over the network in performing a specific text and data processing function is substantially less than that needed for a multiprocessing computer system. At the same time, the system is more user-friendly in providing prompting and forgiving handling errors.

A myriaprocessor is also fault-tolerant in that the breakdown of any one component does not result in the loss of effectiveness of the entire aggregate. The system protects the security and privacy of information. Security should be implemented in a multilevel scheme so that different users are allowed access to only the information for which they are authorized.

Data integrity over the network can be maintained without having a large portion of processor time dedicated to network overhead. This is another way in which myriaprocessors excel over the more classical star or cluster approaches, whether based on mainframes or on minicomputers.

MAJOR ADVANCED-TECHNOLOGY FINDINGS

The research done coast-to-coast in October and November 1982 involved not only leading computer and communications manufacturers but also banks, insurance companies, and manufacturing concerns. The results have confirmed the trend toward the application of PCs and LANs in financial and industrial environments. First of all is a validation of strategic perspectives in the banking industry:

- Home banking (HB) and electronic tellers are going well beyond the automatic teller machine (ATM) level.
- Both HB and electronic tellers are based on PCs, and the newer branch office application is LAN-oriented.

Home banking has reached its first level of maturity. Broadly, there are three basic solutions: Videotex; on/off intelligence through professional PCs, and an intermediate stage using very low cost home computers. At the same time, banking and insurance companies demonstrate a steady evolution of and improvements in LAN implementation.

Computer and communications manufacturers increasingly focus on LAN architectures; the second generation arrived in early 1983. On the user side, top management is one of the areas in which myriaprocessors are put into practice to advantage. Many companies are already replacing the minicomputers with PCs and LANs.

The market is expanding, but competition gets stiffer. In the exploding PC market there were, in 1983, an estimated 105 competing firms offering some 150 products. A shakedown is inevitable. It is projected that, by 1988, only five or six companies will remain in the PC arena. Something similar can be said of the LAN.

Not surprisingly, there is a strong IBM thrust into personal computers, with a very important market impact. At the same time, IBM is changing its price structure of key products from mainframes to minicomputers. This turnaround is most significant. Mainframes are being phased out of processing, which is increasingly distributed by means of LANs and PCs. The mainframe remains as a text and data warehouse and also as a central switch.

Word processing and data processing tend to merge. Indeed, technological trends and market considerations indicate that word processing as a dedicated terminal entity will cease to exist during the 1980s. DP and WP require the same technologies, and only for historical reasons are the two considered separate now. The data communication nodes and microfiles get distributed, with personal computers increasingly able to run large disks. To answer the data communication requirements, networks are designed for a certain scale of implementation over a certain distance.

The argument over the choice between broadband and baseband is still hot, but in pursuing it we tend to forget practicality. There is a place for baseband; we don't need broadband to wire the president's office.

As in all areas of information systems work, there are rules to guide us toward successful implementation. Analysts and designers must remember that documented results of an application study are not only the best basis but the only acceptable basis for myriaprocessor use:

1. The study of the workplace and the establishment of the goals to be reached are prerequisites.
2. All system analysis and programming must be *structured.*
3. All analysis and programming must be fully *documented.*
4. Analysis, programming, and documentation must use a *data dictionary* and generally be computer-assisted.
5. Every *file must be structured as a message*, and every message must be a file in the local database.

With messages usually handled on a LAN as datagrams, files and messages must be designed accordingly.

6. There should be no direct WS/WS communication. All messages and file transfers should transit through the local text and database.
7. There is no point in replacing what's available in maxi and minicomputers. We should put our attention on end-user functions.
8. With PCs and LANs, we should definitely choose among existing application packages. We should not write software.
9. The user must be an integral part of the system design and his reactions the foundation for making choices.
10. Lifelong learning should characterize any myriaprocessor implementation.

The closer we bring computers and communications to the user, the more we need to upgrade, and update, user skills. How much time and know-how should be invested in the analysis depends on the application and on what is already available: the degree of end user functions to be supported, the interactivity , the linkage to the central resources, the distribution at the WS level, and the security and uptime prerequisites to be observed.

Here is how the Chemical Bank of New York attacked this problem. First management chose *one application* and stressed it; it was PC-based teller terminals with signature recognition capability linked through a LAN. The goal was an automated branch model. Second, a valid R&D budget was set up, and authorization to go ahead was given.

The choice of application, the goal, and the budget constituted the first step. The steps which followed help identify the extremes of a valid timetable:

1. January 1982, identification of the LAN to be used (Nestar).
2. February 1982, system goes into development.
3. July 1982, programming phase is completed.
4. August 1982, demonstration to management.
5. September 1982, first live test pilot Nestar in a branch, followed by user training.
6. September 1982, based on the positive results, three more LANs ordered for the next three installations.
7. October 1982, first LAN installation goes into production.
8. November 1982, second, third, and fourth installations start operations.

The key to Chemical Bank's success is that management took the time to set goals, took care to understand the system, and took the pilot to the branch—it did not let it rot in DP shop. Management also had the courage to make tough decisions. Early results led it to order a stop to the other lines of development and concentrate on the promising PC and LAN combination. It took a lot of discipline to reach results: one step at a time. And the results are very positive.

That's the way management must work if it wants to achieve commendable goals. The myriaprocessor technology is new, and there may be failures along the way. But if the aim to be reached is clear—and the timetable reasonable—the aim will be reached. Said the senior executive of a manufacturing firm who faced the same problems: "We understand we may have to throw away some of the application software or rewrite it. But above all we want to understand what we do and learn from the experience."

In fact, the American financial community seems determined to go a long way in the implementation of PCs and LANs. Nestar is only one of the LANs. Yet among its references we find an impressive list of financial institutions: Detroit Bank and Trust, for administrative duties; Smith, Barney, for the financial analysts section; Brown Brothers; Bank of America; Bank of Louisville; Harriman; Citibank; Merrill Lynch; and Goldsmith Sachs, for the MIS system and financial services.

The St. Paul Insurance Companies uses PCs and LANs for financial analysis pertaining to insurance and has installed a LAN in each of its offices. Bangor Punta implemented a LAN to serve the offices of the president and his main assistants. Bell Laboratories uses a LAN for planning and administration, and Visicalc is one of the applications.

Several industrial users employ PC-based business graphics on the LAN. In one installation a two-color Hewlett-Packard plotter is connected to a PC. The network takes files from the file server and brings them to the Apple III for graphics by using PC-based business graphics software. Significantly, the plotter prepares monthly reports for the board of directors.

LAN EXPERIENCE AT THE CHEMICAL BANK

Dynamic signature verification is the next step in the effort to keep track of who is withdrawing cash from a teller window or a remote ATM or point of sales equipment (POS). The technology is dynamic in comparison with the classical signature reproduction in paper files, which requires the teller to verify signatures for customer identification. Dynamic signature technology captures a customer's signature in realtime while he is writing it, usually by means of a special electronic pen and digitizer. Pressure, speed of writing, acceleration, and movements on and off the surface by the pen are captured and compared with an existing digitized record of the customer's signature.

The magnetic stripe card and personal identification number (PIN), in widespread use to assure security of bank accounts, have a fundamental weakness. Anything possessed by an individual, such as a bank card, is vulnerable to loss or theft. While use of electronic online authorization systems helps control fraud, current techniques do not allow timely reporting of loss of cards and disseminating that information back to the industry. Once someone has acquired another person's bank card and knows its assigned PIN, he is capable of using the card to gain access to a customer's account through a self-service banking unit, such as an ATM, or at the retail location.

For these reasons, signature verification will gain acceptance as transactions by self-service banking machines increase in number and losses to banks from an associated rise in fraud increase in amount. The cost of a computer-based signature verification device is expected to dip to a few hundred dollars as implementation grows and the design characteristics settle down.

Two types of devices are in the foreground. The one particularly suitable for teller stations uses a graphic tablet (or camera) and projects on the teller's screen two signature windows: one stored in the local database and the other the realtime signature of the client. It is then up to the teller to compare the two signatures. A projected cost per station is less than $200.

The other alternative is fully automatic, more costly, and still not fully perfected. It has its origins in a signature verification system which originated in the early 1970s as a research project at the National Physical Laboratory in England. The results were promising, and research staff from several organizations (IBI, SRI, etc.) showed interest in the technology. In this solution, each signature feature is described as a statistical distribution which reflects the normal variations in each person's signature style and rhythm.

Verification is a matter of probability theory, determining whether a signature feature is valid or invalid. The next question is the probability that the customer's dynamic signature will fall within the normal tolerances of the customer's reference signature. These normal tolerances are held in computer memory. Certain people exhibit a broad distribution of signature features, whereas others show a narrow distribution of signature features.

With this background, let's look at the experience the Chemical Bank has acquired in implementing PCs and LANs for client identification purposes and signature verification. When a new account is opened at a branch, the following data are recorded through the PC at the teller station:

1. Account opening date
2. Account number
3. Account type
4. Account title
5. Home address

6. Social security number
7. Citizenship
8. Date of birth
9. Place of birth
10. Name and address of employer
11. Business telephone
12. Home telephone
13. Mother's maiden name
14. Signature

If the account is joint, some or all of items 5 to 14 may be recorded twice. Classically this has been done on paper in more than one copy for filing purposes, even with the realtime banking systems in existence. With PC and LAN it is done online to the local database. In addition to the generic information entered through the keyboard, the signature is recorded by means of a graphic tablet with its own interface software attached to an Apple II.

Although the procedure is quite successful, the system designers look to the alternative of a Sanyo Videocamera ($140 with $300 supporting software) to capture the image and store it on disk. The camera solution presents a clear crisp image with improved contrast and curves and hence reduced storage requirements. It also permits the bulk transfer to the database of signatures already on client cards without having to ask the clients for new signature registration. Two features of this procedure are outstanding:

- First, it only takes 2 h of teller training to become proficient in the WS usage, including the online signature capability.
- Second, whereas other signature systems require 1500 bytes as a minimum on the disk, this solution demands 490 bytes as a maximum.

The software is projected to handle up to two signatures per account. Response time is very fast. Removal of signatures is not allowed.

The next LAN application being projected at the branch level is relative to the back office, more specifically the clearance system: bookkeeping, general ledger, incoming and outgoing work to/from the main office, and the handling of all bad checks, dividend checks, and account information. So far, even with online systems, such information was typed and was largely redundant. The back office implementation under development will prepare the forms and also the charges.

All this will be handled on the same 33-MB database as that used for the signature system. The applications, including the driver for the graphic tablet and the generalized routines, are written in Pascal with the exception of lower-level primitives, which are in assembler. (Apple II is too slow for Pascal in highly repetitive operations.)

At the branch office where it is currently under test, signature and account information concern the management of about 12,000 accounts. All information elements are accessed through the client account number as primary key and the full name as secondary key.

The 3270 bisynchronous protocol is used for communication between the LAN and the central computer resources. The information goes to a tandem computer, and so do all ATM and the Pronto/Home Banking project. Significantly, bank management decided to implement one standard protocol and one standard database.

Related to this experience is the electronic teller (ET) capability. It involved microcomputer-based devices on the LAN that were totally interactive with the customer and supported:

1. Dual cash dispensing (to serve two customers)
2. Online inquiries
3. Money transfers
4. All sorts of payments
5. Online account statements

The electronic teller can be best described as home banking in the bank's own environment. It will substitute for the ATM in the lobby and fulfill the commitment made by leading banks to replace *all* tellers by 1988. Early ET installations will run in two modes: in full capability and cash only. They will also allow entry for new accounts by means of a smart (microprocessor-based) interaction through function keys.

PERSONAL COMPUTERS IN AN INSURANCE ENVIRONMENT

The St. Paul Insurance Companies is one of the six or seven independent insurance firms in the United States. It handles property, casualty, and life insurance, grosses about $2 billion per year, and operates coast-to-coast. To manage its commercial property, liability, homeownership, and automobile insurance, it operates through a network of agents and employs about 9000 people (one-third of them in St. Paul and the balance in its 45 offices in the United States and Canada).

Responsibilities at the home office are policy making, product development, marketing, accounting, and data processing. Operations at offices include underwriting, handling claims, and managing the agent accounts. The major effort in automation, particularly the PC and LAN, is directed at this level.

Insurance products are sold by independent agents, who quote premiums. Since the agents have access to several insurance companies, it is competitively important that the insurance company be able to quote risk at the agent's terminal. The St. Paul Insurance Companies realtime dealer service developed in three steps.

First, from mainframe use, the company moved in the 1970s to distributed data processing with Datapoint installations at the regional office. The Datapoint units were basically used for data entry and the handling of files and as commercial processors.

Second, the proliferating Datapoint Units at the offices were wired together through ARC. The same thing was done at the headquarters for WP. Use of the ARC local area networks began in 1980 and expanded within one year as the company converted to LAN from stand-alone. "We used to have Datapoint and diskette," said a senior executive, "but as the diskettes multiplied, it got messy."

Quite significantly, there has been an easy software conversion. The process took about three months, and the stand-alone machines became part of a LAN operating environment. Performance and reliability have increased; per office it now stands at 99 percent. Reliability of stand-alone units was 95 percent and never dropped during the conversion.

The third step in developing realtime dealer service was to place personal computers in agents' offices. The IBM PC has been chosen for this application, but the implementation plan goes much further. It includes linking long haul the agents' PC to the LAN and the LAN to the mainframes.

The implementation problem is not unique to any one firm; every major computer user has it. For that reason, eight companies sponsored a research project and requested proposals. Several value-added networks responded. The finish was IBM versus American Bell: INS versus Net 1. IBM won the bid. The goal is to:

1. Tie together the company's own offices rather than use leased lines.

2. Tie the agents to the offices and the headquarters.

LAN and PC will be communicating through automatic modems. At the same time every effort is made to convert the users' mentality to interactive systems, because office automation is not going anywhere unless most senior executives and middle managers use workstations as an everyday tool. Only when most executives, middle managers, and professionals start using the microprocessor-based workstation of the automated office will the new system perspectives emerge. In clear-eyed companies like St. Paul, management is convinced of the need. Workstations are no longer expensive, but training a vast group of diversified individuals is a complicated task.

Management characterized the education task as much more complex and challenging than, for instance, the power problem faced during installation: "Yes, when we started in some of the buildings there were some problems. Stabilizers were not used from the beginning, and the office managers did not do what they were instructed to do." But these difficulties were soon corrected, and there have been no problems in some time. Neither are there any problems with the LAN's hub.

There have been however, procedural problems, and they also relate to people. Editing is a prime example. There are unique tables, rates, structures, and values in every state. In insurance the quality of the data calls for a lot of editing, which wasn't done when all operations were manual. With formal controls the error rates have significantly decreased, and that's another advantage of the PC and LAN.

Procedural issues and error rates have a common denominator: people. Now we are back again to subject number 1. Of all the barriers, training is the biggest. Training concerns people, whereas pricing and applications are functions of the marketplace. It is quite important that better software with greater capacity show up as the use of workstations expands; but unless an organization handles its training problems successfully, there will not be general acceptance and utilization.

Only training and use can make evident the fact that the executive-level workstation allows the manager to access instantaneously the information processed by subordinates and communicate with both subordinates and peers. And if the executive needs more assistance, he can get it from the terminal itself. This is true of all levels of management from the highest to the lowest.

A NETWORK CONTROL CENTER

As the St. Paul Insurance Companies' experience helps show, a number of key components must be considered when we speak of the functioning of a total information system. Within a distributed environment with PCs and minicomputers, the mainframe will be a main switch—not the DP handler—and it has to be examined as such.

Another main switch is the PBX. In many major U.S. companies, five or ten different LAN technologies may be implemented from headquarters to the most remote locations. The PBX can serve as the interconnection. Furthermore, just as the PBX switches lines in a building, so the action switch switches trunks. It optimizes FX, WATS, and pay lines (dial up). This, too, is necessary to keep costs under control, the more so because for many companies, the data communication expenses have really doubled each year since the late 1970s. This helps reduce the workforce in the field through greater productivity, but it has its own cost factors.

When we enter the PBX into the equation, we should also recall the coming integration of text, data, and image with voice and the wiring of the building necessary to handle the load. The telephone set, as we know it, is empty now because all the electronics fit on a chip. The size remains the same because it fits our hand; hence the drive to integrate the telephone set and the terminal.

If we put developments in the proper perspective, what we see happening is an integration of videotex, personal computers, word processing, and generic applications into a professional WS including voice. Some LAN offerings capitalize on the second and third telephone twisted pair running through the buildings for expansion purposes. Borrowing data communication concepts from long haul, other benefits come from the implementation of a network control center (NCC).

The object of a network control center is to assure needed services for smooth, uninterruptable operation of the LAN. The various NCC functions can be invoked manually by a terminal operator, automatically on NCC start-up, or remotely by special request over the network. Tasks involving important data should be performed automatically without operator intervention. They include network status monitoring, network activity monitoring, quality histories, and identification of malfunctioning components.

If abnormal conditions occur, the operator should be alerted by special messages on the control WS. The NCC should have a menu of commands available for network control, security, remote diagnosis, and generation of different operating reports. These commands should be executed in a foreground-background mode without interfering with the normal functioning of the LAN.

Remotely initiated tasks will typically be used for access to the local or remote databases. For instance, requests for downline loading of executable files will be executed through software in BIUs, gateways, and workstations. Downline dumping and upline loading may involve text and data files, programs, and directory files needed for logical addressing or other inquiries by network users. They must be handled automatically by the NCC.

BIU status messages are a primary input to the NCC for monitoring purposes. NCC control messages are used for control and reconfiguration. Logical and physical network configuration involves communications links, nodes, workstation BIUs, gateways, servers, hosts, and the NCC itself. Not only the physical processing and transmission media but also the software support can be affected.

Network status information to be maintained includes traffic (load on channels, BIU, statistics of sessions, messages, peak periods); performance (throughput, response time, uptime, availability); and equipment status (state of BIU, gateways, servers, and workstations). Note, however, that network management is an area in which little standards work has been done despite its significance for users. On the one hand there is a lack of standardization, and on the other there is a user demand for network monitoring systems. With them, network managers can count on maintaining performance and avoiding pitfalls in implementation. Among the benefits to be gained when we talk of NCC at large (both long-haul and local) we note:

1. Automatic remote monitoring, which enables the central operator to obtain all pertinent network status information and eliminates the need for remote-site test personnel
2. Color-graphics monitoring, displaying line, modem, and terminal status in easy-to-read color charts
3. Management reporting, which enables central site equipment to prepare comprehensive reports on system trends and behavior
4. Network system restoration from a remote site

Polyvalent NCCs are software-based and are capable of monitoring today's most sophisticated online communications systems.

Computer-based controllers can easily supervise multipoint and distributed text and data-processing networks. Each control module maintains an ongoing check by collecting status data and responding to commands from the main controller. Quality histories permit the diagnosis of faults in the network and the making of necessary corrections rapidly.

At the current state of the art, the NCC should maintain a database of network resource information collected from BIU status reporting messages, provide an interactive, standardized interface for control purposes, and make it feasible to analyze the network traffic load. A more sophisticated unit would simulate the behavior of attached devices on the basis of warning signals and thus provide a forward control capability. Preventive maintenance is a must. The NCC should periodically check circuits to detect gradual, marginal degradation, which under normal circumstance goes unnoticed.

Isolation of network failures by maintenance personnel must be facilitated. This involves the ability to remotely execute diagnostic tests to isolate workstation, server, or network problems. Intermittent software problems should also be analyzed by dumping the memory contents of the component to the NCC. Maintenance-related data should be integrated into the network database. Related activities consist of fault detection, isolation, repair, and preventive maintenance. The log produced when the remote diagnostics function is performed is a major source of this information.

As the LAN implementation expands to sensitive areas, other necessary activities are security and user access control. The latter occurs during log-in and log-out. The minimum level of validation consists of authentication of a user password. Log-in permits the user to initiate a network session; thus an association between the user's workstation and other network nodes can take place.

To perform these functions in an able manner, the NCC requires administrative information. A network hardware directory will typically contain a list of all registered hardware devices and their descriptions, including names and chassis serial numbers. A network configuration table will include a current configuration description: nodes, workstations, servers, communication link, and channel parameter and also a history of all reconfiguration changes including the description, date, and time.

A configuration status table will stress current operational status of hardware and software components. A list of all registered network software names, release versions, source codes, and object codes should be found in the network software directory. The traffic log files will contain the traffic measurements from the network data collection points plus traffic statistics computed through a traffic analysis tool.

The object of a user directory file is to list user names, addresses, and authorized functions; that of a function directory file is to list functions and names and addresses. The user menu file will contain a list of all user menus framed on pages or screens for display at workstations, and the operator command file will contain a list of all operator commands.

This brief description of enhanced functioning helps document that, although PCs and LANs are the way to go in the new era of computing, we have to do considerable preparatory work to make the system successful. People get great productivity from PCs, but if we don't find the right standards and implement them, this information system, like so many others before it, can become a bottleneck.

Some of the special software is transferable and know-how is the key to its use, but the applications which are destined to be successful must be studied case by case within their environments. We have to look with great care at the details. Ford found that, with the same PCs and the same applications, people used different features, employed them in different ways, and got quite different results.

We cannot afford to stereotype our conceptions, and we can afford even less to be sloppy and careless. *The larger framework in which we operate as people who design and apply computers and communications involves much more than mechanical action.* If we wish to employ intelligent machines in an able manner, we must act with insight and foresight—which means with more intelligence.

LIST OF INITIAL-LETTER ABBREVIATIONS*

ac alternating current

A/D analog to digital

ADLC advanced data link control

AGC automatic gain control

***AI** artificial intelligence

AIM associative index method

ALAN advanced local area network (tentative name for the 3M/IS offering)

AP applications programming

ARC attached resource computer

ATM automatic teller machine

***BAB** baseband

BER bit error rate

***BIU** bus interface unit

bps bits per second

***BPW** bits per word

***BRB** broadband

BSC bisynch

CAD computer-aided design

***CATV** community antenna television; cable television

*The abbreviations marked with an asterisk are included in the Glossary.

CC connection confirm

***CCITT** Consultative Committee for International Telephone & Telegraph

CEI Commission Electrotechnique Internationale

CIU cable interface unit

CP/M control program for microcomputers

CPU central processing unit

CR connection request

***CRC** cyclic redundancy check

***CSMA** carrier-sensing multiple access

CSMA/CA carrier-sensing multiple access with collision avoidance

CSMA/CD carrier-sensing multiple access with collision detection

D/A digital to analog

DB database

DBMS database management systems

dc direct current

DC data communication

DCE data communication equipment

DCIO direct channel interface option

***DDB** distributed database

DIS distributed information system

DLC data link control

DMA direct memory access

DP data processing

DTE data terminating equipment

DVX digital voice exchange

ECMA European Computer Manufacturers Association

ET electronic teller

FCC Federal Communications Commission

FCS frame check sequence

***FDM** frequency division multiplexing

FP file processor

FSK frequency shift key

FTS file transfer server

GB gigabyte

KHz kilohertz

GHz gigahertz

HB home banking

Hz Hertz; cycles per second

HDLC higher-level data link control

ID identification

IDN integrated digital network

***IE** information element

I/O input/output

ISAM index sequential access method

ISDN Integrated Systems Digital Network

ISX information switching exchange

ITI Interactive Terminal Interface

***JND** just noticeable difference

kbps kilobits per second

kB kilobyte

kBps kilobytes per second

KB keyboard

***LAN** local area network

LAP line access protocol

***LHN** long-haul network

LLC logical link control

LSI large-scale integration

MAC media access control

MAU media access unit

MB megabyte

***Mbps** megabits per second

MHz megahertz

NBS National Bureau of Standards

***NCC** network control center

NFT Network File Transfer

NPDN Nordic Public Data Network

NIM network interface message processor

NPL nonprocedural language

NRZ nonreturn to zero

NUA Network Users Association

OEM original equipment manufacturers

OIS office information system

***OS** operating system

OSI Open System Interconnection

PAD packet assembly-disassembly

***PBX** private branch exchange

***PC** personal computer

PCB printed-circuit board

***PCM** plug compatible manufacturers

PCU packet communication unit

PI priority indicator

PIN personal identification number

PLP presentation level protocol

POS point of sales

PSI packet system interface

PTT Post, Telephone, and Telegraph

RAM random-access memory

RF radio frequency

RIM resource interface module

ROM read-only memory

RS recommended standard

SBS satellite business

SDM space division multiplaning

SNA System Network Architecture

S/S start/stop

TC transport control

***TDB** text and database

***TDM** time division multiplexing

***TK** token

TM traffic mode

UIT Union International des Telecommunications

USART Universal Synchronous Asynchronous Receive/Transmit

VAN value-added network

***VC** virtual circuit

UCS user communications facility

VCR video cassette recorder

VLSI very large scale integration

WP word processing

***WS** workstation

GLOSSARY

Address: An entity specifying a particular point of attachment. It may be a port, workstation, or location in memory.

Amplifier: A device that boosts the strength of an electronic signal. Amplifiers are installed at intervals throughout a cable system to rebuild the data signals, which weaken as they pass through the network.

Artificial intelligence Machine capacity that approximates human intelligence, which is the ability to learn or understand from experience, to acquire and retain knowledge; mental ability.

Human intelligence involves insight and foresight, memory, calculation, extrapolation, and imagination. As man-made systems exhibit some of these characteristics and their capacities are increased, we make more references to AI. "Expert systems" in this decade and teachable computers, as well as machines able to learn from environmental stimuli, may be the first manifestations of AI.

Auto answer The ability of a machine to answer a telephone without human intervention.

Autodial A telephonic device that automatically dials prerecorded telephone numbers.

Audio annotation Audio comments about a text document. The comments are stored with the document on a computer or word processor.

Baseband local area network Typically, a network operating in the 0 to 10-Mbps range; transmission speed is a basic reference in characterizing a family of LANs. Baseband, like broadband, also describes bandwidth equipment or systems that can carry a large proportion of the electromagnetic spectrum.

Binary Of or pertaining to the digits or numbers used in binary notation (0,1).

Bandwidth A measure of frequency use or capacity. Voice transmission requires a bandwidth of 3000 to 4000 cycles per second (3 to 4 kHz). A TV channel occupies a bandwidth of 5 to 6 million cycles per second (5 to 6 MHz; 5 MHz is the European standard, and 6 MHz is the American standard).

Bit Binary digit.

Bits per word (BPW) The number of bits, 4, 8, 16, 32, 64, . . . , handled as a unit by the microprocessor; a significant characteristic of the processor design.

Bridge: A specialized packet gateway used to route packets among carrier channels, as in the case of LocalNet implementation.

Broadband Industry standard CATV distribution using digital channels and modulating RF carriers. Typically, a broadband network is an analog information distribution system permitting both digital services and conventional analog information services to coexist on the same cable system. Also typically, BRB handles BAB channels on the same corner.

Bus interface unit A standard local area network device used to interface workstations and servers to the carrier. Also known as the CIU (cable interface unit) and by other names specific to manufacturers.

Byte A sequence of adjacent binary digits operated upon as a unit and usually shorter than a word.

Cable powering Supplying operating power to active CATV equipment by using the coaxial cable to carry the power along with the information signal.

Cable tilt A reduction in the level of an RF signal passing through a cable as it sweeps from low to high frequency. It is caused by an increase in cable attenuation as the frequency increases.

Carrier The medium on which a circuit is laid out: telephone communications line, an IC chip in a gate array environment, a printed-circuit board, and so on.

Carrier-sensing multiple access A technique by means of which many independent nodes (workstations) can share a common broadcast communication channel without requiring a central transmission allocation authority. One of the basic solutions to LAN operation implemented through collision detection (CD) or collision avoidance (CA) algorithms.

CATV Community antenna television, or cable TV, a generic term for broadband networks that employ coaxial cable and are used for information distribution in cities, campuses, and buildings. The objective is clear signals.

Channel A set of adjacent physical or logical lanes unblocked by other components or obstacles. Usually much longer than average component length, a channel is typically bound on each side.

A frequency division, multiplexed, multipoint, or point-to-point carrier. Also, a preestablished fraction of the available bandwidth. One of the BRB advantages is the ease with which channels can be configured on a broadband cable; each channel can be shared among a number of workstations and servers.

Channel number A numeric value identifying one of the available channels.

Channel route A system that routes wiring or logical paths along predefined channels on a carrier.

Communications tools Devices that make communication more efficient. They include voice, text, and electronic mail.

Main trunk The major link(s) from the head end to downstream branches.

Megabits per second (Mbps) A measure of channel capacity in terms of data rate; a common unit of measurement in present-day systems.

Message A logical partition of a terminating equipment's data stream to and from another data terminating equipment. A basic unit of reference in voice, text, and data communications.

Microwave transmission The transmission of sound over distance by using ultrahigh frequencies and line-of-sight transmission between sending and receiving towers.

Modem An A/D and D/A conversion device (modulator-demodulator) interfacing the data terminating equipment and the analog transmission lines. The modem codes or decodes an information signal onto or off an analog carrier signal by varying the amplitude, frequency, or phase of the resulting signal, and also detecting the variation.

Network A collection of nodes (hosts and switches) and trunks that interconnect the nodes. Intelligent networks are software-driven.

Network control center A network center that provides enhanced services to users and network managers through diagnostic and maintenance facilities, network start-up and shutdown, performance monitoring, reconfiguration, network security, and so on.

Networking layer In the ISO/OSI networking model, the layer that provides the addressing and routing of packets. The principle may be virtual circuit (as in X.25) or datagram (as with most LANs).

Node An identifiable point in a design that must be electrically connected to other nodes. A node may or may not be associated with a specific device or topology.

Noise Any unwanted input to an electric circuit such as random spurts of energy or interference. Heavy noise is sometimes called snow.

Operating system The basic software that drives the hardware, that is, the resource management programs: monitor routines, input/output control, allocation capabilities, interrupt processing, swapping in central memory, job scheduling, and management of peripherals. The kernel of any computer.

Packet A unit of data handling that contains the header, trailer (control information), and user information.

Parity Originally, a horizontal 1's complement check sum of each byte transmitted and/or received. Parity may be even, odd, or none. The concept has been developed into a more complete protection of all information included in a packet through redundancy checks.

Peripheral Pertaining to, situated in, or constituting the periphery of a computer or communications system.

Personal computer A microprocessor-based unit (8, 16, or 32 BPW) with a central memory typically ranging between 64 kB and 1 MB. It has soft- and hardcopy facilities and floppy and/or hard disk storage. Its capacity is that of the mainframes of the 1960s and early 1970s but its cost ranges from $200 to $8000.

Physical layer The combination of two sublayers in a local area network: the broadband cable (data distribution system) and the media access unit (MAU) attached to the carrier. A simple layer in a long-haul network, typically the modem.

Plug compatible manufacturer A vendor that orients its design and marketing services toward the equipment produced by leaders in the computer and communications industry. The objective is to offer alternatives, particularly in peripherals and memory devices, which are more cost-effective than those of the original equipment manufacturer (OEM).

Port A socket to which a user device attaches; a point of access. Typically, each port has an identifying number.

Presentation layer The layer of the ISO/OSI model that provides data communication through a virtual terminal service. It consists of a connection constructed from the network layer virtual circuit or datagram packets, and it assures the finer programmatic interfaces of functions treated by the session layer.

Private branch exchange (PBX) A private telephone exchange that services an individual organization and has connections to a public telephone exchange. The computer-based telephone exchange is a descendant of the old electromechanical switchboard that is able to execute a complete range of services (hold, follow me, unattended operation, call accounting, and so on) and also handle data as well as voice.

Protocol A rule of conduct, a procedure for ordering the exchange of formatted information packets between correspondents. Protocols are interpreted through hardware and software. They may be layered: one protocol interpreter may use a lower protocol for the transport of its packets to its correspondent protocol interpreter.

Record Information in a design file that is organized and structured according to a predefined design model.

Server A software driver dedicated to specific functions. A LAN typically has a file server, print server, and communications server (gateway).

Session The data transport connection resulting from a call from one to another of two user devices attached to a network. The network service assured by the session layer.

Session layer The layer that provides packet communication units with network management functions. Its protocols are responsible for resource protection, data security, access control, network authentication, symbolic name translation, service accounting, name directory, and extended addressing services.

Signal A representation of information; part of a message.

Signal balancing The equalizing of the attenuation that a signal encounters through the network in the forward direction so that its level is essentially the same at all outlets. Also, the production of nearly equal inputs to the head end from a fixed-level transmitter in the reverse sense.

Software Programs and routines that drive computer hardware and extend its capabilities. Broadly, it divides into three classes: *Basic software*: the operating system(s), languages, compilers, and fundamental utilities. *Horizontal software*: generally applicable programs, like spreadsheet, that are valid for a variety of organizations and applications domains. *Vertical software*: the specific application programs generally available as packages to serve the user's needs.

Speech generation The ability of a machine to produce speech from prerecorded sounds.

Speech synthesis Speech generation by the assembling of separate phonetic units to form words and sentences.

Splitter A device coupled online to a main trunk or branch for dividing the power and information signal in two or more ways on a coaxial network.

Tap A passive boxlike device normally installed online to serve a feeder or branch cable.

Tap outlet A connector port on a tap used to attach a drop cable. The information signal is carried through this port.

Text and database An organized, orderly collection of information elements designed in an applications independent manner to serve data and word processing purposes. It includes all files stored in an organized, planned fashion and constitutes a storehouse of information for all corporate data for any purpose. It is a corporate resource.

Text to speech technology The means of converting text information stored on a computer or word processor to synthetic speech.

Time division multiplexing Channel separation by time. It is becoming common in carrier transmission systems and data multiplexing.

Token (TK) A bit pattern circulating around the corner—whether physical or logical ring.

Transport layer The ISO/OSI layer, the most important function of which is flow and error-controlled connection between units of communicating equipment.

Trunk line A communications channel between two switching stations or between PBX switching stations and a central office.

Unity gain A standard design parameter used in CATV that is kept at unity or less. It is the signal output level of a head-end frequency translator divided by the signal level of an external transmitter attached to the network. It implies that the output of any amplifier is equal to or less than the output of the preceding cascaded amplifier in the network.

Virtual circuit A point-to-point switched (or permanent, nonswitched) circuit, over which data, text and commands (reset, interrupt, flow control) packets can flow.

Virtual connection A bounded, numbered, sequenced stream of network messages that passes user data and control information between correspondent units of data terminating equipment. A connection is established and broken by the transport layer.

Virtual terminal A service oriented toward the support of many low-speed devices transmitting essentially character-by-character traffic. It provides a host interface that maximizes host terminal buffer utilization and assures tools for controlling the format of data presented to and received from remote terminals attached to the LAN.

Voice mail A message system that permits users to create, send, and or store voice messages. Delivery to other users can be either immediate or delayed.

Workstation Any microprocessor-supported workplace to which information is routed and at which direct data collection, basing, and processing operations are performed. A place where work can be done in accordance with computer-based procedures, text and data can be stored and retrieved, and messages can be created and exchanged with other workstations.

INDEX

ABOUT THE AUTHOR

Dimitris N. Chorafas is an "old timer" in a young industry—his involvement in the computer field dates back to 1953. A Fulbright Scholar, Dr. Chorafas received his doctorate in mathematics at the Sorbonne in Paris. He is a graduate electrical and mechanical engineer, has a Master of Science degree in computers from the University of California, Los Angeles, and has done doctoral studies in production management and human engineering at UCLA, and in other fields at the University of Denver and George Washington University. He has worked as a university professor, programmer, analyst, designer, and project manager, and, since 1961, has had his own practice as a corporate consultant to the banking and manufacturing industries. As a consultant he has been associated with: General Electric, IBM, Univac, Honeywell, Olivetti, Nestlé, Omega, AEG-Telefunken, Osram, Worthington, Italcementi, Commerzbank, Dresdner Bank, Istituto Bancario Italiano, Banca Provinciale Lombarda, Credito Commerciale, and a host of other client firms in 50 countries.

Dr. Chorafas has been on the faculty of the Catholic University of America, Washington, D.C., and has lectured as visiting professor at the Technical University of Karlsruhe, the George Washington University, the University of Florida, Washington State University, the Georgia Institute of Technology, the University of Alberta, the Polish Academy of Sciences, and the Russian Academy of Sciences.

He has written 35 books published in 14 languages and numerous technical articles.